Linguistic Representations
— The Road Ahead —

Hyderabad Studies in Philosophy

1. *Philosophy of Wittgenstein: Indian Responses* by R.C. Pradhan (ISBN 978-81-86921-15-9)
2. *The Philosophy of Language in Classical Indian Tradition* by K.S. Prasad (ISBN 978-81-86921-20-3)
3. *Indian Philosophy of Religion* by A. Ramamurty (ISBN 978-81-86921-22-7)
4. *Language and Mind*, vol. 1: *A Western Perspective* ed. R.C. Pradhan (ISBN 978-81-86921-34-0)
5. *Language and Mind*, vol. 2: *The Classical Indian Perspective* ed. K.S. Prasad (ISBN 978-81-86921-45-6)
6. *Epistemology, Science and Cognition* ed. Prajit K. Basu and S.G. Kulkarni (ISBN 978-81-86921-54-8)
7. *Communicate Self and Other Essays: Philosophy of Ramchandra Gandhi* ed. R. Raghuramaraju (forthcoming)
8. *Language: An Instrument of Knowing* ed. Ananda V. Wazalwar (forthcoming)
9. *Mind and Meaning* ed. Prajit K. Basu (forthcoming)

Hyderabad Studies in Philosophy, no. 10

Linguistic Representations

— The Road Ahead —

Edited by

R.C. Pradhan

Decent Books
New Delhi

Cataloging in Publication Data — DK
[Courtesy: D.K. Agencies (P) Ltd. <docinfo@dkagencies.com>]

Linguistic representations: the road ahead/edited
by R.C. Pradhan.
p. cm.
Includes bibliographical references and index.
ISBN 13: 9788186921586

1. Realization (Linguistics) — Congresses. 2. Analysis (Philosophy) — Congresses. I. Pradhan, R.C.

DDC 401.41 23

ISBN 13: 978-81-86921-58-6 ISBN 10: 81-86921-58-3
First published in India, 2012

Published and printed by:
Decent Books
D-36/A-1, Mohan Garden
Najafgarh Road, New Delhi - 110 059
Ph. (011) 2535 3435

Distributed by:
D.K. Printworld (P) Ltd.
Regd. office : *"Vedaśrī,"* F-395, Sudarshan Park
(Metro Station: Ramesh Nagar)
New Delhi - 110 015
Phones : (011) 2545 3975, 2546 6019; *Fax* : (011) 2546 5926
E-mail : indology@dkprintworld.com
Web : www.dkprintworld.com

Contents

	Acknowledgements	vii
	Introduction	1
1.	Linguistic Representation: A Philosophical View — *P.R. Bhat*	18
2.	First-Personal Self-Reference — *Bijoy H. Boruah*	59
3.	On the Irreducibility of the Semantical — *Nirmalya Narayana Chakraborty*	75
4.	Representation, Meaning and Truth — *Sadhan Chakraborty*	93
5.	On the Impossibility of Language–Reality Divide: Arguments from the Standpoint of Reference — *Amitabha Dasgupta*	110
6.	On Grice's Analysis of Meaning — *Laxminarayana Lenka*	129
7.	Discrete versus Distributive Representation: The Debate Between the Classicist and the Connectionist — *Ram C. Majhi*	153
8.	Wittgenstein and Derrida on Representation — *Muhammedaly P.P.*	168
9.	Is there a Private Language called the Language of Thought? — *Sreekala M. Nair*	183

10. Communicative Intentionality: An Analysis of "The Rules of Statement Making" 197
— *Ranjan K. Panda*

11. Linguistic Representations, Mind-World Relations and the Encounter with Truth 216
— *R.C. Pradhan*

12. Epistemic Autonomy of Śabda-pramāṇa: Revisiting Classical Indian debates 248
— *K.S. Prasad*

13. Minding Language and Languaging Reality 275
— *Manidipa Sanyal*

14. Metaphoric Understanding and Mental Representations of Moral Concepts 295
— *Smita Sirker*

15. The Mentalistic Turn in Analytical Philosophy 319
— *Madhucchanda Sen*

16. Limits of Linguistic Representations: Wittgenstein and the Unrepresentable that Shows Forth 338
— *Muhammad Maroof Shah*

17. Hermeneutics and Language Analysis: Gadamer and Wittgenstein on the Nature of Language 391
— *Sreekumar Nellickappilly*

18. The Nature of Linguistic Representations 414
— *C.A.Tomy*

Contributors 438

Index 440

Acknowledgements

THIS volume under the Hyderabad Studies in Philosophy Series is the result of the seminar conducted under the UGC-SAP programme in 2011 with the title "Linguistic Representations: The Road Ahead". All the papers presented in the seminar have been included in the volume after sufficient revisions and additions by the authors. Besides, many invited articles such as those of Professor Sadhan Chakraborty, Professor Amitabha Dasgupta, Dr. K.S. Prasad and Dr. Madhucchanda Sen have been included. We are thankful to all the authors for contributing to this volume.

In the preparation of this volume, I have been helped immensely by Dr. K.S. Prasad in terms of technical expertise and practical guidance. I am thankful to him for this help.

I am thankful to Professor Prajit K. Basu, the co-ordinator of SAP and to Professor Amitabha Dasgupta, the former co-ordinator of SAP for their guidance and help in making the volume possible. Besides, I am thankful to all our colleagues in the Department of Philosophy for their help not only in organizing the seminar but also in making the publication possible.

We at the Department of Philosophy are also thankful to Professor Ramakrishna Ramaswamy, the Vice-chancellor who is the Chairman of the SAP Advisory Committee and the external members of the Committee for their guidance in the matters of publication and conduct of seminars.

We have special thanks for the external referee of this volume, Professor P.K. Mohapatra, for his encouraging comments and useful suggestions in making this volume publication worthy.

Last but not the least, we are thankful to the staff, students and research scholars in the Department for their co-operation in this regard.

We owe special thanks to M/s Decent Books for undertaking publication of this volume.

Introduction

IN this collection of essays the central focus is on the nature of linguistic representations as distinguished from other types of representations, such as mental representations. It takes into account other related concepts such as understanding, meaning, reference, truth, etc. which constitute the core of contemporary philosophy of language. Many of the debates in present philosophy of language, especially in the West are concerning how the language/reality divide is to be understood and how much of the linguistic representations are to be accommodated within the broad framework of truth-based semantics. Besides, there is a raging debate as to whether truth can be saved at all with all the objectivity it deserves and whether reference can be saved from indeterminacy and inscrutability.

While analytic philosophers are engaged in a truth-centred debate, the continental philosophers are concerned with understanding and the linguistic practices in less representationalist terms. In fact, some of them take a dim view of the notion of linguistic representations. That does not, however, deflect them from serious engagement with language as such and its multi-dimensional facets. The hermeneutic tradition provides a framework of language engagement within a broader vision of multiple horizons.

In addition to the above two traditions in philosophy of language, the Indian philosophical tradition has highlighted some of the key issues relating to language as a source of knowledge, the structure of language and meaning and the relation between language and reality. The rich resources of the Indian grammatical tradition throws light on some of the central problems of the Western philosophy of language relating to the nature of linguistic representations.

The essays in this volume have been attempts to study language and the linguistic representations from the points of view of the above-mentioned traditions. Of course, the attempt made here is very modest in view of the vastness of the traditions represented in this volume. I will make an attempt in this introductory essay to bring out the main themes of the essays included here.

Linguistic Representations: What and Why?

It is, no doubt, true that philosophy of language across centuries has been concerned with the nature of language, its structures and contents as these have been manifested in the broad framework of linguistic representations. Language has been broadly defined as the system of representations in the medium of symbols and their constitutive rules. Since language basically developed as a natural medium of communication in the life of the human species, it is but natural to take language as species-specific, though it is not necessarily confined to the human species alone. The idea of animal languages, the language of the computers or the machine languages and other forms of linguistic representations are not ruled out. But here the focus is on the human linguistic representations for obvious reasons.

P.R. Bhat and C.A. Tomy have addressed the question of the nature of linguistic representations in their respective papers. Bhat in his paper "Linguistic Representations: A Philosophical View" has argued that language provides the representation of reality through its various modes with a well-designed structure of syntax and semantics. It is, however, not confined only to represent the actual world, because it can also represent the possible as well as plausible worlds which are counterfactual in nature. Bhat makes a distinction between the possible worlds and plausible worlds such that the latter are a subset of the former. The plausible worlds are various scientific accounts of the actual world such that they are set up within the framework of natural laws. The linguistic representations of the plausible worlds save truth and reference to the actual world as much as possible. But the possible worlds can be far away from the actual world and so truth and reference to the actual world cannot be saved at all. They therefore become fictional or stipulated worlds. However, Bhat observes, we require language even to represent the fictional worlds as much as we need language to represent the actual world. He does not confine language and its representations to science alone but extends it to the realm of the fictions and to also the realm of Artificial Intelligence where machines have well-designed languages.

Tomy, in his paper "The Nature of Linguistic Representations" focuses on the nature of language and its representations with reference to the actual world such that what we refer to and describe in language are the items in the actual world. Taking the concept of linguistic representation as central to philosophy of language, Tomy develops the idea that there is a natural as well as conventional relation between the linguistic representations and the objects and states of affairs in the world, such that the words and sentences in language have their counterparts in the world. The relation between language and the world no doubt is man-made, but at the same time it is not arbitrary, because of the deep-seated conventions in logic and semantics which constitute such a relation. In this context, Tomy argues that the semantic question of meaning cannot be solved without granting the ontology of linguistic universals because the linguistic tokens used in language use must be instantiation of the linguistic universals. He also argues for an ontology of universals even in the realm of objects and states of affairs in view of his contention that both the linguistic representations and the world must subscribe to the ontology of universals for any representation to be possible at all.

The Language/Reality Divide: Is it Dispensable?

The idea of linguistic representation has implicit in it the language/reality divide which is in a sense crucial to the realist semantics of truth and reference. Realists in semantics assume that such a divide alone makes truth possible as the goal of inquiry. But the opponents of semantic realism take the opposite stand that no such divide is tenable and that we need to dispense with the notion of truth as correspondence at any cost to save language and reality.

Amitabha Dasgupta in his paper "On the Impossibility of Language? Reality Divide: Arguments from the Standpoint of Reference" has taken up Putnam's argument against the language/reality divide and has shown that if we follow Putnam's internal realist arguments, then we cannot save such a divide in view of the fact that this divide is a dogma of metaphysical realism. The metaphysical realists take it for granted that there is a world independent of our language and conceptual scheme and that the world is a fixed totality of readymade objects. Such a world view obviously is committed to the idea that language represents the world in a unique way which gives rise to the idea of truth as correspondence. Thus truth is central to the idea of linguistic representations of the world.

Putnam, as Dasgupta has shown, has debunked the whole idea of truth as correspondence and the associated language/reality divide by showing that reference which is central to the realist semantics, is itself not fixed and determinate.

Reference, though causal, is still relative to a conceptual framework and is underdetermined by the interests of the speakers in a language. Besides, there is no metaphysically necessary relation between language and reality as it is causal in nature and not magical. The realist notion of reference is magical because it is committed to the view that reference is already fixed pre-linguistically and hence must be taken to be necessary at any cost. Putnam shows in his Brain in the Vat argument that if such were the relations between language and the world then we can never go wrong in reference to the world. But we can go wrong like the Brain in Vat, which is disconnected from the world. The metaphysical realist position can lead to such a situation in which we can get distanced from the world and thus world may prove to be illusory as reference is not causally and humanly determined. Thus Dasgupta argues that Putnam has decisively proved that the realist idea of language as a logical picture of the world must be laid to rest and we must reconsider our notion of truth as correspondence.

Muhammedaly in his paper "Wittgenstein and Derrida on Representation" has taken up for discussion the anti-representationalist stand of the later Wittgenstein and Derrida. Wittgenstein's later philosophy is well known as an attack on the realist picture of language and world which he himself defended in his *Tractatus.* Wittgenstein's main argument is that language is a form of life and hence we understand it better in terms of the language-games we play and not in terms of the propositions which make truth-claims regarding the world. The language-games not only encode the activities we do but also embody whatever references we make regarding the world. As Muhammedaly has argued, for Wittgenstein both reference and the referent, the signifier and the signified are in language and hence there is no question of reality being posited outside the world. Language is basically a rule-based practice wherein all the transactions of language take place and hence it is a myth that language represents reality which is outside the world. Comparing Derrida's position on language with that of Wittgenstein's, Muhammedaly further points out that Derrida has gone to the extent of saying that language has no structure of its own except that which it exhibits in use of the signs along with other signs which are related by difference and differance. The relation of differance shows that the signs themselves deny their own identity and thus dissolve themselves in the flow of the language use. Thus, Muhammedaly argues, both Wittgenstein and Derrida reject the logocentric view of language and meaning and opt for a non-representational view of language.

Truth, Objectivity and the World

Those who argue that language/divide is relevant to the problem of meaning and truth agree like Davidson, McDowell, Brandom and others that the anti-representationalist framework is not all that well as it is claimed to be, because there are still the remnants of meaning that hinge on truth-conditions of statements regarding the world. Besides, truth and objectivity can be saved against the anti-representationalist's attack mounted by Richard Rorty in his rejection of the mirror theory of language.

R.C. Pradhan in his paper "Linguistic Representations, Mind-World Relations and the Encounter with Truth" has argued that language can still be held as the representation of the world because it is in language that we make truth-claims regarding the world and that truth is central to the very idea of language as a representation of the world. Though in a metaphorical way we can say that we "see the world through language" without admitting language as an intermediary, we need not have to admit that there is a metaphysical gap between language and the world. Language represents the world directly without the gap because of the fact that the gap is a myth created by the empiricists. Taking the clue from McDowell, Pradhan argues that there is already a grammatical space — like the space of reasons, according to Sellars and McDowell — in which the world is situated. Besides, it is because of the nature of language–world relationship that truth can be situated in language.

Pradhan further argues that truth cannot be displaced by justification as Rorty argues, because justification can fail us owing to its being conditioned on the interests of the language community. Rorty's ethnocentric view of truth and knowledge leaves no room for the objectivity of truth. Following McDowell and Bilgrami, he argues that truth is still the goal of inquiry and that we can safeguard truth best in the transcendental idealist framework in which truth is not beyond our mind and language and that the world is not lost as argued by Rorty.

Sadhan Chakraborty in his paper "Represenation, Meaning and Truth" highlights the importance of linguistic representations in the Western philosophy of language and mind. He argues that linguistic representations account for the way we can describe the world and can also account for the meaning and truth of the sentences. He argues for an externalist theory of meaning according to which sentence-meaning is world-directed and hence is intentional in nature.

Chakraborty further argues that just as the mental representations are directed at the world , so also the linguistic representations are referentially directed at the world thus making room for truth in language. Both the mental and linguistic representations are directed at the external world. Hence representationalism is entrenched in the way we relate mind and language to the external world.

Meaning, Communication and Intentionality

The question of meaning is central to the representationalist way of understanding language. Language not only represents the world but also accounts for the way we understand the world through our linguistic performances. The interpretation and understanding of the linguistic performances take place within the intentional horizon of language.

L.N. Lenka in his paper "On Grice's Analysis of Meaning" has pointed out that the non-natural meaning of the signs in language are dependent on the speaker's intentions. Grice's analysis of meaning differs from the analysis offered by the truth-conditional theory on the ground that meaning NN is singularly a feature of how the speech acts are performed. Lenka considers many counter-examples to Grice's proposal in terms of speaker's intentions. Grice's theory of meaning is relevant to the mainstream semantics because it puts forward the view that language is a performance rather than a representation of the world. But as can be seen from the cases of utterances of sentences taken for consideration by Grice, all of them are directed at the world although within the speaker-hearer context.

Ranjan K. Panda in his paper "Communicative Intentionality: An Analysis of 'The Rules of Statement Making'" has argued that meaning has to be understood only within an intentional framework as shown by Searle and Ramchandra Gandhi. While analysing the intentionalist account of meaning in Searle's philosophy of biological naturalism, Panda holds that meanings are not causal in their nature but are normative because they are embedded in the communicative network woven around speaker's mental contents. These contents fulfil the direction of fit as well the conditions of satisfaction within the speech acts. Taking Gandhi's theory of language and meaning into account, Panda has shown that Gandhi has a far more sophisticated account of meaning than Searle's because

Gandhi has introduced the notion of address to the audience in the speech acts which bring in the elements of normativity in a more forceful manner. There is no causal basis of our address to the hearer and so there is no way we can derive meaning from the speaker-hearer nexus except through the communicative intentionality that characterizes our hearer-targeted utterances.

Panda further holds that human beings are already born into a speech situation with all kinds of norms making communication possible. That is why we can say that human beings are intrinsically linguistic beings having to participate in the communicative situation within a gamut of semantic and epistemological values. Linguistic representations, according to Panda, are intrinsic to the communicative linguistic field.

N. Sreekumar in his paper "Hermeneutics and Language Analysis" has brought out the hermeneutic account of meaning and understanding by comparing and contrasting the views of Wittgenstein and Gadamer. Wittgenstein's use theory of meaning and understanding is embedded in a view of language that identifies language with forms of life which are given in the historical situation. Language is historical for him, though the rule-structure is placed in a grammatical space. He banishes mentalism from semantics thus paving the way for a hermeneutics of language-games which situates understanding and meaning in the life-forms themselves. Gadamer goes further in bringing in the hermeneutics of the linguistic horizons within which understanding takes place in an ontological space. Understanding and interpretation of language and texts is ontologically structured within the fusion of horizons such that man encounters meaning and truth within this horizon.

Sreekumar argues that Gadamer's hermeneutics is far superior to Wittgenstein's because the latter did not take into account the ontology of understanding and meaning. Though he takes into account the forms of life, but he does not go far into the ontology of the human traditions expressed in language. Therefore, he has fallen short of making the real hermeneutic move to unravel the deep ontological structures of language and man wherein the spiritual reality of language unifies the I and Thou.

Self, Self-incarnation and Limits of Linguistic Representations

The nature of self or the I is necessarily related to the use of language. Therefore, there has always been a philosophical puzzle as to how the self is to be situated in language. Wittgenstein in his *Tractatus* declared that self in the transcendental sense cannot be part of language and the world and so must be outside the world. However, in his later works he modified his view and allowed the self to be incarnated in the world as indicated by the first-personal pronoun I. He still maintains that the I does not stand for an objective entity like "LW"; it only refers the subject indicated by "I" from the subjective point of view.

Bijoy Boruah in his paper "First-personal Self-reference" has brought out the logic of the first-personal use of "I" by distinguishing between the objective use of "I" and the subjective use of it. It is the subjective use of "I" to state subjective facts about oneself which is the proper use of the first-personal pronoun "I". It is the non-objectifying self-reference which underlines the metaphysical subjectivity of the I and it cannot be substituted by any objectifying use of "I" standing for the body of the self. This unique use of "I" is the very point which Wittgenstein emphasized in his early philosophy, though he characterized it as the transcendental I.

Boruah brings K.C. Bhattacharyya's notion of self-incarnation to highlight Wittgenstein's subjective notion of the I. For Bhattacharyya, the "I" does not stand for a meant content, because "I" is always the subject and can never be the object of thought at all. The self is incarnated in the utterance of the "I" and thus is embodied in the use of the word in self-reference. The use of "I" is in a sense the self-articulation of the introspective self-knowledge. The I or the self is the centre of consciousness and is the locus of the first-person perspective.

Wittgenstein was haunted by the fact that the self or I always slips away from the grip of the objective language used for representing the world and the objects in it. In that sense he was forced to make use of the transcendental notion of self to distinguish it from the ordinary objective notion of self prevalent in philosophy of language and mind. For that reason he talked about bringing out the limits of language and thus to find out what cannot be said in language. The idea of the mystical was the intrinsic part of this discourse of the limits of language and its objective representations.

Muhamad Maroof Shah in his paper "Limits of Linguistic Representations: Wittgenstein and the Unrepresentable that Shows Forth" has argued that Wittgenstein is a deeply mystical thinker because he believes that there are things that can never be expressed in language. He identified the realm of ethics, aesthetics and religion to be the realm of the unsayable because it is this realm that defies any linguistic representation. Shah holds that the mystical and transcendental aspects of Wittgenstein are the deepest aspects of his philosophy. It is not that the transcendental aspects are incidental to Wittgenstein's philosophy and that he could be understood without them. But, according to Shah, they are the most fundamental aspects of his philosophy which must be given due importance.

Shah compares Wittgenstein's mystic thought with that of Ibn Arabi, the great sūfī mystic who shows that the deepest reality is that which can never be said and theorized about. The sūfī mysticism is unique in the sense that God or the ultimate reality is beyond words and can only be experienced within oneself. Wittgenstein, Shah holds, was by nature and inclination a deeply religious thinker though he believed that religion is not a matter of doctrine but of faith and experience.

The Mentalistic Turn

Consciously or unconsciously, analytic philosophy of language has taken a mentalistic turn because language involves thought and that meaning is no less related to our beliefs and intentions. Madhucchanda Sen in her paper "The Mentalistic Turn in Analytic Philosophy" has argued that it was inevitable that philosophy of language has turned towards philosophy of mind for a full comprehension of the nature of meaning. She has argued that without the help of the beliefs and their intentional contents we cannot understand the linguistic meaning itself because there is a lot of give-and-take between language and mind. She has taken into account the two types of mental contents, narrow and broad, to define how the theory of meaning is divided into internalism and externalism while analysing the nature of meaning of our language.

Sen has further argued that those who have turned towards the mental contents are not against analytic philosophy as such as it is defined narrowly by Dummett who holds that analytic philosophy is concerned with language rather than thought. She has taken into account Evans's analysis of singular thoughts for pointing out that these thoughts are regarding the world on the basis of Russell's Principle and that these have broad contents in the sense that they are regarding the external objects. The Cartesian self-containedness thesis, according to her, is not sufficient to guarantee meaning of the singular demonstrative thoughts. Thus Sen defends the mentalist turn in philosophy of language and meaning without inviting Cartesian internalism into the theory of meaning.

Sreekala Nair in her paper "Is There a Private Language Called the Language of Thought?" brings out the implications of Fodor's Language of Thought to show that even our mental operations need a language different from the natural languages. Nair examines Fodor's arguments for the Language of Thought hypothesis to show that such a language is needed not only for the human mental computations, but also for the mental activities of the sub-human animals and the non-verbal infants. Such a language is not private in the way Wittgenstein has characterized it, but it is the internal language that functions in terms of the formal structures appropriate for making thoughts possible. Fodor's Computational Representational Theory of Mind explains how the mental contents need a system of representations for tracking down our interactions with the world. This system of representations called the Mentalese is well designed to take account of the mental representations in a formal way such that we can account for the meanings which we associate with the natural language terms.

Nair further holds that the Language of Thought is the basis of our natural languages themselves because the latter are to be learnt on the basis of the innate structures of the former which is not to be acquired like the natural languages.

R.C. Majhi in his paper "Discrete Versus Distributed Representations: Classicist and the Connectionist" argues against the notion of mental representation found in Fodor's representational theory of mind. He takes the connectionist model of mental representations as the alternative to the model of discrete mental representation in order to explain the nature of cognitions. Human cognitions do not take place in a discrete and linear manner but in a connectionist framework where all the mental representations are connected together in a system.

Fodor and Pylyshyn hold that the Language of Thought (LOT) alone can explain the productivity, systematicity, coherence and compositionality of the human cognitions. But Majhi argues that the connectionist model is better placed to explain these features without committing itself to a formal and innate language of thought. The connectionist neural networks can better explain how human beings actually think and mentally represent the world.

Smita Sirker in her paper "Metaphoric Understanding and Mental Representations of Moral Concepts" has undertaken a study of the moral thinking and understanding of moral concepts in terms of mental representations. She holds that the moral concepts like good, right, etc. have their representations in the mind more like the non-moral concepts like cat, tree, etc. The moral concepts like well-being have their analogical or metaphorical use in the domain of commodity transactions. The moral thought is better explained by the Moral Accounting Metaphor which relates the concepts in the economic domain with those in the moral domain. Sirker holds that moral language is replete with metaphors such as "Kingdom of Ends" and can be understood at three different levels such as Internal System Level, the Network Level and Application Level. In all these levels the moral concepts get codified and applied in moral reasoning.

The study of the mental representations involved in moral thinking brings out a new dimension of the moral thinking which is more often relegated to the background when talking about the computational language of thought. Moral thinking, as Sirker shows, is no less an integral part of thought in terms of concepts and their networks in the mind.

Knowing from Words: Autonomy and Irreducibility of the Testimonial Knowledge

The Indian systems of thought, especially Nyāya, Mīmāṁsā,

Buddhism and grammarians have been engaged in a serious debate on the nature of language, meaning, the knowledge produced by language, etc. since time immemorial. *Śabda-pramāṇa* has been recognized as a valid and independent source of knowledge by Nyāya, Pūrva-Mīmāṁsā and Vedānta for the reason that it provides knowledge on part with perception and inference, besides giving us knowledge about the transcendental objects like self, God, etc. But this has been challenged by the opponents like Buddhism, Vaiśeṣika, etc.

Nirmalya Narayana Chakraborty in his paper "The Irreducibility of the Semantical" has defended the Nyāya position as enunciated by Jagadisha who holds that knowledge gained through language (*śabda*) is independent of other kinds of knowledge and is irreducible to other forms of knowledge. His argument is that knowledge through language arises from the hearing of the words. Knowledge gained through language is true and justified depending upon how it tells us about reality. Language has a unique epistemic power to generate knowledge about the world such that even without perceiving or inferring anything, one can arrive at true knowledge of the world. Thus Chakarborty argues that testimonial knowledge cannot be subsumed under either perceptual or inferential knowledge, because such a reduction will deny the autonomy of verbal or testimonial knowledge.

K.S. Prasad in his paper "Epistemic Autonomy of Śabda-pramāṇa: Revisiting Classical Indian Debates" has argued that testimonial knowledge, according to Nyāya, is independent and irreducible because of the very nature of verbal cognition which takes place without the involvement of the sense organs. For the Naiyāyikas testimonial knowledge does not involve inference either, because of the transparent nature of the cognition in language. Defending the autonomy and irreducibility thesis, Prasad argues that if testimonial knowledge had been a form of inference, then there would have been the presence of premises including *vyāpti* in verbal cognition. But actually that is not the case. Verbal knowledge or linguistic understanding stands alone in its own validity and justification. He further argues that the domain of transcendental objects such as self, god, moral obligations, etc. cannot be subjected either to perception or to inference. Therefore testimonial knowledge is the only knowledge available in this domain.

Prasad's account of testimonial knowledge makes it clear that language as a representation of the world leads us to truth or true cognition even where our perceptual and inferential apparatus is absent. Language itself is pre-perceptual and pre-inferential and so linguistic knowledge is autonomous of the perceptual and inferential knowledge.

Manidipa Sanyal in her paper "Minding Language and Languaging Reality" argues for the thesis that linguistic understanding is a genuine form of knowledge of the world even though the Buddhists have rejected such a knowledge as illusory. She defends the theory of determinate perception which admits concepts into its fold against the Buddhist attack. The idea of pre-conceptualized and pre-verbal knowledge is a myth because knowledge in any form involves concepts. She takes the view of the Western thinkers such as Dummett and Davidson to support her claim that thought and language pervade our knowledge of the world and that there is no pre-verbal thought or knowledge worth the name.

She further explores the Grammarian point of view in understanding the nature of language and thought. According to Bhartṛhari, our knowledge and consciousness are already infused with language, and therefore, language is there all the way down to the world. For the grammarians the knowledge that we have of the world is already encoded in language and meaning is already innately involved in all our linguistic utterances. This she calls the languaging of reality because what we call real is already linguistic in structure.

Thus the idea of linguistic representation is already implicit in the grammarians' notion of language. Language has its semantic potency to express meaning and to represent the world with which it is connected because of its inherent representational capacity. Indian theory of grammar shows the way as to how we can never disown the linguistic representation of reality.

1

Linguistic Representation
A Philosophical View

P.R. Bhat

Introduction

THIS essay is intended to examine the possibility and the difficulties associated with linguistic representation. To begin with what is to be represented is discussed. Having realized that it is the reality that has to be represented, some discussion on what is reality is entertained. In order to make the idea clear as to what is actual, we entertain the notion of possible word. A clear distinction between logically possible world and a plausible world is made so that the idea of what is real is sharpened. Furthermore, a discussion on counterfactual situation is discussed relating the discussion of plausible world and counterfactual situation. We find no serious difference between counterfactual situation and a plausible world. This would give us the semantics of the contingent, empirical statements. A real world that gives the truth-conditions of the contingent proposition also gives the meaning of the empirical propositions.

All the rules of language including grammatical rules, besides all the conventions of language, form the syntax of the language. One need not go beyond the language in order to generate meaningful sentences if one has the list of ontology. The words in a language can be generally clubbed into two basic categories: referring expressions and predicate expressions. However, this is not a rigid classification. Given the linguistic freedom and competence of the user of language, one can use a proper name or referring expression predicatively and a predicate expression referentially. When we describe something we would at once do two things: refer and predicate. One needs to map how this can happen when we speak of linguistic representation. Normally proper names, demonstrative pronouns and pronouns do the function of referring and general terms like common names, universals, etc. do the function of predicating. However, one can also use predicate expression referentially to economize on the linguistic vocabulary.

An important aspect of identifying the statements, which are empirical, one requires the fixing of the reference. This is done by using an empirical statement as a criterion. We might introduce someone by saying "This is Mr. *X*" or we might introduce the person by saying, "This is my colleague". In either case we have fixed the referent of these expressions. We have the linguistic licence to use these words again and again in our subsequent discourse by using the proper name or the pronoun. Thus, we can generate a number of meaningful sentences that are contingent and meaningful. Once we are able to fix the reference, we are sure that we are in the domain of reality.

In contrast, the language of fiction, epics and possible world talk may not meet truth-conditionality. There would be no empirical statement that links the fictional dimension of such language to the real world. There is no way to come out of fiction and link the discourse to reality without an empirical statement that is found to be true. Those who treat epics to be history tend to do this by claiming that the names of the places mentioned in the epics do exist. However, no such transition from fictional world to the real is possible unless we exit the fictional mode of speaking. We can, when we want, exit fictional mode to semantics of ordinary language, only by getting out of the discourse.

The mind that has the cognitive ability to recognize the conceptual relations and logical laws has also the ability to arbitrarily assign meaning to certain symbols. This ability of the mind may be called stipulating or conventionalizing ability. This ability to stipulate is responsible for a developed language with semantics. Animals too have some resemblance of language that is causally and psychologically evolved. Causal conditioning is an essential feature of such undeveloped languages. However, this is not enough for human language. Human language involves conventions, which are basically stipulations. Thus, human mind is capable of perceiving, and perception is a cognitive activity, is capable of conceiving that is a conceptual activity and is capable of imagining that is a psychological activity. When we identify a counterfactual statement, we only cognize the possibility; similarly when we argue with possible world scenario, we are conceiving of such a logical possibility. However, our imagination might help us in using our familiar experiences to aid our conceivability. All the three, perceiving, conceiving and imagination are cognitive activities of the mind.

One can develop a formal semantics, which would give us the formal features of the representable statements. All the syntactic rules, all the laws of nature, tautologies, contradictions, can be fed into the logical syntax. Thus, we would be in a position to formally decide whether a statement is likely to linguistically represent reality. All the cultural dimensions are kept away from our discussion of linguistic representation. However, it would be possible to develop a model for linguistic representation of cultural dimension for each society differing from one another. The difficulty one may foresee here is the difficulty in isolating what is cultural fact and what is value. All the cultural facts can be represented. Thus, even cultural representation cannot take care of values.

Our last section would be on the Artificial Intelligence and the human mind where we find that human mind is different from the computers, yet the computer in principle can be made capable of linguistic representation. What is required is to have some mechanism to receive data from different dimensions of reality. Human beings perceive through five senses and we need to find ways of capturing the data received through all the five senses. So far, we have succeeded in coding visual sensation and auditory sensation. If we are able to find ways of representing the sense of taste, sense of smell and the sense of touch, we would be in a position to have all the channels open for feeding information into the system. The cognitive processing is not difficult for a computer to perform the way human beings do. The arbitrariness that human beings exercise in deciding certain things is not granted to computers. This is not to say, computers are incapable of offering operational definitions or stipulative definitions. They are not yet granted this autonomy. Not designing the computer to stipulate and then declaring that it cannot do these things, which are not granted, would be self-defeating. If powerful computers are programmed to handle such cases and computers can behave better than human beings then there is no reason why linguistic representation is not possible. The function of referring and the function of decision-making and acting on the decisions can be found in the computer deriving the intentions and decision-taking from human beings. Absolute autonomy like human beings is not required to do all these. One can very well imagine that a human being does not coin a new word, does not deviate from the conventions of others and also one can imagine a human action only in accordance with the decision taken by their elders following the social norms. Thus, if such human beings can use "language entry rules" and "language exit rules" even computers can perform these.

From time immemorial the issue of what is real has remained unsettled. This is because we are in touch with reality in several different ways. One way is that we know reality through different sense organs. Our knowledge of the reality helps us to generate new thoughts about them. When we plan to do certain things, we cannot avoid confronting reality. Every aspect of our life is linked to reality in one way or the other. We perceive them, think of them, imagine them, conceive them, talk about them, modify them, and use them and so on.

It is but natural that human beings want to capture reality as much as possible. And the modern days of computing can make it possible. Given the problem at hand, one may tend to do what is relatively easy first, i.e. representing the reality in a computer. Thus, perceptions of reality have to be represented first. Not that there are no hallucinations or erroneous perceptions, even these hallucinations and erroneous perceptions are identified by using the means of one or the other sense perception. Given the importance of what is real, one would be naturally interested in solving the issue of linguistic representation.[1]

In order to know the reality in a better manner, one may invoke the notion of possible world,[2] scientific fiction, and rational argument and so on. Often philosophers entangle themselves by raising wrong questions by invoking certain scientific fictions. As if that is not enough, they stipulate possible world, build arguments to prove something of genuine interest on ground. Sometimes such arguments cloud one's thinking rather than clarify or sharpen one's vision. Linguistic

---

1. Jerry Fodor first tried the idea of linguistic representation in the book *Language of Thought*, New York: Thomas Y. Crowell Company, Inc, 1975, and revised the views in *LOT 2*, Oxford: Oxford University Press, 2008.
2. S. Kripke, *Naming and Necessity*, Cambridge, Mass.: Harvard University Press, 1980, p. 18.

representation seems to be one such issue where clarity seems to be lacking.

For simplicity, we shall distinguish only two functions of language: referring function and predicative function. The semantics of a sentence is defined in terms of truth-condition. The assumption made here is simple: all those who know the meaning of a declarative sentence know the circumstances under which the statement would be considered as true or false. It may be difficult for many to have the competence to conclude whether a statement is true or false since they may not be experts on certain matters, or the situation might lend itself to multiple interpretations, but there is nothing wrong in believing in this thesis in principle. All contingent observable statements are covered by this thesis. In other words, the semantics of all empirical statements can be given in terms of their truth-conditions.

There are other forms of statements known as analytic statements, conceptual statements, universal statements, tautologies, etc. These statements do not require going beyond the language to provide semantics for them. There would be no linguistic representation that would be required for them. We claim that the analyticity depends on meaning. That is to say, if one knows all the rules for the use of words in an analytic sentence, one also knows whether the sentence is true. Similarly, one knows that a definition is true because it is a way of initiating a word into language by offering meaning to certain words. The other statements are universal in nature. One can further divide universal statements into conceptual statements, general statements and logical statements. An example of conceptual statement is "All trees are plants". These statements are true because of the conceptual relation between trees and plants. Plants are of wider scope than trees and inclusive of trees. The concept of plant is genus and the concept of tree is species and hence every tree would be a plant. The general statements that are true because of their logical form may be called logical statements. "X is either a male or not a male" is an example of this sort. This statement is universal since the variable can be replaced by any constant and yet the statement would remain true. One might find some of the necessary statements that are intuitively true, having the structure of a universal statement. An identity statement of the kind "Water is H_2O" would be one that belongs to this category. "A stick must have two ends" would be another which Wittgenstein might call a grammatical statement. It should not matter whether we call these statements as conceptual, logical or of other types if we wish not to accept a separate category for them. General statements as opposed to all these, may not have any conceptual relation and any logical form. There can be contingent general statements. All law-like statements fall under this category. "Creatures with kidneys are creatures with heart" would be one such example. So far human beings have not found any exception to this general statement. No human being is in a position to verify this statement conclusively. This statement is neither true because of its structure, nor true because it itself is a natural law or application of a scientific law. The truth of this statement depends on the human history, cultural faith in human observations. It is a working hypothesis and one is ready to modify one's belief if and when there is a counter-example. There is yet another kind of statement which is considered universal. "All students in this class are males" for instance would take a universal quantifier. However, such statements can be verified and hence they do not belong to this category of universal statements.

Truth-conditions cannot give the semantics of all the statements which are universal in nature. This is because there is condition of the world that would satisfy the truth-conditions of these statements. Hence the issue of linguistic representation also would not arise because there is nothing to be represented. There is no fact, corresponding to these statements that one has to represent them. However, all these universal statements, except the contingent ones, can be represented in computer as rules or general statements. They do not interfere with the process of representations. However, all of them and the grammatical and conventional rules put together form what one may call the syntax part of the language as opposed to semantics. Syntax would be needed to generate meaningful sentences, but they would not be performing the function of linking the language with reality. To be more specific, syntax would not perform the referring function of the language.

Of the universal statements mentioned above, it is only some general statements which need to be linguistically represented. Statements having universal quantifiers applicable only in specific contexts need to be linguistically represented since they are verifiable. As mentioned earlier, "all the students in my class are males" would be such a statement requiring linguistic representation. All other conceptual statements, logical statements, tautologies, analytical statements can be fed into the computer and they can function as principles and rules. The truth of these statements does not depend on extra-linguistic factors and hence there is no need to revise their truth values.

A question may arise regarding the laws of nature. From a certain point of view, they are universal since they apply without exceptions. Time and space factor do not come into the picture even when time and space dimensions are part of our formulation of the law. If the distance figures in explaining the speed of an object, that occurs as a variable and not as a constant; similarly if time figures there, it figures as a variable and not as a constant. If the constants are put in place of variables, then it would be a case of application of the law and not law itself. Thus, it would not be wrong to say that the laws of nature are universal. However, one might have a lurking doubt about the manner in which we discover the laws. As we know, laws of nature are not tautologies or analytic statements. By denying the laws of nature, one does not obtain a self-contradictory statement or a contradictory statement. Given this, one realizes that the laws of nature are synthetic, informative. One may recollect Kant's vision here. The laws of nature are both synthetic and a priori.

We may note here that since the laws of nature are universal and since they do not undergo any change, their truth value cannot change. Thus, they are like universal statements and therefore, we can feed them into computers as rules, and thus will form a part of syntax rather than semantics. However, we also should note that the application of the laws needs to be linguistically represented. For instance, though law of gravitation is true universally, an incident where law of gravitation applies such as a satellite falling to the ground needs to be recognized and linguistically represented linking language with reality. This is so because it is an event of the real world and statements about the world require linguistic representations.

A more basic notion of human ability needs to be highlighted in the context of linguistic representation. What constitutes the basis of human language needs to be explained adequately. Human language is qualitatively different from animal language. All the psychological associations, causal and perceptual explanations are inadequate in explaining human language. It is not possible to speak of syntax of animal languages, so is the case with language based on psychological associations or causal perceptual mode of accounting for human language. Grammar is conventional; and anything conventional might become the base of psychological association when repeated. But, in the initial few cases, every convention is different from psychological association. If we explain even the beginning of a convention as a form of psychological association, we have fundamentally misunderstood what is conventional. Pavlov's experiment on dogs indicated that even animals could learn the convention. However, this learning is not different from learning the causal relationship. Human beings too exhibit similar behaviour like animals. Children in a kindergarten school start salivating after the long bell indicative of lunch break waiting to open their tiffin box and eat the delicious food carried from home. But, these children know the difference between the conventional relationship and the causal relationship between the bell and the food.

Causal relationship and conventional relationship are different though at a certain level they seem to be similar. In the case of children mentioned above they also exhibit similar behaviour as that of dogs in the Pavlov's experiment. However, there is a fundamental difference between the two. Dogs cannot start a convention, though they can be conditioned following the theory of classical conditioning. Children, on the other hand, are capable of forming a convention often exhibited in their role-playing games. A child might assume the role of a mother; another child might play the role of a teacher and so on. Every child knows the role it is playing and the convention exists only within the framework of the game. The convention comes to an end when they stop playing the game.

Conventional causes should be distinguished from natural causes including perceptions. It is but natural to feel threatened when one sees a cobra in his garden, but to feel threatened when one sees the death warrant is different. In the former case, there is no role of convention and in the latter it is only because of the linguistic convention that the warrant generates fear. Perception through senses also comes under natural causes. It is but natural that when the light hits your retina, you would have visual perception; and similarly when sound waves reach your eardrum, you hear the sound. Thus the causal theory of perception gives the account of perception in the form of cause and effect. This kind of causal perception should be distinguished from the conventional perception of traffic lights. Red light at the traffic junction does not cause the vehicles to stop, but the vehicles are stopped when red light is seen at the traffic junction. If the same causal explanation is offered for both the examples just mentioned, we have failed to recognize the role of convention in our social behaviour.

The ability of human beings to conventionalize something is at the core of human civilization. This ability springs from human nature itself. Human beings are autonomous and they have this ability to take something for something else. Animals too use tools, but whether they can conventionalize something is doubtful. Conventionalizing would involve making a choice. If *X* has to be taken as conventionally representing *Y*, then *Z* could have done the job equally well. Furthermore, if *X* becomes a part of our natural language by virtue of the convention, even *Z* could have served the purpose of *X* equally well. This means, before we conventionalize something, we have the choice; we make something happen as opposed to the rest of the alternatives.

To use the familiar expression, there were several possible worlds out of which only one was converted into actual by our act of convention. Or to put it in another way, there were several real possibilities out of which we chose to do a particular thing. This is nothing but engaging ourselves in the possible world talk.

The possible world talk could be about past, present and future. With reference to past one might say "you could have done other than what you did" or the sequence of events could have been different than what it was; and about present one could say that "Things could have been different than what you think is the case" or looking at the present scenario, I understand something else would have been better and about future one could say "you can act differently than what you plan to do" or the turn of events would be different than what you predict, etc.

Possible world talk can be classified into two groups: possible worlds that are plausible and possible only in the logical sense. The former account of plausible world[3] would be strictly in accordance with laws of nature; and the latter would be construction of possible world strictly in accordance with laws of logic without showing any concern about laws of nature. Thus, an example of a plausible world is that human beings build holiday homes on the Moon and all necessary things that are required if not found on the Moon are supplied from the Earth. An example of logically built possible world would be that which humans discover arresting ageing and live eternally.

Language Entry and Exit Rules

Wittgenstein has drawn our attention to language by declaring language as a form of life. To a very great extent, the language is the window to a culture. By knowing the language of a culture, we get to know the culture itself. Philosophers have pointed out without much clarity that there is some opening and closing phenomena happening when we use language. This opening and closing phenomena are termed as "language entry rule" and "language exit rule".[4] Roughly speaking, one

3. See for some discussion on plausible world, P.R. Bhat "Possible Worlds", in *JICPR,* vol. XXIV, no. 1, 2007 pp. 48-51.
4. H. Putnam, *Reason, Truth and History,* Cambridge: Cambridge University Press, 1981, p. 11.

observes the world and speaks about it and once the speech is over, one makes one's non-verbal move. For example, one sees an apple and describes it as an apple and then one eats it. Observing the apple is "language entry rule" and eating the apple would be "language exit rule" in this example. Since we know how to use language, we begin using the language, say, describe the state of affairs, and then close the language use; we stop talking and start acting. The activities of life go on by intermittently using the language and stop using the language.

Much clarity on the nature of language entry rules and exit rules is not possible. In fact, calling these aspects which link language with reality in some way as rules is misleading. These are non-verbal and non-linguistic aspects. However, any clarity on this would go a long way in understanding the nature of language itself and the use of possible world arguments. We shall turn to this discussion after having more clarity about the functioning of language.

Two Basic Functions of Language

If one were to simplify the functions of language in the cognitive domain, one would speak of referring function of language and predicating function of language. Expressions such as proper names, definite descriptions, referring expressions, demonstrative pronouns do the function of referring and the predicate expressions such as common names do the function of predicating. A declarative sentence has normally both these functions since the description is always description of something and hence referring function, and the other function is of predication, i.e. describing the object referred to. A statement that lacks any predication could be an identity statement between names, and a statement that has no reference could be a tautology or analytic sentence explaining the structure or meaning of the words. A definition, for instance, would offer the meaning of the term defined. It would not have any reference to anything that is external to language.

What is worthy of our attention is the liberty with which a speaker of a language uses these expressions referentially or predicatively. A referring expression can be used attributively and a predicate expression can be used referentially. This has been made amply clear by Donnellan by giving the example of "Smith's murderer is insane". One can use the expression "Smith's murderer" referentially to state a fact or use the same expression to express an opinion. When it is used referentially the sentence means that someone who has murdered Smith is insane asserted truly or falsely; and when it is used attributively, the sentence expresses an opinion the speaker has about the murderer, namely anyone who has murdered such a kind and moral person should be attributed insanity to him.

Referring expressions do the function of relating language with reality and predicating expressions provide us the principle of classification or grouping. A simple subject-predicate sentence consists of a subject term and a predicate term. "Hyderabad is a city" for instance, is a simple declarative sentence where the proper name refers to a particular city in Andhra Pradesh, and the term "city" indicates the grouping principle. All that the statement expresses is that given the grouping principle of city, the place named Hyderabad meets the condition of identifying it as a city. If we know sufficiently enough about Hyderabad, one would be in a position to generate many other meaningful sentences true or false. For instance, Hyderabad is a small city; it is a big city; it has good transport system; it is a metropolitan city; it is a congested city; it is an old city and it is a multicultural city and so on. All these declarative sentences are meaningful whether they are true or false. However, the following would not be meaningful: Hyderabad city is a liquid; Hyderabad city is a number; Hyderabad city is a man, etc. To cut the long story short, such sentences are not meaningful because the names that belong to ontology of a kind will have certain attributes and the terms that belong to another ontology would take different attributes. Not that one cannot name a dog as Hyderabad and claim that Hyderabad barks at strangers. This sentence would be meaningful in such special context, even though the sentence is meaningless when the term Hyderabad is taken as the name of a city.

The Context

A discourse is always in a context. In fact, not all things are spelt out linguistically when we speak. For instance, consider the naming ceremony. A child is baptized in a context and it could be both cultural and linguistic activity. Certain words having religious, historical significance are often used for naming children though these names may not signify anything religious or historical personalities. Contingent statements expressed in the form of sentences or observations are all context specific. These contingent statements or observations help us to fix the referents[5] of proper names, truth-values of empirical statements and so on.

Kripke claimed that definite descriptions are non-rigid designators and proper names are rigid designators.[6] This is because, definite descriptions can fit more than one person in different possible worlds. In the example of Donnellan the punishment that would be recommended to Smith's murderer would depend on the kind of use the expression "Smith's murderer" is put to. If referentially used, that is to say, if the person who murdered Smith is truly insane, then he would be sent to mental hospital rather than to the gallows. And if

5. Kripke, *Naming and Necessity*, p. 75.
6. Ibid., p. 4.

the expression "Smith's murderer" is attributively used and if it is found true, then the minimum punishment is life imprisonment in a country like India. These alternative accounts of "Smith's murderer" would show that the definite description is non-rigid. However, the proper name "Smith" in these alternative accounts is rigid and it designates one and the same person in both these accounts.

Kripke also sees the possibility of two individuals having the same name "Smith" in alternative accounts of the world. Such homonyms would not create practical problems. He invokes the notion of a criterion to fix the reference. In order to link the possible world talk to the actual world, Kripke introduces the notion of fixing the reference using a contingent empirical statement as a criterion. A criterion to fix the reference is a simple observable contingent statement, which in a context identifies the unique person or place, etc. successfully. Donnellan goes one step further. Even a false description of the person may succeed in fixing the reference of a name he opines. The expression "the man with a glass of Champagne in the hand" can succeed to fix the reference even if the drink referred to is only coke. Such isolated cases of false criterion succeeding in fixing the reference should not be generalized. The attempt would have failed if most of the circumstantial evidences were false. A criterion to fix the reference could also be the context where all the statements from observation taken together form a successful criterion. The context might include ostensive definitions, the non-verbal gestures, and body language and so on.

What Kripke failed to note is that any expression can be used rigidly or flexibly. It all depends on the speaker.[7] A

---

7. See for discussion on emphasizing the name or its criterion P.R. Bhat "Pragmatic Principles and Language", *Indian Philosophical Quarterly*, vol. XVIII, no. 1, 1991 pp. 301-06.

definite description may not fit more than one person if the speaker insists that the definite description should be used rigidly. For instance, the first president of India could be used as a rigid designator. If we mean by "rigid designator" a designator which designates the same person or object in different possible worlds wherever the designated person or object exists, we can use that expression rigidly. A definite description is a unique description which helps us to pick out only one individual in a context. Kripke invokes several competing contexts and applies this definite description to all those contexts and insists that the description does not remain unique and the description picks up different individuals in different competing contexts. That is to say, the definite description does not pick up the same individual in different possible worlds. This argument is flawed because the term "definite description" is no more a definite description if one invokes different possible competing worlds. The definite description will not have the property of unique description when applied across possible worlds. Yet the notion of rigid designator brings out one powerful thing that the speakers of language often use. We could use two expressions, a proper name or a definite description to do the function of referring. For instance, "Venus" or "morning star" could be used for referring to a particular planet. One could say "Venus is a planet that goes around the Sun"; one could as well say "Morning star is a planet that goes around the Sun". However, one might be very particular about a certain use. One might insist that the expression "morning star" should be used rigidly. If this expression is used rigidly, evening star cannot be the morning star. Furthermore, the speaker might insist that morning star cannot be a planet since no star can be a planet. One may stick to one's position tightly and not allow any change in the manner in which a referring expression is used. Let us now examine the other sentence "Venus is a planet that goes around the Sun." If one wants to use this name "Venus" rigidly, then one cannot replace "morning star" in its place. If we do so, we might face the problem of picking up different things in different possible worlds. But if we do not insist on using the name and we are willing to use any expression that uniquely identifies the same object in the actual world, then both "morning star" and "evening star" do the job equally well. If someone knows only "morning star" or "evening star" it would enhance his knowledge if one gives the information that the planet called Venus appears both in the morning and in the evening and is known as the morning star as well as the evening star. We are using all the three expressions "Venus", "morning star" and "evening star" here non-rigidly and interchangeably.

Not necessarily everyone wants to use these referring expressions interchangeably. When we refuse to use them interchangeably, the expression is said to be referentially opaque. When we allow them to be used interchangeably they are said to be referentially transparent. When proper names are used as rigid designators, we might be willing to provide different criteria to fix the reference. In one context, the ostensive definition might work as a criterion if the person is present. If one has to introduce the person in absentia, then a definite description might work. In yet another context, we might provide yet another definite description as criterion to fix the reference. The speaker retains the linguistic right to provide appropriate criterion to fix the reference and there is no rider as to which one the speaker should provide. Each and every criterion might work well. The success of the criterion is the mark of a good criterion. Any criterion is perfectly all right if it helps the hearer to identify the object referred to.

The point to be noted is the rigidity with which a referring expression might be used by the speaker. Normally we use proper names as rigid designators. However, one can find the exceptions. A definite description might be used as rigid designator. For instance, the police are investigating a criminal act of Smith's murderer. Let us assume that at a certain stage of investigation, they prepare a list of two individuals having identical names as possible shooters. Eventually, it is the definite description "Smith's murderer" that fixes one individual as against the other one with the same name. Here, one could notice that the definite description "Smith's murderer" is used rigidly even though it could have referred to any one individual out of the two. We are not willing to change the criterion to fix the referent. We are willing to replace the name of one person with that of another to retain the criterion. We can imagine other contexts where such a criterion could be used rigidly. In a criminal conspiracy, the criminal don gives instruction to his subordinate to collect a parcel from Mr. *X*, who would be wearing red cap, at a particular bus stop at a particular time, on a particular day. The subordinate is given a code word which he needs to utter to introduce himself. Suppose on enquiry, on the specific date and time, the subordinate found that Mr. *X* is waiting for the bus, and also has a bag in his hand and at the same time he also notices another person in the queue wearing a red cap and has no parcel in his hand. The subordinate of the criminal has to make a choice about whom he should be speaking to. He would speak to the person with red cap instead of the person who is Mr. *X*. He may even discover later that the person named *X* could not come because of some contingency and Mr. *Y* is sent in his place. The parcel was hidden in his overcoat and is handed over to the person concerned once his identity is revealed. In this situation, we would not be wrong if we say that the "red cap" is used as a rigid criterion. Anyone else even with the name *X* would not be contacted for the parcel unless he wears the red cap.

Discourse Opening and Closure

This very ability to use referring expressions rigidly or non-rigidly is indicative of our freedom in linking language with reality. When it is the matter of past actions, we are able to view our past actions against other possible alternatives that existed. Similarly, when we view past events, we have the ability to view them in an alternative perspective. Similar analysis is applicable to present and future actions and events. We can view the present actions in an alternative manner. Instead of my writing the present sentence, I could have written some other sentence. Similarly, instead of today being a bright day, it could have been a cloudy day. With respect to future, one could say that I am going to city and purchase some books instead of going to office. With respect to prediction, one could say that tomorrow is going to be a rainy day. Thus, in all these examples, what is underlying is that human beings are autonomous and they could do things differently than how they did, or are doing or contemplate to do; similarly, they have the ability to view the past, present and future events in an alternative manner. In all these altered modes of viewing, the language and reality relationship gets modified. We might use the referring expression with rigidity or might make an expression flexible and replaceable.

When we use an expression rigidly, we insist that the word should be used with referring function strictly and we are willing to compromise about its predicative function if there is any need. In contrast, when we use the referring expression predicatively or non-rigidly, we are willing to replace the expression with any other expression having the same referring function. However, we might insist that the predication is important and one cannot make compromise on that.

The notion of "discourse" would help us to move forward. This concept of discourse, like the concept of a "text," cuts across several domains. Put in a general way, any theme presented could be a discourse. Discourse would have a beginning and an end in a context. A lecture on something could be a discourse. A discussion session could be a discourse. A gossip session could be a discourse. The theme of the discourse may be of the past, present or future. A discourse could be about an action or about an event. However, the language entry rules and language exit rules would be applicable to these discourses.

A typical example of using the language entry rule in a discourse is when the vice-chancellor explicitly makes the statements "I declare the convocation open" and when the vice-chancellor declares "I declare the convocation closed". In between, the two declarations, the oath taking ceremony is conducted. In normal transactional situations, we might start the conversations with the statement "good morning" or "how are you?" and after the transactions, we may terminate the transaction by making the statement "See you again" or simply "Bye". Conventionally we know how to take these statements. "Good morning" may not mean that the morning is good; it could be cloudy day or a depressing day. "See you again" may not mean that you meet the person again. It is one way of bidding bye to someone.

When we have discourse on epics, we have the mode of story-telling. We may begin by saying "There was a king called Daśaratha". We terminate the story by saying "Thus, they lived happily" if the story is of a happy ending. Similarly, we may have discourse in science. We might explain how scientists in early days were interested in developing the tool for measuring fire. Phlogiston theory treated the oxidization problem in a certain manner. Similarly, one could also have long debate using counterfactual statements. If certain medicines were discovered early enough, many individuals could have been saved. Discourse could also be about counterfactual situations and possible worlds.

Not always we need to explicitly indicate the language entry rules and language exit rules in discourses. We are experienced enough to know that a discourse in history is different from discourse in epics or scientific fiction. For instance, the daily TV serial shows do not have entry rules and exit rules explicitly stated. Sometimes, there is recap of the story so far, sometimes there is also some introduction to the next episode before the programme is ended. But inclusion of these in a TV serial is not a must. We know how to link the previous episode with the next one. But all the episodes put together form one story.

Fixing the Frame of a Discourse

If the discourse is about the daily affairs, the same criterion which fixes the reference of a name can be used to link the language of the discourse with that of reality. However, every discourse may not be about the reality. There could be a discourse about the theme of epics, theme of scientific fiction or philosophical theme of a possible world. One might wonder how the referring expressions succeed in referring to anything in these discourses.

We noted that referring expressions could be used rigidly or non-rigidly in normal circumstances. When we use proper names rigidly, they do the basic function of referring and their criteria are not strict. If we use definite descriptions rigidly, they too do the function of referring rigidly, i.e. they become the defining criteria. With reference to possible worlds, the method of fixing the criterion gets altered. As we noted earlier, the criterion to fix the designator could be any contingent property of the designated. However, one cannot observe a fictional entity in an epical discourse or in a scientific fiction. Given this special situation, how can one handle the issue of providing a criterion to fix the reference?

The criterion for a character in a fictional discourse is

offered only by description. Speaking of definite description would not make sense in a fictional discourse. Rāma is the first son of Daśaratha would never become a definite description. When in the actual world, it is possible to identify the person referred to if a unique description is offered. In a fictional discourse, such a thing is not possible since there is no independent way of discovering the truth other than the one provided by the fictional discourse itself. Given this analysis, it is not possible even to interchangeably use different criteria to fix the reference. One may further note that there is no way one can distinguish referential use or attributive use of definite description in a fictional world. Thus, in a fictional discourse like epics and science fiction, the discourse itself is fixed by the language entry rules and language exit rules. If one begins by initiating the discourse by stating "let us assume . . .", "let us suppose . . .", etc. we are expected to take these sentences as language entry rules. In a story-telling mode, "There was a king named . . ." would be enough to give us an idea that this is to be taken as language entry rule for the discourse that would follow. The language exit rule is when the discourse is stopped. Individuals begin to engage themselves in something else once the discourse is over.

Children, when they hear stories, they know that stories should not be mistaken for histories. The stories have the domain of their own, especially when animals and birds are said to speak to one another, when they are said to be friends or enemies, children learn how to take them. However, the child might fail to distinguish between history and historical fiction. There might be some overlap of descriptions, proper names, time frame, etc. and it is quite difficult for the child to conclude one way or the other. Similar is the situation with elders if the markers are not clearly visible between history and fiction in certain cases. Certain historical films are made attractive by adding certain fictional elements to them. To be on the safer side, the producer may also add a note in the beginning that the characters that he depicts in the film are only fictional and any resemblances to living human beings are incidental. If such a note is there, it is clear that the film is only fictional and any reference to any place or person should be taken only as incidental and not purposeful.

Philosophers are not unaware of such exercises. In fact, they are experts in presenting fictional characters as if they are real. This is done in several ways. They invent new epistemology; they invent new metaphysics and ethics, and narrate the stories as if they are true. Apart from such grand exercises, they also have short scripts sometimes to help them raise important questions. "Brain in a Vat" and the issue of "Water on Twin Earth" thought experiments, for instance, would help philosophers to raise the issue of reference. These short stipulations work like mini-islands in the ocean. They create a world view that has no link to the world in which we live. But there are resemblances between the actual world and this fictional world, which mislead us to believe that the issue raised is genuine.

Possible World Talk

The concept of possible world, though in some sense stipulative, is not fictional like epics or scientific fictions. There is one important difference between the two: plausible worlds, a subset of possible worlds, are competing account of the actual world, whereas a fictional world does not compete at all with the account of the actual world. This makes a substantial difference between the two. When a referring expression is used in a plausible world, a criterion can be offered to fix the reference unlike in a fictional world. Similarly, it is possible to use a definite description referentially or attributively in a plausible world and this is not possible in a fictional world. Let us consider an example to elicit the point. In the early stages of development in science, scientists believed that there were two bright stars, the morning star and the evening star based on their observations. However, a competing account was developed where the two stars seen were not actually stars but the planet Venus which is quite close to the Sun and appears both in the morning before sunrise and in the evening immediately after the sunset. Similarly, there were two accounts about the relationship between the Sun and the Moon. One group gave geocentric account of the relationship and the other group gave the heliocentric account. Both gave alternative criteria in support of their theses. Both theses were plausible accounts. Heliocentric account was accepted as actual when the observations were made about the galaxy and the position of the Sun in the galaxy.

When scientific progress is made, what is done is to give up the earlier world view and replace it by a new world view. The new world view would be considered actual and the old world view is no more held to be correct. That is to say, the new world view is adopted and the old world view is relegated to the status of possible world. Whether such a world view is only possible or plausible would depend on whether scientific progress is marginal or fundamental. If a new law of nature is discovered or the present understanding is modified, then the change is fundamental, and the old world view would be only logically possible and not scientifically possible.

We have ingenius way of suspending our world view and begin a fictional world view in our thought experiments. We do this by stipulating certain things. Not many seem to have examined the role of "stipulation" in a philosophical argument. Let us ask the question: Why do we not question a stipulative definition? Or, when someone remarks: "That is true by definition" why are we satisfied? For instance, an infant is defined as "one to four-year-old child" in a research study. This definition is offered by the researcher and the findings are that 80 per cent of infant mortality in India is due to dehydration. This finding changes if the definition of infant is "one to four-and-half-year-old child". If the researcher takes it one way or the other, we grant the definition and respect the findings of the researcher. To consider a more familiar philosophical example, if the thinker defines "real" as something that can never change, and show that any contingent object that we know through sense perception cannot be real since all of them do change, we accept the definition and agree that the conclusion follows. We get puzzled at the end that we know no reality. This philosophical trap is inevitable because all of us are trained to grant what is stipulated is true by definition.

A basic linguistic habit of human beings is to accept the stipulative definition offered to us. That is to say, meaning-giving activity is most fundamental to learning of language. When we name a thing or a place, we offer stipulative definition. When we use pronouns, we cannot but use stipulative definition. In all these, we are habituated to grant what is asserted. This is a requirement in the use of language. When someone is named as *X*, subsequent reference to *X* would naturally be taken as reference to the same person. Similarly, when I use the pronoun "he" subsequently, I could replace "he" with *X* without loss of meaning or without adding anything substantial to that sentence. That is to say, stipulative definition gives the meaning of the expression. Of course, a word cannot be used in a sentence having no meaning. Therefore, as communicative beings, we cannot question the very basis of communication and hence we accept anything said to be true by definition. Defining a term is the manner in which we introduce a term in our language-game, to borrow Wittgenstein's terminology.

"Possible world" arguments and science fictions make use of the provision of stipulation, which are of course legitimate rights of the language user. Let us raise Wittgenstein's question and make the point clear: What is the colour of the red rose in a dark room? This question has two legitimate answers. Given the analytic bent of mind, one might be tempted to think that this is an analytic sentence and answer: Of course, "a red rose is red" is analytic and hence irrespective of what is the context, one might say that the colour of the red rose even in a dark room is red. The second legitimate response is going by the epistemic nature of the statement. Colour of a thing is known through sense perception and human beings cannot perceive the colour of anything in the dark. And hence, by considering the statement to be empirical, one claims that one cannot perceive the colour of a red rose in the dark room.

The situation is not quite different in the case of scientific fiction of "Brain in a Vat". It all depends on what one would consider this fictional being to be. If it is taken to be a human being with all human abilities, then there is no reason why the brain in a vat cannot refer to the things that we refer normally by using certain words. Assume that a brain in a vat had personal history. It was one like us till it lived for twenty years. The scientist then put this brain in a vat as Putnam stipulates.[8] We would have said then the brain in the vat is capable of referring to itself as well as to others since it had learnt how to use referring expressions. That is to say, if the brain in a vat uses our language with our meaning and reference, then there cannot be any surprises that it is capable of handling referring expressions the way we use them. If it is constantly under illusion or delusion about everything, then it is impossible for the brain in a vat to refer to the things we normally can, including the self-referential statement that I am a brain in a vat. By stipulation, brain in a vat is incapable of using any criterion to fix the world view. The marks that

8. Putnam, *Reason, Truth and History*, pp. 1-8.

are made by an ant or any other animal cannot be part of human language and hence the question of reference does not arise. Stipulation is essential for human language. Causal, perceptual relationship is not enough for the creation of a human language as we noted earlier in this essay. Human beings are capable of taking natural signs as signs, but that is not all. Cloud can be taken as sign of rain, and heavy rain may be sign of flood, yet our language cannot be explained only in terms of these associations. We require stipulations, conventions and other digital ways of relating to things using arbitrary signs and sounds. Natural language explained in terms of causal or psychological principles cannot have syntactic rules in the form of a grammar. The word order in a sentence has nothing to do with the causes in the nature. However, word order in a sentence is important for human construction of meaningful sentences.

The supposition that the whole world has come into being five minutes ago with all its complexity suffers from the same problem as above. A date on which a file that is created in a computer can be changed at will. First, one should change the system date of the stand-alone computer and put the desired value. Create and edit the file and save it. It would have the attribute of date and time you desired. Now you can change the system date and time as desired. The file would show the date and time of the system on which it has been created and not the real date and time. Inspired by such exercise a sceptic poses the question: If the whole world were created with all its complexity five minutes ago, can one disprove this hypothesis? Yes, one can. What we have missed in the whole argument is that the causal laws of nature cannot be fictional. One cannot implant the causal law in a plausible world where it has come into existence only from five minutes ago but give us the complexity of having existed for millions of years. Causal laws are atemporal, beyond time and hence the construction of plausible world where it has come into being only five minutes ago is an inconsistent supposition. This is a logical fiction, but not a plausible world.

Thus, we bracket our ordinary life and create certain stipulated world view to construct a sceptical argument. This is what happens often in scientific fiction or epic story or historical fiction. What a sceptic does is he begins with "suppose . . ." and makes us believe in certain things as given, and then the further story is constructed; and in the end certain paradoxes are created. In fact, we do not know when the supposition is terminated. Consider the following: I begin by saying, "imagine that you are on planet Mars and you discover that the human beings there breathe nitrogen and eat nitrogen compounds. But they are like human beings on Earth, talk to each other, marry one another and so on". Should we consider them to be human beings?

In the above case, we do not know when the supposition is terminated. "Is the last question: Should we consider them to be human beings?" outside the framework of stipulation or is it part of the supposition itself? When such doubt arises, one needs to fix the reference of the perspective itself. Is the perspective the stipulated perspective of the Martians or is it one of human beings on Earth? From the point of view of Earth, such Martians cannot exist and hence the question whether they are human beings does not arise. But from the point of view of stipulated perspective, it does not matter whether they consider themselves to be human beings or not, since this stipulation also would be in continuation of the stipulation we began with. We need some mechanism to know the closure of the stipulation. That is often done by the philosophers by beginning the new paragraph with the word "now" or putting the whole episode within quotes as we did above.

Consider the issue of Water on Twin Earth in Putnam's

science fiction. Everything else is the same on both Earth and Twin Earth except water on Earth is constituted of H_2O and water-like substance on Twin Earth is constituted by *XYZ*. Furthermore, it is supposed that the experience of water on Earth by human beings and experience of human-like beings on Twin Earth are identical. When a question is asked: Would these human beings on Earth and Twin Earth refer to different substances when they use the expression "water"? is a philosophical question. We need to know whether this question is asked after terminating the stipulative mode or before. If the question is asked before the stipulative mode of presentation is terminated, then one needs to continue the stipulated mode of answering the question either in an assertive manner or in a negative manner. After all, this too would be in continuation of the stipulation. If the stipulation is terminated and this question is asked from the point of view of ordinary life on Earth, the answer is simple: we have never come across such a planet and such a substance and it is highly improbable that such a substance on another planet exists. If such an issue ever confronts us we would be competent enough to resolve this issue in one way or the other.

Possible and the Plausible World

Philosopher's thought experiment does not match the rigour of a scientist's experiment in the lab simply because a scientist does not stipulate in an unrealistic manner. Philosophers are known for their unreasonable supposition in order to make a philosophical point, but the scientist often finds philosophical arguments amusing. Let us now turn to philosophers and make them realistic and see the consequence.

The expression "possible world" is quite familiar to all of us though we mean different things by this expression. Instead of entering into a debate, one thing seems to be clear that a possible world does not physically exist elsewhere

where my duplicate exists and does everything the way I do. A possible world is an alternative way of viewing this world. That is to say, between two perspectives a large number of common elements would be there, only certain elements in these perspectives would be different. An ideal example of a possible world is an experimental set-up where one or two natural variables are controlled. For instance, in a thought experiment, if we build the perspective with the known laws of nature, then it is a plausible world. In an experimental set-up, normally we meet all conditions and take the measurement of certain things. If we have to measure the hardness of an alloy that has to be used in an aircraft that moves with certain speed at a certain height facing resistance of air with certain friction at a certain temperature, we may make a wind tunnel where we blow the air which meets all the required parameters mentioned just now and we measure the hardness of the material in the laboratory. The force, resistance, temperature of the aircraft is measured in relative terms with the wind that blows in the tunnel. Certain observations made there would be exactly the same as could have been made in the real world where aircraft is flown with certain speed at a certain height. A thought experiment can be taken as true experiment provided it is built keeping all the known laws of nature in place. Definitely the miniature world created in the laboratory is not the actual world. It is a plausible alternative to the world in the laboratory where certain things have been tested out. It is not necessary that even the conditions created in the lab actually prevail yet; still it would have been an alternative account of the world. To make the point obvious, let us consider the experiments conducted at the level of -72°C about superconductivity. Scientists have shown how at this level of temperature superconductivity is possible using certain alloys. The result found is useless since we want to have superconductivity at the room temperature. This experiment gives us an alternative picture of the mini world where superconductivity is a reality, yet it is not the case with our normal everyday world. A plausible world is one like an experimental set-up in a lab with the rest of the factors of the world remaining the same. When we extend this concept of experimental set-up to the whole world view, it can be considered as an alternative account of the world which we prefer to call as "plausible world".

A plausible world is not a stipulated world the way Kripke conceives. Logically possible world too is a stipulation, but has no value. But a plausible world is different than the actual world where no variable is controlled, but an experimental set-up is a plausible world exactly like the one in a natural uncontrolled situation but is artificially created controlling the variables which are relevant from the point of view of all known natural laws. To the extent they are artificially created, they can be called stipulations, but they are different from arbitrarily assigned meaning of words or worlds. Hence they have the value of a real world. Furthermore, a stipulated statement is true by definition, and here a stipulated experimental set-up is not true by definition, it is true by observation like any other observation.

Let me repeat the main point here: an experimental set-up where relevant variables are taken care is the same as actualizing a plausible world. Instead of conducting an experiment on how the living being would react to the gravitational force at the gravitationally neutral level up above the Earth, an experiment can be conducted on Earth by making gravitational force zero in a special chamber by using magnets with certain power. This experimental set-up is nothing but a plausible world, not simply a logically constructed possible world. Hence what is discovered, the truth is the same or identical with that of actual world in the space between the Earth and the Moon. Furthermore, there is no inductive leap involved here since the identical experiment can be conducted infinite times and yet the understanding would be the same. Without conducting the experiments innumerable times, one can conclude that this experiment has the same value as is conducted innumerable times. It is one like saying that 2+5 is 7 and I found it so in innumerable cases.

A possible world includes all plausible worlds and a large number of logically consistently constructed world views often discarding the known laws of nature. Our construction of Martians who breathe nitrogen is blatantly against the known laws of nature. It is not possible to have combustion to produce energy using nitrogen and nitrogen compounds. Yet, it is possible to stipulate such a condition in our fictional account of a possible world. Arguments constructed on such fictional world often lead to self-contradiction; however one might have to labour much to discover self-contradiction. It is possible to think of a sheep and its clone Dolly. Assuming that the two clones have been obtained from the same donor sheep, we can have two Dollies with identical attributes. A genuine metaphysical issue can arise if we think that soul is an indivisible substance, for how can the donor sheep and the two cloned Dollies having distinct bodies share the indivisible singular self? We are compelled to modify our notion of self because Dolly experiment has given us an alternative account of the world including the nature of self. A thought experiment, which does not violate any known laws of nature, can truly throw light on some of our philosophical issues.

The Issue of Reference

The issue of reference in the case of the trace made by an ant, or the brain in a vat or that of water on Twin Earth is not a genuine issue since the possible world constructed violates the laws of nature. Ants do not have the stipulating power, they do not use developed human language and hence cannot have the referring ability through diagram or sketch. In the thought experiment of water on Twin Earth, the supposition itself is arbitrary. It violates the principle of identity. If the liquid that appears to be like water, it cannot be water though it is called water. A fool's gold (iron ferrite) appears to be gold, but is not gold. If the liquid has all the properties of water on the Earth but is not water on the Earth, then the supposition itself is self-contradictory.

If the question is: how are you sure that you are not a brain in a vat?, this question is comparable to the question: how are you sure that you are not dreaming now? The difficulty arises because there is no neutral ground on which you stand and answer this question. There is no metre to measure whether you are in the dreaming state or you are in the waking state. The question expects a state where you can measure whether you are in a dreaming state or a waking state. This question cannot be answered to the satisfaction of a sceptic. The brain in a vat is also constructed science fiction in a similar line. The brain in a vat thought experiment though stipulates the sense organs like those of human beings, has a brain like that of human beings, but lacks connection with the world by stipulation. It lives in a stipulated state all the time and hence whether brain in a vat refers to what we refer by certain expressions also has to be stipulated and answered. If the question is raised from the point of view of the world we live in, then there cannot be a brain in a vat of this kind. We gain nothing by creating a brain in a vat. It also lacks the ability to refer to itself as brain in a vat by stipulation. It works in a causal way and hence is incapable of having developed language. The brain in a vat has no ability to know its own state by definition and hence it cannot answer the question when one is a brain in a vat. Similarly, by definition one is not in a position to know whether one is dreaming, therefore one cannot answer whether one is dreaming when one is dreaming.

However, one can surely answer that one is not dreaming because one can verify whether one is dreaming by walking, talking and interacting with others and checking whether anything is missed. In a dream state, all laws of nature do not work in a normal way; there are surprises; but that does not happen in the waking state. Though one may not be sure whether one is dreaming or not while in dream, one can be very sure whether one is dreaming or not while one is wide awake. Asking a question that is meaningful in one world view and demanding that it should make sense in another world view goes against the very nature of human language. The so-called language entry rules and language exit rules would be different for these two world views and hence the same question does not apply equally to both the world views.

Human Mind

We are examining the human mind in the context of linguistic representation. There is some harmony between language and reality. Even to claim that there is no harmony between language and reality, we need to make use of this harmony. This harmony is due to the nature of our mind that gets reflected in our language. The human mind is such that it cannot think in a different manner than the way it thinks with reference to reality. The way human mind thinks is its nature and anything that is natural is factual. A relation may be transitive or opaque. For instance, a sister is a sibling, but a sibling need not be a sister. *X* is my father, *Y* is my father's father, then *Y* is not my father, but is called my grandfather. If *X* is to my right and if *Y* is to the right of *X*, then *Y* is to my right. This relation is transitive. What we learn from this is that we can produce meaningful sentences when the relation is transitive. If the relation is intransitive, we cannot generate meaningful sentences by logical operations.

Conceptual relations work as facilitators sometimes and

as hindrance in certain ways. We are governed by conceptual rules and these rules seem to be basic even if they seem to be conventional. Why they are so fundamental is an interesting question to be raised. That is to say, even the arbitrary nature of language is not all that arbitrary is made clear. Given this, what is it that is part of fundamental nature of human thought that cannot allow certain things to happen? Or, what is it that makes these conceptual rules binding on human mind? needs to be explored further.

What is important to note is that there are certain facts about minds. These facts are like laws of nature. They are facts and at the same time logical laws since they are about thoughts. We may identify some of them: Mind cannot combine opposites to produce a synthesis. Hegel demanded that thesis and anti-thesis should emerge into synthesis. This synthesis is a gestalt exercise. It is a contingent exercise. We can only recognize that such a synthesis has occurred but not derive such a synthesis. Therefore, this dialectic is not logical, but a creative happening. The second, we may produce a dichotomy, or binary, we cannot produce a third value on the same plane. Sāṁkhya appeared to have created the three: *sattva, rajas* and *tamas*. However, their internal relationship is not of logical kind, but of creative synthetic kind. Similarly, we have four colours as basic. One can produce all other colours as combinations of these basic four colours. One might wonder why four-colour theorem is true: one can map successfully the most complex geographical area with just four colours.

One may wonder why the following happens: following the use theory of meaning one may think that the meanings of the words are acquired from the use and usages of words. That is to say, one can arbitrarily assign meaning to words and if these words are used in that particular manner one can naturalize those meanings. However, this seems to be impossible in certain cases. Despite our efforts, we may not succeed in assigning certain meanings to certain terms. A familiar example that proves this point is the computer device called "mouse". When this term is picked up from the natural language, the resemblance must have played an important role in calling this device a mouse. The computer device is not a living being, nor is it something, which has birth and death. It also does not require oxygen, food and rest. It also does not have something called ageing though there might be wear and tear. These features which lack in this device are all applicable to the mammal mouse. Anyone who is aware of both the uses of the word knows that the word can have an ambiguous meaning in an ambiguous sentence like this: "I have a mouse in my house". How does one know that a word is likely to produce an ambiguous meaning if used in a certain manner? What makes us believe that there are two senses to this word "mouse"? If use-theory of meaning is a theory of meaning, then when someone insists on claiming that computers have mind, we would have started attributing mind to computers.

Note that there are limitations to use-theory. What stumbles use-theory is the ontological category. Certain ontology is such that you cannot bridge their gap and make them a continuum. For instance, you cannot bridge the dichotomy and make them the widest one category. There seems to be some fundamental concept of being. You cannot make being and non-being a continuum. Similarly, existence and non-existence cannot be put into a continuum. Substance and quality cannot be put into a continuum. Derrida has a point here. A use-theory which tries to combine both the meaning of opposites would fundamentally fail.

What is important is the human ability to suppose. That is to say, human ability of stipulating something is unique. This is what is known as arbitrariness or ability to take something as something else. Animals cannot do this. They cannot take picture to stand for human beings. What they perceive is causally connected to what they would react to. Human beings are capable of reacting to symbols, something that stands for something else. Memory standing for sense perception is direct causal reference. However, a word or thought standing for the object is arbitrary. We can have second and third order symbolism. Money itself is a symbol; we can have interest on money, interest on interest and so on. Therefore, it is important to know what is it this particular function has in our natural language that lacks in the brain in a vat a stipulated being.

Supposing is a logical act. This logical act can be anything. For instance, suppose that everything that I say hereafter is false. We do not know when this supposition has to be terminated. Even if I say that now you terminate the supposition, but one cannot know whether that is part of the supposition or termination of the supposition. This supposition can be terminated only in this way: any of the descriptions of the world whether that is true or false independent of the internal relation that is assumed to be true. That is to say, the table in my office is brown. I can independently verify this statement whether it is true or false. If it is not false, then the supposition is terminated. As noted earlier, we terminate the supposition after ending the quote in a written discourse or by beginning new paragraph or by changing the tone and beginning with the expression, "now", etc.

Only human beings have this ability to suppose. That is to say, they arbitrarily make a rule for the use of words and follow them, maybe, in a limited discourse. We are able to have a thought experiment because we have the ability to suppose. Where such suppositions are simply logical exercise and where these thought experiments have genuine point needs to be noted. A thought experiment pictures a counterfactual situation or a possible world. It is possible to picture a world where gravitational force works differently. Following the observation that we cannot have a lump of uranium with the diameter of a mile, is an important observation and based on this one can stipulate a possible world where gravitational force acts on smaller things, but not on larger things. Or, one can think of the whole universe based on repulsion rather than attraction. It is possible to think that the Moon moves around the Earth because of the repulsion. If we can explain what is the case given the condition of other things, it is also possible to say what is the case because of the conditions of what other things are not. It is like saying p is true and hence not p is false or not p is false and hence p is true. If the world order is what it is because of the gravitational force, one can equally say that the world order is what it is because of the repulsion.

Artificial Intelligence and Human Mind

As of now, we have not taken sufficient interest in creating computers with all human abilities. We have concentrated more on feasible project of making computer more effective in cognitive domain. Even if one contemplates on creating one such huge computer with all the abilities, cloning may work out cheaper than creating such a computer. However, let us make certain general comments since such an issue has been already raised earlier in philosophical literature.

The above limitations of both human mind and human language do not come in the way of linguistic representation. A big "if" is there in recognizing computers as human beings. This has something to do with the human attitude. One may be surprised to know that human beings were not considered as human beings once upon a time when there was the concept of slavery. Slaves were treated as animals and not as human beings. If this could happen the reverse too can happen. It would not be too far where we would be faced with the genuine issue of granting citizenship to clones. We need to modify our inheritance laws. We already entertain the idea of animal rights and so on. Given the manner in which we progress, it would not be quite surprising that we grant computers with certain abilities to exercise certain freedom and come to their own conclusion and thus give them the status of an entity with autonomy. Can a computer be a human being? — is not an epistemic or a metaphysical question. As long as we are able to distinguish computers from human beings, obviously they are not human beings. If we ask the functional issue, can a computer do in the distant future, all that human beings can do, the answer is in the positive.

As we have noted earlier, linguistic representation is easily possible. All the conceptual relations can be fed into computer. All the universal statements can be fed into computer. All the syntactic rules can be easily fed into a computer. All the laws of nature can be fed into the computer and so on. We have computer with the ability to perceive visual signals and audio signals. Computer can stipulate and follow its own stipulation systematically. All that we need to do is to work in the direction of perceiving other data, which our other sense organs give us. Though not easy, such a computer is conceivable in distant future. A powerful computer has good memory, good central processing unit, and it has high ability to receive data from hundreds of sources at a time and so on. Given all these, it would be wrong to say that computer cannot match the competence of a human being in linguistic representation. However, if the question is: can a computer bleed, can it love like human beings, etc. the answer is in the negative. We better not create computers, which can do these things as well. The limited task of linguistic representation in the domain of cognitive science is perfectly possible if we improve the capacity of computers in the desired direction.

The so-called language entry rules and language exit rules can also be used by computers. They too can make observations to meet the language entry rules and they too can perform certain actions after the language exit rules, depending on what has gone on in-between. Part of the problem is that we are using computers as our slaves and not willing to elevate them to the status of a human being. Not because, they lack autonomy and intentionality, but because our attitude towards them is that of a machine. Even if there are human beings who cannot behave like autonomous beings with independent ability to stipulate, etc. we consider them as human beings though deficient. Computers can have far better abilities, yet we are not willing to grant them the status of human beings. Thus, the question "can computers be one like human beings?" is a politically loaded question. In terms of limited abilities, computers can perform large part of the activities that human beings are capable of performing, including linguistic representation, having limited autonomy, intentionality and so on. However, the act of referring which the computer does may not be called referring even if a computer announces "Your flight is ready for boarding, please proceed for boarding from Gate No. 4" and a philosopher might sit up in his chair just wondering how a computer can refer to anything!

2

First-personal Self-reference

Bijoy H. Boruah

"I am LW": Wittgenstein on Self-Reference

In *The Blue and the Brown Books*, Wittgenstein writes:

> The word "I" does not mean the same things as "LW" even if I am LW, nor does it mean the same as the expression "the person who is now speaking". But that does not mean that "LW" and "I" mean different things. All it means is that these words are different instruments in our language.[1]

Wittgenstein is telling us that we must distinguish between the first-personal pronoun "I", the proper name "LW", and the description "the person who is now speaking". The reason why we must do so is, according to him, difference in the *meaning* of the two terms. But, then, dramatically qualifying the opening statement, he immediately makes the enigmatic remark, that the two terms do not mean different *things*. It, of course, is obvious that one and the same thing, same person, is intended to be picked out by the two terms. So, these two terms differ in meaning without there being any difference in the things they each mean (or intend) to get hold of.

Since, by using both these terms LW manages to get hold of *himself* and nobody else, LW can only make *self-referential*

1. Ludwig Wittgenstein, *The Blue and the Brown Books*, Oxford: Basil Blackwell, 1958, p. 67.

use of these two terms. Does this common feature of their use by LW mean that we cannot figure out why they differ in *meaning* by attending to the ways LW might *use* them? The general question at issue here is whether a person's self-referential use of the first-personal singular pronoun differs in meaning from his equally self-referential use of his own (proper) name.

Bringing in the matter of *use* is relevant here in view of Wittgenstein's contention that these two terms are "different instruments" in our language. This contention implies that LW is making self-referential use of two different linguistic instruments (subject terms) when he says (a) and (b):

(a) I am fond of Vienna

(b) LW is fond of Vienna

Does LW's utterance of (a) differ in sense from his utterance of (b), despite the fact that whoever is referred to as the person fond of Vienna in statement (a) is identical with the person referred to in statement (b) as being fond of Vienna?

There is, of course, an obvious difference between these two statements seen from the grammatical perspective: (a) is a first-personal report of what LW is fond of whereas (b) is a third-personal report of the same fact of his fondness for Vienna. But this is difference in grammatical sense, whereas what we are wondering is whether there is a *semantic* difference as well.

Statement (b) is LW's third-personal statement of a first-personal fact, i.e. the fact of his own fondness for Vienna, or how Vienna fares from his first-person perspective. In making this statement, LW is making use of an "objective" grammatical device, as it were, in order to report a "subjective" or attitudinal fact. Another way of putting this point — which would be a substantive rather than a formal-grammatical way — is to say that LW is stating "from the outside" an attitudinal fact to which he is related "from the inside" as the *subject* of that particular attitude.

It is this very attitudinal fact, to which LW is *internally* related, that is *directly* stated in his utterance of (a). The "directness" of the statement implies that the utterance conveys the experiencing subject's attitudinal state without abstracting the state from the subject's first-personal perspective, or from the subjective perspective which makes it a subjective attitudinal state. In this I-sentence, the perspective of the subject *I* is inherent in what is expressed by the predicate-expression "am fond of Vienna".

By contrast, LW's utterance of (b) is evidently *indirect* in that a first-personal attitudinal fact is being conveyed by the first person *under the guise of* a third person. An objective third-personal channel, through which objective third-personal facts are naturally transmitted, is resorted to by the subject for the transmission of a first-personal fact. However, the indirect and "disguised" transmission of a first-personal fact does not betray the direct or internal relation the subject has with the fact so transmitted. In other words, the *external* mode LW has chosen to say something in uttering sentence (b) does in no way affect the *internal* or subjective perspective — that is, the first-person perspective of LW — with which the content of the saying is inextricably connected.

If I, Bijoy Boruah (BB), were to utter sentence (b) instead of LW, then I would be using the external, objective, third-personal mode as a natural channel for conveying a third-personal fact, namely the fact that so-and-so (who is other than me) is fond of Vienna. I would be using the modality of *oratio obliqua* which happens to be the standard way of stating objective facts, or facts with which the speaking subject does not stand in an internal or subjective relation. So the feature of externality occurs twice in the case of BB uttering (b): that is, BB not only speaks in the (grammatically) external mode, or from the third-person perspective; BB also stands in a non-internal, third-personal (semantic) relation with the spoken fact.

What, then, is the difference in *use* between sentences (a) and (b)? One difference is that (b) can be used by *both* LW and BB, or, for that matter, any other person than LW, to make the same point, namely LW's fondness for Vienna. The meaning of (b) remains unaffected whether Wittgenstein himself utters it to convey his fondness for Vienna, or Bijoy Boruah utters it to make that very point. It is the same predicate, *his fondness for Vienna*, which is predicated of the same person, LW, in both instances of utterance. It is the same proposition, or the same statement-type, of which the LW-utterance and the BB-utterance are distinct tokens.

Of course, what is conveyed when LW utters it is a first-personal fact, whereas what is conveyed by BB's utterance of it is a third-personal fact. But this difference is not within the scope of either of the utterance tokens. As far as the "face value" (i.e. the propositional content) of the utterance tokens is concerned, both the token utterances represent a third-personal attitudinal fact. It is *his* fondness for Vienna which is reported in either utterance. And the fact that LW is talking about his *own* fondness for Vienna when he utters (b) is outside the scope of either utterance. That the predicate *fondness for Vienna* is intrinsically tied to LW's first-person perspective remains concealed, until it is known, and thereby revealed, that the utterer of (b) is identical with the subject, of whom the predicate in question is predicated.

As far as LW is concerned, the difference between (a) and (b) is, respectively, that of first-personal self-reference and third-personal self-reference. First-personal self-reference is uniquely subjective in that it is the only mode of conveying self-awareness. Unlike statement (b) which can be made by both LW and BB (and by any other person), statement (a) can *exclusively* be understood as being made by LW. This is because, unlike the utterance of (b), the fact that *being fond of Vienna* is inseparably linked with the first-person point of view of LW cannot remain undisclosed in the utterance of (a). The use of the first-personal pronoun *is* a disclosure of that link.

Two Uses of "I"

In the same book mentioned above,[2] Wittgenstein distinguishes between two uses of the first-person singular pronoun: the *subject*-use and the *object*-use. The object-use is exemplified in remarks like "I have grown six inches" or "I have a bump on my forehead". The "I" here refers to me as a bodily object or in my bodily dimension. That is, I identify the body in question as myself. While any such I-statement is grammatically first-personal, it is not *subjectively* first-personal. For it makes no sense to say that I have grown six inches *from the first-person point of view*, nor does it make any sense to say that *having a bump on my forehead* is graspable only from the first-person perspective of the person whose forehead it is. In either case, the predicate-expression expresses a third-person fact about me in respect of my physical existence.

Indeed, I stand in *external* or objective relation with the states of affairs predicated of me in these I-statements. That there is a bump on my forehead, or an increase in my bodily height by 6 inches, will be true *of* me even if I am not *aware* of these physical developments in me. While these physical developments are likely to have a psychological impact on me, my psychological orientation towards these developments does not shape the physical parameters of these developments.

Wittgenstein draws our attention to a logico-epistemic feature of the object-use of "I" in terms of which the subject-use of "I" can be interestingly distinguished. The feature is

2. Wittgenstein, op. cit. pp. 66-7.

that the former use is susceptible to the possibility of error. For example, standing in front of a mirror and looking into it alongside my brother, I may mistake a bump on *his* forehead for one on mine. Likewise, in wrestling with someone, and catching the sight of a leg bleeding, I might say "I am bleeding"; but the fact could be that it is the leg of my wrestling partner which is bleeding, and I am not bleeding at all. Thus, these self-ascriptive judgements lack immunity to error in so far as the identification of the subject of ascription is concerned.

By contrast, the subject-use of "I", exemplified in assertions like "I have toothache" or "I try to lift my arm", is characterized by what Sydney Shoemaker famously describes as "immunity to error through misidentification" of the first-personal pronoun.[3] There is no question of misrecognizing the person who has toothache when I say that I have toothache. Wittgenstein writes:

> [I]t is as impossible that in making the statement "I have toothache" I should have mistaken another person for myself, as it is to moan with pain by mistake, having mistaken someone else for me.[4]

The reason for this immunity to erroneous identification or misrecognition of the subject of ascription of mental attributes such as *having toothache* is that the self-ascriptive judgement is based on one's introspective awareness of that attribute. And introspective awareness is neither observational nor inferential. In self-ascribing pain in a tooth on the basis of introspective awareness, my judgement does not depend on my observation of myself as an object, whose behaviour is taken to be a

3. Sydney Shoemaker, "Self-Reference and Self-Awareness", *Journal of Philosophy* 65 (1968), pp. 555-67, reprinted in Quasim Cassam (ed.), *Self-Knowledge*, Oxford: Oxford University Press, 1994, 80-93.

4. Wittgenstein, op. cit., p. 67.

symptom of such a pain and hence a reason for that self-ascription. Rather, the very occurrence of the pain intimates its self-ascription in a direct, criterionless way.

Shoemaker analytically sharpens the point by adding that "in being aware that one feels pain one is, tautologically, aware, not simply that the attribute *feels pain* is instantiated, but that it is instantiated *in oneself*".[5] Introspective self-ascription of psychological predicates of this kind in the subject-use of "I" is immune to erroneous self-identification because of the fact that knowing such a predicate to be *instantiated* is tantamount to knowing it to be *instantiated in oneself*.

The Proper Use

Which of the two uses of "I" discussed in the above is the proper one? Grammatically, of course, the answer to this question is trivially yes; we *do* have first-personal pronominal constructions of both kinds. Therefore, the question can be significant only philosophically. Shoemaker has convincingly argued for the priority of the subject-use of "I" over the object-use. The argument shows that the object-uses of "I" are derivative or secondary uses that can readily be eliminated in favour of incorrigible subject-uses. In misidentifying the bleeding body of my wrestling partner as my own body in a state of bleeding, the subject of predication here is a body that is assigned to a *self*, that is, *me*. So, the "I" in this statement can be replaced by "my body", and this brings out the fact that the object of reference which is misidentified is something distinct from the self.

To say that I am bleeding is, of course, to say that my body is bleeding. Shoemaker explicates the sense of "my" in "my body" in terms of the subject-use of "I". To say of a certain body that it is mine is to imply that it is "the body from whose

---

5. Shoemaker, op. cit., pp. 563-64.

eyes I see, the body whose mouth emits sounds when I speak, the body whose arm goes up when I raise my arm, the body that has something pressing against it when I feel pressure, and so on".[6] The "I" that occurs in the explication of the meaning of the phrase "my body" is obviously put to the subject-use. That is, the "my" of "my body" must be understood in its use-as-subject.

The primacy or non-derivative character of the subject-use of "I" in contrast to the object-use also follows from the fact that my physical states are derivatively mine, whereas the psychological states ascribed to me are mine in an original or non-derivative sense. My bodily states are mine only in virtue of being related in the appropriate way to my psychological states. If my psychological states are mine in the non-derivative way, then obviously their subject cannot be the body which is derivatively mine.[7] This point can be understood to imply that the object-use of "I" is not really the use of "I" as *subject*. This particular use of "I" is a use by default, and as such it always sits parasitically on the subject-use.

To say that the proper, non-derivative use of "I" is its use *as subject* is to make the metaphysically essentialist point about the "subjecthood" of the *I*. If the subject-use of the first-personal pronoun is *necessarily* its proper use, then first-personal self-reference involves an essentially *non-objectifying* mode of self-acquaintance. This means that any possibility of "objective" construal of "I" is foreclosed by semantic constraint; that is, the meaning of "I" does not permit its grasp in terms of "objecthood" under any circumstance of first-personal self-reference. Even when I say "I am the object of my neighbour's envy", it does not mean that the "I" in this remark refers to

---

6. Shoemaker, op. cit., p. 567.

7. This argument is essentially made by Thomas Nagel in "Physicalism", *The Philosophical Review* LXXIV, 3 (1965), pp. 339-56.

me understood as an object. If the neighbour envies me because of my impressively well-structured body, the "my-ness" ascribed to the body indicates the subject, of which the attribute *well-structured body* is predicated. Indeed, the body that captures the enviable attention of my neighbour cannot be detached from the subjective fact that I own it. The attitude of envy is directed, not at the body viewed as an impressive objective item, but at the body viewed as "belonging" to a conscious fellow person.

Even when I refer to myself as owning a well-structured body, it is not by way of identifying the well-structured body that I become aware of it as *my* body. Rather, I am directly (introspectively) aware of myself as the subject of the bodily attribute in question. This is true of any first-personal self-referential thought, which may be characterized as self-reference without identification. Self-reference through self-awareness is not a type of object-consciousness or objectifying self-acquaintance. Dan Zahavi neatly describes the difference of first-personal self-reference from third-personal self-reference in the words:

> [F]irst-personal self-reference owes its uniqueness to the fact that we are acquainted with our own subjectivity in a way that differs from the way in which we are acquainted with objects. In first-personal self-reference one is not aware of oneself as an object that happens to be oneself, nor is one aware of oneself as one specific object rather than another. Rather, first-personal self-reference involves a non-objectifying self-acquaintance.[8]

Perhaps the non-objectifying mode of self-reference, or self-reference without identification, is clear in the very logic of the use of "I". If I say "I", it is not necessary for me to look for

---

8. Dan Zahavi, *Subjectivity and Selfhood: Investigating the First-Person Perspective,* Cambridge, Mass.: MIT Press, 2005, p. 27.

who says it, in the way I have to look for, and identify, who the utterer is if it is spoken by another person. The simple and straight fact of using "I" picks me out as the intended subject. It is this logical feature of the use of "I" that has been effectively brought to light by Anscombe's following remark:

> If you are a speaker who says "I" you do not find out what is saying "I". You do not for example look to see what apparatus the noise comes out of and assume that that is the sayer; or frame the hypothesis of something connected with it that is the sayer. If that were in question, you could doubt whether anything was saying "I".[9]

The "I" of Self-incarnation

The notion of "non-objectifying introspective self-acquaintance" illuminates, and thereby captures, the idea of what it is to be a mental subject, the self of self-ascription of mental and physical attributes. Perhaps this notion of a subject or self is synonymous with that of the first-person perspective that characterizes consciousness. To be a subject *is* to instantiate a first-person point of view towards the world, and whatever is the target of this point of view is an *object*. In this sense, then, there is no objective content to "I", and it is used as a projection of the perspective of consciousness on a perspectiveless world which constitutes its "object pole". "I" represents the empty subject of consciousness that acquires contentful states through its projective perspectival relation with the world.

The notion of "empty" subject understood to represent the first-person point of view on the world, whereby it becomes a bearer of states with content, is in sharp contrast to the notion of an object. Krishna Chandra Bhattacharyya

9. Elizabeth Anscombe, "The First Person", in Samuel Guttenplan (ed.), *Mind and Language*, Oxford: Clarendon Press, 1975, p. 55.

(KCB) has dealt with this contrast in a way that illuminates the special character of the first-personal pronoun. He writes:

> The word *I* expresses a unique and unanalysable content from which all that is meant is distinct and which is yet understood and unquestioningly believed. The belief cannot be called a grammatical superstition, though the fact believed is inexpressible except in language by a grammatical pronoun. The subject appears as a known fact, *only as it is spoken of through a personal pronoun or conceived to be so speakable*. One's private awareness of *I* before its expression in speech is indeed knowledge, but the *I* here does not appear as a known fact distinct from the knower. *To be aware of the subject as a known fact is to be aware of it as a spoken fact*. It is not so about the object of which one may be aware as known even if unnamed.[10]

The striking observation of KCB is that the content of "I" is not a *meant* content, because the *I* is a subject, and what is meant is always an object. An object is what is referred to by a subject, and it can be an object of identifying reference by different subjects at one and the same time. But no two persons would use the term "I" to refer to the same thing, "not being applied to more than one thing at a time".[11] Because of this uniqueness in the use of "I", the speaker understands "the thing intended by the speaker through the word but not through the *meaning* of the word".[12]

There is a further explanatory point regarding the "unmeant" character of the use of "I". It is that "the communicating act of the speaker, which is never a part of the

---

10. Krishna Chandra Bhattacharyya, "The Subject as Freedom", included in *Studies in Philosophy*, ed. Gopinath Bhattacharya, 2nd rev. edn. Delhi: Motilal Banarsidass, 1983, p. 386. Emphasis added.
11. K.C. Bhattacharyya, op. cit., p. 445.
12. Ibid., p. 381.

meaning of a word, is itself conveyed by the word *I*".[13] This is an extremely important point with which KCB offers a most original account of the nature of the first-personal pronoun and its peculiar relation with the self or subject. The illuminating originality of this account is articulated in terms of the dichotomy of object-consciousness and self-consciousness.

When I as a speaker communicate my consciousness of an object, what is understood to be meant by the communicative act does not include that act as part of the meant content. It is the object, and not the *speaking* of the object or the object-as-spoken by me, which is intended to be meant by my speech act. The matter is quite different when it comes to the communication of self-consciousness. In this communicative act, what I communicate is not the consciousness of my self *per se*, but the speaking-self, the self-as-communicatively-expressing-itself in the speech act. In other words, the intended self of self-awareness is not merely expressed *by* the speech act of saying "I". Rather, the intended self is expressed *in* and *through* the utterance of the word "I", so that the speech act is part of the communicative intention of expressing the intended subject of awareness.

The subject of self-awareness is thus a *spoken* subject; the self of first-personal self-reference is a *communicative* self.[14] KCB captures the essence of this feature of self-awareness by exploiting an illuminating metaphor when he says that my "self-consciousness may in this sense be said to be not merely expressed but *incarnated* in the word *I*".[15] What is implied here

13. K.C. Bhattacharyya, op. cit., p. 381.
14. The idea of a communicative self finds its resonance in the analysis of self offered by Ramchandra Gandhi in terms of the addressive act of communication. See his discussion in the chapter entitled "Soul" in Ramchandra Gandhi, *The Availability of Religious Ideas*, London: Macmillan, 1976.
15. K.C. Bhattacharyya, op. cit., p. 381-82.

is that when the utterance of the word "I" is understood by the hearer to stand for the speaker, this understanding does not consist in grasping the meaning of the word. Rather, the utterance of the word itself, and not its meaning, carries the intention of the speaker. The speaker's *speaking* of the word "I" and the speaker's *being* I or the self are indistinguishable. Apart from its spoken status, the word "I" does not have any meaning or meant content. Nevertheless, the speaking of the word communicates the intention of the speaker, which is the self-awareness of the speaker. Hence, despite not having any meaning-*content* in it, the word "I" is said to have a meaning-*function*. KCB writes:

> The word ["I"] here has a meaning function but not a meaning: it is the expression of introspection or what may be called the *I*-function.[16]

The metaphor of "incarnation" is uniquely apt here, because it captures the special intimacy of the connection between the first-person perspective of self-consciousness and the first-personal pronoun — between *I* and "I". If the speaker's self-consciousness or *I*-ness is incarnated in speaking the word "I", then there is no gap between (the speaker's) being *I* and being the "I"-speaker in question.[17] This is quite unlike the situation, for example, of the speaker's being an astronaut and her saying, "I am an astronaut". The difference is one of

16. K.C. Bhattacharyya, op. cit., p. 445.

17. J.N. Mohanty remarks: "[T]he I (who is incarnated in any use of "I") is just and simply the function of speaking. The speaker (who utters "I") is not first someone who then says "I". She is rather one who is the I in the sense of the "I"-speaker . . . . Being *I* and being "I"-speaking are one and the same." — J.N. Mohanty, "Krishna Chandra Bhattacharyya's Theory of Meaning", in Bina Gupta (ed.), *Exploration in Philosophy: Essays by J.N. Mohanty*, New Delhi: Oxford University Press, 2001, p. 184-85.

incarnation and designation. If I am, as a matter of fact, an astronaut, then the utterance of the predicate "am an astronaut" serves the purpose of designating me as an astronaut. But my saying "I" (as an expression of my self-consciousness) is not a speech act by which I designate myself as *I*. It is not with designative intention — the intention of designating something as *me* or *I* — that I engage in the "I"-speaking act. Rather, my self-consciousness, or my being *I*, is directly or literally communicated by the unique "I"-speaking function.

Another way the alleged intimacy is brought out is in terms of the difference KCB shows between "This is I" and "I am this". "This" is a demonstrative that refers to an object in a context-relative sense. In saying "This is I" the speaker would be referring to an independently existing object and identifying herself with that object. The speaker would then be making a self-referential statement in the objectifying mode. For, she would at first identify something *and* then identify herself *as* that thing. It would sound like saying that there exists an object such that I am (identical with) that object. It would also mean that there is an object which is a subject. KCB therefore considers this statement to be a false statement of self-awareness.

When I say, instead, that "I am this" (where "this" means "this speaker of the first-personal pronoun), the announcement is not a judgement of self-recognition in terms of an objective "this", but an expression of the felt awareness of self-identity. In other words, the statement "I am this" is not to be understood as the *assertion* that I am anything, but as expressive of the inward *feeling* of selfhood — of being oneself — that one experiences in sincerely saying "I". Here the demonstrative "this" is to be understood as performing the self-referential function of pointing inwardly at myself, rather than pointing outwardly (in the objectifying mode) at something with which I identify myself.

The interpretation that I am presenting here of the statement "I am this" finds support in what KCB seems to suggest in this remark: In saying "I am this" what I am actually doing is introspectively getting hold of my self, which implies that the demonstrative is used to play the introspective "*I*-function". It is intrinsic to the *I*-function in "I am this" that *this* not only points to the subject or *I*, but the pointing is meant, as it were, for its full "absorption" in the subject. To be strict, the so-called "pointing" function of the demonstrative *this* is actually an expressive gesture at my own being. *This* in this context simply stands for *I*.

Support for the above interpretation can be gleaned from what KCB says on introspection *vis-à-vis* the first person:

> It [i.e. introspection] is just the first person I, the speaker who is not an object to introspection but simply the function of speaking ["I"]. Introspection is not believing *in* the *I*: it *is* the *I*. . . .[18]

This remark clearly indicates that introspection is the inward phenomenon of self-consciousness, of which the *I*-functional act, or the act of saying "I" is the outward manifestation. Hence talk about introspective self-acquaintance, or introspectively "getting hold" of myself, must not be mistaken as referring to introspection as a special intentional act of cognizing the self.

The unique use of "I" is the articulation of introspective self-acquaintance. The "I"-speaker puts the word "I" to the *I*-functional use, not in order to mean (refer to) the speaker herself, but as an *expressive instantiation* of her introspective self-awareness. The "meaning function" of the "I" is already performed by the "I"-speaker inasmuch as this speech act is coterminus with the speaker's introspective self-intimation. Conversely, the speaker's introspective self-intimation is a testimony to the successful *I*-functional use of the first-personal pronoun.

18. K.C. Bhattacharyya, op. cit., p. 443. The latter emphasis added.

What, then, is the crux of the appropriateness of the metaphor of incarnation to the use of "I"? To say that *I*, the subject or self, is incarnated in the speaking of the word "I" is to bring the *ontic* and the *linguistic* together, which would appear to be a category mistake. How does this metaphor play its explanatory role in making us understand this uncanny nexus of "I" and *I*? I think that the phenomenon of introspection implying self-awareness provides a clue to answering this question. Saying "I" is typically a moment of giving expression to introspective self-acquaintance, which in turn is a translucent realization of one's being a subject of consciousness. As soon as I sincerely *speak* in the first person, I *become* a first person inasmuch as the locus of the speaking subject is a centre of consciousness. This centre of consciousness is also the locus of the first-person perspective that sets this speaker as *me*, as *I*.

By way of Concluding . . .

What I have tried to do in this paper may be summarized as a sketchy account of first-personal self-reference in the light of ideas provided mainly by Wittgenstein and K.C. Bhattacharyya. In this excursus from Wittgenstein to KCB I have traversed through the subtle and illuminating observations of Sydney Shoemaker. The thrust of my discussion has been to show that the proper use of the first-personal singular pronoun is the "subject-use", which is interpreted as "non-objectifying" mode of making *I*-statements. First-personal self-referential statements are claimed to be self-ascriptions without identification on the ground that they are grounded in direct introspective self-acquaintance. Finally, the unique intimacy of the relation between "I" and *I* is shown to be captured by the metaphorical contention that self-consciousness, or *I*-ness, is incarnated in the speaking of "I". The *I*-function of "self-incarnation" is again held to be explicable in terms of introspective self-acquaintance.

3

On the Irreducibility of the Semantical

Nirmalya Narayan Chakraborty

WE acquire knowledge in various ways. Sometimes we see things happening. Sometimes we infer from the available evidence. And we also know various things by listening to others. This understanding of people's utterances and the resultant knowledge that we get have been the objects of inquiry among philosophers since antiquity. In classical Indian philosophical tradition several systems of thought made valuable contribution to an analysis of knowledge that we acquire by listening what other people say. Presently, I shall be concerned with such an analysis, viz. the way Jagadīśa has elaborated in his *Śabdaśaktiprakāśikā*. Jagadīśa concludes that testimonial knowledge cannot be reduced to other kinds of knowledge like perception or inference. I agree with this conclusion of Jagadīśa, but move further by claiming that in so far as the justificatory status of testimonial knowledge is concerned, we have to go beyond knowing through words alone. Many other sources of knowledge will have to be accommodated in order to do justice to the full-blooded notion of testimonial knowledge. And here I heavily draw on John McDowell's insights.

Jagadīśa promises to write *Śabdaśaktiprakāśikā*, a text that will satisfy the needs of those who want to gain expertise in the analysis of word.[1] Jagadīśa claims to have knowledge of Nyāya and Grammar (Vyākaraṇa). This implies that in the present text analysis of different aspects of grammar has been undertaken from a Nyāya perspective. Although the name of the text is *Śabdaśaktiprakāśikā*, the work does not contain an analysis of *śakti* (semantic power) only; the text contains analysis of many other related concepts like *lakṣaṇā* (metaphorical meaning), etc. So *śabdaśakti* here means anything that is required to be able to (*sāmarthya*) understand people's utterances, i.e. linguistic understanding in general.

Jagadīśa starts the text with an invocation (*maṅgala*) addressed to Goddess Sarasvatī. It is interesting to note that the invocation verse could be interpreted in two ways: one consists in taking "Sarasvatī" to mean the Goddess, the other consists in taking "Sarasvatī" to mean words (or collection of words having expectancy (*ākāṅkṣā*), etc.). The former could be called "The Divine Interpretation" (*devī pakṣa*) while the latter could be called "The Linguistic Interpretation" (*vākya pakṣa*). In the divine interpretation, Sarasvatī is the cause of all our knowledge. She is the presiding deity of knowledge in general. By "knowledge" here we mean direct awareness of reality (*tattva*). In the linguistic interpretation, we should interpret this as saying knowledge of words having expectancy, etc. is the cause of the knowledge of meaning (*vākyārthabodha*). In the divine interpretation, Sarasvatī appears in front of the devotees. In the linguistic interpretation, Sarasvatī in the form of knowledge of words that appears in front of people who are interested in acquiring knowledge of words. Three terms have been used here, viz. *sākāṅkṣā*, *āsannā* and *yogyā* as adjectives of Sarasvatī.[2] In the divine interpretation, *sākāṅkṣā* means

1. Jagadīśa, *Śabdaśaktiprakāśikā*, ed. & tr. Madhusudan Nyayacharya, Kolkata: Sanskrit College, 1980, p. 3.
2. *Śabdaśaktiprakāśikā*, p. 5.

compassionate and kind, *āsannā* means staying close or near and *yogyā* means ability to offer the desired result to the devotee. In the linguistic interpretation, *ākāṅkṣā* means the special order among the words, *āsatti* stands for the ability of the words to present a corresponding object immediately and *yogyā* means the relation among the objects denoted by the corresponding words. Following the divine interpretation, it could be said that when Goddess Sarasvatī is prayed and worshipped properly, she appears to her devotee and immediately (*sadyaḥ*) grants him or her the boon, viz. the knowledge of reality. In the linguistic interpretation, knowledge of meaning is produced immediately after knowledge of words having *ākāṅkṣā*, *yogyatā* and *sannidhi*.

If we follow the divine interpretation of the invocation verse, Jagadīśa seems to be claiming that Goddess Sarasvatī has certain abilities that other deities don't have and so we should pray to Sarasvatī and not to anyone else. Sarasvatī is kind, stays in close proximity to us, able to grant us the desired result; she produces the result immediately, without any delay. Other gods and goddesses might have some of these attributes, but only Sarasvatī has all these properties together. So ignoring all the gods and goddesses, it is Sarasvatī who we should pray to.

If we follow the linguistic interpretation, Jagadīśa claims that immediately after knowing the words having *ākāṅkṣā*, *yogyatā* and *āsatti*, knowledge of the meaning of the sentence arises. According to Naiyāyikas, knowing through words is a distinct kind of knowledge. Knowledge through words is called *śābdabodha* in Nyāya. Linguistic understanding (*śābdabodha*), to be precise, stands for that kind of judgemental knowledge which has as its object (*viṣaya*) one thing related to another thing (*anvaya*). This relation is not present in other kinds of knowledge like perception, inference, etc. Thus *anvayabodha*, *vākyārthabodha* and *śābdabodha* are synonymous. This *anvaya* relation could either be (1) Identity (*abheda*) relation or (2) Difference (*bheda*) relation. In the knowledge "Blue pot", we have the knowledge of blue predicate as related to pot in identity relation. This identity relation is nothing more than the blueness residing in the pot. Difference relation could be of different types like *ādheyatā*, *pratiyogitva*, etc. In "Bring the pot" (*gahaṭam ānaya*), the "am" suffix denotes objecthood (*karmatva*) which resides in pot in the relation of *ādheyatā*.

However, as we have understood *Śābdabodha*, knowledge of word (*padajñāna*) is the *kāraṇa* and presence of the objects is the *vyāpāra*. When we talk of knowledge of word, we mean knowledge of word having *vr̥tti*. The relation between word (*pada*) and object (*padārtha*) that is likely to generate linguistic understanding is called *vr̥tti*. This *vr̥tti* is of two types: (a) *saṅketa* and (b) *lakṣaṇā*. By *saṅketa* we mean the intention that let this word be the producer of knowledge of this meaning. If this *saṅketa* is eternal, i.e. divine in nature, then this is called *śakti*.

In the example *gaṅgāyāṁ ghoṣaḥ*, the word *gaṅgā* has its *śakti* in the flow of water. The bank of the river is related to the "flow of water". Since in *gaṅgāyāṁ ghoṣaḥ* we mean the bank of the river, we can say that the "bank of the river" is the *lakṣyārtha* and it is related to the *śakyārtha* of *Gaṅgā*, viz. "the flow of water".

Thus when there arises knowledge of words having *vr̥tti* as its predicate (*viśeṣaṇa*), this knowledge of words is the cause of linguistic understanding. Out of this knowledge of words, there arises presence of objects and this is the immediate cause of linguistic understanding. But mere presence of object is not sufficient to produce linguistic understanding, we need auxiliary causes like knowledge of *ākāṅkṣā*, *yogyatā*, and *āsatti*.

Ākāṅkṣā (expectancy) between the words hold only when without one particular word the other word fails to produce any knowledge of *anvaya*. The order of the words in a sentence is also called *ākāṅkṣā*. In "Bring the cow", the form of *anvayabodha* is *goniṣṭha karmatvanirūpaka ānayānukūla kṛtimān*. When the order of the elements in a sentence becomes *prakāra* in a knowledge and the last word in the sentence becomes *viśeṣya*, such knowledge is called *ākāṅkṣā jñāna*. *Ghaṭaḥ, karmatvaṁ, anayānaṁ, kṛtiḥ* — all these elements without expectancy relation (*nirākāṅkṣā*) cannot produce linguistic understanding. Knowledge of *saṁsarga* (between the earlier object and the latter) is not possible without *ākāṅkṣā jñāna*. Words not having any *ākāṅkṣā* relation cannot produce linguistic understanding.

Knowledge of mutual fitness (*yogyatā jñāna*) involves one thing as *prakāraka* and another thing as *viśeṣya* (*eka padārtha prakāraka, apara padārtha viśeṣyaka*). This *yogyatā jñāna* is present both in *saṁśaya* and *niścaya jñāna*. Knowledge of mutual fitness is the cause of *anvayabodha*. "Sprinkling with fire" — here we do not have any *anvayabodha*. Here in the meaning of *sic* verb *bahnikaraṇakatva* is *bādhita*. Because of this *bādhajñāna*, knowledge of *vahnikaraṇakatva* in the sprinkling activity is not *yogya*, such *yogyatā jñāna* is not possible. So this sentence fails to generate linguistic understanding. Thus *yogyatā jñāna* has to be accepted as a cause of linguistic understanding.

Contiguity (*āsatti*) refers to the immediate presence of objects arising out of words having *vṛtti*. If the presence of words or objects gets delayed, linguistic understanding cannot be produced. For example, *girirbhuktam agniman devadattena*. *Giriragniman bhuktam devadattena* — this *anvayabodha* is not produced.

Intention (*tātparya*) is the intention of the speaker. Take the example, "Bring saindhava" (*saindhavam ānaya)*. From the context we have to find out whether the speaker means a kind of salt or a kind of horse by the word *saindhava* and we will have the corresponding linguistic understanding accordingly.

As we have seen, knowledge of meaning arises immediately after the knowledge of words having expectancy, etc. So knowledge of words having expectancy is the cause of knowledge of corresponding objects (*artha*). But this knowledge of corresponding objects could very well be treated as a case of perception involving memory (*pratyakṣika eva aupanāyika*). The idea is as follows: Presence of word is not required in perception. But in case of words referring to supra-sensual things (*atīndriya*) perception does not play any role. But before linguistic understanding arises, presence of objects (*padārthopasthiti*) caused by knowledge of word having *vṛtti* is constantly required. And so, presence of objects through *upanaya sannikarṣa* could be treated as a cause of *anvayabodha*, and then *anvayabodha* could be treated as a case of *jñāna lakṣaṇa pratyāsatti*, which is a case of *alaukika pratyakṣa*.[3]

Let us explain this further. In Nyāya one talks about two types of perception: (1) *laukika* and (2) *alaukika*. *Laukika* perception arises out of *laukika sannikarṣa* and *alaukika* perception arises out of *alaukika sannikarṣa*. This *alaukika sannikarṣa* is of three types: (1) *sāmānya lakṣaṇa*, (2) *jñāna lakṣaṇa* and (3) *yogaja*. *Pratyāsatti* refers to this *sannikarṣa*. When we have the knowledge where *ghaṭa* is the *viśeṣya*, and *ghaṭatva* is the *prakāraka* (this is *savikalpaka* knowledge), in this visual perception there is a *sāmānya lakṣaṇa pratyāsatti* with the universal *ghaṭatva* and then taking *ghaṭatva* as *viśeṣaṇa*, we have *alaukika pratyakṣa* of all the *ghaṭa*s as the residence of *ghaṭatva*. From knowledge of universal property residing in an object, we come to perceive all the *adhikaraṇa*s of such a property and this perception is *alaukika* perception.

Jñāna lakṣaṇa pratyāsatti refers to *jñāna lakṣaṇa sannikarṣa*. *Jñāna lakṣaṇa pratyāsatti* does not produce knowledge of *āśraya* like that of *sāmānya lakṣaṇa*. In case of "fragrant sandalwood"

---

3. *Śabdaśaktiprakāśikā*, p. 9.

(*surabhi candanam*), we have the eye contact with sandalwood. At the same time even though fragrance (the predicate of sandalwood) and fragrancehood [*saurabhatva* (the predicate of fragrance)] are not subject to eye contact, before eye contact we have *jñāna lakṣaṇa pratyāsatti* with the presence of fragrance in the form of fragrancehood. Out of this *pratyāsatti,* we have *jñāna lakṣaṇa sannikarṣa* presenting *alaukika pratyakṣa* of fragrancehood in the part fragrance and of fragrance in the part sandalwood.

Yogaja perception involves the perception of the subtle objects by the *yogī*s who possess special power to see them.

Now we can see that linguistic understanding is not included in perception, inference, etc. Whenever we use the word "*sākāṅkṣa*", we mean *ākāṅkṣā, yogyatā, sannidhi*. It is to be noted that in Nyāya knowledge of words is the cause of linguistic understanding. Word alone is not the cause of linguistic understanding. *Anvaya* means relation. Out of the *sākāṅkṣa* words, objects present themselves and then knowledge of objects in subject-predicate (*viśeṣya-viśeṣaṇa*) form arises. The relation that is known in the rise of linguistic understanding out of subject-predicate relation is called *anvaya*, and knowledge of this *anvaya* is called *anvayabodha*. Jagadīśa argues that we have the knowledge of objects (in subject-predicate relation) presented by the *sākāṅkṣa* words. And, this knowledge is of a specific kind in the sense that this knowledge centres round only those objects that are presented by the corresponding words. This is why it is different from perception, etc.

Jagadīśa offers an inference to prove the non-inclusion of linguistic understanding in other kinds of knowledge like perception, etc.[4]

> *soyam bodhaḥ pratyakṣānumityādibhyoḥ bhinnaḥ sākāṅkṣapadopasthāpyapadārthamātraviṣayakatvāt*

4. *Śabdaśaktiprakāśikā*, p. 12.

One could argue that this *anvayabodha* could well be a unique one, but why should it rise out of knowledge of words having expectancy, etc.? Jagadīśa's answer is that there is *anvaya-vyatireka* relation between unique (*vilakṣaṇa*) *anvyabodha* and knowledge of words having expectancy, etc.[5] The idea is that we determine cause-effect relation by *anvaya-vyatireka bhāva*. When *x* precedes *y* and whenever there is *x*, there is *y* and whenever there is no *x*, there is no *y*, we say that there is *anvaya* (*sadbhāva*) *vyatireka* (*asadbhāva*) relation between *x* and *y*. And then *x* could be regarded as a cause of *y*. This is how we determine cause and effect. Similarly, we have *anvaya-vyatireka* between knowledge of words having expectancy, etc. and linguistic understanding. Thus we have to accept linguistic understanding, i.e. testimonial knowledge as a unique kind of knowledge arising out of knowledge of words having expectancy, etc.

Jagadīśa argues that presence of individual objects arising out of knowledge of words with expectancy, etc. is not the ultimate product of linguistic understanding. Presence of individual objects is not what is meant by linguistic understanding. Had it been the case, then our reflective knowledge (*anuvyavasāya*) would be "I remember cow" (*gam smarāmi*), "I remember existence" (*astitvam smarāmi*), etc. The form of reflective knowledge implies the form of pre-reflective knowledge. After listening to the utterance "There is a cow" (*gaurasti*), we have the reflective knowledge "I have the linguistic understanding of cow through its existence" (*astitvena gāṁ śābdayāmi*). If one denies that the form of reflective knowledge determines the form of the original pre-reflective knowledge, then similar thing could be said about inference and other sources of knowledge.

In the analysis of reflective knowledge what we have seen

5. *Śabdaśaktiprakāśikā*, p. 14.

is that linguistic understanding is predicative knowledge (*viśiṣṭa buddhi*); it is a knowledge where a predicate is attributed to a subject. But then this predicative knowledge possesses *śabdatva jāti* and not *anumititva, upamititva* or *smṛtitva* — there does not seem to be any argument for this thesis. The *anvayabodha* theorists argue that the typical *anvayabodha* is not produced without the memory (*smṛti*) of objects that have been known beforehand. Along the same line memory theorists could also argue that knowledge of word having *vṛtti* inspires the impression (*saṁskāra*) and out of this impression there arises the knowledge where existence (*astitva*) is predicate (*prakāra*) and cow (*go*) is subject (*viśeṣya*). So, this line of argument concludes that linguistic understanding is actually a knowledge of memory.

Jagadīśa argues that it is undeniable that impression (*saṁskāra* in the form of *astitvaprakāraka go viśeṣyaka*) is the cause of the corresponding memory. And without this cause, memory cannot arise. But this impression is not required to be present before the appearance of *anvayabodha* of "There is a cow" (*gaurasti*).[6] Impression is regularly present before the rise of memory. But impression is not regularly present before *anvayabodha*. First we have the knowledge of words having *vṛtti*s, out of this knowledge appear the individual objects (*viṣakalika*), which lies at the root of the impression of the objects. And once these individual discrete objects appear, this is enough to generate *anvayabodha*. Before the rise of this *anvayabodha*, presence of corresponding impression is not required to be present. As a result treating *anvayabodha* as memory is not defendable.

Lokāyatas accept perception as the only source of knowledge (*pramāṇa*). Naturally, they try to reduce testimonial knowledge to perception.

---

6. *Śabdaśaktiprakāśikā*, p. 19.

Jagadīśa responds to this "only perception theorists" by arguing that if testimonial knowledge is to be included in perception, and since perception is of two kinds, viz: (1) *laukika* and (2) *alaukika*, testimonial knowledge could be included either in *laukika* or in *alaukika*. Linguistic understanding cannot be included in *laukika* perception, for we recognize contact (*sannikarṣas*) as the cause of *laukika* perception and in case of *anvayabodha* no such contact is present. Could testimonial knowledge be included in *alaukika* perception? *Alaukika* perception is of three kinds: (1) *sāmānya lakṣaṇa*, (2) *jñāna lakṣaṇa* and (3) *yogaja*. In *sāmānya lakṣaṇa* perception, presence of perceived object with which *laukika* contact has been established is required. And in *jñāna lakṣaṇa* perception, all the residences (*adhikaraṇas*) of the universal (*sāmānya*) become objects of knowledge. When we have linguistic understanding from "There is a cow" (*gaurasti*), individual cow becomes the object of knowledge and not all the cows. Moreover, *laukika* contact is not required to be present before linguistic understanding.

Also linguistic understanding cannot be included in *yogaja* perception. *Yaugika* contact with suprasensuous objects is not possible before the *anvayabodha* arising out of knowledge of "There is a cow".

If at all testimonial knowledge is to be included in perception, it has to be *jñāna lakṣaṇa* perception. "Only perception theorists" accept this. According to them, out of knowledge of words having expectancy, etc. The corresponding objects appear and with these objects we have *jñāna lakṣaṇa pratyāsatti* and results in the *anvayabodha* (involving memory), viz. *astitva viśiṣṭa go viśeṣyaka*.

If testimonial knowledge is considered *alaukika* perception resulting from *jñāna lakṣaṇa pratyāsatti*, it amounts to saying that as the appearance of objects out of knowledge of words results in testimonial knowledge, similarly, the presence of objects out of inference, etc. with which *jñāna lakṣaṇa* contact is present could be objects of linguistic understanding.

This, however, goes against our experience. Only those objects that present themselves by words become the objects of *anvayabodha*. If objects present themselves through something other than words, such knowledge is not called linguistic understanding in our common experience.

Moreover, when objects present themselves banking on linguistic understanding, we have the reflective knowledge (*anuvyavasāya*) of linguistic understanding. But if "Only Perception Theorists" are correct, then objects which present themselves by something other than words, that knowledge would also become the object of reflective linguistic knowledge (*śabdānuvyavasāya*). In other words, all kinds of reflective knowledge (of perception, inference, etc.) would turn out to be reflective testimonial knowledge (*śabdānuvyavasāya*).[7]

So, as we have seen, "Only Perception Theorists" hold that the objection that objects present themselves in ways other than word would become objects of reflective testimonial knowledge (*śabdānuvyavasāya*) does not stand. They hold that the cause of reflective testimonial knowledge is the knowledge as presented by wordness (*śabdatva*), arising out of knowledge of words having expectancy, etc. This precludes the possibility of object being present in ways other than through word becoming objects of reflective testimonial knowledge. Objects presenting themselves through ways other than word will never present themselves as predicated by wordness (*śabdatva*).

Jagadīśa holds that this causal relation is not acceptable, for this relation suffers from *vyabhicāra*. If something is a cause of an effect, then such relation holds because of our knowledge of *anvaya* and *vyatireka*. In the present context, reflective testimonial knowledge (*śabdānuvyavasāya*) centring round

7. *Śabdaśaktiprakāśikā*, p. 19.

specific object is the effect. And the cause is the linguistic understanding centring objects presenting themselves out of knowledge of words having expectancy, etc. For this causal relation to obtain, there should be *anvaya* and *vyatireka* between these two.

The anti-reductionist Nyāya holds that even if there is *anvaya* between the two, there is no *vyatireka* relation.[8] There are cases where the effect is produced overriding the cause, i.e. in absence of cause. Because of this *vyabhicāra*, the alleged causal relation advocated by "Only Perception Theorists" does not obtain.

Let us see how this *vyabhicāra* can be shown. The alleged *vyabhicāra* obtains between reflective testimonial knowledge (*śabdānuvyavasāya*), i.e. the effect and testimonial knowledge arising out of knowledge of words having expectancy, etc., i.e. the cause. Take the example "Bring water by a jar" (*ghaṭena jalamāhara*). Out of these words having expectancy, etc. arise objects like *ghaṭa*, *karaṇatva*, *jala*, *karmatva*, *āharaṇa* and *kṛti*. And during these objects presenting themselves, there is a certain knowledge of block (*bāddha niścaya*) of the form "jar with a hole cannot be the instrument of bringing water" (*jalāharaṇam na sacchidrakaraṇakam*). And, at the next moment arises the linguistic understanding of the form "bringing of water by a jar other than that which has a hole" (*chidretara ghaṭakaraṇaka jalāharaṇagocara*) and then comes reflective knowledge centring round the linguistic understanding regarding jar different from that having a hole (*chidretara ghaṭa*). Now notice that even in the absence of linguistic understanding arising out of presence of objects due to knowledge of words having expectancy, etc. centring round the object not presenting itself through words, linguistic understanding and corresponding reflective knowledge arise. Thus there is no causal relation between linguistic understanding centring round objects presenting

8. *Śabdaśaktiprakāśikā*, p. 22.

themselves out of knowledge of words having expectancy, etc. and the corresponding reflective knowledge.

Analysis of linguistic understanding is undertaken by philosophers since this is one of the important ways in which we acquire knowledge. Epistemic progress is tied up with our ability to understand people's utterance. Epistemology matters to philosophy of language in two ways: (1) The first is the simple fact, when we listen to utterance or read and understand a sentence, we come to acquire knowledge; (2). The second, and no less significant, concerns the fact that growing into language is growing into being in possession of a world. The way we slice up the reality is tinged by the language we possess. In the present essay, however, I shall be concerned with the first: Gaining knowledge by understanding what one is told.

When we acquire knowledge, we also want knowledge to be true and capable of being justified. Justification comes in, for otherwise we would fail to distinguish between knowledge and fluke guess or happy coincidence. Knowledge would fail to account for epistemic advancement unless justification is tied to it. In order to account for this full-fledged conception of knowledge, we need to view knowledge (linguistic understanding in the present context) "as standing in the space of reasons". Let me clarify this idea of "standing in the space of reason".[9] As I understand it, when I hear an utterance and understand it, I acquire a piece of knowledge. In order to rule out the possibility of me making a lucky guess, I as a knower must epistemically satisfactorily stand in the space of reason with respect to the particular knowledge. This means that my satisfactory standing is constituted by the validity of an argument that is said to be ascribed to its

9. John McDowell, "Knowledge by Hearsay", in his *Meaning, Knowledge and Reality*, Cambridge, Mass.: Harvard University Press, 1998, p. 415.

possessor (the speaker), with the knowledge in question as its conclusion. So, after I acquire knowledge, for that piece of information to be knowledge proper, in order for me to be in an epistemically satisfactory standing, I need to articulate that knowledge in the form of an argument that I can ascribe to the speaker. This epistemically satisfactory standing can be called "mediated standing". Once we accept this idea of mediated standing, we are tempted to suppose that mediated standing in the space of reasons for the justificatory argument must start somewhere. One could, of course, try to argue that all epistemically satisfactory standings are mediated. This is an important issue, but none the less we need not bother with this at present.

This is the right occasion to understand the concept of mediated understanding deeper. It makes perfect sense to say that since someone sees things as this and so, she concludes that things are thus and so. But the person's satisfactory epistemic seeing that things are thus and so demands justification. The concept of seeing that things are thus and so already involves the concept of epistemically satisfactory standing with regard to the fact that things are thus and so. A genuine mediated epistemic understanding should consist of an argument without begging the question about the relevant epistemic standing. So, on this view, one's epistemically satisfactory standing with regard to the knowledge that things are thus and so must be constituted by the availability of an argument to the informant where the premises are to be different from merely seeing that things are thus and so to be followed by the conclusion that things are thus and so.

If this analysis of mediated satisfactory epistemic understanding comes through, then how does it affect the notion of linguistic understanding, i.e. the knowledge through testimony? Knowing through understanding an utterance requires the knower to stand in the space of reasons and this standing is a mediated one, for the speaker does not force the hearer with the information. It is rather the hearer who depends on the speaker for the former's understanding and this dependence is more rational than causal in nature.

Consider a tourist looking for the museum in a city. She asks a passerby who is a resident of that city and told where the museum is. The tourist hears and understands the passerby's utterance and finds out the museum where it is told to be situated. This is the core of any account of knowledge through testimony.

If our earlier analysis of epistemically satisfactory mediated standing is correct, then the tourist must be credited with a cogent argument to the conclusion about the location of the museum where the tourist's epistemically satisfactory standing with regard to the premises must require further justification. Of course, here one could talk of the tourist armed with ancillary premises like the informant being competent, trustworthy, etc. But can we explain the tourist's epistemically satisfactory standing with regard to these ancillary premises in a non-question begging way? A positive answer does not sound promising.

The underlying idea of the uneasiness that I am expressing regarding the analysis of the hearer's epistemically satisfactory mediated standing to the knowledge that she acquires through testimony, is that for the hearer's belief to be counted as knowledge the argument that the hearer possesses must not leave open the possibility that things are not as she believes them to be. Claim of knowledge carries along with it the claims of justification and truth. I do not mean to suggest that the only alternatives left are intolerable scepticism on the one hand and impossibility of any knowledge claim whatsoever on the other. I would like to uphold knowledge claims carrying with it claims of truth and justification, at the same time, without giving undue concession to scepticism.

Consider a person who keeps himself abreast with the latest developments by regularly listening to news broadcast at 6'o clock every evening. Can we attribute to her at 3'o clock in the afternoon on some day late in the life of say Gandhi that Gandhi is alive (assuming that Gandhi is not in the news lately)? Many of us would be inclined to say "Yes". Something similar happens to a large number of our knowledge claims concerning durable but impermanent states of affairs to which we have only occasional epistemic access. Here, we seem to rely on the principle that we can have knowledge claims that things are thus the way we knew them until a change has been reported, which has not yet been. This intuition seems reasonable, for if we deny this, much of knowledge claims would be lost to us. This much of risk one has to take to do justice to our epistemology of retained knowledge. Otherwise, we would end up in supposing we know much less than what we ordinarily think we know. What our intuition suggests is that we think of knowledge claim as a kind of continuant. It needs nutrition, occasionally through intermittent confirmatory experience.

If knowledge is a standing in the space of reasons, then knowing that things are thus and so must have a reason for taking things to be thus and so. Not that inferential transitions are irrelevant, but one could offer a better explanation of such relevance.

In the epistemology of retained knowledge one cannot stick to one's knowledge claim if one's epistemic access to the impermanent but durable states of affairs has lapsed for long. Knowledge claim demands its claimant to be doxastically responsible. Being doxastically responsible is obviously an exercise of rationality. And this accounts for the thought that knowledge is standing in the space of reasons.

In the backdrop of the above discussion, one could explain "standing in the space of reason" in terms of "mediation by the rational force of surrounding consideration". One cannot claim to have an epistemically satisfactory standing unless one is sensitive to rational force. The epistemic satisfactoriness of the knowledge claimant's mediated standing does not consist in the cogency of the argument from the mediating considerations, but the knowledge claimant could not even have a standing in the space of reasons without being rationally sensitive to the mediating considerations. We are interested in the epistemic standing of the knower who has acquired knowledge by listening to her interlocutor's utterance. One cannot claim to have testimonial knowledge that things are thus and so unless one claims having heard from the interlocutor by virtue of understanding what the interlocutor says that things are thus and so. "Acquiring knowledge by testimony is not a mindless reception of something that has nothing to do with rationality; it yields a standing in the space of reason."[10] And this idea can be buttressed by stressing the point that one can claim to have acquired knowledge from one's interlocutor by exhibiting doxastic responsibility. There are many ways one could be doxastically irresponsible, for example, by believing someone who is not trustworthy or who is not informed about the subject matter that she speaks about.

Of course, doxastic responsibility paving the way towards knowledge claim leaves room for subtle nuances. Consider the story of the boy crying "wolf". After many a fake call made by the boy, people who knew the boy consider it doxastically irresponsible to derive knowledge claims even when there was a wolf and knowledge claim could have been derived. But think of a stranger present on that occasion, having no knowledge of the previous fake calls of the boy. It would be doxastically irresponsible for the stranger not to derive

10. John McDowell, "Knowledge by Hearsay", p. 434.

any knowledge claim. This goes well with our intuition. This rational responsiveness that is crucial to testimonial knowledge claim, rather than the idea of cogency of argument involving a leap from a lesser informational state to a greater informational state. This fits well with our idea of testimonial knowledge where knowledge gets transmitted from one to another, unless violation of doxastic responsibility takes place. I would like to conclude that in so far as its epistemic status is concerned, testimonial knowledge could not be reduced to other ways of knowing. But in so far as its justificatory status is concerned, testimonial knowledge involves many other sources of knowledge.

4

Representation, Meaning and Truth

Sadhan Chakraborti

THE divide between inferential role semantics and truth conditional semantics in philosophy of language has been revitalized by Brandom's forceful attempt to defend inferentialism[1] considering it as opposed to representationalism. Putting Brandom's inferentialism kind of philosophical view aside we can say that philosophy of language in the West is concerned with three broad questions: (1) What is the relationship between language and the world ? ; (2) What is the relationship between our mind and the world ?; and (3) What is the relationship between our language and our mind ?

In the context of the first question it is commonly said that speakers use language to describe how the world is. Typically, the use of language to describe the world is glossed by saying that language is a type of *representation*, and that words or sentences stand for the world (or chunks of it). The word "parrot", for example, can represent a particular red-beaked bird and the sentence "that parrot can speak" can represent the fact that the bird in question can speak. The philosophical question that has bothered philosophers is how is it possible for language to represent the world ?

1. Robert Brandom: (a) *Articulating Reasons: An Introduction to Inferentialism*, Cambridge, Mass.: Harvard University Press, 2000.

   (b) "Inferentialism and Some of Its Challenges", *Philosophy and Phenomenological Research*, 74, 2007, 651-76.

Representationalism in philosophy of language has a long tradition. Many philosophers before the twentieth century held that mental images form the basis of the power of language to represent things. Hume,[2] for example, explicitly identified ideas as images and observed that language represents the world through ideas associated with it. In the beginning of twentieth century Russell wrote:

> We must attach some meaning to the words we use, if we are to speak significantly and not utter mere noise; and the meaning we attach to our words must be something with which we are acquainted.[3]

According to Russell, we are confronted with things (entities) and somehow make our words stand for them. Representing or standing for things in the world makes our words meaningful. Many philosophers of the twentieth century took some form of representationalism for granted. Wittgenstein's earlier theory in *Tractatus*,[4] Etchemendy's[5] representational semantics, Fodor's[6] notion of semantics as an annex to his representational theory of mind, Devitt's[7] semantics based on the concept of reference are taken to be some of the examples of the twentieth-century representationalism in philosophy of language.

The second question, i.e. the question regarding the

2. David Hume, *An Enquiry concerning Human Understanding*, Calcutta: Progressive Publishers, 1967.
3. Bertrand Russell, *The Problems of Philosophy*, Home University Library, 1912.
4. Ludwig Wittgenstein, *Tractatus Logico-Philosophicus*, London: Routledge and Kegan Paul 1961.
5. J. Etchemendy, *The Concept of Logical Consequence*, Cambridge, Mass.: Harvard University Press, 1990.
6. J. Fodor: (a) *Representations*, Cambridge, Mass.: MIT Press, 1981; (b) *Concepts*, Oxford: Clarendon Press, 1998.
7. M. Devitt, "The Methodology of Naturalistic Semantics", *Journal of Philosophy*, 91, 545-72.

relationship between mind and world, or thought and world is seen to be answered in two different ways. Some philosophers contend that our mind represents the world through images. This view can be traced back to the classical Greek philosophy. Aristotle,[8] for example, said, "The soul never thinks without a mental image". This view was almost universally accepted in the philosophical tradition from the Greek philosophy uptil the emergence of twentieth-century philosophy. Of course, there are some dissenting voices, e.g. the voices of Ryle,[9] Wittgenstein, Schlick, Sartre,[10] etc., which contributed to the decline of interest in imagery in both, analytical and phenomenological tradition. Although imagery lost its earlier glory in the twentieth century, a significant number of philosophers continued admitting image-like entities through which our mind was claimed to represent the world. After the rise of cognitive science this was prominent. In cognitive science, cognition is viewed as computational manipulation of symbols expressed in mentalese — language of thought. Fodor championed this view. Kosslyn[11] developed a *quasi-pictorial* computational theory of visual imagery. *Description* and *quasi-pictorial* theorists disagreed sharply over what sorts of computational symbols or data structures are acceptable within cognitive theory.

However, one thing that philosophers are not inclined to deny is ingeniously formulated by Brentano[12] in characterizing

8. Aristotle, *De Anima*, 431a, 15-20.
9. G. Ryle, *The Concept of Mind*, Penguin Books, 1963: 1st published 1949.
10. J.P. Sartre, *Imagination, A Psychological Critique*, tr. F. Williams, University of Michigan Press, 1962.
11. S.M. Kosslyn, *Ghosts in the Mind's Machine: Creating and Using Images in the Brain*, Norton, 1983.
12. F. Brentano, *Psychology from an Empirical Standpoint*, tr. Antos C. Rancurello, D.B. Terrel and Linda L. McAlister, Routledge, 1995.

the thought or the mental, viz. intentionality. According to him, mind or thought is intentional. It is directed towards objects. In characterizing the mental in terms of intentionality Brentano maintains neutrality regarding the nature of objects towards which our mind or thought is directed. Neither mental inexistence nor real existence of things is committed in such characterization.

"Intentionality" is often used interchangeably with "representationlity". "Mental states are intentional" is used to mean that mental states represent things towards which they are directed. Taken in this sense, an external realist who admits external objects and contends that mental states are directed towards external objects, may be said to hold a representationalist theory of mind. Now one may subscribe to the view that mental states are directed to the external objects not through any intermediary, entity like idea or imagery or entities having mental inexistence. One may hold that mental states are directly directed to the external objects. Philosophers advocating this view are called "naïve realists". The above sense of "representationality" entitles inclusion of naïve realists in the camp of representationalists.

The above exposition of representationality suggests that the content of a sentence, for both a naïve realist and a representative realist, is an external state of affairs. Both of them would adhere to the view that a sentence represents an external state of affairs. The only difference between them would be that a naïve realist would contend that a sentence represents, whatever it represents, directly, not through any intermediary, whereas a representationalist would hold that the external state of affairs is represented by a sentence through an intermediary.

A representative realist, who is also an external realist, upholds the view that our thoughts are directed towards external objects only through intermediaries constituted by ideas or imagery or similar entities. These are the direct (immediate) objects of our thought. External objects are thought of by us through our thinking of the immediate objects of our thoughts. If "representationality" is used interchangeably with "intentionality" then representative realists can also be called representationalists.

Even those who restrict our thoughts to be directed to internal entities, cannot be barred from being included in the camp of representationalists under the above interpretation of the term "representationality".

There is a similarity between representationality and intentionality. When we say that thought is intentional, what we intend to say is that thought is always a thought *of* something. This holds in the case of representationality too. "Our thoughts are representational" means our thoughts are thoughts of something. What can be disputed — is that representationality like intentionality consists in *being of something*. One may contend that apart from being of something representationality involves *indirectness*. On this view *when* we say our thoughts are representational in nature what we intend to say is (i) a thought is *of* something and (ii) a thought provides a model of the thing of which it is a thought. So it is argued that intentionality is one of the components of representationality.

A representationalist about mind or thought in this sense would say that the content of our thought is a model of reality. The content of propositional attitude, for example, is a model of reality. *X*'s belief to the effect that Delhi is to the north of Kolkata is a depiction of the geographical relationship between Delhi and Kolkata. It is through this depiction (model) that *X*'s belief represents the geographical relationship between Delhi and Kolkata.

The theory of truth that is compatible with this kind of representationality thesis about thought characterizes truth in terms of correspondence. A representationalist would say that a belief is true if and only if the content of it corresponds to the reality of which the content is a model.

Regarding the question of the relationship between language and mind it is commonly held that speakers use language to express, more or less accurately, what they are thinking. If Sabina is thinking that children are playing merrily, she can say that. Here priority of thought over language is envisaged. Language is viewed as a vehicle of thought. Language represents the content of thought. Mental representation and linguistic representation are two ways of representing the same thing. The content in mental representation is the same as the content in linguistic representation. The content may be claimed to consist in the external situation or in some internal situation or in some inexistents or concepts.

The received opinion of our time is *that* linguistic representation is a derivative of mental representation. So emphasis is being given on the study of mental representation.

Of different forms of representationalism, mental or linguistic, those which aim at giving an account of how our language or mind represents the empirical reality has always been fascinating for philosophers. Those philosophical theories of mental/linguistic representation of empirical reality have drawn much attention of thinkers in this area which endorse the human predicament pointed out by Kant, viz. that our knowledge of external reality is possible only through our senses.

The cognitive neuroscientist's account of our mind representing the world endorsing the above human predicament is now believed to be the scientific account of it. So having an idea of the neuroscientist's account of our mind's representation of the world helps in engaging ourselves in a meaningful discussion about the philosophical issues centring linguistic/mental representationalism.

The neuroscientists' account of the neurological processes which generate perceptual experience gives an idea of their view of mind's representing the empirical world. Neuroscientists have given much emphasis on the visual system, because it is fairly similar in man and the higher primates and so appropriate experiments on such animals may be relevant to the study of neural mechanism underlying perceptual experience in humans; indeed 50 per cent of the cortex in the Macaque monkey is devoted to visual perception. Another reason why vision is so important is that it enables us to perceive information at a distance, to engage in remote sensing by which we can avoid a predator better — it is too late to flee once sharp teeth pierce the skin. If the neurological processes involved in visual perception are understood then it will be easier to understand the neurological processes involved in other modalities of perception.

Visual information is contained in the light reflected from an object. To perceive an object we need sensory receptors that respond to the reflected light. As light passes through the lens of the eye, the image is inverted and focused to project on the back surface of the eye, the retina comprises millions of photoreceptors, each containing light-sensitive molecules or photopigments. When exposed to light, the photopigments become unstable and split apart. Then decomposition alters the flow of the electrical current around the photoreceptors. This light-induced change triggers action potentials in downstream neurons. Then photoreceptors provide for translation from an external stimulus, light, into an internal neural signal, the detection of that stimulus.

Photoreceptors are of two types — rods and cones. Rods are sensitive to low-level stimulation and so useful at night when light energy is reduced. Cones require more intense levels of light and so they are active during daytime vision. Cones are essential for colour vision.

Extensive signal processing of visual information is performed within the retina. The output from the photoreceptors is first processed in the bipolar cells and from there in the ganglion cells. Extensive convergence of information happens within this processing layer of the retina. Axons of the ganglion cells form a bundle, the optic nerve. By way of this nerve, visual information is transmitted to the central nervous system. Within the brain each optic nerve divides into pathways that differ where they terminate within the subcortex. One such pathway starting from the retina reaches the lateral geniculate nuclei (LGN) of the thalamus. This pathway contains more than 90 per cent of the axons in the optic nerve and provides input to the cortex. The remaining 10% of the fibres innervate other subcortical structures including the pulvinar nucleus of the midbrain. The final projection to the visual cortex is via the geniculo-cortical pathway. This bundle of axons exits from the LGN and ascends to the cortex, with almost all of the fibres terminating in primary visual area of the occipital lobe. Thus visual information in the cortex is processed by at least five distinct neurons: photoreceptors, bipolar cells, ganglion cells, LGN cells and cortical cells.

The strongest hypothesis in visual perception is that visual information is distributed across distinct subsystems. On this view perception is analytic. Early processes are devoted to analysing attributes of a stimulus: some processes represent shape, some other processes focus on colour, and the rest provide information about the dynamics or movement in the visual scene.

Distinct regions of visual processing are identified in the cortex like V_1, V_2, V_3, V_4, etc. Each visual area has a topographic representation of external space in the contralateral hemifield. An area is defined by a discontinuity in the retinotropic representation of the cells. Neurons within an area not only decode where an object is located in visual space, but also provide vivid information about the object's external attributes.

Visual perception is a divide-and-conquer strategy. Rather than each visual area representing all attributes of an object, each provides its own limited analysis. Processing is distributed and specialized. As we advance through the visual system, different areas elaborate on the initial information in V_1 and begin to integrate this information across dimensions to form recognizable percepts.

Neuroimaging studies (mainly based on FMRI and PET) have opened a new window for studying visual perception. The results of these studies suggest that perception involves higher visual areas rather than the primary visual cortex. Features like colour, shape and motion are processed along distinct neural pathways. But perception requires more than simply perceiving the features of objects. When we look at an object we perceive a unified object. Object recognition is more than linking features to trigger memories.

Failures of perception can occur even when processes, such as the analysis of colour, shape and motion are intact. This disorder is limited to the visual modality. The syndrome is referred as visual agnosia. Neuroscientists have identified two pathways in higher visual areas, viz. the virtual or occipito-temporal pathway and the dorsal or occipito-parietal pathway. The former is specialized for object perception for determining what it is we are looking at and the latter is specialized for spatial perception, for determining where an object is, and for analysing the spatial configuration between different objects in a sense. "What" and "Where" are the two basic questions in visual perception which are answered by these two pathways.[13] The neuroscientists appear to say that the

13. Michael S. Gazzaniga, Richard B. Ivry and George Mangun, *Cognitive Neuroscience: The Biology of the Mind,* 2nd edn. Norton, 2002.

external reality consists of waves and particles, which are imperceptible, but they are causally responsible for generating inner representations in the form of nerve signals the processing of which ultimately generates perceptual experience. Thus it seems that the neurophysical account of perception is a form of representationalism.

Representationalists generally make use of what is dubbed as "the argument from illusion" to show that direct realism is impossible, and that there must be sensory inputs that are directly (immediately) grasped by our perceptual experience. The argument from illusion may be formulated thus:

(a) Cases of perceptual illusion are facts.

(b) What we are immediately aware of in such an illusion are not the external objects but the sensory inputs the indubitability of which is guaranteed by the perceptual experience itself.

(c) In respect of epistemic status there is no difference between veridical perception and illusory perception.

(d) Therefore, like the objects of illusory experience objects of veridical perception are also sensory inputs, not external objects.

The argument from variability is also levelled by representationalists against direct realism. In spite of the object constancy we have different perceptual experiences at different moments as is the case with face-vase variability. So what we directly experience in perception cannot be the external object, it is rather our internal representation.

In neurophysical account, perception is explained as a modification of the brain that comprehends the specific nature of the external object. The external object is actually inferred from the internal representation of it.

One of the problems encountered by the upholders of the

neurophysical theory of perception, who seem to be representationalists, is that if it is said that we infer the external objects on the basis of inner representations, where inner representations are taken to be caused by the waves and particles which constitute the external world then a direct knowledge of certain relation is to be admitted between inner representations and external objects (waves and particles). Now, in order to have this knowledge we must have knowledge of inner representations and external waves and particles separately. According to the neurophysical theory of perception inner representations are known directly but we do not have direct knowledge of the external waves and particles. It is difficult to account for how one can have inferential knowledge of waves and particles, which cause inner representations, on the basis of knowledge of inner representations.

Such an inferential knowledge could be admitted had the argument been a transcendetal one. The argument that this theory resorts to is rather a causal argument. Knowledge of causality between *A* and *B* requires independent knowledge of *A* and that of *B*.

If the neurophysical theory of perception is not treated as representationalism then it tantamounts to phenomenalism. Phenomenalists, unlike representationalists, do not claim to have inferential knowledge of external reality. They hold that what we perceive is our construction from the sensory inputs that we receive.

Some neuroscientists tend to view the neurophysical theory of perception as a form of phenomenalism. Semir Zeki, for example, quotes the following passage from Kant:

> All presentations have a necessary reference to a *possible* empirical consciousness, for if they did not have this reference, and becoming conscious of them were entirely

> impossible, then this would be tantamount to saying that they do not exist at all. But all empirical consciousnesses have a necessary reference to a transcendental consciousness (a consciousness that precedes all particular experience), viz. the consciousness of myself as original apperception.

Then he says,

> Here, I disagree only with the suggestion that the "empirical" (micro) consciousness has a necessary reference to the unified, transcendental consciousness.[14]

If the neurophysical account is taken as a form of phenomenalism then it has to admit like Kant, noumena (things-in-themselves) which consists of things unknown and unknowable, or the propounders of this theory have to sever the relationship of inner representations from external reality and thus conceding much to the sceptics.

If we do not deny or doubt the existence of external reality, if we are not idealists or sceptics, then the only option seems to be to admit that the external objects and events are perceived directly. Thus direct realism seems to be the only plausible view of our representation of the external world. But perhaps this goes against the neurophysical account of it.

Quine views the above neuro-scientific account of our experience of the empirical world as naturalism. It is a rational reconstruction of the individual's and/or the race's actual acquisition of a responsible theory of the external world. It would address the question how we, physical denizens of the physical world, can have projected our scientific theory of the world from our meagre contacts with it: from the mere impacts of rays and particles on our surfaces and a few odds and ends such as the strain of walking uphill.

---

14. Semir Zeki, "The Disunity of Consciousness", *Trends in Cognitive Science*, vol. 7, no. 5, 2003.

The kind of naturalism Quine advocates takes, as a physical analogue of Carnap's elementary experience, *global stimulus* as the foundation of naturalism. By "global stimulus" he means the class of all sensory receptors that are triggered at a moment — the temporally ordered class of receptors triggered during the specious present.

Each global stimulus is an ordered subject of the subject's nerve-endings. Two global stimuli are said to be receptually similar if they comprise more or less the same nerve-endings in more or less the same order.

Receptual similarity is distinguished by Quine from perceptual similarity. Perceptual similarity is the effect on the subject. Two receptually very similar global stimuli are indeed apt to be perceptually similar, but two receptually very dissimilar ones can be perceptually similar too.

Another factor responsible for perceptual similarity is *salience*. Most of the receptors triggered on any occasion are not perceptually effective. Only the salient ones determine perceptual similarity among global stimuli. Quine says that the salient part is the part by virtue of which a global stimulus is perceptually similar to other global stimuli despite divergence of other parts.

Salience is, says Quine, the operative factor in ostensive definition. Sweeping or pointing gestures in the vicinity or direction of the intended portion of the scene implement the desired association with the spoken word.

Quine observes that perceptual similarity is the basis of all learning. It operates through our propensity to expect perceptually similar situations to have sequels perceptually similar to each other. Since learning hinges on perceptual similarity, perceptual similarity is not itself learned. It is innate. It can also be moulded by experience. Natural selection has endowed us with standard of perceptual similarity. Perceptual similarity of global stimuli of an individual is, in part innate and in part moulded by experience, private, but there is a public harmony of private standards of perceptual similarity. If two scenes trigger perceptually similar global stimuli in one individual they are apt to do so in another.

Learning of language, according to Quine, is based on public harmony of private standards of perceptual similarity and it is made possible by natural selection. Observation sentences constitute the building-blocks of human languages. Examples are "It is raining", It's cold, "Dog!". They report intersubjectively observable situations, observable outright. Within the individual the observation sentence is keyed to a range of perceptually fairly similar global stimuli. They qualify as observation sentences across the community. Observation sentences are the inception of language.

It seems from the kind of naturalism advocated by Quine that words are tied down to the effects in an individual of global stimuli. So sentences are tied down to the relationships between the effects of global stimuli. If such a relationship between effects of global stimuli constitutes the content of a sentence, how is it possible for a sentence to be in touch with the world at all? How is it possible for our language to represent the world at all?

This "How question" cannot be answered by giving a description of the reality. It is not a descriptive question at all. Rather it is a question of a familiar philosophical kind.

McDowell[15] raises a similar question in the context of the relation between mind and world. He argues that talk of impressions, impingements by the world on a possessor of sensory capacities is empirical description. The idea of receiving an impression is the idea of a transaction in nature. Such a description cannot give an answer to the philosophical question

15. J. McDowell, *Mind and World*, Cambridge, Mass.: Harvard University Press, 1994.

"How can our thinking be directed to the world?" An answer to this question can be given in terms of placing certain things in the logical space of reason, which is contrasted with the logical space of nature.

Quine's naturalism, as an account of the intersubjectivity of linguistic representation, may be admitted, but it is not clear about the way in which it addresses the "How possible?" philosophical question. Since observation sentences are the inception of language, Quine's success in addressing the question in general depends upon his success in addressing the issue in particular for observation sentences. Observation sentences are learned by an individual through keying them to perceptually similar global stimuli. The public character of our observation sentences is ensured by pre-established harmony.

What do these observation sentences represent? Do they represent global stimuli? If yes, then Quine's naturalism can be considered as an adequate account of linguistic representation. The Wittgensteinian charge of impossibility of private language may be avoided in terms of naturalistic idea of pre-established harmony.

The further question that Quine has to answer is "Are truth-matters of observation sentences confined to global stimuli?" The issue of truth is closely related with the issue of linguistic representation. If a sentence represents something then the obtaining of that thing makes the sentence true. Thus if an observation sentence represents certain perceptually similar global stimuli, then it is true, if and only if such a stimulus occurs. This form of naturalism does not seem to be very different from Carnapian phenomenalism from which Quine explicitly distinguishes his naturalism.

The "How possible?" philosophical question comes in with all of its force as soon as it is admitted that truth-matters of observation sentences are outside our global stimuli. Quine seems to hold that truth-matters of observation sentences are external to our global stimuli. He says that all members of the language community are disposed to agree on the truth or falsity of such a sentence on the spot, if they have normal perception and witness to the occasion.[16] What constitutes the spot, the occasion? If it is considered to be the external situation the obtaining of which makes the observation sentence true then it becomes difficult to give an account of how the observation sentence represents the external situation.

Davidson differs from Quine with respect to what constitutes the communicable content of our sentences. For Quine, it is the global stimulus that constitutes the communicable content. An observation sentence is stimulus synonymous for two users of the concerned language between whom communication in terms of the observation sentence takes place. They are prompted to accept or reject the sentence by the same patterns of proximal stimulation.

Davidson is an externalist. He suggests that semantic content is determined by external objects and events, salient to both speaker and interpreter It is determined by the very objects and events the speaker's words are taken by the interpreter to have as the subject matter. Davidson says, "It is the distal stimulus that matters to interpretation".[17] Davidson's distal theory of reference and meaning can, unlike Quine's proximal theory of reference and meaning, avoid the philosophical "How possible?" puzzle of linguistic representation. No such issue arises in the Davidsonian framework as meaning of a sentence in this framework is tied down to external objects and events.

---

16. W.V. Quine, *From Stimulus to Science*, Cambridge, Mass.: Harvard University Press, 1995, p. 22.
17. Donald Davidson, *The Structure and Content of Truth*, p. 321.

One difficulty often pointed out against the Davidsonian distal theory is that it makes error hard to explain, the crucial gap between what is believed to be true and what is true; since the distal theory bases truth on belief, the problem is crucial.

Davidson has attempted to give his solution to this problem. Davidson's distal theory of reference and meaning encounters another difficulty that I think cannot be addressed so easily. Davidson is a direct realist. He contends that the real objects and events in the external world can be represented directly by our language.

The neuro-scientific studies provide a ground to the claim that the neural system of humans puts the limit to our knowledge of the external world. Our knowledge of the external world is shaped by our neural apparatus. A brief account of how it is so is given above. The neuro-scientific account of our knowledge of the external world suggests that the neural limit to our knowledge of the external world is a human predicament. So the Davidsonian distal theory of linguistic representation has to refute the claim of human predicament pointed out by neuro-scientists in order to achieve its strength, which, I think, is not so easy a task. Quine accommodates the predicament but fails to answer the "How possible?" question; Davidson can answer the "How possible?" question but fails to accommodate the predicament. This Quine-Davidson conflict stands in the way to the progress in the area of linguistic representation in the Western philosophy of language.

5

On the Impossibility of Language–Reality Divide

Arguments from the Standpoint of Reference

Amitabha Dasgupta

THE language-reality relationship gives rise to two views of the world or reality. The one is the impersonal view of the world which is also described as the God's-eye view of the world. The other is the speaker's view of the world. The God's-eye view of the world is essentially a view from nowhere. Whereas, the speaker's point of view of the world is essentially associated with a human point of view. As we can see, these are the two conflicting views of reality whose basis lies in the way language is related to reality. In other words, these two views of the world follow from the two different ways in which the language-reality relationship is conceptualized in these two traditions. That is, each tradition has a distinctive way of conceiving this relationship. The God's-eye view of the world is associated with classical realism. Classical realism due to its metaphysical orientation defines the relationship between language and reality at a purely objective level. Language is thus conceived as a picture or mirror of reality — the reality that is lying outside and independent of us. Accordingly, how is language hooked onto reality becomes a singularly important question for realism. Since reality is conceived as independent of language, the language–reality divide becomes inevitable. The language–reality divide defines the core of the realist world view.

In the other perspective, language-reality relationship is defined from the point of view of human subject or speaker. Thus, the relationship between language and the world is not that of correspondence or mirroring. Language does not mirror the world. It is the speaker who mirrors the world. He mirrors the world through the use of language. This perspective thus does not admit of language–reality divide. The reason is reality is largely determined by the conceptual categories that we impose on to the world. These categories are linguistic in nature and it is through these categories that we experience the world.

The present paper will argue against the language–reality divide on the ground that such a divide is not possible. It is not related to reality in the way it is conceptualized in classical realism or, what Hilary Putnam calls metaphysical realism. In this respect, the bulk of the argument comes from the theory of reference developed by Putnam. The two fundamental claims to be made in this paper are: First, metaphysical realist notion of reference allows language–reality divide and second, this divide is not possible because of the untenability of the supporting theory of reference. Accordingly, this paper will have three sections. The first section will be concerned with the theory of reality as proposed in metaphysical realism. The second section will be concerned with metaphysical realists' notion of truth and reference. The third section will offer Putnam's critique of metaphysical realism whose main thrust is to show that language–reality divide is untenable. Its untenability lies on the ground of theory of reference.

I

Language–reality Divide and the Emerging Theory of Reality

Historically, realism or metaphysical realism stands for a theory of reality. Its basic concern is to describe the ultimate nature of reality which actually means delineating the essential structure of reality. The essential structure is one which explicates the essential nature of reality and is distinguished from the appearance of reality. The notion of reality includes both, its appearance and the essential inner structure. It is because of this reason traditionally there is a constant attempt on the part of philosophers to separate the elements that are essential from those that are non-essential in their description of reality. Reality has an essential nature and it is the one which makes reality what it is. The distinction between reality conceived in terms of its essential nature and the appearance of it thus becomes a necessary requirement for having a theory of reality. Such a notion of reality defined strictly in terms of its essential nature makes it evident that it is independent of the comprehensive power of human mind. It exists, no matter whether we recognize it or not. Now the question arises: If reality is independent of us, how could we talk about it? It is, of course, language that comes here as a medium that enables us to get to reality. The mechanism that operates here is that we comprehend reality by virtue of representing it in language. Its ultimate structure can be revealed in language and thus allows us to talk about the essential nature of reality. Language, in this sense, is often thought of as a mirror of reality.

Wittgenstein's *Tractatus* is a celebrated attempt that seeks to show the connection that exists between language and the world. The precise nature of this connection is established by making the correlation between the ultimate elements of thought and the simplest of atoms which constitute the substance of the world. This forms the background of his famous picture theory of meaning. The theory holds that language is a body of propositions which picture the world. Propositions are significant by virtue of being perceptible expressions of thoughts where thoughts are viewed as logical pictures of facts.[1] Wittgenstein regards propositions and thoughts as pictures not only in a metaphorical sense but also in a literal sense. But there is always a possibility that there may be a sentence which does not look like a picture. Wittgenstein's answer is that this failure is due to the reason that language disguises thought so much so that the sentence fails to be a picture in a literal sense.

Now, the next question that arises is how do sentences become pictures of reality? For this, consider the two following sentences: "My fork is to the left of my knife" and "My knife is to the left of my fork". Note that these two sentences, though different from what they are saying, contain the same words. Their difference lies in their spatial arrangement of words. The meaning of the first sentence, for example, is different from the second because the words "my fork" occurs to the left of the words "my knife". Here spatial relationship between words symbolize a spatial relationship between things. The sentence thus expresses a spatial representation of spatial relationship.[2]

Now suppose, the same sentence "My fork is to the left of my knife" is spoken instead of written. It would then be expressing a temporal relationship between the spoken words representing spatial relationship between the physical objects. This is possible because both the temporal sequence of spoken

1. L. Wittgenstein, *Tractatus Logico-Philosophicus,* tr., D.F. Pears and B.F. Mc Guinness, London: Routledge & Kegan Paul, 1961, 3.5, 4,4.001.
2. Ibid., 4.002.

words and the spatial array of written words share a common abstract structure. In Wittgenstein's example, the score of a song, the notes sung by a singer and the grooves of a record of the song, though all are different, share a common structure.[3] *Tractatus* thus makes the claim that a picture of any kind must have in common with what it depicts. This condition must hold even if the picture depicts incorrectly. This assumes that there must be an element that is an irreducible shared minimum existing between the picture and what it depicts. Wittgenstein calls it logical form. A proposition is thus called a picture because of its shared form.

From this idea of shared form conveying the idea of irreducible shared minimum, we can reconstruct Wittgenstein's search for the ultimate constituents of the world through his picture theory of meaning. *Tractatus* offers an ontological scheme which may be roughly explicated in terms of the three basic concepts — names, objects and fact. They are so interconnected that they form a system — a system of the world. A sentence when analysed shows that it is made of names and each name refers to an object. A sentence thus, in its capacity as a picture, pictures a particular configuration of objects. Further, a name is logically simple which cannot be analysed into any other expressions as its constituents. In this sense, they are primitive. Correspondingly, objects too are metaphysically simple and hence, are not amenable to farther decomposition. Objects are constituents of the world and they do not undergo any change. They are unalterable. They are the building-blocks out of which possible and the actual world is composed. The actual world is the one where the constituting objects are arranged in a particular way and thus form a configuration. Here, at this stage, the notion of fact

3. L. Wittgenstein, *Tractatus Logico-Philosophicus*, tr., D.F. Pears and B.F. Mc Guinness, London: Routledge & Kegan Paul, 1961, 4.001.

comes into the picture. Facts unlike objects are contingent and they form the contingent aspects of reality. However, the ontological importance of fact is that the world is necessarily represented in terms of facts and not in terms of isolated things. The relationship between facts and objects is that facts are a combination of objects. A particular combination of objects gives rise to a particular fact — indicating the existence of a state of affairs. Facts are thus possible due to the existence of objects. Objects in this sense are constituents of facts. As Wittgenstein remarks, they are the unalterable forms of the world and thus without them the world will not be possible. They constitute the essential structure of the world which is eternal and unchanging.

The picture of reality that is sketched here, is drawn from the point of view of God's-eye view of the world. It expresses an impersonal and objective world view which evidently follows from metaphysical realists' desire to discover the ultimate constituents of the world. It is thus found that the objects or entities in the sense of unalterable forms are necessarily accepted in metaphysical realism. These objects or entities are thought to be eternal which are not restricted by space-time boundary. They are pure objects of the Platonic variety and thus they are qualified to be called the ultimate stuff of the world. To put it in the traditional vocabulary, they are the essences which are unaffected by the changing character of the world associated with facts.

From this discussion it is evident that in metaphysical realism what is called real is independent of what we think about it. It is independent of our language or conceptual scheme. It results into a purely objective, absolutist and impersonal viewpoint. Metaphysical realism in this sense serves as providing the philosophical foundation of natural science. With this discussion, we now got to the second section where our main objective is to offer a critique of metaphysical realism in the light of Putnam's theory of reference.

II

The Language–reality Divide and the Supporting Theory of Reference

It has been said in the first section that the impersonal world view that metaphysical realism offers which is expressed through its proposed theory of reality is largely supported by the language–reality divide that it presupposes in its philosophical persuasion. In this respect, the two notions — truth and reference — play a vital role providing the justification for a language–reality divide. In fact, language–reality divide is an outcome of the theory of reference that metaphysical realism holds.

Metaphysical realist view of truth and reference, following Putnam, can be expressed in terms of the three following theses:

First: The world consists of a fixed totality of mind-independent objects.

Second: There must be one true and complete description of the world possible.

And

Third: Truth is the result of correspondence that holds between the word and the object designated by it in the world outside.

The implication of these three theses can be further elaborated. The first thesis is a commonly available principle accepted in all versions of metaphysical realism including the traditional one. It is a thesis which is linked with epistemological realism subscribing to the view that a cognitive subject can, in principle, attain the absolute perspective of the world characterized as a view from nowhere. From this it follows that how a cognitive subject is situated in the world and how the perspective of his inquiry influences his approach to the world, are of no epistemological importance. In this respect, it is specially important to note that this view rules out the possibility of forming a picture of the world worked out by our cognitive apparatus, such as, language. Its fundamental plea is that the description of the world must be given through a neutral medium.

The second and the third thesis may be approached together because the possibility of the second thesis depends on the third one. For exactly one true and complete description of the world to be possible, it is required that truth must be independent and bears uniqueness relationship with the world. The idea of truth as correspondence thus includes, as Putnam pointed out, such properties as uniqueness, independence and bivalence. They make truth non-epistemic, which rules out the possibility of offering justification while making a truth claim because the truth or falsity of a statement is not decided on the ground of how it is being justified, but on the ground of its correspondence with mind-independent reality. In this context, as Putnam[4] further clarifies, even an idealized justification will not do since for theorists of metaphysical realism the notion of truth is not constrained by any epistemic consideration and thus it can "outrun even idealized justification". In metaphysical realism, a rigid distinction is thus maintained between truth-conditions and assertability condition of a statement. Truth is defined in terms of purely correspondence relation. Truth as correspondence, as the claim made, will ensure the objectivity of truth.

From this definition of truth one can now make sense of the second thesis mentioned above regarding the possibility of obtaining exactly one true and complete description of the world. The latter is a consequence which follows from the idea of truth defined in terms of independence and uniqueness.

4. H. Putnam, *Reason, Truth and History*, Cambridge: Cambridge University Press, 1981, p. 15.

If truth is independent and also exhibits a uniqueness relationship between the word and the object, then an exactly one true and complete description of the world, in principle, should be possible. On the other hand, to accept the possibility of multiple descriptions will have serious consequences that will amount to be the denial of realism as such. The possibility of multiple descriptions will mean that there are multiple ways in which descriptions correspond to the world. This allows room for an idea of having many types of correspondences to be available between descriptions and the world. As a result, it defies the uniqueness claim of correspondence, since there is not one description which will uniquely correspond to the world. There is a further problem with the idea of multiple descriptions. The problem comes from the reality itself. It is assumed in metaphysical realism that reality has an intrinsic nature and the validity of a theory is judged in the light of this nature. But this will not be possible because reality will no longer have intrinsic nature in view of the fact that there can be multiple descriptions of reality possible. This implies that we can never know the reality by itself except through theories. Indeed, this will be a collapse of metaphysical realism. Hence, in order to protect itself, metaphysical realism demands that there should be exactly one true and complete description of the world.

These three interrelated theses, as Putnam claims, assume the notion of a determinate reference. The picture of the world that emerges from these three theses requires this notion of reference. To elaborate, the central to the metaphysical realist picture of the world is the non-epistemic notion of truth, which will be unattainable without the support of the notion of a determinate reference. This will be evident from the claim made by metaphysical realism that even an ideal theory may turn out to be false; because the object projected in the theory may not be the same object actually situated in the world. A true correspondence will take place only when there is a specific referential relation that exists between the theory and the object. This implies that the idea of truth as correspondence presupposes the notion of a determinate reference. A statement will be true only when it is in correct referential relationship with the world. In the light of this exposition narrating the essential structure of metaphysical realism, Putnam then constructs his critique exposing the untenability of metaphysical realism on the ground of its unreal nature of realism itself.

III

Why is the Language–reality Divide Untenable?: Putnam's Arguments

The untenability of metaphysical realism becomes evident if we see how it is far removed from the real world, both in epistemic and in semantic terms. In this respect, the critique of metaphysical realism that Putnam offers can be brought under three heads. The first is epistemological. The metaphysical realist's theory of the world, as Putnam argues, can lead to a situation which is epistemologically disastrous because ironically at the end it denies the existence of the world. The second is about reference. The theory of the world as formulated in metaphysical realism is supported by its theory of reference which is equally untenable. Its untenability lies on the ground that the relation of reference (i.e., the relation between language and reality) is constructed without looking into the actual world and the objects situated therein. The fixing of reference thus turns out to be magical since no rational account of the process involved can be given. The third, which follows from the second, challenges the possibility of a unique determinate referential relation. Reference, as it argues, is essentially situation-specific.

Argument 1: Brain in a Vat

The metaphysical realism is based on the premise that the world exists on its own independently of our language and mind. Putnam argues that given this premise there is a sceptical conclusion that can be derived from it which rules out the possibility of our having the knowledge of the world at all. Putnam construes this argument in terms of a thought experiment which he calls "Brains in a Vat".

As Putnam presents, let us imagine a world where brains of all human beings are removed from their respective bodies and are kept in a vat being controlled by a super computer. The persons whose brains are kept in a vat seem to have the same experiences like us whose brains are not in vat. But what they are experiencing is not a real experience since it is not connected to objects of the real world. It is a hallucination mechanically caused by the computer. The experience that they have of the world cannot be thus said to be the experience of the real world, but of the vat world where the objects are perceived. Though they appear to be same as the objects of the real world they are actually illusory. If this is so, how do inhabitants of this world refer to objects? It is quite likely that those objects may have reference in the language that they use which is characterized as vat-English. But, now the question is, as Putnam puts it, can the words of vat-English have the same reference as that of English? For reference to be successful there must be a causal connection between the word and the object. As Putnam argues,[5] in order to refer to an object, such as, a tree, the speaker must be in a "causal interaction" with the object. From this it follows that in vat-English there is no scope for making reference to the real world.

The argument that Putnam puts forward through this

5. H. Putnam, *Reason, Truth and History*, Cambridge: Cambridge University Press, 1981, pp. 16-17.

thought experiment is that metaphysical realism may be found to be facing with a similar situation as that of the vat world. The reason is since the reality that we know is independent of our human minds and the conceptual system it is quite possible the objects that we experience and the reference that we make to such objects are manipulated. They are the parts of hallucinating world. Metaphysical realism in this sense can be construed as a form of scepticism leading to the denial of the reality of the world.

There is a second implication which follows from this argument. The first one reveals the paradoxical nature of metaphysical realism, while the second implication of the argument, on the other hand, exposes the falsity of the assumption that we are brains in a vat. The second implication of the argument may be construed as an anti-sceptical argument whose main thrust is to show that we are not brains in a vat and thus to make the contrary claim will be self-refuting.

The conceptual orientation of metaphysical realism assumes the possibility that we are all brains in a vat. Putnam points out the logical flaw involved in this position. Putnam's major contention is that while we are brains in a vat we cannot legitimately say that we are brains in a vat. To say this will imply that we are not brains in a vat. Or, as Putnam[6] puts it, to say this will imply that the statement "we are brains in a vat" is necessarily false. But, why is it necessarily false? It has been pointed out earlier that according to Putnam referring to an object requires that the speaker must be causally connected to the object. Unless this condition is satisfied there will be no successful reference. But people living in the vat world cannot make such causal connection because they do not have any contact with the real world. The references that

6. H. Putnam, *Reason, Truth and History*, Cambridge: Cambridge University Press, 1981, p. 15

they make are essentially restricted within the range of "electronic impulses travelling from the computer to their nerve-endings". As a result, the statements that they make cannot go beyond the vat world and they are true only in relation to that world. They become subjective and, thereby, lack objective truth. This situation thus prevents those who are brains in a vat to say that they are brains in a vat. They cannot make this statement in the same way in which those who are not brains in a vat.

On the consideration of the same logic, we can make a claim that we are not brains in a vat. We can make this claim solely on the criteria that we can make a true statement that we are not brains in a vat. Our claim to make a true statement is based on the consideration that we are causally connected to the real world. This causal connection shows that we cannot be always wrong about what we say. This is a story of the real world which is completely different from the vat world since brains in that world are always in error regarding what they know because they are not causally connected to the real world. In the absence of this requirement the statement that we are brains in a vat is necessarily false. With this, we now come to the second issue involving Putnam's critique of metaphysical realism. It is an issue about reference which follows from the earlier discussion.

Argument 2: Is Reference a Metaphysically Necessary Relation?

We start with a few of questions: Does language refer to reality without taking into account objects of the world? Is their any ideal and unique referring relation that exists between a word and an object? Can mental representation of the meaning of a word fix the reference of word? All these questions are raised at the background of an influential assumption of metaphysical realism that reference is an independent relation which need not be anchored in the world. The reason is that the referring function is the one which is intrinsic to language itself, and thus, it can carry out its function without taking into account the actual world. The referring relation that exists between the word and the object is thus thought to be representing an ideal and unique relationship which can be rightly characterized as metaphysical. Putnam finds this view of reference is an expression of "magical thinking". It is a case of magical thinking because the idea of referring relation projected here as metaphysically necessary is based on what Putnam calls, a "magical connection" holding between the word and its referent. A mechanism, such as this, which operates without the concern for the actual world turns out to be a magical theory of reference. In Putnam's reading, metaphysical realism subscribes to the magical theory of reference which is totally removed from the way language refers to reality. Fixing of reference is not an outcome of any magical connection but of a connection which is contextual, contingent and conventional. Putnam's rejection of the magical theory of reference can be broadly discussed under three heads.

First: Putnam's first argument is that reference is causal, not magical. For to show the absurdity of the ideas that reference is magical, Putnam[7] takes the help of a simple illustration. An ant while crawling on sand, traces a line in the sand. Now the line that it traces and the various curves formed out of it taken together express a human figure, which by chance looks like the picture of Winston Churchill. The question that inevitably arises, as Putnam pointed out, "Has the ant traced the picture of Churchill?" No one will say that it has done it on the basis of such reasoning, like the ant has never seen Churchill, nor has any knowledge about Churchill

7. H. Putnam, *Reason, Truth and History*, Cambridge: Cambridge University Press, 1981, p. 48

or it is possible that it does not have the intention to draw the picture of Churchill. Citing such grounds is irrelevant because the fact of the matter is that it unintentionally draws a line which we "see as a picture of Churchill". The whole thing takes place accidentally and thus there is no necessary connection involved between ant's picture and Churchill. The magical theory, on the other hand, will not arrive at this conclusion. The theory will compel its proponents to accept that the line accidentally drawn by the ant is a picture of Churchill. This compulsion comes due to the magical power ascribed to words and to language. The magical theory thus reduces itself to absurdity by admitting a situation which is far removed from the way language functions in the actual world. The use of language reveals that language does not have any magical power. Reference is not an outcome of a magical connection, but of a causal connection existing between a word and the object.

Second: Putnam rules out reference to be a mental act. Mental act by itself cannot fix the reference. It cannot do it precisely on the ground that without the medium of language no reference can be made. The question of its actual operation becomes important while we make reference. To think to the contrary, is to assume that there is a magical relation existing due to which mental representations themselves can relate to their objects in the physical world without the means of language. But mental content does not have any such magical power which will enable it to fix its referent. The reason is that its nature is largely determined by the external world and thus the act of referring cannot be a mental act since it is controlled by the specificities of the actual world.

In this context, Putnam's narrative on the "Twin Earth"[8]

8. H. Putnam, "The Meaning of 'Meaning'" in *Mind Language and Reality*, Philosophical Papers, vol. 2, Cambridge: Cambridge University Press, 1983.

is specially instructive because it refutes the mentalistic basis of meaning by its argument that meanings are not in the head. We take meaning to be mental because we tend to think that meaning and in the same way reference are both determined by, to put it in Putnam's phrase, "what goes on inside our heads". The reason for the "Brain in a Vat" hypothesis is found to be incoherent because of the same tendency of our queer way of looking at meaning.

Putnam's story of the "Twin Earth" reveals a significant fact. As the story goes, people who are living on Earth and those who are living on Twin Earth may have the same mental content with regard to the concept of water. However, in spite of their same mental content they differ in terms of their reference. That is, when they use the expression "water" they refers to two different substances. In the context of the Earthians "water" refers to H_2O, whereas for the Twin Earthions "water" refers to XYZ. The significant result that follows from it is that for both of them the word is same, i.e. "water" but the corresponding referents are different. In view of this, we can no longer say that the reference of a word is determined by the mental content or "what goes on in people's head". Its reference, on the other hand, is determined by the world or, as Putnam puts it, by using Mill's phrase "the substance itself. Reference is not the result of some prior magical connection but it is the one which is causally fixed by the world.

Putnam's analysis shows that metaphysical realism, instead of embracing realism, ironically enters into a subjective world which Putnam calls, following Dennett, a notional world. Engagement with the notional world becomes inevitable if meaning is taken to be a matter of what goes on in the head. The notional world of the speaker determines the intention of the term, and accordingly, the reference is directed to the fictitious object of the notional world. But reference derives its legitimacy only in relation to the objects of the actual world. Hence, the idea of reference, as found in the notional world, turns out to be a mere notional reference which does not suggest that an actual reference is made to the real world and thus without this latter condition, there cannot be any referring relation possible. Metaphysical realism thus forecloses all its avenues to the real world and instead takes notional world to be the real world. The situation portrayed here is not different from that of "Brain in a Vat" situation.

Argument 3: The Indeterminacy of Reference

The third argument of Putnam against the metaphysical realist's ideas of reference is that reference, by nature, is indeterminate and this indeterminacy follows from the way language interacts with the reality. Putnam is essentially using here Quine's idea of indeterminacy and insecurability of reference to establish the following points. First, reference does not express any fixed determinate and a priori relation between the word and the object. Second, it is always relative to a conceptual scheme or a framework and third, a single system providing a unique description of the world is not possible.

To put it briefly, the main thrust of Quine's argument is that reference becomes indeterminate due to the reason that there are alternative ways of fixing reference. This implies that the same object can be referred to in several ways. This situation arises because of the data which is not subjected to one interpretation. Consider Quine's example. The native's utterance of "gavagai" in the presence of a rabbit, for instance, can be equally translated as "undetached rabbit parts", "an instance of rabbit-hood", "a slice of rabbitness in space and time", depending on what the manuals for translation or the conceptual scheme that we use. Further, all these translations or interpretations are equally acceptable since there is no fact of the matter which can decide what is a right or a wrong translation. The reference of a term cannot be thus fixed in absolute terms. It can be fixed only within a background of some specific manual of translation or theory. The indeterminacy of reference thus leads to ontological relativity.

Putnam uses Quine's argument regarding indeterminacy of reference in a distinctive way. Putnam, while developing his model theoretic argument against the metaphysical realist idea of the determinacy of reference, considers Quine's argument to be largely a version of model theoretic argument. But what is important to note at this stage is the similarity between the structure of these two forms of argument advanced by Quine and Putnam regarding indeterminacy of reference. Putnam, along with Quine, argues that there cannot be one single system available that decides the fixing of the reference of a term. The reason is that a term in a language may have any number of interpretations and thus it allows multiple ways of fixing reference. This rules out the possibility of having one fixed reference for anything and instead grants the availability of having a number of references to be possible, in accordance with the conceptual scheme that one holds.

The idea that reference is relative to a conceptual scheme takes us to the view of what Quine calls ontological relativity. Quine demonstrates how accepting a conceptual scheme leads us to commit to a particular ontology. In a similar way, Putnam, while arguing against the monolithic picture of reality that metaphysical realism projects, adopts the same view of ontological relativity and says that realism has many faces.[9] The force of this argument will be evident if we consider the issue in the context of scientific theory, whereby accepting a particular physical theory, we commit ourselves to an ontology of particles and atoms and, on the other hand, by accepting

9. H. Putnam, *The Many Faces of Realism*, La Salle, Open Court, 1987.

another physical theory we commit ourselves to an ontology of quarks and so on. Ontological relativity, that we are experiencing, is the outcome of indeterminacy of reference. In this context, Putnam argues that for metaphysical realism to prove itself to be viable it must refute such a fact like ontological relativity, but because of its inherent lacuna, it fails to do so and this explains why it is untenable.

To sum up, the language–reality divide that metaphysical realism accepts as a part of its theory of reality is fundamentally flawed. That is why an approach to reality cannot be intelligibly pursued without the involvement or the intervention of the speaker. In this respect, the nature of language–reality relationship that metaphysical realism conceived is misleading if not erroneous. Language does not mirror the world. It is the speaker who mirrors the world through the use of language. The main contention of Putnam's critique is to show the importance of the constructive role that the speaker plays in shaping the reality. As he argues, no formulation of realism is possible that does not take speaker's contribution into account. This brings a radical change in our approach to truth, reference and explanation.

6

On Grice's Analysis of Meaning

Laxminarayan Lenka

THE first part of this paper contains a presentation of Grice's distinction between natural meaning and non-natural meaning; and a statement of the three Gricean conditions of meaning. The second part contains an outline of some important criticisms on Grice's account of meaning. In the third part, an assessment of those criticisms is followed by some observations.

I

Grice (1957) distinguishes non-natural meaning (Meaning-NN) from natural meaning.[1] For example, "mean" in "Those spots mean you have got measles" and "mean" in "Those three rings on the bell (of the bus) mean that the bus is full", are in the natural sense and non-natural sense of "mean", respectively. The natural sense is associated with what a natural symptom, event or thing shows or indicates. The non-natural sense is associated with speaker's meaning something by producing certain utterance (verbal or non-verbal). For example,[2] in "The

1. H.P. Grice, 1957, "Meaning", *The Philosophical Review*, LXVI, no. 3, pp 377-88. In H.P. Grice (1989), *Studies in the Way of Words*, Cambridge, Massachusetts: Harvard University Press, pp. 213-23.
2. This example is from Max Black, 1973, "Meaning and Intention: An Examination of Grice's Views", *New Literary History*, vol. 4, no. 2, pp. 257-79. See p. 259. Black's criticism on Grice's account has not been discussed in this paper.

twittering of the fledgelings *meant* that they were hungry", *meant* is in natural sense; in "When I said 'The fledgelings are hungry', I *meant* that the fledgelings were hungry", *meant* is in non-natural sense. The five points of difference between the two senses *mean* can be presented through "Yes" or "No" answer to the following five different questions.

1. Does *x mean that p* entails p?

("Yes" for the natural sense of *mean* and "No" for the non-natural sense.)

2. Can it be concluded from *x means that p* that what is meant by x is that p?

("No" for the natural sense and "Yes" for the non-natural sense.)

3. Does it follow from *x means that p* that somebody or other meant by x that p?

("No" for the natural sense and "Yes" for the non-natural sense.)

4. Can *x means that p* be reformulated as *x means 'p'* ?

("No" for the natural sense and "Yes" for the non-natural sense.)

5. Can *x means that p* be restated as "The fact that . . ."?

("Yes" for the natural sense and "No" for the non-natural sense.)

Each of the five points of difference presupposes the presence of the utterer's intention in non-natural meaning and its absence in natural meaning. This is briefly explained below.[3]

3. More on it can be found in L. Lenka, 1990, "MeaningN and MeaningNN: An Exposition of the Unformed Gricean Intention", *Indian Philosophical Quarterly, Students' Supplement*, vol. XVII, no. 2, pp. 1-9.

If no intention is involved in producing *x*, there is no chance of producing *x* by mistake, unintentionally, or by mischief, deliberately, when it is not the case that *p* but *x* means that *p*. For no mistake or mischief makes sense without reference to intention; and it amounts to a kind of mistake or mischief if *x* is produced in a context of ~*p*, when x means that *p*. In a non-natural sense of "mean", *x* means that *p* even if it is not the case that *p*. For example, even if the bus is not full, the three rings on the bell of the bus means that the bus is full. The conductor of the bus might have made the mistake of ringing the bell three times even if the bus was not full. On the other hand, in a natural sense of "mean", it is odd to say that *x* means that *p* when it is not the case that *p*. For example, it is odd to say that those red spots mean that you have got measles, but you have not got measles. This explains the first point of difference.

What is meant by *x* counts as a natural symptom or cause of a fact or event that *p*, not as a conventional linguistic meaning that *p*, unless people intend to mean that *p* by *x*. In a non-natural sense of "mean", the utterance is treated as a linguistic utterance, such that a linguistic relation exists between the utterance and what the utterance means. Therefore, from *x means that p*, we can conclude that what is linguistically meant by *x* is *p*. On the other hand, the relation between *x* and *p* is factive relation when "mean" is used in natural sense in "*x* means that *p*". Therefore, here, we do not conclude that what is (linguistically) meant by *x* is *p*. For Grice, the factive relation between *x* and *p* (e.g., red spots and you have got measles) does not involve any intention, whereas the linguistic relation between *x* and *p* (e.g., the three rings and the bus is full) involve communicative intentions. This explains the second point of difference.

There is no necessity of presupposing the existence of an utterer (somebody with intention), if *p* could be meant by *x* without an utterer's intention. This condition of meaning that *p* from *x* without utterer's intention is satisfied by a natural sense of "mean". Because, in this sense, although *x* (red spots) means that *p* (You have got measles), *x* is not produced by a human being to communicate something. But, in meaning-NN, *x* (the three rings) is produced by a human being (the conductor) with some intention to communicate something. This explains the third point of difference, namely that somebody or other meant by *x* that *p* when "mean" is used in non-natural sense in "*x* means that *p*" and it is not so in natural sense of "mean".

Unless we introduce intentions, there would not be any ontological difference between *x* and *p*, hence, no sense of separating the two by using quotation (" ") on one and not on the other of the two — *x* and *p*. The intentionality factor involved in meaning-NN puts a level difference between the utterance produced with an intention to communicate and the fact referred to, through what is meant by that utterance. This difference is not found in natural sense of "mean". For example, the red spots and the measles are at the same ontological level. On the other hand, the three rings produced with certain communicative intention and the bus being full are not at the same ontological level. This explains the fourth point of difference.

An instance of meaning something could be reduced to natural facts, had there been no requirement of utterer's intention. As utterer's intention is present in case of meaning-NN, *x* means-NN that *p* cannot be reformulated as "The fact that it is *x*, it is *p*." It can be reformulated so in case of natural meaning. For example, "Those spots means that you have got measles" can be expressed as "The fact that you have got those spots means that you have got measles". This explains the fifth point of difference.

For Grice, "*A* meant-NN something by *x*" is roughly equivalent to "*A* uttered *x* with the intention of inducing a belief by means of the recognition of this intention".[4] To include imperatives, that is, cases other than "informative", "*A* meant-NN something by *x*" is equivalent to "*A* intended the utterance of *x* to produce some effect in audience by means of the recognition of this intention".[5] Accordingly, meaning-NN has been defined in the following way.[6]

"*U* meant something by uttering *x*" is true if, for some audience *A*, *U* uttered *x* intending

(1) *A* to produce a particular response *r*

(2) *A* to think (recognize) that *U* intends (1) and

(3) *A* to fulfil (1) on the basis of his fulfilment of (2).

II

Urmson's counter-example[7]

When the captors of a prisoner of war torture the prisoner by applying thumbscrews in order to obtain some information from him, they do not mean anything but do satisfy the three Gricean conditions. They applied the thumbscrews with the intention of producing a certain response on the part of the victim; they intended him to recognize their intention; and they intended that the prisoner should produce the response on the basis of recognizing that they intended him of producing the response.

Responding to Urmson's counter-example, Grice amends his definition. The amended version is this:[8]

"*U* meant something by uttering *x*" is true iff

---

4. Grice, 1989, p. 219.
5. Ibid., p. 220.
6. Ibid., p. 92.
7. Urmson's counter-example is raised by him in conversation with Grice. See Grice, 1989, p. 93.
8. Ibid., p. 94.

(1) *U* intended, by uttering *x*, to induce a certain response in *A*,

(2) *U* intended *A* to recognize, *at least in part from the utterance of x*, that *U* intended to produce that response, and

(3) *U* intended the fulfilment of intention mentioned in (2) to be at least in part *A*'s reason for fulfilling the intention mentioned in (1).

Stampe's counter-example:[9]

U is playing bridge against his boss. To get his boss's favour, *U* wants his boss to win and wants his boss to know that *U* wants him to win. When *U* has a good hand, *U* smiles in a certain way; "the smile is *very* like, but not *quite* like a spontaneous smile of pleasure". Thus when producing the smile *U* intends

(1) the boss to think that *U* has a good hand,

(2) the boss to think, at least in part because of the smile, that *U* intended the boss to think that *U* has a good hand, and

(3) at least part of the boss's reason for thinking that *U* has a good hand should be that *U* intended him to think just that.

According to Stampe, since Grice's three conditions are satisfied but this can hardly be counted as a case of *U*'s meaning that *U* has a good hand, the three Gricean conditions are not sufficient for meaning something.

Strawson's counter-example:[10]

S produces certain action *x* before *A* with the intention that *A*

9. Stampe raised the counter-example in conversation with Grice. See Grice, 1989, p. 94.

10. P.F. Strawson, 1964, "Intention and Convention in Speech Acts", *Philosophical Review*, 73, pp. 439-60.

will believe that *p*. But it all happens in a peculiar situation. The situation includes that

(i) *S* is arranging convincing-looking "evidence" that *p*,

(ii) *A* is watching *S* at work,

(iii) *S* knows (ii),

(iv) *A* does not know (iii), and

(v) *S* knows (iv).

As *S* intends *A* to believe that *p*, *S* satisfies the first Gricean condition. The second condition is satisfied if *S* can intend *A* to recognize that *S* intends *A* to believe that *p*. *S* can intend so in this way: *S* thinks that *A* will not count *S*'s arranged evidence as a genuine or natural evidence that *p* but take it as a ground for thinking that *S* intends to induce in *A* the belief that *p*. The third condition is satisfied as *S* knows that A will think that *S* will not make *A* to think that *p* unless *S* knows that it is the case that *p*. *A*'s recognition of *S*'s intention of getting *A*, believed that p becomes sufficient reason for *A* to believe that *p*. However, even if all the three Gricean conditions are satisfied, this cannot be an instance of *S*'s meaning that *p*.

Strawson suggests that at least one more condition is required to overcome such counter-examples. The fourth condition is the recognition of the recognition-condition. That is, not only that *U* should intend *A* to recognize that *U* intends *A* to believe that p, but also intends *A* to recognize that *U* intends *A* to recognize that *U* intends *A* to believe that *p*. Accordingly, if we employ this condition in Stampe's counter-example, the employee further intends the boss to think that the boss is intended to think that the employee wants him to think that the employee has a good hand.

Schiffer's counter-example:[11]

A is notoriously avaricious but has a certain pride. *A* is in *U*'s room. *U* wants to get rid of *A*. *U* tosses a five-pound note out of the window. *U* intends *A* to think the following:

> *U* wants to get me to leave the room, thinking that I shall run after the money. He also wants me to know that he wants me to go (so contemptuous was his performance). But I am not going to demean myself by going after the banknote; I shall go, but shall go because he wants me to go. I do not care to be where I am not wanted.[12]

Although we will not count this case as an instance of *U*'s meaning that *A* should go away, the four conditions are fulfilled.

In throwing the banknote, *U* intended that

(1) *A* should leave the room,

(2) *A* should recognize that *U* intended (1),

(3) *A* should leave the room on the basis of recognizing that *U* intends *A* to leave the room, and

(4) *A* should recognize that *U* intended (2).

The further restriction required in order to exclude such instances from meaning something is given as the fifth condition: that *U* should intend *A* to recognize that *U* intends (3). In the counter-example, *U* intended *A* to leave the room on the basis of recognizing that *U* intends *A* to leave the room, but *U* did not intend this to be recognized by *A*. *A* was intended to think that *U*'s purpose was to get him to leave in pursuit of the five-pound note. To incorporate the further restriction, Grice reformulates the definition as follows.

---

11. Schiffer too raised the counter-example in conversation with Grice. See Grice, 1989, p. 95.

12. Ibid., p. 96.

"*U* meant something by *x*" is true if *U* uttered *x* intending:

(1) that *A* should produce response *r*

(2) that *A* should, at least partly on the basis of *x*, think that *U* intends (1)

(3) that *A* should think that *U* intended (2)

(4) that *A*'s production of *r* should be based (at least in part) on *A*'s thought that *U* intended that (1) (that is, on *A*'s fulfilment of [2])

(5) that *A* should think that *U* intended (4).

The fundamental feature of the counter-examples which require additional conditions is that they construct a situation such that

> *U* intends *A*, in the reflection process by which *A* is supposed to reach his response, *both* to rely on some "inference-element" (some premise or some inferential step) *E and* also to think that *U* intends *A not* to rely on *E*.[13]

To eliminate such counter-examples, to prevent *U* from having such complex intentions, Grice provides us with a different version of the definition of meaning-NN as follows.[14]

"*U* meant something by uttering *x*" is true iff (for some *A* and for some *r*)

(a) *U* uttered *x* intending (1) *A* to produce *r*

(2) *A* to think *U* to intend (1)

(3) *A*'s fulfilment of (1) to be based on *A*'s fulfilment of (2)

(b) there is no inference-element *E* such that *U* uttered *x* intending both (1′) that A's determination of r should rely on *E* and (2′) that *A* should think *U* to intend that (1′) be false.

---

13. See Grice, 1989, p. 99.

14. Ibid., pp. 99-100.

Searle's counter-example:[15]

In the Second World War, an American soldier is captured by Italian troops. The American soldier utters *"kennst du das Land, wo die Zitronen blühen"*. He utters it with the intention that the Italian troops will release him thinking that he is a German officer. Searle argues that even if this instance can satisfy Gricean conditions, it is not a case of meaning something. The American soldier can intend the Italian troops to believe that he is a German officer, can intend them to think that he wants them to believe that he is a German officer, can intend them to believe that he is a German officer on the basis of their recognizing that he wants them to believe that he is a German officer. But, as he remembers that the sentence in German is learnt in his school days and it means "Knowest thou the land where the lemon trees bloom", he does not mean by uttering the sentence that he is a German officer.

Grice suspects that Searle wants him to incorporate the element of convention. That is,

> *U* intends *A*'s recognition of *U*'s intention (to produce the effect) to be achieved by means of the recognition the sentence uttered is conventionally used to produce such an effect.[16]

Grice does not consider the way out, in terms of convention, proper to his framework. Because, for him, though convention does matter in correlating an utterance and what is meant by the utterance, it is just one way of correlating the two. It cannot be the defining element in general.

Moreover, Grice considers Searle's counter-example "underdescribed".[17] In one sense, the American soldier does

---

15. J.R. Searle, 1970, *Speech Acts*, Cambridge: Cambridge University Press, pp. 44-45.
16. Grice, 1989, p. 100.
17. Ibid., p. 101.

not satisfy the Gricean conditions. For, even if he intends the Italian troops to believe that he is a German officer, he would not intend them to believe this on the basis of their recognition of his intention. This will be so if the situation is described as a case of persuading somebody to believe that *p* when it is false that *p*. In another sense, the American soldier means that he is a German officer and does satisfy the Gricean conditions. For example, the situation is such that the meaning of the German line becomes irrelevant and what matters is the way, the gestures, stress, intonation, etc. in which the line has been uttered with the accompanying suitable intentions. Grice cites a parallel example here. In Port Said, a shop owner standing in his doorway, and with an alluring smile, says to a British tourist the Arabic for "You pig of an Englishman". He meant that the visitor was to come in; he has satisfied the three Gricean conditions. The utterance does not matter here, what matters is the way the utterance is presented, to correlate the utterance with what is meant by uttering that.

One more example Grice cites to explain meaning something by satisfying Gricean conditions, even if the utterance conventionally does not mean what is successfully meant in the context. He notices that a child learning French wrongly thinks that a French sentence means "Help yourself to a piece of cake", though the French sentence means something quite different. Now when there is some cake nearby, Grice utters the same French sentence before her and, as he intended, the girl helps herself. Grice summarizes the way in which one correlates his intentions with the response he intends from the audience as follows:

> Characteristically, an utterer intends an audience to recognize (and to think himself intended to recognize) some "crucial" feature *F*, and to think of *F* (and to think himself intended to think of *F*) as correlated in a certain way with some response which the utterer intends the audience to

> produce. It does not matter, so far as the attribution of the speaker's meaning is concerned, whether *F* is thought by *U* to be *really* correlated in that way with the response or not; though of course in normal case *U* will think F to be so correlated.[18]

Accordingly, Grice finally puts forth his definition as follows.[19]

Range of variables:

A: audiences

f: features of utterance

r: responses

c: modes of correlation (such as iconic, associative, conventional)

U meant something by *x* iff

(∃*A*) (∃*f*) (∃*r*) (∃*c*):

(a) *U* uttered *x* intending

(1) *A* to think x possesses *f*,

(2) *A* to think *f* correlated in a way *c* with the type to which *r* belongs,

(3) *A* to think, on the basis of the fulfilment (1) and
(2) that *U* intends *A* to produce *r*,

(4) *A*, on the basis of the fulfilment of (3) to produce *r*,

and

(b) there is no inference-element E such that *U* intends both

(1′) A in his determination of *r* to rely on *E* and

(2′) A to think *U* to intend (1^1) to be false.

---

18. Grice (1989), pp. 102-03.

19. Ibid., pp. 104-05.

Ziff's counter-examples[20]

George is an irritable academic. Being in army, he was compelled to take a test to establish his sanity. An army officer asked him "What would you say if you were asked to identify yourself?" George said, "Ugh Ugh blugh blugh ugh blug blug", intending

(i) the officer to be offended,

(ii) the officer to recognize that George intended (i), and

(iii) the officer to be offended on the basis of fulfilling George's intention (ii).

As a result, George meant-NN that the officer would be offended, but George did not mean anything by the utterance. Therefore, meaning-NN ‡ Meaning.

Once more George gave the test, to another officer, and said "Pi.hi.y pi.hi.y", intending the above (i), (ii) and (iii). Accordingly, what George meant-NN by "Ugh ugh blugh blugh ugh blug blug" = what George meant-NN by "Pi.hi.y pi.hi.y". But, in Hopi, "Pi.hi.y pi.hi.y" means that one does not know oneself and George knows what the utterance means in Hopi. Hence, Ziff argues that what George meant-NN by "Pi.hi.y pi.hi.y" (the officer would be offended) ‡ what George meant by "pi.hi.y pi.hi.y" (I do not know who am I). Therefore, meaning-NN ‡ Meaning. Both of the counter-examples are attempts to show that meaning-NN ‡ Meaning. The first one attempts to show it by establishing that *U* meant nothing by *x* but meant-NN something by *x*; the second by establishing that *U* meant something by *x* but what he meant was different from what he meant-NN by *x*.

Ziff's third counter-example too, leads to the same conclusion, namely meaning-NN ‡ Meaning. George uttered "Claudius murdered my father" on three different occasions:

20. P. Ziff, 1967, "On H.P. Grice's Account of Meaning", *Analysis*, XXVIII, 1967, pp. 1-8.

(a) in the course of morning soliloquy,

(b) in the course of discussion with Josef in the afternoon,

(c) in the evening while delirious with fever.

Utterance of *x* on different occasions is taken as three different tokens of the same utterance type such that *x* does mean the same thing as an utterance type on different occasions. But, in accordance to Gricean analysis, in (a) and (c), *x* cannot mean-NN something though it may mean-NN something in (b). Hence, meaning-NN ‡ Meaning.

Further, we may take up Ziff's fourth counter-example. George's head has been tampered with. Electrodes have been inserted, plates mounted. He was asked, "How do you feel?" He said, "Glyting elly beleg". Afterwards, he was asked why he said so. He replied that, somehow, he thought/believed that what he was saying was synonymous with that he was feeling fine and, also, believed that everyone else knew that. Thus George meant-NN something but did not mean anything by x. Hence, meaning-NN ‡ Meaning.

Another counter-example, similar to the above but simpler one follows like this. A man suddenly cried out "Gleeg gleeg gleeg", intending to produce some effect in an audience by means of the recognition of his intention. He wanted his audience to believe that it was snowing in Tibet. Later on he was sent to a psychiatrist. However, Ziff would argue that since he could manage to meant-NN something but did not mean anything by that utterance, meaning-NN ‡ Meaning.

Wilson's ultimate counter-example:[21]

Since for Grice what *U* means is equivalent to certain intentions of *U*, Wilson argues that, in so far as *U*'s intentions are under *U*'s control, *U* can mean anything by uttering any statement.

---

21. N.L. Wilson, 1970, "Grice on Meaning: The Ultimate Counter-example", *Nous*, IV, pp. 295-302.

But one cannot mean anything whatsoever he wishes by uttering any statement. In other words, *U* does not have independent control over *U*'s meaning something but has independent control over *U*'s intentions, hence, *U*'s meaning something cannot be made equivalent to the conjunction of any of *U*'s intentions.

Wilson argues that Grice has confused primary (linguistic) intention with secondary intention (what one intends to accomplish by saying). A primary linguistic intention and a secondary intention may vary independently. The same utterance *x* can be made in different contexts to accomplish different things. So also, the same effect can be accomplished through different utterances. According to Wilson, Grice fails to distinguish the two types of intentions and, hence, to explicate meaning, Grice attempts to explicate the primary linguistic intentions in terms of the secondary linguistic intentions. Wilson argues that there is no covariance between meaning and intended effect. For example, "Kindly leave me alone", "It is already 7 p.m.", "It may rain now", and "Get out" do not mean the same thing but the intended effect may be the same, viz. to get rid of the audience. Consequently, for Wilson, the meaning of a sentence cannot be explicated by means of an utterer's intention when the utterer's intention is taken in the sense of secondary intentions. The ultimate counter-example is put forth to claim that fulfilment of Grice's three conditions with respect to *U* means that *p* does not guarantee that *U* means that *p*. Wilson claims that Grice fails in his analysis because he has overlooked the fact that there is no covariance between meaning and intended effect and that primary linguistic intention is different from secondary intention.

The ultimate counter-example is this. Grice and Wilson are discussing Grice's analysis of meaning and, in this context, Wilson utters "Snow is white" intending (i) Grice to believe that Wilson wants Grice to be defeated (or dislodged from his position or proved to be wrong), (ii) Grice to recognize that Wilson intends (i), and (iii) Grice would believe that Wilson wants him to be defeated partly because of the fact that Grice has recognized that Wilson intends (i). All the three Gricean conditions have been fulfilled. But, by uttering "Snow is white", neither Wilson means nor the utterance literally means that Grice should be dislodged from his position.

One may argue that, even if "Snow is white" does not literally means that Grice should be proved to be wrong or dislodged from his position, by uttering "Snow is white", Wilson must have meant that Grice should be dislodged from his position since he had the appropriate Gricean intentions to mean that Grice should be dislodged from his position. Wilson's reply to this explains why he calls his counter-example the ultimate counter-example. In this counter-example, the intended effect or response Wilson puts forth is that Grice should believe that Grice is wrong. If the above argument holds good, that is, if Wilson means that Grice should be dislodged from his position since he has the appropriate intentions, then, Grice will not believe that he is wrong. Wilson cannot intend Grice to believe that Grice is wrong if Wilson has the reason to believe that Grice will not believe that Grice is wrong. In other words, if Grice's analysis is correct then the ultimate counter-example's utterer's first intention is not possible. Since the said intention is possible, for Wilson, Grice's analysis is wrong.

III

An Assessment

Grice makes a distinction between primary intention and secondary intention.[22] If, for example, a traffic policeman stops a car, in order to check the smuggled items inside the car, by

22. See Grice, 1957, p. 386.

signalling to stop the car, the primary intended effect is to get the car stopped and the secondary intended effect is to check the smuggled items inside the car. According to Grice, it is the primary intended effect, not the secondary intended effect, which becomes relevant for his analysis of meaning. Wilson's distinction between primary intention and secondary intention is different from that of Grice, and Wilson's distinction is no less vulnerable to criticism than the Austinian locutionary-illocutionary distinction which presupposes a distinction between force-neutral meaning and meaning with a force.[23]

Wilson's ultimate counter-example is inconsistent in that on the one hand he accepts that, by uttering "Snow is white", he intends to believe that Grice is wrong and, on the other hand, he denies the possibility of his intending so. The acceptance is based on the ground that he intends Grice to be defeated. The denial is based on that, if he really means that Grice is wrong by fulfilling the Gricean conditions, he cannot expect Grice to believe that Grice is wrong.

Instead of taking the ultimate counter-example as a counter-example, we can take it as to be expressing the following paradoxical situation: If Grice's analysis is correct, Wilson means that Grice's analysis is wrong by uttering "Snow is white" and having the required intentions to mean that. But, at the same time, if the Gricean analysis is not wrong, Wilson cannot intend Grice to believe that Grice is wrong, thereby, not fulfilling the first intention, Wilson cannot mean that Grice's analysis is wrong.

In the conclusion of each of Ziff's counter-examples, we find that meaning-NN ‡ Meaning. It is true that what an utterance x literally means is not the same as what an utterer means by uttering x. It is the latter meaning, the utterer's

23. Criticism on Austin's locutionary-illocutionary distinction can be found in Searle 1968, "Austin on Locutionary and Illocutionary Acts", *Philosophical Review*, LXXVII, pp. 405-24.

meaning something in a particular occasion, and not the timeless meaning of *x*, for which Grice has offered the three conditions (intentions). Grice does make a distinction between the two — utterer's occasion meaning and timeless meaning; and suggests that the latter can be ultimately explicated in terms of the former.

"Ugh Ugh blugh blugh ugh blug blug" itself does not mean anything. What is wrong to say that George did mean something by uttering it? Following Ziff, one could say that if there is nothing wrong in that, then, "good intentions suffice to convert nonsense to sense".[24] In this regard, it can be pointed out that sense or meaning is not the copyright of some particular range of sounds themselves that we are closely acquainted with. As a mere sound, every word is nonsense. As a sound in our communication, that is, as a sound that is audience-directed and "meaning-intended" by the utterer, any sound is having sense. Is not it true that even the utterance "Ugh Ugh blugh blugh ugh blug blug" has some sense of representing the nonsense that Ziff is alleging against it, at least among some philosophers?

Moreover, if we go by the Wittgensteinian dictum that meaning is in use, we cannot accept that an expression can have meaning independent of its use. It may be crude to say but, in a certain way, both Wilson and Ziff are in the grip of the idea that meaning is embedded in a dead sign (spoken, written or non-verbal) itself and a secondary meaning is derived from them when they are used in situations of linguistic communication.

Searle's American soldier, as pointed out by Grice, may or may not succeed in meaning something. It depends on the way we interpret the situation. If it is interpreted as a case of unsuccessful persuasion, the Italian troop's recognition of the

24. P. Ziff, 1967, p. 5.

American soldier's first intention becomes counter-productive; the soldier cannot mean that he is a German officer. If it is interpreted as a case of successfully meaning something, then, the soldier somehow presents his utterance in a way that goes consistent with the required intentions. But what the soldier means by uttering that German sentence is different from what that sentence conventionally means. This is possible because the correlation between an utterance and what the utterer means by that utterance need not be conventional.

We have already noted how Grice responds to the type of counter-examples contrived by Strawson and Schiffer, by disallowing inference-element *E* that paves the way for such counter-examples. The inference-element *E* consists of a reasoning on which the audience depends to respond in a particular way. However, even if the utterer thinks that the audience will depend on that reasoning, he does not want the audience to recognize that the utterer thought it so. This element of *E* works well in cases of cheating, not in normal sincere cases of meaning.

For example, I note down all the moves I have planned for a chess match. Later on, I have decided to change my gameplan. But I leave that piece of paper on my table knowing well that my opponent player will come to my room and that he does not know that I know that he will come to my room. Let us try to fit this situation to Gricean conditions as follows:

(i) I intend my opponent to believe that the piece of paper contains my gameplan;

(ii) I intend my opponent to recognize that (i); and

(iii) I intend that my opponent's recognition of my intention (i) should function as a reason for him to believe that the piece of paper contains my gameplan.

No doubt it is possible that (i). But how can (ii) be possible? If my opponent recognizes (i), he is most likely to believe that

I have a different gameplan and, hence, (iii) becomes impossible. Why at all he will recognize (i) and at the same time trust me and fulfil my intention (iii). He can trust me only if he is "worthy of a Tertullian".[25] But I cannot take my opponent to be so bogus.

If at all I succeed in cheating my opponent, my opponent does not believe that the piece of paper contains a false gameplan. He believes that it contains my true gameplan; and he can believe so only if he thinks that I have the intention of carrying out that gameplan, and not that I have no intention of carrying out that gameplan. In short, although I have left the paper on the table in order to cheat him, this is not recognized by my opponent, if at all I succeed in cheating. Thus the reorganization condition fails if we put the first condition as that I intend my opponent to be cheated. I never intend my opponent to recognize that I intend him to be cheated, if I sincerely and seriously intend him to be cheated. However, making the first condition as that I intend my opponent to believe that the piece of paper contains my gameplan, the recognition-condition may be fulfilled in a contrived situation where my opponent is somehow under the impression that I want him to become the winner, although I actually do not intend so, but the opposite. In this situation, where the recognition-condition is fulfilled and yet I succeed in cheating, the inference element *E* plays the significant role. For, in this case, I intend my opponent to rely on a reasoning to think that I intend him to win the game but I do not intend him to recognize this very intention. If he recognizes it, no more I succeed in cheating him. Thus the inference element is to be blocked in every case of normal meaning, and incorporable in cases of lying, persuading and cheating, etc.

25. A.P. Martinich, 1984, *Communication and Reference*, New York: Walter de Gruyter, p. 119. (Tertullian declared that he believed in Jesus' resurrection because it was absurd.)

Some observations

When I say "We are in a classroom" to assert that we are in a classroom, I do believe that we are in a classroom. Although, when I mean to say we are in a classroom, in uttering the sentence "We are in a classroom", I succeed in doing that without explicitly stating that I do believe that we are in a classroom. This shows that what follows from an assertion need not be asserted explicitly. But, for sure, it is asserted implicitly in the sense that neither implicitly nor explicitly its denial can be asserted. Asserting that we are in a classroom, for example, neither implicitly nor explicitly, I can tell that I do not believe that we are in a classroom. The act of asserting demands that if I assert that *p*, I do believe that *p*. This demand is to be fulfilled both in public speech acts and private thought acts, in explicit assertions and implicit assertions. It is absurd if I seriously tell you that I assert that I am an Indian, but I do not believe that I am an Indian. No less absurd it would be if I think or tell to myself that I assert that I am an Indian, but I do not believe that I am an Indian. The point I underline here is that what follows from an assertion cannot be denied (implicitly or explicitly) without absurdity, although what follows from an assertion need not be stated or asserted explicitly. Analogously, without making the utterer's intentions explicit, an utterer means something. In so far as utterer's certain intentions follow from the utterer's meaning something; no less than his believing that *p* follows from his asserting that *p*, we cannot, without absurdity, hold that the utterer does not have those intentions and yet means something.

As in the case of making a non-defective sincere promise, the sincerity condition[26] demands that *S* intends to do *A* if *S*

26. Sincerity Condition is one of the nine conditions proffered by Searle for a non-defective sincere promise. The nine conditions can be found in Searle's "What is a Speech Act?" in J.R. Searle, 1971, *The Philosophy of Language,* Oxford: Clarendon Press, pp. 48-51.

promises to do *A*, so also, in case of meaning (in non-natural sense), *S* intends to mean that *p* if *S* means that *p*. Never an utterer means that *p* seriously and sincerely, and, at the same time, the utterer does not intend to mean that *p*. That the utterer's intention is a necessary condition of an utterer's meaning something cannot be denied. Now, in Gricean framework, this intention has been further specified as to be the conjunction of three certain intentions. The necessity of the three intentions can be easily made out from the absurdity involved in each of the following three sentences.

(a) I intend to mean that *p* but do not intend my audience to believe that *p*.

(b) I intend my audience to believe that *p* but without his thinking that I intend him to believe that *p*.

(c) I intend my audience to believe that *p* with any reason except that he has thought that I intend him to believe that *p*.

Note that we are analysing normal cases of non-natural meaning, not the cases of cheating, telling lies or deceiving. Each of the above three sentences may hold well with respect to cheating, telling lies or deceiving, not with respect to normal cases of meaning.

If believing that *p* does not follow from asserting that *p*, then it is possible to assert both *p* and not-*p* without inviting contradictory beliefs and, hence, without making no sense of *p* and not-*p*. For, in that case, one would claim that even if she is asserting both *p* and not-*p*, neither she believes that *p* and not-*p*, nor does she expect others taking her to believe that *p* and not-*p*. Similarly, if the Gricean conditions do not follow from an utterer's meaning something, then it is possible to mean something without having some or all of the Gricean intentions. Now, as we find it implausible to say that one does not believe that *p*, even if one asserts that *p*, it is equally implausible to say that one does not intend some or all of the Gricean intentions, even if one means something. For example, if I do not intend my audience to close the door, I do not mean my utterance "Close the door!" to be a request or order to close the door. Nor do I mean it so, if I do not intend my audience to think that I intend him/her to close the door. Again, I do not mean it so, if I do not intend my audience to close the door on the basis of his thinking that I intend him/her to close the door.

From the above discussion it is clear that we cannot deny the necessity of the Gricean three conditions. Criticisms against the sufficiency of the Gricean conditions are largely dependent on counter-examples which incorporate the inference element *E* disallowed by Grice for normal cases of meaning-NN something. We can observe that the said element *E* can be made idle by putting forth the mutual awareness between the utterer and the audience as a background condition of linguistic communication.

The Gricean second condition, the recognition-condition, suggests that mutual awareness works as a background condition in every successful linguistic communication. This second condition demands the utterer to acknowledge that he/she has produced the utterance, and this acknowledgement is an acknowledgement served by the utterer to the hearer who is aware of the utterer's production of the utterance. For example, if *A* leaves *B*'s handkerchief near *C* in order to get *D* believe that *C* has been murdered by *B*, this is not counted as a case of *A*'s meaning to D that *B* is *C*'s murderer. Because, even if *A* intends *D* to believe that *B* is *C*'s murderer, *A* does not intend *D* to recognize that *A* intends so. The second Gricean condition is not satisfied. It so happens because, *A* does not acknowledge that it is *A* who has placed *B*'s handkerchief near *C* and, thereby, also, does not acknowledge that he wants *D* to believe that *B* is *C*'s murderer. In this case, even if *A* is aware that *D* will investigate the case, *D* is not aware that *A* has produced the utterance (placed *B*'s handkerchief near *C*) to mean something. This suggests that the normal cases of successful linguistic communication are in a sense open, not surreptitious, not confined to the utterer's awareness of the hearer. The hearer's awareness of the utterer is as much inevitable as the utterer's awareness of the hearer.

To conclude, I would suggest that the above-said mutual awareness between the utterer and the hearer works at every level. That is, if the fulfilment of first and second Gricean conditions reveal that the utterer and the hearer have mutual awareness at level 1, then, the contexts which fulfil the Gricean second condition and the Strawsonian fourth condition (the recognition of the recognition-condition) reveal the mutual awareness at level 2. Thus, putting the mutual awareness at every level as a background condition of every linguistic communication, we can get rid of the counter-examples raised by Strawson and Schiffer, without adding more complex conditions to the Gricean three conditions.

7

Discrete versus Distributive Representation
The Debate between the Classicist and the Connectionist

Ram C. Majhi

WE use language to talk about the world. It is important to note that only living language is capable of expressing things about the world. A language no longer in use is dead and hence cannot express the world. Language is a concatenation of symbols to which meanings are assigned by a group of speakers through conventions and practices. Thus, symbols are artificial in the sense that there is no natural connection between a symbol and what it symbolizes. For example, the symbol "cat" would not mean cat if there would not be a convention or practice of using "cat" to refer to cat. This picture of language presupposes a representation (symbol), the object of representation, i.e. the thing represented (the thing the symbol stands for) and a system in which a representation is interpreted as expressing the object.

If the use of language is an indication of cognition, then explanation of cognition must assume the notion of representation because cognition comprises, among other things, recognition, and classification, and finding relations among the classified objects of the world and talk of these activities cannot be possible without this notion. The notion of representation, which requires at least a cognitive system, a representation and the object represented, is assumed in cognitive science that aims at explaining human cognition. But there is a crucial difference between the notion of representation assumed with regard to a living language and the notion assumed in cognitive science. There is no interpretation going on in a cognitive system that connects the representation and the object represented. This is because the assumption of such a process leads to regression problem. But then, no one knows yet how the cognitive system is able to represent the objects of the world (Dietrich 2007).

Cognitive science supposes that human cognition can mechanically and computationally be explained. Fodor's language of thought hypothesis (Fodor 1975) assumes that human thinking uses meaningful symbols. There are physical bearers of symbols and there is a causal relation among these bearers. In addition to that, structural relations among the semantically evaluable objects are also assumed. The expectation is that an adequate mechanical and computational explanation of the functions of symbols will give an explanation of the relation among the meanings of the symbols, thereby explaining human thinking.

Language of thought (LOT) assumes computational theory of mind (CTM) and representational theory of mind (RTM) which further assumes the notion of discrete representation. Connectionism which is also a representational system, on the other hand, assumes the notion of distributed representation. Fodor claims that a connectionist model cannot be the right kind of model for explaining human cognition (Fodor & Pylyshyn 2007). There are counter-claims by Rumelhart (McClelland, Rumelhart, & Hinton 2007), Smolensky (Smolensky 2007) and Gelder (Gelder 2007). Interestingly, there are also claims that there is deep problem at the heart of the LOT/CTM programme (Schneider 2009) and that folk psychological theories, because of the kind of entities and processes posited, are unlikely to fare better against connectionist theories (Ramsey, Stich, & Garon 2007). I take up the controversy here to find out which group makes sense with regard to explanation of human cognition. Since both the classicists (Fodor et al. 1975) and the connectionists (Smolensky et al. 2007) are talking about two different representational systems and that notion of representation is at the core of such a system, it will be fruitful to examine this core concept. Let us look at the concept of discrete representation first.

I

A system has discrete representations if it contains more than one representation, and the representations are bounded and uniquely identifiable. They are composable, enduring and make finite, localizable, and precise contribution to larger states. Categorization is one of the important reasons for the necessity of discrete representation. Categorization takes place when a system's internal states impose classes of sameness to two different inputs without discerning the differences. Enduring classes of sameness are also required for such activity. A system has discrete representations if and only if it can discriminate its inputs. It follows that if a system categorizes, that is, discriminates inputs at the level of conceptualization, then it has discrete representations (Dietrich 2007).

Concepts combine in a cognitive process. This is typically evident in case of language use. We use primitive concepts to form complex ones. Because we combine concepts freely and easily in this manner, Fodor, McLaughlin and Pylyshyn assume that representations have a compositional, or role-argument structure that facilitates combination (Dietrich 2007). Mental representations which are discrete, according to LOT, must have combinatorial syntax and semantics. There are structurally atomic and molecular representations. Molecular representations have syntactic constituents that are themselves either molecular or atomic. The semantic content of a molecular representation is a function of the semantic contents of its syntactic parts, together with its constituent structure.

LOT also assumes the structural sensitivity of the process. Mental operations are possible by working on the form of the representations. For example, in a model of inference, an operation may take a representation of the form *P&Q* and transform it into a representation of the form *P*. Such an operation can apply equally to representations that differ widely in their structural complexity. For example, the operation is satisfied when "AvBvC" is derived from "AvBvC & DvEvF" (Fodor & Pylyshyn 2007). In a computational system, if mental operations succeed in transforming one syntactic form to another through causal relation, then what more the symbol system, with its semantic properties, is supposed to do? It seems to be redundant (Schneider 2009).

Fodor and Pylyshyn, however, think that an adequate explanation of human cognition must talk of a symbol system because it can capture the characteristics of human cognition-productivity, systematicity, compositionality and inferential coherence. They support their claim by offering arguments from consideration of these characteristics. Let us look at these arguments. The basic idea of the argument from productivity is that a language has the capacity to express indefinitely many propositions from a finite number of means. The correspondence between a representation and the proposition it expresses is built up recursively out of correspondences between parts of the expression and parts of the proposition. LOT is a representational system like a language is. So, it captures the productivity of the human cognition. Now, the methodological reason for assuming that human cognition is productive is that a human cognitive task is performed within the constraint of limited resources. There will be large demands on memory unless productivity is assumed. The empirical reason comes from the observation that a speaker could, in fact, utter or understand tokens of a finite number of sentence types, but his knowledge of his language supports an unbounded productive capacity. One, who works out a few additions, can do an unbounded number of sums.

The systematicity argument holds that cognitive capacity is systematic. Since language comprehension and production is systematic, the capacity that facilitates that comprehension is systematic. The systematicity of a linguistic capacity consisting in the ability to produce or understand some sentences is intrinsically connected to the ability to produce or understand certain others. It is a property of the mastery of the syntax of a language, not of its lexicon. For example, one who produces or understands the sentence "John loves the girl" can produce or understand the sentence "The girl loves John". This capacity shows that sentences must have both syntactic and semantic structures. This is an argument from systematicity of linguistic capacity to construct structures of sentences. A parallel argument goes from systematicity of thought to syntactic and semantic structures of mental representations. The systematicity of thought follows from the systematicity of language provided that understanding a sentence involves entertaining the thought that it expresses.

The argument from compositionality arrives at the compositionality of human cognition from the compositionality of language. The principle of compositionality requires that a lexical item must make approximately the same semantic contribution to each expression in which it occurs. It is, for example, in so far as "the", "girl", "loves" and "John" make the same semantic contribution to "John loves the girl" that they make to "the girl loves John". Similarity of constituent structures accounts for the semantic relatedness between systematically related sentences only to the extent that the semantic properties of the shared constituents are context-independent. Further, acceptance of the principle of compositionality explains how a finitely representable language can contain indefinitely many non-synonymous expressions. A further argument for the principle comes from consideration of entailment. Predicates like ". . . is a brown cow" severally entails semantically ". . . is brown" and ". . . is a cow" and is entailed by their conjunction. The adjective "brown" retains its semantic value under the simplification of conjunction.

The evidence for the compositionality of mental representation comes from the compositionality of sentences via the psycholinguistic premise that one uses language to express one's thoughts. If the ability to use some sentences is connected with the ability to use some other semantically related sentences, then, given the premise it implies the ability to think some thoughts which are correspondingly connected to some other semantically related thoughts. Thoughts are thoughts through mental representations. This implies that mental representations must be semantically connected.

The argument from inferential coherence is made from assumptions to adequate explanation of psychological phenomena to the justification of the assumptions. It is assumed that the combinatorial semantics of mental representations is sensitive to their syntax and that mental processes apply to mental representations by virtue of their constituent structure. These assumptions explain why people tend to think that *P* from the thought that *P&Q*. Further, there is hardly any case where one thinks that *P* from thinking that *P&Q&R* but doesn't infer *P* from thinking that *P&Q*.

The basic line of reasoning that Fodor follows is the following:

1. Natural language *L* is productive, systematic, compositional and coherent.

2. Speakers of *L* use *L* to express their thoughts.
3. The language the speakers use to express their thoughts corresponds to the language of his thoughts.
4. Therefore, the language of thought is productive, systematic, compositional and coherent.

Once the premises are accepted the conclusion is inevitable. Further, the discreteness of mental representation fits into the features of the language of thought. The first premise is well argued for. The second premise may be taken as a matter of fact. But the third premise is really problematic. There is virtually no argument for this premise. This is the crucial bridging premise without which the conclusion does not follow. There are good reasons to be sceptical about the plausibility of the premise. There is an alternative explanation for human cognition without assumptions of discreteness of mental representation and the alleged characteristics of the language of thought. Further, in this connection it is important to take note of an observation by Harré:

> We must beware of the product/process fallacy. It does not follow that the products of a process bear any resemblance to the process by which the product has been produced. To assume that there must be such a resemblance is to fall prey to the product/process fallacy. In psychology cognitive *products*, intentional entities and processes of many types are characterized by the demands of public meaningfulness. However, cognitive *processes* are constrained by the architecture and neurophysiology of the cluster of cells we call the brain. Beware of the product/process fallacy. The second "cognitive" above, in the phrase "cognitive process", is defined by picking out some relevant neural process that, meaningless in itself, has an outcome that displays intentionality and meaning. The generative process is not cognitive in that sense. This is a subtle point but of the greatest significance in understanding the strengths and

> the limits of cognitive "science". — Harré 2002: 112.

Fodor would presumably not deny the distinction nor would he disagree with the observation. Cognitive processes at the level of neurophysiology are different from psychological processes and entities. The former need not resemble the latter. The former are the workings at the implementation level while psychological processes and entities are at the implemented level. What he would emphatically assert is that the cognitive phenomena are the functions of a representational system that closely resemble the functions of a natural language. But the question is: should we assume this? Do these two representational systems have to resemble each other? Connectionists answer the questions in the negative. They take the notion of representation as primitive but work with a notion of distributed representation which is different from the discrete representation assumed in case of LOT and natural language.

II

Perhaps the most authoritative version of distributed representation (Hinton, McLelland, and Rumelhart 1986: 77) is:

> Each entity is represented by a pattern of activity distributed over many computing elements, and each computing element is involved in representing many different entities.
> — Gelder 2007: 923

However, for various reasons, Gelder disapproves the definition; one reason being that both patterns of activity over computing elements and patterns of connectivity that mediate their transformation are considered as distributed representations. He introduces the notion of extended representation. In typical connectionist networks, the benchmark is one computing unit for every item, a representation is extended if it uses many units for every item. Here, as it seems, distinctive patterns over computing units are crucial since they represent the item which the individual units do not. One such connectionist scheme is to assign one microfeature to one unit and group of units with their interconnectedness will give rise to a distinctive pattern that can be said to represent the item. For example, Smolensky gives the following account of how a network of units can represent an item as a result of processing the microfeatures (Smolensky 2007: 970-71):

Units Microfeatures

- • upright container
- • hot liquid
- o glass contacting wood
- • porcelain curved surface
- • burnt odour
- • brown liquid contacting porcelain
- • porcelain curved surface
- o oblong silver object
- • finger-sized handle
- • brown liquid with curved sides and bottom

Figure 80.2: Representation of *cup* with *coffee*

Units Microfeatures

- • upright container
- o hot liquid
- o glass contacting wood
- • porcelain curved surface
- o burnt odour
- o brown liquid contacting prorcelain
- • porcelain curved surface
- o oblong silver object

- • finger-sized handle
- o brown liquid with curved sides and bottom

Figure 80.3: Representation of *cup* without *coffee*

Units Microfeatures

- o upright container
- • hot liquid
- o glass contacting wood
- o porcelain curved surface
- • burnt odour
- • brown liquid contacting porcelain
- o porcelain curved surface
- o oblong silver object
- o finger-sized handle
- • brown liquid with curved sides and bottom

Figure 80.4: Representation of *coffee*

Microfeatures-based schemes, however, are not the only kind in which distributed representation can be worked out. Connectionist network is also not committed, according to Gelder, to the existence of microfeatural analysis of task domains, or to simple feature-based semantics for their representation. Internal structure of the representation is essential for reflecting the semantic properties. The way a group of units is connected constitutes the internal structure of a representation. The pattern of activity used to represent an item is determined by the nature of that item. Thus, similarities and differences among the items to be represented will be directly reflected in similarities and dissimilarities among the representation themselves. Further, each unit will be involved in representing many different entities, because the representations of other items are simply different patterns of activity over the same group of units. The representations of the two different entities can in this way be superimposed on each other and moreover, it is possible to superimpose patterns while preserving the functional independence of the representations (Gelder 2007). For some technical reasons Gelder prefers the term *superposed* in place of the term *superimposed*.

The representations of two distinct items are superposed if they are coextensive, i.e. if they occupy the same portion of the resources available for representing. Thus, in connectionist networks one can have different items stored as patterns of activity over the same set of units. When two representations are effectively superposed, they become a single new item representing both the original contents. The two representations now become a single superposed representation.

The often used metaphor of filing cabinet illustrates the difference between discrete representation and superposed representation. In the ideal filing cabinet, every distinct item to be represented is encoded on a separate paper, and the sheets are then placed side by side in cabinet, drawers. Every paper can be accessed, modified, removed or destroyed without affecting the other. A discrete representation encoded by binary unit strings and stored in registers can similarly be treated. In case of superposed representation, by contrast, there would not be any separate location for each distinct item in the cabinet. The whole cabinet would be representing every item without any more fine-grained correspondence of sheets or locations for individual items. Accessing the representation of one item is accessing the representations of all items. Modifying or representing of one item cannot but affect the representing of all items.

The schemes of discrete representation assume an isomorphic correspondence in the sense that there is a distinct representation for every item to be represented and the structure of the space of representations systematically corresponds to the structure of the space of possible contents. The way it corresponds can only be characterized relative to the scheme in question. Languages usually define an infinite array of distinct expression types, which are then put in correspondence with distinct items or state of affairs. In a scheme of discrete representations a representation is stored as it is and retrieved as it is.

The notion of superposed representation overthrows this whole familiar picture. In superposition one point in space of representations can serve as the representation of multiple contents. Here, some non-arbitrary structural or functional relationship between a representation *R* and its content *C* ensures that *R* is the representation of *C*. When a single point of space functions as the representation of every item to be stored, the storage involves transformation. In order to recover a representation in its original form the transformation is to be reversed. Actually the original or something like it is recreated as Rumelhart and Norman stated, "Information is better thought of as 'evoked' than 'found'" (Gelder 2007).

III

We have seen in the previous sections that the notion of discrete representation is radically different from the notion of distributed representation (superposed representation). The desiderata formulated for schemes explaining human cognition within a framework need not be the desiderata for another for the simple reason that it is meant for former. If schemes explain cognition in the latter framework that do not take into account the desiderata of the former, that should not be the ground for rejecting the schemes of the latter. The schemes that assume discrete representation are formulated in the framework of symbol system of CTM, the classical framework. The schemes that assume distributed representation are formulated within the connectionist framework. The desiderata of systematicity and compositionality are such that they require a symbol system that CTM stands for. The failure to comply with the desiderata need not be the deciding factors for rejecting the connectionist schemes. Whether the connectionist schemes effectively portray human cognition and that they have better explanatory power over the schemes in a symbol system framework has to be decided on their capacity to explain widely acknowledged cognitive activities that the latter schemes cannot. It is too early to decide this, given the present developmental stage of connectionism.

The appeal of LOT supported by CTM lies with the hypothesis that concepts are involved in highly abstract thinking and concept combining seems to have an affinity with the way expressions of a language are manipulated. In addition to that, the use of language to talk about oneself and the objects of the external world presupposes language processing. This may suggest that a mental language at the stage of abstract thinking is a good working hypothesis. But to assume it to be the hypothesis for all kinds of cognitive phenomena is to make a very strong claim. Developmental psychology speaks of cognitive phenomena at the initial stages of object recognition by infants where LOT does not seem to have any role to play (Dietrich 2007).

The appeal of connectionism lies in that the neural network of the brain is supposed to be the base of the cognitive architecture and accepting this basic assumption connectionist network models are designed to explain human cognition. Now the challenge for connectionism is that network modelling not only has to explain the simple cognitive phenomena of object recognition but also has to explain the highly abstract thinking. Even the explanation of the so-called simple object recognition is highly complex itself. But to argue against connectionist approach, because it is rooted in distributed representations, and claim that it is theoretically unsuitable to handle high complexity of abstract thinking is unwarranted.

References

Copeland, B.J. & Proudfoot, D. (2007), in P. Thagard (ed.), *The Philosophy of Psychology and Cognitive Science* North Holland, pp. 429-82.

Davies, M. (2007), "Cognitive Science," in F. Jackson & M. Smith (eds.), *The Oxford Handbook of Contemporary Philosophy* New York: Oxford University Press, pp. 358-94.

Dietrich, E. (2007), "Representation," in P. Thagard (ed.), *The Philosophy of Psychology and Cognitive Science* North Holland, pp. 1-29.

Dietrich, E. & Markman, A.B. (2003), "Discrete Thoughts: Why Cognition must Use Discrete Representations," *Mind and Language*, vol. 18, no. 1, pp. 95-119.

Dretske, F. (2007), "Misrepresentation", in F. Jackson & P. Ludlow (eds.), *The Phiosophy of Mind*, New Delhi: Prentice-Hall of India Pvt. Ltd, pp. 597-610.

Fodor, J.A. (2007), "Methodological Solipcism as a Research Strategy in Cognitive Psychology", in B. Beakely & A.P. Ludlow (eds.), *The Philosophy of Mind*, New Delhi: Prentic-Hall of India Pvt. Ltd., pp. 575-96.

Fodor, J.A. (1975), *The Language of Thought*. Sussex: Harvester Press (Harvard University Press paperback).

Fodor, J.A., & Mclaughlin, B.P. (2007), "Connectonism and the Problem of Systematicity: Why Smolensky's Soluton Doesn't Work", in F. Jackson & P. Ludlow (eds.), *The Philosophy of Mind*, New Delhi: Prentice-Hall of India Pvt. Ltd., pp. 983-1000.

Fodor, J.A. & Pylyshyn, Z.W. (2007), "Connectionism and Cognitive Architecture: A Critical Analysis", in F. Jackson & P. Ludlow (eds.), *The Philosophy of Mind* New Delhi: Prentice-Hall of India Pvt. Ltd., pp. 921-60.

Gelder, T.V. (2007), "What is the "D" in "PDP"? A Survey of the Concept of Distribution", In F. Jackson & P. Ludlow (eds.), *The*

Philosophy of Mind, New Delhi: Prentice-Hall of India Pvt. Ltd., pp. 1001-1026.

Harré, R. (2002), *Cognitive Science: A Philosophical Introducton,* London: Sage Publications India Pvt. Ltd.

McClelland, J.L., D.E. Rumelhart, & G.E. Hinton, (2007), "The Appeal of Parallel Distributed Processing", in F. Jackson, & P. Ludlow (eds.), *The Philosophy of Mind,* New Delhi: Prentice-Hall of India Pvt. Ltd., pp. 899-920.

Perry, J. (1998), *Some Puzzles about Beliefs,* Home Page of Perry, Princeton University.

Pitt, D. (2008), "Mental Representation", *Stanford Encyclopedia of Philosophy.*

Ramsey, W., S.P Stich, & J. Garon (2007), "Connectionism, Eliminativism, and the Future of Folk Psychology", in F. Jackson & P. Ludlow (eds.), *The Philosophy of Mind,* New Delhi: Prentice-Hall of India Pvt. Ltd., pp. 1027-48.

Schneider, S. (2009), "LOT, CTM, and the Elephant in the Room", *Synthese,* 170: 235-50.

Smolensky, P. (2007), "The Constituent Structure of Connectionist Mental States: A Reply to Fodor and Pylyshyn", in F. Jackson & P. Ludlow (eds.), *The Philosophy of Mind,* New Delhi: Prentice-Hall of India Pvt. Ltd., pp. 961-82.

Solomon, M. (2007), "Situated Cognition", in P. Thagard (ed.), *The Philosophy of Psychology and Cognitive Science,* North Holland, pp. 413-28.

Stich, S. (1992), "What is a Theory of Mental Representation?" *Mind,* vol. 101, 243-61, 402. April.

Wilson, R.A. & C.F. Craver (2007), "Realization: Metaphysical And Scientific Perspectives", in P. Thagard (ed.), *The Philosophy of Psychology and Cognitive Science,* North Holland, pp. 105-58.

Wright, C. & W. Bechtel (2007), "Mechanisms and Psychological Explanation", in P. Thagard (ed.), *Philosophy of Psychology and Cognitive Science,* North Holland, pp. 30-79.

8

Wittgenstein and Derrida on Representation

Muhammedaly P.P.

THE later Wittgenstein and Derrida share the view that language does not refer to anything whatsoever. In his *Philosophical Investigations* Wittgenstein articulates his view that language is a rule-governed activity. It is a set of socially determined rules that makes language possible for us. Other than the social determination, rules of language have no base. If one who uses language intends to violate these rules any time, nothing can prevent one from doing so. If references of the uses of words are represented by means of linguistic rules, a violation of these rules implies a possibility of dismantling the system of references we have through them. This is the reason why Wittgenstein says in his *On Certainty*[1] that we can have only a mythical account of why we follow a set of rules that makes language possible for us. This means that the linguistic representation of "what there is" is a myth for him. A myth, which is sustained in what we call a *systematic uses of words* that makes it look deceptively objective. Derrida, in a related

1. He says: "The propositions describing this world-picture might be part of a kind of mythology. And their role is like that of rules of a game; and the game can be learned purely practically, without learning any explicit rules." Ludwig Wittgenstein, *On Certainty*, tr. Denis Paul and G.E.M. Anscombe, Oxford: Basil Blackwell, 1977, 15e.

manner, sees language as a play of signifiers which constructs the signified by means of the *relations of difference and deference* that exist between them. For him, the relations of difference and deference that exist between signifiers lead to the deconstruction of the presence of being of meanings and thereby that of the world, which is a function of the web of signifiers. He believes that language represents (or constructs) the being of the world through a *detour*, which in turn calls into question the ability of language to represent.

In his earlier work *Tractatus*[2] Wittgenstein believed that words had meanings by virtue of the fact that they referred to objects. It is this view that he questions in his *Philosophical Investigations,* which largely determines his later views on language and heralds a new way of looking at the world. In *Tractatus*, he thought that a word referred to an object *eternally*. Let us explain this view with the help of the example of the word "Excalibur". If the sword that is meant by this word is destroyed, then it is not the case that this word ceases to have meaning. How does the meaning of this word survive the destruction of the object it referred to? It is because of the fact that the word "Excalibur" consists of simple names, which refer to simple objects which constituted the sword Excalibur, which has been destroyed now. Wittgenstein argued in *Tractatus* that an object was an arrangement of simple objects, which were not in space and time.

An arrangement of simple objects, which constituted a material object, could be in space and time, but not the simple objects as they really were. Destruction of an object meant only a change in the configuration of simple objects, which were referred to by simple names, which were also beyond spatio-temporal existence and so indestructible. It explains the

2. Ludwig Wittgenstein, *Tractatus Logico-philosophicus*, tr. D.F. Pears & B.F. McGuinness, London: Routledge & Kegan Paul, 1969.

reason for the early Wittgenstein why the destruction of the sword Excalibur did not entail the destruction of the simple objects of which it was made owing to a configuration of theirs. And these simple objects were the base for the meaning of the word "Excalibur" because they were referred to by the simple names of this word.

Wittgenstein now says that there is no rationale for such a picture of language and meaning, and that he constructed it under an illusion that made him believe that language referred to things and its meanings outlived the destruction of things in question.

In *Philosophical Investigations* he says that such an illusion is created in our minds by the very nature of language. Take for example our belief that the word "red" refers to the colour red. Does this word really refer to the colour red? Wittgenstein's view is that we can only say that we *use* this word in order to refer to what we call the colour red and we have no way to determine whether it *really refers to* the colour in question. This is his celebrated use-theory of meaning which states that the references of language are determined by the uses of words and not vice versa. When we use the word "red" to refer to the colour red continuously we, as it were, lose sight of the fact that it is the use of it that makes the colour red as its reference possible for us, and begin to believe that a magical relation exists between the word "red" and the colour red and that his ethereal relation is referential in nature. The word "red" seems to utter by way of a joke: "there is something behind me that determines my being as a name for it", and we are ever ready to take this joke seriously!

If references cannot determine the uses of words, what does determine them so that they are used by their users in the same way? Wittgenstein's answer to this question is that it is the rules of language that determine their uses. Here comes the problem of the objectivity of the rules. Are they objective?

For Wittgenstein they are not objective but *means of representations* which make references possible for us. Let us see how he explains this view.

Wittgenstein compares a rule with the standard metre kept in Paris which is the means of representation for 1 m. length as it is used in our measurements now. There is nothing inviolable about this standard metre which has been hermetically sealed and kept in Paris. One can remove or change its length and this, in turn, shall either remove or change what is represented through it, which is 1 m. length as we understand it now. Wittgenstein asks us to imagine a situation in which all the samples of colours with their names attached to them (which will have the form "This length = One metre") have been kept in Paris as the rules for the uses of the colour words. These rules then will determine how we use the colour words in language. It shows how the rules of language create an order in our use of language so that we can talk about things in an order. Once these rules are not followed, they will no longer represent the relation between words and things as we have them now. To quote Wittgenstein:

> There is *one* thing of which one can say neither that it is one metre long, nor that it is not one metre long, and that is the standard metre in Paris. — But this is, of course, not to ascribe any extraordinary property to it, but only to mark its peculiar role in the language game of measuring with a metre-rule. — Let us imagine samples of colour being preserved in Paris like the standard metre. We define: "sepia" means the colour of the standard sepia which is there kept hermetically sealed. Then it will make no sense to say of this sample either that it is of this colour or that it is not.[3]

One may be tempted to think here that in language rules come

3. Ludwig Wittgenstein, *Philosophical Investigations*, tr. G.E.M. Anscombe, Oxford: Basil Blackwell, 1976, 25e.

first and then the uses of words, which are determined by them. Wittgenstein does not think so as is evident from his view that rules are not extraordinary but are as ordinary as the uses of words that they determine. Rules have their base in the uses of words. When a word is used *regularly* to denote a thing it becomes a rule such that it is expected to determine the uses of that word further. This is reflected in the statement of Wittgenstein that the use of the word "same" and the use of the word "rule" are interwoven. In a form of life people *agree* to use a word to refer to a thing and it thus becomes a linguistic rule of representation of that thing. Wittgenstein calls the word "agreement" the cousin of the word "rule". For Wittgenstein language is possible only as a form of life where people agree on the uses of words by following their rules to represent things.

When language has no foundation in physical things, which are situated in our life as functions of the uses of words, can it have a base in our mental world? Wittgenstein says that what is called "mental" is defined in language. So it means that language *in a way* precedes (or should we say here that it is contingently simultaneous with?) what is being called "Physical" and also what is being called "mental". He says that to understand the meaning of a word is nothing more or less than to understand its uses in the relevant contexts which is not a mental phenomenon. To understand the use of a word is not like "being depressed" or "being happy", which are instances of mental phenomena. The plane on which language makes its being known to us is the plane of our social life and this implies not only the infinite possibilities of language but also its infinite limitations. What does it mean to understand the use of a word? Wittgenstein says that it is like understanding an algebraic formula.

Wittgenstein takes an example where *A* writes down the series: 1, 5, 11, 19, 29. . . . . and *B* watches it trying to make sense of it. Suddenly the formula $an = n^2 + n - 1$ occurs to him as the rule of this series and he then exclaims that he now knows how to go on. That the formula occurs to him presupposes that *B* has been trained in mathematics as it is used in our society and also that he knows how to substitute an algebraic formula for a number series. Someone may think that the mere occurrence of the formula to *B* does not constitute his knowing it because it may be the case that a formula occurs to *B* as a rule for a series of numbers, but he will not be able to apply it to predict the next number in it. So to understand a formula means something more than its having occurred to one and what is this "more than" must be a mental process. Wittgenstein opposes such a view. To quote him:

> . . . . - does it follow from this that I employ the sentence "Now I understand . . . . ." or
>
> "Now I can go on" as a description of a process occurring behind or side by side with that of saying the formula?
>
> If there has to be anything "behind the utterance of the formula" it is *particular circumstances*, which justify me in saying I can go on — when the formula occurs to me.[4]

Language has neither a mental nor a physical foundation, for what is either physical or mental is defined and made sense of in and through language. Its base lies in the acceptance of its rules in a form of life. Wittgenstein sees language as an indistinct picture, which can never be replaced by a sharp one. It is the very nature of language to be indistinct and it is not its imperfection. A rule of it implies a possibility where it can be followed in infinitely different ways which at times include the ones, which will negate its accepted connotation radically. So how will we define the social acceptance of a linguistic rule and its being obeyed by a community as a result? To quote Wittgenstein:

4. Ludwig Wittgenstein, *Philosophical Investigations*, tr. G.E.M. Anscombe, Oxford: Basil Blackwell, 1976, 60e.

> "How am I able to obey a rule?" — If this is not a question about causes, then it is about the justification for my following the rule in the way I do.
>
> If I have exhausted the justifications I have reached the bedrock, and my spade is turned. Then I am inclined to say: "This is simply what I do."[5]

Wittgenstein says symbolically that when a rule is "stamped with a particular meaning" it "traces the lines along with which it is to be followed through the whole of the space". He believes that one obeys a rule *blindly* as if it were laid for the use of a word which extends over an infinite space and time. It may give us the impression that a rule is determined not causally but logically. Though this impression helps us understand a difference between being causally determined and being logically determined, for Wittgenstein a rule cannot be determined either causally or logically.

Wittgenstein writes:

> But what is the purpose of that symbolical proposition? It was supposed to bring into prominence a difference between being causally determined and being logically determined.
>
> My symbolical expression was really a mythological description of the use of a rule.[6]

A rule is not a superlative phenomenon either. It can be disobeyed if one chooses to do so either intentionally or unintentionally. Suppose a child is taught how he is to complete a series of numbers adding 2 to the preceding digits in it and has been tested and trained in it only up to 1,000 and not beyond that, and now he has been given the order "add 2" to complete a long series of numbers. He adds 2 up to 1,000 and

5. Ludwig Wittgenstein, *Philosophical Investigations*, tr. G.E.M. Anscombe, Oxford: Basil Blackwell, 1976, 85e.

6. Ibid., 85e.

after that he adds 4 to continue it. We try to get him "right" by saying that he is supposed to add 2 even after 1,000 and not 4, but he will not understand what we say. He is not convinced of the way we follow the rule of the order "add 2". Wittgenstein writes:

> In such a case we might say, perhaps: It comes natural to this person to understand our order with our explanations as *we* should understand the order: "Add 2 up to 1,000, 4 up to 2,000, 6 up to 3,000 and so on."
>
> Such a case would present similarities with one in which a person naturally reacted to the gesture of pointing with the hand by looking in the direction of the line from fingertip to wrist, not from wrist to fingertip.[7]

The word "cube", for example, suggests a use to us and we sometimes think that we can grasp its meaning in a flash. Wittgenstein says that it only shows that we know that this word has been used in several contexts in a particular way and how it should be used in similar contexts in the future. That is, it only implies that we know how to follow a rule meant for it in the normal cases of its use, not in the abnormal ones. One may object to it saying that the word "cube" brings a picture of the cube before our minds, which in turn determines the uses of it. Wittgenstein says that it does not matter what picture it brings before our minds, but what matters is the way it is used in the circumstances where it is supposed to be used. If at all it brings a picture of the cube before our minds (what kind of mental picture it would be?), it can no way be different from a picture which we may draw of it on a piece of paper. Wittgenstein's question is: how can a picture of the cube, whether it is mental or non-mental, determine the use of the word "cube"? It can be put in a

7. Ludwig Wittgenstein, *Philosophical Investigations*, tr. G.E.M. Anscombe, Oxford: Basil Blackwell, 1976, 75e.

different way: how can the object called cube, let alone its picture, determine the use of the word "cube"? His answer to this is that the abnormal uses of this word are as natural as its normal uses and that there is no way to determine what sense we can make of the use of this word, for that matter the use of any word, except in the case of its normal uses. It leads us to conclude that Wittgenstein does not accord language the ability to represent things as they are because they are for him defined solely in terms of the varied uses of its words, whose base lies in their being accepted in a community of speakers. That is, we make sense of the world through language, whose normalcy can always be questioned.

Now we would make an attempt to relate Wittgenstein's view on language to Derrida's approach to representation of meaning and object. Just as Wittgenstein says that objects are a part of our referential framework owing to the fact that they are being implied through our uses of words, so Derrida defines them as functions of the uses of signs. A sign for him is given in a web of relations that exist between signs. This is similar to Wittgenstein's position that a sentence is functional only in the whole context of the language which it belongs to. Wittgenstein compares a sentence to a brake lever, which is what it is in the context of the whole mechanism of an engine, and separated from it, it can be anything or nothing. If a sign is what it is owing to its position in a web of relations of signs, Derrida says that the uniqueness of a sign dissipates as it cannot exist in isolation. Further he adds to this that the relations between signs are those of difference and deference, which make a proper definition of a sign impossible as a sign is accorded its being in the criss-crossings of these relations.

For him if the differences of signs are the very condition of the possibility of language, the same differences dig the grave of it because a difference between two signs or more brings into play a postponement or a deference of their coming together, which in turn makes possible their significance as signs heralding their own insignificance. If "good" is "bad differed and deferred", where do we find good as such? "Good" is something that is *different* from "bad" and it then leads to a *deferential* relation between them which, by not allowing them to be together, makes their existence possible through an irony.

Reminding us of a Heraclitean flux where the difference between elements in a series is the condition of the disappearance of each element in it and that of the series itself as a result, Derrida articulates a unity of the concepts "difference" and "deference" through another concept (or non-concept) called *differance,* which makes the appearance of *being* possible as a disappearance of it at the same time. He calls the "a" in *differance* a spelling mistake that characterizes the very nature of our discourse of the signified, which is a function of the signifiers.

It is a spelling mistake for Derrida that there is an "a" in the word *differance,* which means both "to differ" and "to defer". In this spelling mistake we see what is wrong with our entire use of language. We can ignore this awareness of what is wrong with our uses of words in the same way that we learn to overlook the Wittgensteinian notion of abnormality that has been written into a linguistic rule when we follow it. The very fact that we ignore it constitutes its importance for Derrida. He writes:

> The *a* of *differance,* thus, is not heard; it remains silent, secret and discreet as a tomb: *oikesis.* And thereby let us anticipate the delineation of a site, the familial residence and tomb of the proper in which is produced, by *differance,* the *economy of death.* This stone — provided that one knows how to decipher its inscription — is not far from announcing the death of the tyrant.[8]

8. Jacques Derrida, "Differance" in *Margins of Philosophy,* tr. Alan Bass Sussex: The Harvester Press Limited, 1986, 4.

It is speech, which is the tyrant that attributes meanings to words. A script, which cannot be made sense of through speech, is a script which is written without being spoken. When it is spoken it becomes a phonetic script which creates an order in our uses of words which, in turn, produces a world of beings for us. When the phonetic dimension of speech or (phonetic) writing which can be read is absent in a script, what does it signify? What does define its being as a rule? What can it represent? Isn't it like a linguistic rule which has no direction whatsoever? — That this non-phonetic script defines our phonetic speech and phonetic writing creates a void in our uses of words in general. To quote Derrida:

> If there is no purely phonetic writing, it is that there is no purely phonetic *phone*. The difference which establishes phonemes and lets them be heard remains in and of itself inaudible, in every sense of the word.[9]

Differance is not a mere absence of this or that because such an absence makes sense only in terms of something that is negated. It is also not a phenomenon that can be arrived at by means of a method akin to that of a negative theology where the Supreme Being is defined as someone who cannot be defined by any means. Negative theology refuses God the predicate of existence only to affirm "his superior, inconceivable, and ineffable mode of being". But a possible description of *differance* after the manner of negative theology does not point to anything, which would make it superior and ineffable. Wittgenstein says in *Philosophical Investigations* that theology is possible only as a grammar. The grammar of our language with all its uncertainty articulates a notion of God for us. It means that our knowledge of God is grammatical in nature. The means by which we reach a concept of God is

9. Jacques Derrida, "Differance" in *Margins of Philosophy*, tr. Alan Bass (Sussex: The Harvester Press Limited, 1986, 5.

uncertain, and at times hides an irony in its very nature. When Derrida says that *differance* is not a thing akin to God as it is understood in negative theology what he means is that there is nothing solid about the nature of *differance*. It cannot be known either through senses or through intelligence.

It is in language that we define what must be called intelligible and what must be called sensible. But the very condition of language is *differance*, which makes it a "bottomless chessboard" on which the game called life with its myriad implications has been played out like a non-mysterious mystery. Placed between speech and writing, and thus defining them in their very being which is the impossibility of what is possible and vice versa, *differance* belongs to an order which "resists the opposition between the sensible and the intelligible". To quote Derrida:

> Here, therefore, we must let ourselves refer to an order that resists the opposition, one of the founding oppositions of philosophy, between the sensible and the intelligible. The order which resists this opposition, and resists it because it transports it, is announced in a movement of *differance* (with an *a*) between two differences or two letters, a *differance* which belongs neither to the voice nor to writing in the usual sense, and which is located, as the strange space that will keep us together here for an hour, *between* speech and writing, and beyond the tranquil familiarity which links us to one and the other, occasionally reassuring us in our illusion that they are two.[10]

Here one can perceive a striking similarity between *Differance*, which is the condition of language for Derrida, and Wittgenstein's notion of language as *a mythical phenomenon* which brings into being all categories of existence, which include what we call mental ones and also what we call

10. Jacques Derrida, "Differance" in *Margins of Philosophy*, tr. Alan Bass (Sussex: The Harvester Press Limited, 1986, 5.

physical ones. For Wittgenstein, like Derrida, the distinction between the sensible and the intelligible cannot be anything other than a grammatical one. *Differance* cannot be talked about and defined. But Derrida does that precisely. He justifies his "attempted discourse" on *differance* (in a speech that lasted an hour) by calling it "strategic and adventurous". It is strategic since it has no base in a transcendental notion of meaning which alone can account for meaning proper. It is adventurous because this strategy involves tactics, which are blind in their operation.

There is a certain wandering in the tracing of *differance* which does not acquire its meaning either empirically or logically. It is a *play* that breaks with the distinction between the empirical and the logical even when it becomes the source of such a distinction. Derrida writes that this play keeps itself beyond the opposition between the lines of "philosophical logical discourse" and those of "its symmetrical and integral inverse", which he calls "empirical logical discourse" to announce "the unity of chance and necessity in calculations without end". Derrida writes about the aim of his analysis of *difference*:

> Even though *differance* is neither a word nor a concept, let us nevertheless attempt a simple and approximate semantic analysis that will take us to within sight of what is at stake.[11]

Differance is *temporization*, which Derrida defines as temporalization and spacing in their inseparable unity. It is time that makes space porous and it is space that makes time porous. What is it that fills the enigmatic *hiatus* that defines space as an *entity*? What is it that makes time, which is porous being united with space, a positive phenomenon of our life? If

11. Jacques Derrida, "Differance" in *Margins of Philosophy*, tr. Alan Bass (Sussex: The Harvester Press Limited, 1986, 7.

it is the "desire" or "will" of the community of speakers that answers the above questions, Derrida shows that "the accomplishment or fulfilment" of them is suspended when they are seen in the light or darkness of *differance* which questions the very possibility of the *detour* that allows us to represent the being of things by means of language. When Derrida defines an object or a subject as something given as a series of elements, which are conceived as related to one another, he calls the otherness that divides these elements infinitely within themselves "allergic or polemical otherness". He calls the otherness, which defines the relations between plurality of objects or subjects as the condition of their absence, "dissimilar otherness". It shows that *differance* deconstructs the individual entities and their relations not only from within but also from without.

But, for Derrida, an entity, whether it is a subject or an object, is a function of language. So when we say that an entity is assailed by *differance* that deconstructs it what we question is a construction effected through language. Our access to a thing is through the uses of words because it is words which construct it. To quote Derrida:

> Let us start, since we are already there, from the problematic of the sign and of writing.
>
> The sign is usually said to be put in the place of the thing itself, the present thing, "thing" here standing equally for meaning or referent. The sign presents the present in its absence. It takes the place of the present. When we cannot grasp or show the thing, state the present, the being-present, when the present cannot be presented, we signify, we go through the detour of the sign. We take or give signs. We signal. The sign, in this sense, is deferred presence. Whether we are concerned with the verbal or the written sign, with the monetary sign, or electoral delegation and political representation, the circulation of signs defers the moment

> in which we can encounter the thing itself, make it ours, consume or expend it, touch it, see it, intuit its presence.[12]

Language constructs things for us through an ironical detour and gives us the impression that they exist beyond the limits of it. In our attempt to reach out to them the head of our understanding, to quote a Wittgensteinian phrase, moves against the limits of language, which creates bumps on it. Whereas Wittgenstein sees the similarities and differences between language games and at the same time tries to show that representation through language is impossible because of the abnormality that attends the nature of the being of their rules, Derrida's emphasis is largely on differences between the signs that constitute language through a web which heralds its impossibility even when it is there for us as *a or the* means of communication.

---

12. Jacques Derrida, "Differance" in *Margins of Philosophy*, tr. Alan Bass (Sussex: The Harvester Press Limited, 1986, 9.

9

Is There a Private Language Called the Language of Thought?

Sreekala M. Nair

DURING the second half of the bygone century there was a proliferation of psychological research activities predicating the view that mental processes, by and large, are computational processes, from which we may derive the conclusion that the higher cognitive behaviour is rule-governed.

Currently, on a variety of disciplines such as, linguistics, simulation psychology, cognitive psychology, psychoanalysis etc. the techniques of the analysis of rule-governed behaviours have already been implemented. It is good that things have changed, but it is less clear where we have gotten. As a matter of fact, many practitioners feel increasingly unclear about the general character of the theoretical framework that they are working in and are equally quite uncertain about what should happen next. With the aim of providing insight into the current research and to aid in guiding future inquiry, Jerry Fodor, in his work *The Language of Thought* published in 1975, offered a bold hypothesis: the medium of thought is an innate language that is distinct from all spoken languages and is semantically as also expressively complete. The so-called *mentalese* is supposed to be an inner language that contains all of the conceptual resources necessary for any of the propositions that humans can grasp, think or express — in short, the basis of thought and meaning. To present his case, Fodor resorts to speculative psychology claiming that it has an upper hand over both, philosophy and empirical psychology. Speculative psychology, according to Fodor, is a discipline that holds a midway position: it is not quite a philosophy because it is concerned with empirical theory construction. It is not quite a psychology also because it is not an experimental science. But it uses the methods of both philosophy and psychology because it is dedicated to the notion that scientific theories should be both conceptually disciplined and empirically constrained. True, that the best answer to the question how the mind works is *ipso facto,* the best answer that is currently available in psychology, but the best psychology we have is still research in progress. Therefore it is ideal that one contributes for the advancement of this research.

Language of Thought Hypothesis Introduced

If we go by the kind of approach accepted by current psychological research, then one is committed to the view that perceptual process involves computing a series of re-descriptions of events stimulated by our immediate environment. This is to acknowledge that perception presupposes a representational system, a system rich enough to distinguish between the members of sets of properties, all of which are exhibited by the same event. For example, if *e* is a token of a sentence type, and if perceptually analysing *e* requires determining which sentence type it is a token of, then on the current view of perceptual analysis a series of representations of *e* will have to be computed. And this series will have to include and distinguish between representations which specify the acoustic, phonological, morphological and syntactic properties of the token. It will also include all these representations since for anyone who knows, each is essential for determining the type/token relation for the utterances of sentences.[1]

1. Type/token distinction of sentence is something popular in the analytic tradition.

If we come to an agreement that psychological processes are typically computational, then computation presupposes a medium for representing the structures over which the computational operations are defined, i.e. the organism has access to a language in which the computations are carried through. Fodor, even as he argues for a language of thought, does not maintain that thinking is purely attributable to the organisms themselves. It turns out that while drawing ordinary distinctions between what an organism thinks, does or knows, what happens in its nervous system does not seem to be important. The natural kinds appear to include some things that the organism does, some things that happen in the nervous system of the organism, and some things in its environment. It is simply no good for philosophers to urge that since this sort of theory does not draw the usual distinctions, it must be a muddle. If psychological theories fail to draw usual distinctions between some of the things that happen to organisms and some of the things that organisms do, that does not imply that such distinctions should be denied. What is implied is that the distinction between actions and happenings isn't a psychological distinction. Lots of very fine distinctions, after all, aren't psychological distinctions.

With the stage thus set, let us get straight to the theory: LOT hypothesis. Any theory of higher cognitive processes currently available adopts as one of its presuppositions that organism has a representational system in which the individual makes responses of its environment.

Representational realists would maintain that to think a thought with a given content is to be appropriately related to a representation with the right meaning, e.g. to have the belief that capitalism breeds greed is to have a representational token with the content "capitalism breeds greed" in one's belief box. Representation presupposes a medium of representation and there is no symbolization without symbols. Specifically there is no internal representation without an internal language.[2]

The representational system that underlies human thought, and perhaps that underlies thought in other species too, is semantically and syntactically *language-like*, i.e. it is similar to the spoken human languages. Specifically this representational system consists of syntactic tokens that are capable of expressing propositional meanings in virtue of the semantic compositionality of the syntactic elements. There are a number of considerations that lend very strong support to the view that thought is linguistic, for instance, productivity. Humans are able to entertain an indefinitely large number of semantically distinct thoughts. The obvious explanation of our ability to entertain indefinitely many thoughts is that thought consists of linguistic elements that can be combined in indefinitely many ways. Likewise, features like systematicity, semantic compositionality, complexity, introspection, etc. too support the view that thought is linguistic in nature.

Granted that thoughts are linguistic, there are different ways of construing these. For example, one may argue that, of course, there is a medium of representation and it is a language, that is what we call natural language. With regard to this response Fodor remarks:

> . . . the argument which seemed to lead to exciting and paradoxical conclusions thus leads only to one's front door . . . you suppose that natural language is the medium in which we express our thoughts; in fact, it is the medium in which we *think* them.[3]

---

2. Jerry A. Fodor, *The Language of Thought*, Cambridge, Massachusetts: Harvard University Press, 1979, p. 55.

3. Ibid., p. 56.

Conceiving natural language as the medium of thought is appealing as it allows the theorists both to admit the essential role of computation in the production of behaviour and to resist the scarifying implication of the notion of a language of thought. This assumption that LOT is drawn from one of the public languages has some inherent difficulties. The obvious (and for Fodor sufficient) reason for the refutation of the claim that natural languages are the medium of thought is that there are non-verbal organisms that think.

Now here one can engage herself quibbling about what to count as thinking.

There are three known processes considered as thought-contributing namely, considered action, concept-learning and perceptual integration — and all these three are familiar achievements of infrahuman organisms and preverbal children. Computational models of such processes are the only ones we've got, and computational models presuppose representational systems. But the representational systems of preverbal and infrahuman organisms surely cannot be natural language. So we either abandon infrahuman psychology we've so far pieced together or we admit that some thinking at least isn't done in natural language.[4]

Again, there is no internal reason for supposing that our psychology applies only to organisms that talk; although computation presupposes a representative language, it does not necessitate that it must be one that functions as a vehicle of communication. The nativistic argument claims that there is a single genetically determined mental language possessed by humans and all other thinking species. This way, by extending our psychology to infrahuman species, we commit ourselves to cognitive processes mediated by representational systems other than natural language.

4. Jerry A. Fodor, *The Language of Thought*, Cambridge, Massachusetts: Harvard University Press, 1979, p. 56.

From the above discussion, if you got impressed that the so-called extension is not a question of fact, but a linguistic policy, a matter of decision, for after all it's *our word* to credit thought to animals, we got it all wrong. The issue isn't whether we ought to be polite to animals. The appeal is clearly to the fact that there are homogeneities between the mental capacities of infraverbal organisms and those of fluent human beings. For instance, just as human subjects have more trouble mastering disjunctive concepts than they do with conjunctive or negative ones, so have animals. Behavioural facts require us to hypothesize the relevant homogeneities between our representational system and the ones infraverbal organisms use.[5]

These sorts of issues become critical when we consider the preverbal child learning a first language. The first point to make is that we've no notion at all of how a first language might be learned except by hypothesizing formation and confirmation. And learning a language *L* must at least involve learning such concepts as sentence *L*. For example, if Chomsky is right, then learning a first language involves constructive grammars consonant with some innately specified system of language universals.[6] It also involves testing those grammars against a corpus of observational utterances in a prefixed order. And there must be a language in which the universals, the candidate grammars and the observational utterances are represented. This language cannot be a natural language since by hypothesis it is her first language that the child is learning.

To proceed with LOT hypothesis we will have to take

5. That infants have difficulties with disjunctive propositions is experimentally demonstrated in *The Perception of Speech Sounds in Prelinguistic Infants*, Fodor, Garret and Brill, 1975.

6. For a detailed discussion of Chomsky's views on how infants acquire syntax see, N. Chomsky, *Aspects of the Theory of Syntax*, Cambridge, Massachusetts: MIT Press, 1965.

three things for granted: (1) that learning a first language is a matter of hypothesis formation and confirmation, (2) that learning a first language involves at least learning the semantic properties of *p*, (3) *S* can learn the semantic properties of *p* only if *S* learns some generalisation which determines the extension of *p*.[7] The first two assumptions will be granted by anyone who is willing to suppose that there is anything at all to the notion of semantic properties as psychologically real. Let me address the third assumption in detail. What we shall argue here is that you cannot learn a language whose terms express semantic properties not expressed by the terms of some language you are already able to use. Learning a predicate involves learning something which determines its extension. It is convenient to assume that the semantic properties expressed by a predicate are those that determine its extension.

Semantic properties are what you learn when you learn a word. Thus, learning a predicate involves learning a generalisation which determines its extension. For example, to master the predicate "is a chair" one has to learn what falls under such generalisation as "*Y* is a chair" is true *iff Gx*, if, e.g. it is true that "chair" means "portable seat for one" then it is plausible that no one has mastered "is a chair" unless he has learned that it falls under the truth value "*y* is a chair is true *iff* *x* is a portable seat for one". Many philosophers think that truth conditions provide too weak a construal of what we learn when we learn a predicate. Wittgenstein too observes that many ordinary language predicates are open textured. There are indefinitely many objects about which we cannot tell whether they are chairs, not just because the lighting is bad or some of the facts aren't in, but because "is a chair" is, as it were, undefined for objects of those kinds so that whether

7. Fodor, op. cit., p. 59.

they are chairs isn't a question of fact at all (for example, chair made of soap bubbles, the packing case that is used as a chair, etc.). This does not, however, prejudice the notion that learning truth-rules is essential to language learning or the point truth-rules are expressed by biconditional formulae. All it shows is that if the truth condition on "is a chair" is expressed by "is a portable seat for one", then "portable seat for one" must be open textured, undefined, etc., for just those cases where "is a chair" is.[8]

The morals drawn from the above discussions are:

(1) Learning a language involves learning what the predicates of a language mean.

(2) Learning what the predicates of a language mean involves learning a determination of the extension of these predicates.

(3) Learning a determination of the extension of the predicates involves learning that they fall under certain rules.

(4) One cannot learn that *P* falls under *R* unless one has a language in which *P* and *R* can be represented.

(5) This language is expressively semantically complete. That is, any predicate that we are able to semantically comprehend is expressible in this language.[9]

So one cannot learn a first language unless one already has an internal language, a system capable of representing the predicates in that language and their extensions. And on pain of circularity that system cannot be the language that is being learned. This drives us to conclude that at least some cognitive operations are carried out in language other than natural language.

---

8. Fodor, op. cit., p. 62.

9. Ibid., p. 64.

Is Mentalese a Private Language?

In order to proceed with LOT, we must address those objections which purport to show that however plausible this individual steps in an argument favouring LOT may seem, they must be wrong because the conclusions they lead to are incoherent.

The first objection we shall consider is an allegation of an infinite regress. The objection is roughly this: If one cannot learn a language unless one already knows a language, what about that language, the meta language in which representations of the extensions of object language predicates are formulated? Surely learning must involve prior knowledge of a metameta language in which its truth definitions are couched. And so on *ad infinitum*, which is unsatisfactory.[10] Fodor provides a short and decisive answer to this: according to him, you can't learn a language unless you already know one. It isn't that you can't learn a language unless you have already *learned* one. The latter claim leads to infinite regress, the former doesn't; what the objection has in fact shown is that either there is no language of thought as Fodor claims, or at least one of the languages one knows isn't learned. Fodor doesn't find this dilemma embarrassing because the second option seems to him entirely plausible, the language of thought is known (e.g., is the medium for computations underlying cognitive processes), but not learned. That is, it is innate.

Fodor resorts to the function of computers to provide analogy to establish his theory. Real computers characteristically use at least two different languages: an input/output language in which they communicate with their environment and the machine language in which they talk to themselves. Compilers mediate between the two languages

10. Atherton M. and Schwartz, R., "Linguistic Innateness and its Evidence", *Journal of Philosophy*, LXX1, no. 6, pp. 155-68.

in effect by specifying the biconditional whose left-hand side is a formula in the input/output code and whose right-hand side is a formula in the machine code.[11]

Fodor's point is that though the machines have a compiler if it has to use the input/output language, it doesn't also need a compiler for the machine language. What avoids infinite regression of computers is the fact that the machine is built to use the machine language. Roughly, the machine language differs from input/output language in that its formulae correspond directly to computationally relevant physical states and operations of the machine. The physics of the machine thus guarantees that the sequences of states and operations, it runs through in the course of its computations, respect the semantic constraints on formulae in its internal language. This expresses the sense in which machines are *built to use* their machine language and are not built to use their input/output codes. It also suggests an empirical theory: when you find a device using a language it was not built to use, for example, a language that it has *learned*, the way it does it is by translating the formulae of that language into formulae which directly correspond to its computationally relevant physical states. The assumption here is that the truth rules for predicates in that natural language function as part of the translation procedure.[12]

As per this theory we've sketched, what happens when a person understands a sentence. It must be a translation process basically analogous to what happens when a machine understands a sentence in its programming language. The so far sketched view of language-learning does not lead to infinite regress; there is only single stage regress, viz. from the natural language to the internal code and that single stage is empirically rather, than conceptually motivated. That is, we can imagine

11. Fodor, op. cit., p. 66.

12. Ibid., p. 67.

an organism which is born speaking, and born speaking whatever language its nervous system uses for computing.

LOT then figures as a private language in which organisms carry out the computations that underlie their behaviour. The proposal of a private language has been famously rejected by Wittgenstein.[13] I shan't engage myself disputing on private language argument. Instead, I shall just prove that the argument so construed does no damage to the sorts of arguments Fodor has been recommending. To begin with whatever Wittgenstein proved, it cannot be impossible that a language should be private in whatever sense the machine language of a computer is, for there are such things as computers, and whatever is actual is possible. Fodor relies heavily on machine analogy both as an existence proof for devices which don't speak the language they compute in, and as a potential empirical model for the relation between natural languages and the language of thought.

Wittgenstein is basically concerned to show that no definite sense can be attached to the notion of a term in a private language being used coherently. There are two ways of characterizing a private language: either as one whose terms refer to things that only its speaker can experience or as a language for the applicability of whose terms there exists no public criteria. For Wittgenstein's purpose of attacking the idea of a sense-datum these two formulations come to the same thing.[14] On Wittgenstein view, whichever way you may construe, private language is an impossibility.

Responding to Wittgenstein, Fodor maintains that Wittgenstein's private language argument isn't really directed against the sort of theory he has been endorsing. As a mentalist

13. L. Wittgenstein, *Philosophical Investigations*, Oxford: Blackwell, 1953, p. 258.

14. Fodor, op. cit., p. 69.

he need not and should not assume that mental operations exhibit epistemic privacy. Indeed, he had better not assume that if he wants his psychological theories to be compatible with a materialistic ontology, for neurological events are public.

Further, the private language argument isn't really any good. The most that the arguments show is that unless there are public procedures for telling whether a term is coherently applied, there will be no way of knowing whether it is coherently applied. Wittgenstein, Fodor points out, in fact, has a certain picture of what coherence of employment comes to for terms in a public language. Roughly, the use of public language terms is controlled by the conventions of the speech community. These conventions relate the terms to paradigm public situations. To use a term coherently is to use it in accordance with the governing convention. To use it in accordance with the governing conventions is to use it when the paradigms are satisfied. In short, a term is coherently employed when its use is controlled by the facts about the world.[15]

The first point to notice is that this picture Wittgenstein draws can't be right. Suppose I intend to use a term in those situations paradigmatic for that term. Still my verbalizations are determined not just by my intention, but also my beliefs. Hence, the degree of correspondence I can actually effect between my use of *p* and the occurrence of paradigm *p*-situations, depends not only on my linguistic policies with respect to *p* but also on how good I am at determining which situations are *p* situations. The point is that even in the case of public languages coherence does not require a stable relation between the way the terms are used and the way the world is, but rather a relation between the way the terms are used and the way the speaker believes the world to be. We are

15. Fodor, op. cit., p. 70.

thus in a position to say what the analogy between the private and public representations comes to. It's a hard question whether internal as well as natural languages can both be representations in the same sense. Since public languages are conventional and language of thought is not, there is unlikely to be more than an analogy. " If you are impressed", Fodor says, "by the analogy you will want to say that the inner code is a language. If you are unimpressed by the analogy, you will want to say that the inner code is in some sense a representational system, but that it is not a language. But in neither case will what you say affect the ontological status of LOT."[16]

What is Mentalese like?

Any psychological theory that has to be true will have to ascribe a special role to the computational states of organisms, viz. the way that information is stored, computed, accepted, rejected or otherwise processed by the organism explains its cognitive states. To one who worries about the probity of such assumptions Fodor says that our option seems to be either to tolerate them or to do without theories in cognitive psychology altogether.

The following are the methodological assumptions to arrive at how mentalese function or what it is to be like:

1. The computational states ascribable to organisms can be directly explicated as relations between the organisms and formulae in the internal code.
2. The class of basic, theoretically relevant relations between the organism and formulae of the internal code are pretty small, when compared to the relation between the organism and propositions.
3. For any propositional attitude of the organism (e.g.,

16. Fodor, op. cit., p. 71.

> fearing, believing, wanting, etc.), there will be a corresponding computational relation between the organism and some formulae of the internal code such that the organism has the propositional attitude *iff* the organism in that relation is nomologically necessary.[17]

In fact, what we try to do in cognitive psychology is to explain the propositional attitudes of the organism by reference to its (hypothetical) computational operations, by providing for each propositional attitude nomologically necessary and sufficient conditions in terms of computational relations between the organism and formulae of the internal representational system. Now this may suggest the following ontological picture: There are, as it were, two things: the organism's relation to propositions, and the organism's relation to formulae and these two things are so arranged that the latter is causally responsible for the former.

Fodor seems to be denying that one can learn a language whose expressive power is greater than of a language that one already knows. Though the theory of mentalese implies that language of thought is extremely rich and its representational power is all-comprehensive, still it poses some limitations. One can't learn a conceptual system richer than the conceptual system that one starts with, where learning language is construed as a process of hypothesis formation and confirmation. This, Fodor says, is an intrinsic limitation of the model and nothing can be done about this except to learn to live with it.

---

17. Fodor, op. cit., p. 75.

10

Communicative Intentionality

An Analysis of "the rules of statement making"

Ranjan K. Panda

In this paper, I would like to discuss Ramchandra Gandhi's criticism of John Searle's thesis that "speaking a language is performing acts according to the constitutive rules". Searle formulates this hypothesis in the context of the theorization of performative utterances. Following Austin's distinction between *performative* expression and *constative* expression, Searle advocates that the former is about the statement of *institutional* facts, whereas the latter is about the statement of *brute* facts. Institutional facts are grounded on linguistic intentionality. And they represent values. The form of linguistic intentionality is communicative, rather than merely representative. The communicative intentionality shows that various forms of linguistic representation can be realized within the normative framework of language use. The paper delves into the normativity of language use to show that meaning and value can be analysed with reference to the notion of communicative intentionality. The paper is divided into four sections. In the first section, we discuss Searle's theory of communication with reference to the notion of *performative expression* as linguistic representation. The second section deals with the Gandhian critique of Searle's theorization of the *speech act*. Following the arguments of Searle and Gandhi, in the third section, we try to develop the idea of communicative intentionality. In the concluding section we extend the thesis of communicative intentionality to develop further Gandhi's theoretical position that human beings are communicative beings and through linguistic communication we intentionally create the linguistic field in which meaning and values are disclosed.

Performative as Linguistic Representation: The Searlean Thesis of Human Communication

Searle's theorization of *performative utterances* basically elucidates the logical structure of communication, meaning, and understanding. It is through communication that one individual relates to the other. This relationship is mostly based on language. The linguistic expression usually elucidates meaning. In communication, meaning is not only exchanged between the speaker and the hearer but in this process understanding is also being developed. A performative utterance is basically linguistic expression characterized as *speech act*. To issue an expression, whether it is a symbol, word or sentence, signifies the performance of an action. The paradigmatic example of performative utterance is about the expression of promise: "I (*hereby*) promise that *p*". A promise is different from giving a description of a fact. For example, "There is a duster on the whiteboard". This very expression is a constative expression, represents the fact that "there is a duster on the whiteboard". This expression, therefore, has truth value. In other words, if the expression does not represent the fact then it is considered *false* and otherwise it is considered *true*. Performative expressions are not characterized primarily from the viewpoint of truth value. Rather performatives refer to the notion of *performance* in the form of making a statement. To make a statement of promise is to declare or to express it in the presence of the other. This expressive attitude of making a performative statement in public discloses the varying degrees of intention and commitment of the speaker. Performatives in this regard show special case of language use in which *saying* and *meaning* go together. If the speaker does not *mean* what he intended in the expression then the very commitment of the speaker is breached. According to Austin, such a case generates *unhappiness*. (Austin 1971: 18) Austin uses this as a kind of *rule* — "the doctrine of unhappiness" — for making the performative statement explicit. Although there is no fixed and well-defined formula maintained by Austin for the theorization of performative expressions, still the above characteristics are often highlighted to demarcate *performative* expressions from *constative* expressions (Searle 1971 & Jacobsen 1971).

In this connection, analysing further "the doctrine of unhappiness", Searle emphasizes that performative utterances as an integral part of *speech act* theory must result in the *condition of satisfaction*. He writes,

> What is crucially important to see is that for every *speech act* that has a *direction of fit,* the speech act will be satisfied if and only if the expressed psychological state is satisfied, and conditions of satisfaction and psychological states are identical.
> — Searle 1983: 10-11

In the context of *performative* expressions, if the speaker effectively brings about desirable change in the (hearer) world, then it results in establishing the *direction of fit*. The fitness is an intentional relationship that unfolds the communicative engagement between the speaker and the hearer. This engagement is construed by intentionality working in two ways. One intentional way is from *the mind/language-to-the world,* and another intentional way is from the *world-to-the language/ mind*. In the case of the former, the speaker's intention to reach out to the hearer is shown, and in the case of the latter, the reciprocity of the hearer is shown. In accord with performance of the speaker, both complete the two-way intentional relationship. Thus, the *direction of fit* is the result of the satisfaction of the psychological mode of the speaker.

Intentionality is an intrinsic feature of consciousness (Searle 1992: xii), which characterizes the human mind as representational. That is to say, the mind represents the world. The intentionality of the mind shows that thoughts and expressions are *directed about* the objects and the state of affairs in the world. The proper linguistic representation of thought is about the world. Moreover, representations are different from mere expressions. For instance, expressions like Ouch! Hurrah! Wow, etc. are just expressions of different kinds which indicate one's *feelings*. These kinds of expressions do not signify anything beyond themselves, because they lack *propositional content* (Searle 1969: 30). On the other hand, expression of thoughts involves propositional content. For example, the statement "Mr. Barack Obama respects the Gandhian values", describes the fact that Mr. Obama looks up to the Gandhian values as possible alternative to resolve global issues on peace. In the Searlean theorization of *speech act*, the propositional content and psychological mode are two necessary constituents of *speech act* semantics. Propositional content results in condition of satisfaction, whereas *direction of fit* is the result of representation of psychological mode. And, all types of linguistic representation involve a *psychological mode* and *propositional content*.

Linguistic representation is the primary form of linguistic communication. While defining the nature of linguistic representation, Searle maintains a distinction between *representation intention* and *communicative intention*. He writes,

> Communication is a matter of producing effects on one's hearer, but one can intend to represent something without caring at all for the effects on one's hearer. One can make a statement without intending to produce conviction or belief

> in one's hearers or without intending to get them to believe that the speaker believes what he says or intended without even intending to get them to understand it at all.
>
> —Searle 1983: 156

The *representation intention* is something that is very much part of the making of an expression or a statement. That is, a person sometimes is found speaking out something without intending to communicate to anyone. Mere linguistic expressions are expressions without having communicative intention. In this regard, *communicative intention* focuses on the intention of the speaker and the hearer. The speaker finds it certainly awkward to communicate unless he would make an effort to recognize hearer's intention. A mere utterance of a statement (a linguistic representation), in this regard, could be a misfire if it fails to involve the hearer during conversation. The expression here could be treated as a monologue, even if it is uttered in the presence of the audience. Thus, communication intention unfolds the intentionality involved in the very linguistic engagement of the speaker and the hearer in two ways and those result in forming a linguistic field of conversation. The intentionality of the linguistic field represents an intentional structure which has the potential to disclose the intentions of the speaker and the hearer. It also gives an opportunity both to the speaker and the hearer to share the *content*. Thus, performative expression is basically about effective communication, rather than mere representation. The significance of performative lies in *taking effect* into the intentional structure of the linguistic field (Austin 1971: 14).

Moreover, the intentional attitude of communication intention or the communicative intentionality emphasizes that effective representation involves *force* — i.e. the *illocutionary force* of the performative expressions. The *illocutionary force* adds to the semantic content of the statement. In other words, linguistic communication involves two elements, they are, "having meaning" and "meaning something". In a conversation, it might happen that the statement bears a literal meaning and an additional meaning is imposed on it through the *illocutionary force* by the speaker. The imposed meaning, i.e. "meaning something" is expected to be inferred by the hearer. The *illocutionary force* is known through the "stress, word order, intonation, contour, punctuation, the mood of the performative verb" (Austin 1971: 16 and Searle 1971: 43). Hence, in order to capture meaning of performative utterances one must look at the way *illocutionary force* is used in the literal meaning of the expression.

However, to talk about this meaning-force relationship explicitly, Searle advocates normative case of *language use* that maintains the hypothesis that "speaking a language is engaging in rule-governed form of behaviour" (Searle 1969: 16). That is to say, communication as linguistic act is regulated by rules that have normative significance and thereby stand for values. So, communication as valued engagement is grounded on certain norms. In this regard, the *speech act* is considered as a normative act, precisely because language as an institution is not only regulated by rules but also constituted by rules (Searle 1969: 33). Regulative rules operate to monitor the activities which are construed as *if x then y* or *do* (Searle 1969: 34). On the other hand, constitutive rule "creates and defines new forms of behaviours" and is being defined as *x counts as y in the context c* (Searle 1969: 35). It is through the constitutive rule that Searle theorizes the *speech acts* semantics.

The constitutive rule helps in explicating the nature of intended meaning. That to say, constitutive rule shows the intentional mode in which "having meaning" and "meaning something" or *literal meaning* and *intended meaning* are unified in the case of *speech act*. In the Searlean theorization of *speech acts,* all statements potentially involve the *illocutionary force* which characterizes meaning as intentional. The intended meaning as part of the institution of language is considered as *institutional facts*. For instance, when the European Union declared to use€ as symbol of their currency, the Europeans belonging to the union thereby have accepted its economic function. So, here € is used *as* the currency of the European Union, in the framework of the economic, political and the largely social facts. Similarly, when a particular social community formulate a language then the *speech act* emphasizes that all statements are to be articulated and asserted in such a way that it works as narrative of value. Thus, assertions are treated at par with the statement of declaration, promise, etc. It is because assertion involves normative content. In this connection, it is important to note that the whole process of articulation of such beliefs, desires and intentions is not only intentional but also normative.

Gandhi on Presupposition of Communication: The Searlean Hypothesis Rejected

Ramchandra Gandhi, in his book *The Presupposition of Human Communication* (1974), rejects Searle's above hypothesis of *speech act* theory. According to Gandhi, the rules do represent the fact that they are associated with communication, but they do not explain the communicative action. Rules are not explanatory. Since a rule as "institutional fact is not logically independent of the notion of communicative utterances", hence, it cannot explain the nature of communicative utterance (p. 9). Nevertheless, the communicative utterance, particularly the performative expressions remain confined to only a very few exceptional cases of linguistic actions. Whenever we would analyse them, we fall back upon conventions. That is how a typical expression is used regularly within a societal framework. Thus, the explanation of meaning in the theoretical framework of *speech acts* is circular.

In order to avoid that kind of circular explanation, Gandhi

focuses on defining the nature of communicative act. For him, the act of communication must not only involve the act of *telling*, but must also involve the act of *addressing*. The latter exhibits that human communication is a deliberate and intentional fact (p. 42), to be recognized by the audience, whereas the former gives an opportunity to the audience to participate in the *communicatively exhibited act*. The act of *telling* is a communicatively *exhibited* act (p. 63).

Let's discuss the primacy of the *act of addressing*, because that opens up the very structure in which the speaker and the hearer participate. The notion of *addressing* is an intentional act. We although sometimes unintentionally or accidentally try to attract the attention of another person, but in the case of making a case of formal addressing, the speaker exhibits something with an intention of attracting the hearer's attention to a fact. Two things then follow: firstly, one discloses one's location to the other (the hearer); secondly, the hearer is invited to associate with this fact. Gandhi writes, ". . . *S* addresses *A* if and only if *S* attracts *A*'s attention to the fact that *S* is trying to attract *A*'s attention to himself" (pp. 39-40). Thus, the moment the hearer is addressed, he/she gets an opportunity to interact with the speaker. The opportunity is intentionally formed by speaker in order to invite the hearer to participate in the act of communication.

While making a linguistic representation, say, *p* public, "the speaker *brings* the audience to know the fact that he *wants* the audience to know that *p*" (p. 30). To know that *p* is to perceive, recognize and understand the *content* of *p*. In this connection, it is important to note when the speaker intends *to bring out p* to the notice of the audience? That is to say, whether the intended content of *p* is to be brought out to the audience in future or at present, or through *someone* else (p. 32). It depends on the mode in which the speaker makes the representation to the hearer. Because, all acts of bringing out someone to know something, are not the acts of communication. And, it is also true that by *telling p* to someone is not always bringing him to know that *p* (p. 11). This is due to the fact that the speaker, while expressing *p*, can make an insincere assertion of *p*. Gandhi here refers to the possibility of making an *insincere* representation. In such a situation, when insincere representation is made, it is also possible that the speaker can assert *p*, without believing that *p*. Hence, one of the preconditions of making a statement *p* is that the speaker is held *responsible* for making the statement *p*.

The *p* is *told* by *S*, where *A* confronts *p* by virtue of the fact that "*S* wants *A* to believe that *S* believed that *p*". If *S* is a dishonest character, then *S* can express *p* without having any *force*. Nevertheless, the statement *p* as an act would only exhibit the *form*, i.e. the form of a statement, not the *force* in this case. According to Gandhi, *form* and *force* are the two components of communicatively exhibited act (p. 59). *Force* is not part of non-linguistic assertions or indications. Rather, by showing an indication *S* might succeed in communicating some information to *A*, and the *form* of the information here is inferred by the *A*. Whereas *force* is attributed to the act of linguistic representation only. Moreover, linguistic representation as communicatively exhibited act minimally fulfils the condition of passing information to the audience. For instance, if *p* is an assertive statement then the speaker only communicatively brings it to the audience in order to recognize the fact that "something is the case or going to be the case" (p. 52). The act of *issuing p* is essentially a rule-governed act where the speaker *tells p* to the hearer with some sense of authority. Hence, whenever *p* is told by *S* to *A*, *S* assigns *A* the authority of believing *p* (p. 63). In this regard, the construal of the notion of *addressing* and *telling* becomes important as these notions involve the power of simulation to draw the attention of the audience.

Moreover, the preliminary condition of communication is that the speaker must *address* to the audience. The act of addressing would make the communication intention minimally understandable that the speaker *intends* to communicate something. Further, it is important to note that the audience must "perceive, recognize and know something about the world, at any rate about ourselves", that is, "the speaker *brings* the audience to know that he *wants* the audience to know that *p*" (p. 30). Referring to this condition of communicative act of addressing and exhibiting, Gandhi points out that the act is not merely formed to attract the attention of audience, because it would exhibit that the intention of communicating *p* is a "conditioned-response-eliciting action" (p. 104). Had this not been the case, it would have been confined only to reaching out to the state of *attracting the attention of the audience*, but in a communicatively exhibited act "the speaker in addition to that wants *A* to attend to the fact that *S* wanted *A* to attend to the fact that *S* wanted *A* to attend him of his own accord" (ibid.).

So far as human communicative attitude is concerned the conditioning principle is not enough to explain the semantics of communication. This principle would only suggest that humans are intellectually sound to grasp certain facts and develop the pattern of attention attracting stimuli. Children are capable of responding to certain familiar sounds and try to interpret them which initially can go on in "conditioned-response eliciting way". Comparing humans with animals, Gandhi maintains that "humans are capable of exploiting the failure of this condition and also have the intention of enabling their audience to infer" (p. 106). Looking at the development of human condition, Gandhi writes,

> One would say that this results in a situation where a response is not sought to be elicited from audience, but is *solicited* from them. And human beings, because of the form

> of their social life, have good reasons for responding to the solicitation of their human beings. — Gandhi 1974: 107

The condition of solicitation unfolds the normative demand fulfilled by the hearer for the accomplishment of communicatively exhibited act. This interactive mode of engagement helps in the development of language and linguistic *forms of life*. The human social life is essentially language-centric and through language human beings not only address or communicate with one *another* but also represent their respective *self*.

Representation and the Idea of Communicative Intentionality

Human communication is linguistic and intentional. The intentional form of language use is significant not only for the analysis of meaning and understanding, but also for the analysis of the self and its relationship with the world/*the other*. Meaning is disclosed in the intentional representation of language. And, from the above discussions of Searle's theorization of *speech acts* and Gandhi's notion of linguistic representation as communicatively exhibited act, it is at least clear that intentionality is embedded in the linguistic representation and it works as an extraordinary, property of communication intention showing the connection between the speaker and the hearer. It is extraordinary, because it is reflexive in character. In other words, the act of *telling* shows that the intentionality is directed towards the hearer and when the hearer recognizes the meaning of linguistic representation then the act of recognition generates the condition of satisfaction, which shows that intentionality is also directed towards the speaker. Intentionality, functioning in these two ways, not only shows the reflective attitude of human conscious activities but also makes a case for the *communicative intentionality*.

Searle and Gandhi both try to elucidate this form of intentionality. As we have discussed the Searlean notion of *direction of fit* in the first section, we would like to further mention that the *direction of fit* and *condition of satisfaction* are logically connected through intentionality (Panda 2009). The logical relationship between the two structures of representations, that is, the mental representation and the linguistic representation, shows the *flow* of content from the thought to the expression. So far as Gandhi is concerned, he does emphasize that communication involves intentionality. He writes,

> A fundamental and elusive feature of human communication is the sense of the word "to" in which we say that somebody communicated something to him, spoke to him, issued an utterance to him. The sense of the word "to" here is not the sense in which we might say that in painting a white wall black, somebody did something to the wall, or in the case of toothache the dentist did something to him . . . what we want to understand is the sense in which an act of communication is directed by the speaker towards his audience, without the audience being a target, merely of a physical action initiated by the speaker.
>
> — Gandhi 1974: 138

So communication presupposes the presence of the audience with whom the speaker intends to participate in a conversation. And, the speaker also *solicits* the response from the audience. The act of communication is thus defined as *response-soliciting* action. In this regard, the occurrence of this intentional connection between the speaker and the hearer is something very significant for the explanation of meaning and understanding.

Now the question that I would like to bring in here is: "Is linguistic representation essentially intentional?" It is important to illustrate this question because that would throw some light on the *rules of statement making* and would help us to understand the basic difference that lies in the Searlean perspective of linguistic representation and the Gandhian perspective of linguistic representation.

For Searle, linguistic representation is essentially intentional. The intentional content of linguistic representation is derived from the thoughts. And, since mind is intrinsically intentional, the intentionality embedded in linguistic representation is derived from the mind or consciousness. Searle gives a naturalistic interpretation to intentionality. In the theoretical framework of Searle's biological naturalism, intentionality as a semantic property of representation is logically related to the *brute* facts of the brain processes. As he puts it, "It is important to keep reminding ourselves that natural brain processes, at certain level of description, have logical semantic properties" (Searle 2010: 47). The question is how natural these logical semantic properties are? They are not certainly natural to be entirely reducible to the causal process of the brain. If the irreducibility thesis is viable then it also ultimately raises the question about the ontology of representation. And secondly, the neurophysiological properties, the chemical secretion in the brain (that is, "secretion of neurotransmitters into synaptic clefts"), etc. are the *brute facts* about the possibility of the intentional mind. If this naturalistic theory is acceptable, then Searle takes his philosophy of mind and philosophy of language to the theoretical framework of physicalism. To maintain this point of view that semantic properties of representation are associated with the mental as well as the nurophysiological is quite puzzling. It brings out the ontological dualism that infects not only "the intentional utterances of the speaker" and "meaning represented through utterance", but also the statements about the facts and the statements of values.

Gandhi is on the whole critiquing this idea of causal

intentional relationship between the speaker and the hearer. For Gandhi, the notion of communication exhibits reciprocal exchange of information "in the sense that it is a *cooperative* activity" (Gandhi 1974: 47). However, communication is not about causal relation, it rather "opposes to the idea that the speaker causes the audience to respond in a communicative way" (ibid.). As communication has been defined as *response-soliciting* action, hence, it is being presupposed as *cooperative action* which puts a normative demand both on the part of the speaker as well as on the part of the hearer. Searle later realizes this and makes the point very clear to us in his later writings.

However, it is also important to note that Gandhi does not exclude entirely the biological intellectual ability of human mind, particularly the ability of the human infants in acquisition of language. He writes,

> . . . in some sense the infant's mind is already equipped with the intellectual wherewithal in terms of which it grasps the essence of the linguistic structures, and with assistance of which it is able to construct incredible range of linguistic expressions. — Gandhi 1974: 114

So, there is some linguistic ability which is biologically innate and Gandhi argues out it from the point of view of Chomsky's conception of language and mind. For Gandhi, the linguistic skill used in communication develops through constant exposures to language use.

The notion of ability, as Searle defines, refers to *the background*. It is a power to perform various intentional actions including the physical and the linguistic actions. The background is a *basic fact* or *brute fact* about the non-representational power of the being that causes representation (Searle 1983). As the *basic facts* are objectively represented and explained by natural sciences, it can be said that the description of the micro-elements of brain processes are statements of *brute* facts. Hence, these descriptive statements are either true or false. On the other hand, Searle emphasizes that very nature of intentionality is such that,

> [it] *occurs* in a coordinated flow of action and perception, and the *Background* is a condition of possibility of forms taken by the flow. The flow of intentionality tends to rise to the level of the Background ability it reaches all the way down to the bottom of ability. — Searle 1992: 195

Thus, Searle treats intentionality as a persisting feature intrinsic to the mental life which includes thought, experience, reasoning, imagination, etc.

However, communication, whether it is in individual or collective speech acts (Meijers 2007: 93) is grounded on norms. The act of communication is a normative act, precisely because language as an institution is not only regulated by rules but also is constituted by rules. Human intentionality, as the basic constituent of representation, transforms the pre-linguistic intentional capabilities to the form of linguistic intentionality in order to perform cooperative and collective actions. Human beings are linguistic beings who intentionally interact with the world and keep developing their linguistic categories. For Searle, eventually the development of these

> categories help in experiencing change as well as in experiencing individual's own effort of making things happen. In this regard, he considers that the category of identity and individuation are specific to the human linguistic ability. — Searle 2010: 67

So far as linguistic ability is concerned the biological root of human life is not denied. Gandhi to some extent and Searle to a great extent accept this thesis. More importantly, what is critiqued here by Gandhi is that Searle considers language is a social institution and the constitutive rule of language such *as X counted as Y in the context* C is an *institutional fact*. Meaning as a product of this institutional fact does not drop the causal power of the utterance. Although, Searle talks about intentionalization of causation, still the real source of this causal power comes to the realm of the mental from the brain processes. The naturalistic interpretation in this connection can only talk about language and linguistic intentionality adhering to the constructionist point of view of the social. It does not consider language as ontologically significant. Hence, there is a limitation in the Searlean framework in which human communication can be theorized as naturalistic. As a result, language operates with the closure of intentionality grounded in the causal power of the brain processes. The growth of language and language use demands *openness*. Gandhi emphasizes this because it is through language only we can speak about *ourselves*. We are all linguistic beings. So, to put a closure to *language use* by constructing *rules* through the causal theory of intentionality would restrict the scope and the function of language.

The Idea of Linguistic Being and Linguistic Field: Opening the Boundary of Communicative Intentionality

The idea of opening up the boundary of communicative intentionality refers to Gandhi's demand for *openness* in the very act of forming linguistic rules. In fact, this could be well comprehended by construing the fact that language speaks of itself. Language has no boundary as such, except the fact that it constitutes its own boundary referring to the *forms of life*. This is because through language we define the rules. The Searlean notion of *constitutive rules* and *regulative rules* presuppose the ontology of language based on a collective intentionality. This presupposition is logical as well as normative. Gandhi's notion of communication as an intentionally exhibited act *solicits* mutual *cooperation* to represent the fact that language lives in the space of collective intentionality.

Regarding collective intentionality Searle writes:

> Collective intentional behaviour is a primitive phenomenon that can be analysed as just the summation of individual intentional behaviour; collective intention expressed in the form of "we intend to do such-and-such" or "we are doing such-and-such" are also primitive phenomenon and cannot be analysed in terms of individual intention in the form of "I intend such and such" or "I am doing such-and-such".
>
> — Searle 2002: 90

In communication, the individual intentionality discloses the subjective attitude of the self, and it also unfolds collective attitude in which *we believe* and *we intend* to do something for ourselves or for the society as a whole. While believing and intending to act together is the subjective intentionality of the person it gets transformed to an objective reality in language.

Language has the power to disclose the meaning embedded in it. But not the other way, as Searle thinks that "the meaning could be defined only by intentionality". The intentionality of language is intrinsic to life. Human life being language-centric it not only defines the concept "we" and other concepts that we possess in the field of *language use,* but also defines our *being* as "communicative beings" (Gandhi 1976: 21). In communication identity of *being* is revealed. We are linguistically connected with each other. Thus, the communicative intentionality of language creates the *linguistic field*. Defining the notion of linguistic field as disclosure of meaning, Pradhan writes,

> Meaning is the part of the field of language in which it discloses language and the world. The field is the field of language games that make the play of meaning disclosure possible. Thus, there is the possibility of understanding language as a field of linguistic activities in which meaning is necessarily disclosed. — Pradhan 1996: 145

Thus, the communicative intentionality of language can show that enormous linguistic activities are carried out within the realm of language.

In this regard, communicative intentionality has the potential to form the linguistic rule that embodies institutional values. Bringing the intentionality of language into the realm of communication, Searle shows two things: (1) that *semantic power* (Searle 2010: 93) of language that flows through the mental (Panda 2008: 223), and (2) the *deontic power* of language that regulates human conduct. The institutional facts as social reality are constituted of these linguistic elements of human intentionality. Searle places this against the *background* condition of language. Language has the potential to sustain the normativity embedded in the structure of social institutions. The institutional facts such as meaning, governance, rights, duties, commitment, obligation, etc. are the product of human *collective intentionality or the communicative intentionality.*

Commitment and justification essentially add up to making the assertive statement as evaluative statement. As this articulation depends on the speaker's intentional attitude it matters most that the "speaker shows commitment to truth". This very approach emphasizes the internalization of values. As Searle puts it, "deontology in the form of commitment is internal to the performance of speech act" (Searle 2010: 83). The intentional attitude of the speaker involves commitment — it is part of the content, in that sense it is internal. Searle also claims that "language is the basic form of public deontology" and "with a *deontic power* statements are uttered" (Searle 2010: 82). Thus, Searle bestows unique role to the language. Language has the power to hold on to the values. Nevertheless, it is through the *communicative intentionality* we internalize and communicate values.

References

Austin, J.L., 1969, "Performative and Constative", in *Philosophy of Language,* ed. John Searle (1971), Oxford: Oxford University Press.

Gandhi, R., 1974, *Presupposition of Human Communication*, Delhi: Oxford University Press.

———, 1976, *The Availability of Religious Ideas*, London: McMillan.

Jacobsen, Klaus H., 1971, "How to make the Distinction between Constative and Performative Utterances", *The Philosophical Quarterly*, vol. 21, 85.

Meijers, A., 2007, "Collective Speech Acts", in S.L. Tsohatzidis (ed.), *Intentional Acts and Institutional Facts*, Dordrecht: Springer.

Panda, R.K., 2008, *Mind, Language and Intentionality*, New Delhi: Bharatiya Kala Prakashan.

———, 2009, "Searle on Representation: A Relation between Language and Consciousness", in Volker A. Munz, Klaus Puhl and Joseph Wang ed., *Pre-proceedings of 32nd International Wittgenstein Symposium on Language and World*, vol. XVII, Krichberg am Wechesel, Vienna.

Pradhan, R.C., 1996, *Philosophy of Meaning and Representation*, New Delhi: D.K. Printworld.

Searle, John R., 1969, *Speech Acts: An Essay in Philosophy of Language*, Cambridge: Cambridge University Press.

——— (ed.), 1971, *Philosophy of Language* Oxford: Oxford University Press.

———, 1983, *Intentionality: An Essay in Philosophy of Language*, Cambridge: Cambridge University Press.

———, 1992, *The Rediscovery of the Mind*, Massachusetts: The MIT Press.

———, 2002, *Consciousness and Language*, Cambridge: Cambridge University Press.

———, 2010, *Making the Social World: The Structure of Human Civilization*, New York: Oxford University Press.

11

Linguistic Representations, Mind-world Relations and the Encounter with Truth

R.C. Pradhan

THIS paper addresses the question of linguistic representations as distinguished from other types of representations which human beings engage themselves in. Linguistic representations are well known to be the ones which provide us access to the world, i.e. to other human beings and the things which abound in the world.[1] In that sense, there is a logical fit between language and the world. And that also explains how mind and world[2] are related to each other. From the complex relationships between language and the world and between mind and the world, there arises the possibility of our encounter with truth. A semantic way of tracking truth emerges within this spectrum of representations.

My paper takes up some of the issues arising out of the problem of linguistic representations, namely those concerning the necessity of linguistic representations and the nature of truth and those concerning the relations between the mind

1. See Jay F. Rosenberg, *Linguistic Representation*, Dordrecht-Holland/ Boston-USA: D. Reidel Publishing Company, 1974, Chapter 1.
2. See John McDowell, *Mind and World*, Cambridge, Mass., London, England: Harvard University Press, 1994.

and the world. My aim is to establish that, arguments to the contrary notwithstanding, there is a distinct way to establish that language alone tells us what the world is and that our mind and the world have a metaphysical relation which language alone can unfold. I will further argue that some form of transcendental idealism is built into the way the linguistic representations work *vis-à-vis* the world.

"Seeing Through Language": Why Linguistic Representations are Relevant

The metaphor of "seeing through language" is Davidson's, who gives a new meaning to this metaphor by debunking the notion that one can literally see the world through language. What the metaphor really means is that though language is not a medium through which one can access the world, yet one cannot deny that language has something to do with our access to the world. Even if one cannot see the world through language as it were through a window, yet one can see the world only if one has a language. Davidson writes:

> We do not see the world through language any more than we see the world through our eyes. We don't look *through* our eyes, but *with* them. We don't feel through our fingers or hear things through our ears. Well, there is a sense in which we *do* things through, that is, by dint of having eyes. We do cope through having language. There is a *non*-metaphorical point to my title. There is a valid analogy between having eyes and ears, and having language: all three are organs with which we come into direct contact with our environment. They are not intermediaries, screens, media, or windows.[3]

---

3. Donald Davidson, "Seeing Through Language" in *Thought and Language* (Royal Institute of Philosophy Supplement; 42), ed. John Preston, Cambridge: Cambridge University Press, 1997, p. 18.

This long explanation clarifies the exact sense in which we can use the metaphor "seeing through language" without misunderstanding language as a kind of medium or window or intermediary.

Davidson's aim in this essay is straightforward: he wants to get rid of the old idea that language is like a screen which hides things or distorts them. He simply draws our attention to the fact that language is there as a part of us, as a part of our biological make-up and is party to all that we do, such as speaking to others, communicating with them and above all making true or false statements about the world. We do a large number of activities with language and yet we do not feel that language is anything like a medium or an intermediary between us and the world. Thus, Davidson suggests,

> we should banish the idea that language is epistemically something like sense-data, something that embodies what we can take in, but is itself only a token, or representative, of what is out there. Language does not mirror or represent reality, any more than our senses present us with no more than appearances. Presentations and representations, as mere proxies or pictures, will always leave us one step short of what knowledge seeks; scepticism about the power of language to capture what is real is old-fashioned scepticism of the sense given a linguistic twist.[4]

Davidson steers clear of the idea of linguistic representation because he fears it brings back scepticism through the backdoor by creating a chasm between us and the world, that is, they "will always leave us one step short of what knowledge seeks".[5] This, according to him, leads to scepticism "about the

4. Donald Davidson, "Seeing Through Language" in *Thought and Language* (Royal Institute of Philosophy Supplement; 42), ed. John Preston, Cambridge: Cambridge University Press, 1997, p. 18.
5. Ibid., p. 18.

power of language to capture what is real".[6] Davidson's argument regarding why language is not a picture or a representation of the world can be put in the following way:

1. Linguistic representations like pictures create a gap between the representation and what is represented.
2. This gap between language and the world leads to scepticism regarding the power of language to capture the world directly.
3. Scepticism regarding our direct access to the world is impossible because language captures the world directly without any intermediaries.
4. Language does not represent or picture the world from a distance; rather it captures the world directly.
5. Therefore, language cannot be taken as a representation of the world and so there are no linguistic representations.

Davidson argues for direct linguistic realism because he believes that there is no gap between language and the world and that language captures the world directly just as our sense organs do without any intermediary. This theory demolishes all myths regarding how language functions as a "translucent medium, leaving its own character written on everything in its domain".[7] This, in a way, demolishes the myth that language is a model of reality, for "we deceive ourselves when we talk of language representing reality (or anything else) unless we can usefully specify the entities represented".[8]

However, Davidson's arguments can be countered by

6. Donald Davidson, "Seeing Through Language" in *Thought and Language* (Royal Institute of Philosophy Supplement; 42), ed. John Preston, Cambridge: Cambridge University Press, 1997, p. 18.
7. Ibid., p. 17.
8. Ibid.

showing that linguistic representations, correctly interpreted, can be shown to avoid scepticism regarding our knowledge of the world. The counter-argument can run as follows:

1a. There is no gap, ontological or otherwise, between the linguistic representations and what is represented, i.e. the world.

2a. Linguistic representations capture the world directly without any intermediary thus leaving no scope for any gap between us and the world.

3a. Direct access to the world is logically guaranteed and as a result, there is no scope for scepticism.

4a. Linguistic representations are representations of the world and hence their power to capture the world is fully ensured.

5a. Therefore, language functions as a representation of the world and so there must be linguistic representations, if language is to be possible at all.

Davidson characterizes the linguistic representations as old-fashioned because of his belief that language functions directly *vis-à-vis* the world and hence he has with sufficient reason rejected such a myth about language. But the fact of the matter is that the linguistic representations do not function at a distance from reality, for in representing the world, language very much meshes itself with the world and there is no ontological gap between the way language works and the way the world is. The myth of the gap between language and the world is a legacy of the Cartesian dualism between mind and the world. The myth of the Cartesian dualism can be laid to rest without any adverse effect on the language-world relationship. The justification of the linguistic representations does not lie with, as Davidson supposes, the larger question of whether Cartesian scepticism is possible regarding our knowledge of the world. Scepticism is largely an epistemological question which is independent of the semantic question of language-world relationship.

Wittgenstein and the Myth of the Gap between Language and the World

Like Davidson, Wittgenstein is a strong critic of the myth of the gap between language and reality. In his *Tractatus*[9] Wittgenstein demolishes the myth of the gap by showing that there is no ontological gap between what we say about the world and what the world is. His notion of picture in the logical sense, as applied to language, does not revive the myth, but rather demolishes it for the reason that language as a logical picture of the world establishes the identity of the logical form of language and the world.[10] Wittgenstein writes:

> What any picture, of whatever form, must have in common with reality, in order to be able to depict it — correctly or incorrectly — in any way at all, is logical form, i.e. the form of reality.[11]

Thus logical form is that which any logical picture must share with reality so that there could be any picture possible at all. Let us call this the thesis of the identity of logical form. Language, according to this thesis, eminently fulfils this condition by dint of which language can be the picture of the world. Wittgenstein further elaborates this:

> Logical pictures can depict the world.[12]
>
> A picture has a logico-pictorial form in common with what it depicts.[13]

---

9. Wittgenstein, *Tractatus Logico-Philosophicus*, tr. D.F. Pears and B.F. McGuinness, London: Routledge and Kegan Paul, 1961.
10. Cf. ibid., 2.15-2.22.
11. Ibid., 2.18.
12. Ibid., 2.19.
13. Ibid., 2.2.

> A picture depicts reality by representing a possibility of existence and non-existence of states of affairs.[14]

What is emphasized here is that for any representation to be possible at all the representation and the represented must have the same logical form such that we cannot entertain any ontological gap between the two.

Wittgenstein's ontology of logical form is a decisive move to get rid of the myth that language can represent reality only at an ontological distance. The ontological distance is dissolved by pushing forward the thesis that language and the world occupy the same ontological space and that there is no unbridgeable gulf between us and the world. This rules out the possibility that we require another device to make language and world come together. Wittgenstein rejects the empiricist move to make language and world meet only through human contrivances like the so-called conventions which ordinarily make linguistic utterances match the world. Such conventions take away the power of language and logic to capture the world. Therefore, Wittgenstein makes language and logic autonomous in order that they meet the world directly. He writes:

> How can logic — all-embracing logic, which mirrors the world — use such peculiar crotches and contrivances? Only because they are all connected with one another in an infinitely fine network, the great mirror.[15]

Logic mirrors the world just because it works as "an infinitely fine network" with all its contrivances which are part of its autonomous functioning. In that sense, logic along with language is a "great mirror" of the world. The mirror-imagery makes it clear that the world is not stationed far away from

14. Wittgenstein, *Tractatus Logico-Philosophicus*, 2.201.

15. Ibid., 5. 511.

language and logic because it stands exposed to the nuanced functioning of logic and language. It is only in this sense that Wittgenstein can say:

> The limits of my language mean the limits of my world.[16]
>
> Logic pervades the world: the limits of the world are also its limits.[17]

Wittgenstein makes the world as much logic-dependent as he makes logic world-dependent in the sense that logic sets the limits of the world just as the world sets the limits of logic and language. Thus mutual dependence of logic and the world shows that there is no way we can detach the world from logic and language. This ontological dependence of logic on the world and vice versa goes to prove that the classical idea of mapping of the world by logic and language has to be replaced by a stronger thesis declaring the identity of the logical form of language and the world. The classical idea of map-making has a Cartesian thrust because it is assumed that language at best is a map of the world which can conventionally be imposed on the world. In Wittgenstein's theory, however, language reaches the world by virtue of its logic and not because of the intervention of the conventions.

Wittgenstein's theory of logical form brings out the necessity of logical form underlying language and the world. Logical form is pre-linguistic in the sense that language presupposes it as it cannot say what logical form is. Logical form is unsayable, though it is mirrored in language itself. Wittgenstein writes:

> Propositions cannot represent logical form: it is mirrored in them.
>
> What finds reflection in language, language cannot represent.

16. Wittgenstein, *Tractatus Logico-Philosophicus*, 5.6.
17. Ibid., 5.61.

> What expresses itself in language, we cannot express by means of language.
>
> Propositions show the logical form of reality.
>
> They display it.[18]

By being unsayable, but shown in language, logical form makes language itself possible and thus makes it the logical picture or representation of the world. This thesis of Wittgenstein's makes it abundantly clear that language and world share the common logical form and therefore there is no ontological gap between the two to make epistemology at all necessary to fill the gap. Epistemology makes a hasty retreat into the background.[19] Scepticism itself becomes suspect as an epistemological enterprise.[20]

Logic, Semantics and the Missing Gap between Language and the World

Wittgenstein's later philosophy as outlined in the *Philosophical Investigations*[21] carries on the unfinished task of the *Tractatus* by arguing against the myth of the gap between language and the world so much so that it appears as if the gap never existed in his philosophy. Wittgenstein's new techniques of grammatical analysis exhibit no tendency to show that such a gap should ever exist to bother philosophers of language. The remarkable phenomenon of language taking the centre stage of philosophical attention has the tendency to suggest that the linguistic representations of the world do not pose any problem at all, not because they are no more relevant, but because they become so self-evident that language analysis

18. Wittgenstein, *Tractatus Logico-Philosophicus*, 4.121.
19. Ibid., 4.1121.
20. Ibid., 6.51
21. See Wittgenstein, *Philosophical Investigations,* tr. G.E.M. Anscombe, Oxford: Basil Blackwell, 1953.

does not have to presuppose any gap between language and the world. Wittgenstein writes:

> What looks as if it *had* to exist, is part of the language. It is a paradigm in our language-game: something with which comparison is made. And this may be an important observation; but it is none the less an observation concerning our language-game — our method of representation.[22]

What is expressed here is the idea that what exists in the world like colours, for example, is captured in the colour-language through the colour paradigms. Therefore any observation on the colour-objects is really an observation on the colour language-games which are deemed to be the "methods of representation". Here the question is not whether colour-objects exist, but whether colour-words are meaningfully used in a language-game.

If the above passage is further examined, one can decipher a subtle implication that whatever language describes and refers to in the world is already implicitly laid down in language, that is, is already a grammatical fact to be understood within the confines of language and not outside it. Outside the language we cannot describe what exists in the world; inside it, it is already shown in the grammar of language. Wittgenstein puts this in the following passage:

> "The general form of proposition is : This is how things are" — That is the kind of proposition one repeats oneself countless times. One thinks that one is tracing the outline of the thing's nature over and over again, and one is merely tracing round the frame through which we look at it.[23]

One is reminded here of the Tractarian thrust of the argument[24]

---

22. See Wittgenstein, *Philosophical Investigations*, section 50.
23. Ibid., section 114.
24. Wittgenstein, *Tractatus Logico-Philosophicus*, 4.5.

to prove that the logical form of the proposition is enough to show what exists in the world. The same argument reappears here by claiming that language shows through its grammar what the world really is. The so-called gap between language and the world stands dissolved because language alone shows what there is in the world without attempting to say it. Wittgenstein's following remark tells this in so many words:

> When we say, and *mean*, that such-and-such is the case, we —and our meaning — do not stop anywhere short of the facts; but we mean: *this-is-so*.[25]

What comes to our immediate notice is that what we say and mean in language about the world does not stop short of the world; we really mean and say that the world is thus and so. Language says in short what it says, that is, that such and such is the case. There is nothing more to this than meets the eye in the sense that nothing like a gap seems to persist between language and the world.

Logic and semantics, according to Wittgenstein, do not chase the myth of the gap between language and the world just as they do not chase the myth of the Given[26] in the world. It is because there is no gap and also no Given in the sense it has been argued by some philosophers.[27] What makes the gap so threatening is that it makes logic and semantics so alien to the world that the world appears to be totally lost.[28]

Rorty has highlighted the threatening posture of the gap

25. Wittgenstein, *Philosophical Investigations,* section 95.
26. Wilfrid Sellars, "Empiricism and the Philosophy of Mind", in *Minnesota Studies in Philosophy of Science,* vol. 1, ed. Herbert Feigl and Michael Scriven, Minneapolis: University of Minnesota Press, 1956, pp. 253-59.
27. Ibid.
28. Richard Rorty, "The World Well Lost", in *Consequences of Pragmatism* (Essays 1972-1980), Brighton, Sussex: The Harvester Press, 1982, pp. 3-18.

by showing that any attempt to posit a world independent of our conceptual schemes is bound to give rise to the possibility that the world can never be given to our conceptual scheme. That is to say that the world is ever out of the bounds of our conceptual scheme. He writes:

> The notion of "world" as used in a phrase like 'different conceptual schemes carve up the world differently' must be the notion of something *completely* unspecified and unspecifiable — the thing-in-itself, in fact.[29]

Such a notion does not serve any purpose, not even the realist's purpose, because we lose epistemic grasp of it such that it is as good as lost. For Rorty, the Kantian thing-in-itself, like the Kantian distinction between the faculty of sensibility and that of spontaneity, is of no use because it creates a big divide between our conceptual scheme and the world. It makes the notion of the world a vacuous notion. "To sum up this point", says Rorty, ". . . the world is either the purely vacuous notion of the ineffable cause of sense and goal of intellect, or else a name for the objects that inquiry at the moment is leaving alone: those planks in the boat which are at the moment not being moved about."[30] Such being the status of the world, either it is completely lost or it is absolutely pedestrian meriting no philosophical attention. Rorty is clear that we have no reason to talk about the conceptual schemes being able to carve out the world because such a notion does not help us in any way. He agrees with Davidson on this fact that the idea of a conceptual scheme is responsible for the gap between scheme and content which is called the "third dogma of empiricism".[31]

29. Richard Rorty, "The World Well Lost" in *Consequences of Pragmatism* (Essays 1972-1980), Brighton, Sussex: The Harvester Press, 1982, p. 14.

30. Ibid., p. 15.

31. Davidson, "On the Very Idea of a Conceptual Scheme", in *Inquiries into Truth and Interpretation*, Oxford: Clarendon Press, 1984, pp. 183-98, especially p. 189.

With this goes the fine distinction between representation and the represented in the empiricist sense. Rorty, like Davidson, does not entertain the idea of the linguistic representation of the world in the empiricist sense.

But there is still in the logical sense the distinction between what a proposition is and what it is about in the world. Such a distinction is implicit in the idea of language being about the world. No amount of empirical pruning can do away with the idea that language is about the world and so language lights up the world by showing its logical structure. In that sense, "logic pervades the world: the limits of the world are also its limits".[32]

Mind and the World: In Search of the Space of Reasons

In consonance with the logical relationship between language and the world, there is a problem as to how the mind is related to the world which has been discussed by McDowell in his work *Mind and World*.[33] McDowell's attempt is to cement the ontological gap supposedly inserted between the mind and the world by the empiricists through the Myth of the Given. The Myth of the Given which has pervaded the empiricist framework has been attacked by Sellars in his famous paper "Empiricism and the Philosophy of Mind".[34] Sellars's argument against the Myth is that the so-called Given in the form of pre-conceptual sensations does not exist because sensations are already part of our conceptual repertoire and hence are already conceptualized. Sellars writes:

> In characterizing an episode or a state as that of *knowing*, we are not giving an empirical description of that episode

---

32. Wittgenstein, *Tractatus Logico-Philosophicus*, 5.61.
33. Cf. McDowell, *Mind and World.*
34. Cf. Sellars, "Empiricism and the Philosophy of Mind".

> or state; we are placing it in the logical space of reasons, of justifying and being able to justify what one says.[35]

It is this logical space of reasons which holds the ground against the so-called Given thereby demolishing the Myth by declaring it null and void. Sellars goes on to make it clear that a case of knowledge is not that of recording a sensation but rationally justifying and conceptually articulating it in judgements.

McDowell follows Sellars in arguing against the Myth of the Given by strengthening the logical space of reasons in terms of the Kantian notion of the logical space of concepts in which the sensations are synthesized in order to give rise to knowledge. Thus we are led to rehearse the Kantian distinction between the faculty of receptivity and the faculty of spontaneity whereby a definite direction is given by McDowell as to how concepts synthesize the sensations to make knowledge possible. Not only that, he goes forward to argue for the unboundedness of the conceptual realm[36] as against the realm of natural law so as to demonstrate the supremacy of the conceptual over the natural. Thus McDowell arrives at the picture of the mind-world relationship in which the world itself conceived naturally is part of the realm of the concepts. He writes:

> Although reality is independent of thinking, it is not to be pictured as outside an outer boundary that encloses the conceptual sphere. *That things are thus and so* is the conceptual content of an experience, but if the subject of the experience is not misled, that very same thing, *that things are thus and so,* is also a perceptible fact, an aspect of the perceptible world.[37]

---

35. Sellars, "Empiricism and the Philosophy of Mind", pp. 298-99.
36. McDowell, *Mind and World,* pp. 24-45.
37. Ibid., p. 26.

Thus the world though logically independent of the realm of the concepts is yet a part of the realm because it is already represented through the concepts embedded in language. In that sense the world is not alien to the realm of the concepts but is part of it without being completely assimilated into the conceptual realm.

McDowell's conclusions regarding the mind-world relationship are not far from those of Kant, Sellars and Davidson because he shares with them the idea that there is no gap between the world and mind the way it has been projected by the empiricists. The so-called gap is very much cemented by acknowledging the fact that the world is represented in the space of concepts and in language without it being alienated from that space. This is to reiterate that the idea of representation itself is not at fault, but the associated idea that there is a gap between the world and mind. The gap is an empiricist Myth, "the third dogma" which has been subjected to criticism by Davidson.

Language, Truth and the World: Can Truth Be Dispensed With?

Now the question arises, if the gap between language and the world does not exist, how can we then retain the concept of truth as a relation between language and its counterpart, i.e. the world? This question has been answered most decisively, though negatively, by Rorty who rejects the very idea of truth as correspondence[38] between language and the world. Rorty writes:

> Truth is not the name of a property, and in particular not the name of a relational property which ties a statement to

---

38. Rorty, "Solidarity or Objectivity?", in *Objectivity, Relativism and Truth* (Philosophical Papers, vol. 1), Cambridge: Cambridge University Press, 1991, pp. 21-45.

> the world or to a set of semantical rules as followed by an omniscient being.[39]

Rorty thus rejects the very idea of truth as a relation between language and the world because this idea presupposes a gap between the two to be bridged by truth. The classical notion of truth has the following presuppositions which Rorty rejects. They are as follows:

1. Truth is objective and impersonal and is beyond time and context.
2. Truth is transcendental and ahistorical and hence known only to an omniscient being.
3. Truth is absolute and cannot be relativized to any culture or community.
4. Truth can be discovered by reason which can transcend time and history.
5. Truth is transcendental, universal and free from any contingency.

Rorty rejects all the above-mentioned presuppositions 1-5 for the reason that such a conception of truth has outlived its utility in philosophy. With the demise of the representational theory of language, the idea of truth which is the universal property of thought has outlived itself. Rorty is of the opinion that pragmatism to which he owes allegiance does not require the concepts such as "truth", "objectivity", "reason" and "transcendence" because they have no place in the pragmatic vocabulary.[40]

Rorty has brought about a pragmatic turn in philosophy which shows that language is not a representation of reality, but a social practice in which people participate as part of their

39. Rorty, "Representation, Social Practise and Truth", in *Objectivity, Relativism and Truth,* p. 154.
40. Ibid.

ethnocentric life. Adopting the later Wittgensteinian idea that language is basically a form of life,[41] he goes to the extent of saying that in the linguistic practices we are not required to represent reality and so are not in need of a concept of truth as correspondence. This anti-representationalist approach to truth has been the cornerstone of recent anti-realism in semantics and metaphysics.[42]

But it remains to be seen if anti-realism in truth theory can be justified given the fact that much of language remains about the world even if we admit that language is a form of life and not just a rigid logical system of symbols. It is quite obvious that language is about the world, that is, about the way things are in the world. There is no necessity of saying that language is a representation of the world even while accepting that language speaks of the world. There is no metalinguistic way of telling that language is about the world since there is no way we can ascend to a standpoint outside language and the world. But that does not negate the fact that language is about the world the way thought is. That is why we cannot give up the logic which introduces the concept of truth in semantics. This is the reason why truth is retained in language as the standard of justification and not justification as such. Putnam therefore very validly makes a distinction between justification and truth:

> . . . the two key ideas of the idealization theory of truth are (1) that truth is independent of justification here and now, but not independent of *all* justification. To claim a statement is true is to claim it could be justified. (2) truth is expected to be stable or "convergent".[43] . . .

---

41. Wittgenstein, *Philosophical Investigations,* section 23.
42. Hilary Putnam, *Reason, Truth and History,* Cambridge: Cambridge University Press, 1981, Chapter 3.
43. Ibid., p. 56.

What Putnam rescues from the pragmatic de-objectification of truth is its "stability" or "convergence" which if denied can make truth collapse into justification. This would spell disaster to truth as a semantic concept.

Rorty's tirade against objectivity of truth has its relativistic consequences which are far from being less dangerous. Putnam himself draws attention to the dangers in his critique of relativism[44] in view of the fact that truth retains objectivity at any cost in the semantic and epistemological discourse. McDowell makes a concreted effort to "rehabilitate" objectivity in epistemology by arguing that truth in the minimal sense sticks to the very idea of knowledge which is accountable to the world. He writes:

> One could define the discourse of objectivity as involving a certain supposed external use of the semantical notions, and in that sense I have no problem with Rorty's attitudes to it. But Rorty suggests that rejecting these supposed external uses requires rejecting any form of the idea that inquiry is answerable to the world.[45]

McDowell finds it unintelligible that we have to give up the very idea of inquiry being accountable to the world. One cannot give up the very nature of knowledge as knowledge of reality and so one cannot give up truth as such as an objective semantic concept.

Objectivity and Answerability to the World

It is really very surprising that Rorty sacrifices objectivity for solidarity[46] when it is well known that solidarity among the

44. Hilary Putnam, *Reason, Truth and History*, Cambridge: Cambridge University Press, 1981, pp. 54-55.
45. John McDowell, "Towards Rehabilitating Objectivity", in *Rorty and His Critics*, ed. Robert Brandom, Oxford: Blackwell Publishing, 2000, p. 114.
46. Rorty, "Solidarity or Objectivity", in *Objectivity, Relativism and Truth.*

fellow language-speakers itself is in need of some sort of objectivity. His argument is that objectivity leads us in the wrong direction of encountering truth and the world when actually such a goal of inquiry is an illusion. For Rorty, there is no such thing as encountering truth because all that we can hope for is to engage in social practices within the boundary of ethnocentricity. The enthnocentric practices are underlined by solidarity which is nothing but the community agreement. Truth under this interpretation evaporates into justification or communal agreement. Rorty writes:

> For pragmatism, the desire for objectivity is not the desire to escape the limitations of one's community, but simply the desire for as much intersubjective agreement as possible; the desire to extend the reference of "us" as far as we can.[47]

Thus the pragmatic notion of objectivity merges into the ethnocentric notion of communal agreement giving rise to the suspicion that truth has been replaced by the notion of justification within an ethnologically bounded community.[48]

The following objections may be raised against the enthnocentric view of truth and objectivity:

1. Objectivity is not only a metaphysical concept but also a semantic and epistemological one. Rorty's anti-metaphysical stance against objectivity sweeps away the semantic and epistemological notion as well. This seems to be an overreaction on Rorty's part against the concept of truth and objectivity.
2. Ethnocentrism itself is a metaphysical doctrine since it takes for granted the idea of community of human

47. Rorty, "Solidarity or Objectivity", in *Objectivity, Relativism and Truth*, p. 23.
48. Cf. McDowell, "Towards Rehabilitating Objectivity" in *Rorty and His Critics*, pp. 109-21.

beings. Now if the community is the supreme guarantor of what is acceptable in a community, true or false, good or bad, etc., there must be something in terms of which the community does this. In that sense, there is a genuine problem regarding what makes the communal agreement possible. Rorty does not provide any norm for such agreement or solidarity.

3. Abolition of a theory of truth amounts to the abolition of any idea of knowledge of the world and therefore of any idea of accountability to the world.

Rorty's idea of no-truth and no-knowledge approach to philosophy makes philosophy itself redundant in the sense that it has nothing to offer except what human beings in a community actually do. "For the pragmatist . . ." says Rorty,

> 'knowledge' is like 'truth' simply a compliment paid to the beliefs which we think so well justified that, for the moment, further justification is not needed. An inquiry into the nature of knowledge can, on his view, only be a socio-historical account of how various people have tried to reach an agreement on what to believe.[49]

Such being the case, it is difficult to imagine that there is anything that philosophy has to do except recording the socio-historical facts about the community.

But Rorty has to recognize that even within the community, we require justification of what we claim to know to be true and acceptable. How can this be secured if there is no norm or standard within that community? Thus certain criteria of justification have to be smuggled in through the backdoor and so some sort of objectivity has to be grounded within the community practices themselves. Otherwise, there will be complete chaos in the human activities and in human life.

---

49. Rorty, "Solidarity or Objectivity?", in *Objectivity, Relativism and Truth,* p. 24.

Besides, there will be ever present the idea of accessibility to the world which the community must secure for itself. If science of the world is to be possible, then there must be a way of having access to the world which cannot be a mere community-controlled choice. There must be something objectively true about the world which the community must accept as justified. Therefore there cannot be a full stop to the game of community's knowing the world and thus being answerable to the world.

Truth, Justification and the Goal of Inquiry

In this context it is relevant to inquire whether truth is the goal of inquiry or not. This question has been pertinently raised by Bilgrami[50] with reference to Rorty and Davidson. It has been contended by Bilgrami that for both, Davidson and Rorty, truth is not the goal of inquiry because truth is not something one can set as the goal of inquiry into how our beliefs are true. For Rorty, truth slips out of our inquiry because it is out of reach of ours in the way the realists have construed it as correspondence with reality. The only thing which falls within our pragmatic inquiry is the justification of our beliefs within the domain open to our peers or the immediate audience. Beyond that there is no goal of inquiry except in the sense of having extended audiences for securing justification. According to Bilgrami, Rorty makes justification the goal of inquiry because it is all that is needed from a pragmatist point of view.[51]

For Davidson, there is no way truth can be the goal of inquiry because truth itself is a primitive concept which is objective but is not something to be discovered in the process

---

50. Akeel Bilgrami, "Is Truth a Goal of Inquiry? Rorty and Davidson on Truth", in *Rorty and His Critics*, pp. 242-62.
51. Ibid.

of discovering the relation between language and reality. Davidson writes:

> We should not say that truth is correspondence, coherence, warranted assertability, ideally justified assertability, what is accepted in the conversation of the right people, what science will end up maintaining, what explains the success of science or of our ordinary beliefs. To the extent that realism and anti-realism depend on one or another of these views of truth we should refuse to endorse either. Realism, with its insistence on radically non-epistemic correspondence, asks more of truth than we can understand; anti-realism, with its limitation of truth to what can be ascertained, unnecessarily deprives truth of its role as an intersubjective standard. If we want to speak the truth about truth, we should say no more than need be.[52]

For both realism and anti-realism, truth is the goal of inquiry and hence the dispute about its status. Davidson disowns this and makes truth something embedded in the language towards which inquiry is directed.

Rorty and Davidson, however, do not agree on their approach to truth because while Rorty is a pragmatist and hence anti-realist about truth, Davidson is not . He is not a realist either, taking a position against the anti-realist. He takes truth as it is without a supporting epistemology or metaphysics. What makes truth important for language is the fact that semantically we cannot take a sentence without asking for its truth or falsity because of the semantic compulsion rather than of the epistemological demand. Rorty, on the contrary, moves in the opposite direction in which truth is replaced by justification which is an epistemological concept. All that we are left with are the supporting practices which make us accept some statements or beliefs as acceptable or not in the

52. Davidson, "Epistemology and Truth", in *Subjective, Intersubjective, Objective*, Oxford: Clarendon Press, 2001, p. 191.

community to which we belong. Thus Davidson and Rorty stand opposed to each other on the distinction between truth and justification. Though both admit the distinction, while Rorty goes for a full-blooded justification, Davidson remains loyal to truth and gives up justification as redundant.[53]

McDowell raises a pertinent question here regarding the status of truth as the goal of inquiry. In his effort to rehabilitate objectivity of truth, he argues that if truth is retained as the objective accountability to the world, then truth can be the goal of inquiry.[54] There is no doubt that our beliefs are true, not because we have evidence for the truth of a belief but because the belief stands for a state of affairs in the world. It is the world that makes a belief or a statement true. This conformity of a statement to the world is more than a causal relation between language and the world; it is a semantic and normative relation. Given this framework, it is necessary that we recognize the fact that truth is the driving force for any inquiry. McDowell's contention against Rorty is that no amount of effort to make truth unreachable to us so that justification can take its place will succeed because we will be still asked if the justifications themselves are true and if so, whether they are accountable to the world. Rorty makes the world only the causal source of our beliefs, but what is needed is the logical and normative relation between beliefs and the world. Bilgrami writes:

> The only thing to say about these beliefs as inquirers is that they are true. To say that any one of them is true is to say, as McDowell does, that they conform, they have a particular form of normative relatedness, to the world as it figures *in*

53. Rorty, "Universality and Truth", in *Rorty and His Critics*, pp. 1-30.
54. See McDowell, "Towards Rehabilitating Objectivity", in *Rorty and His Critics*, pp. 109-21.

> *our own world view*. So, to repeat, the question is: what does justification apply to, if it does not apply to these beliefs? For surely there must be some distinction between truth and justification.[55]

Thus Bilgrami is sympathetic to the idea that beliefs are true provided they conform to the world, and so he views truth as the goal of inquiry. If justifications are round the corner, truth cannot be far behind. So if truth is reinstated as the goal of inquiry, neither Davidson nor Rorty can have any objection to it because in any case truth is entrenched in our logical thinking.

Bilgrami has brought in a distinction between the first-person and third-person[56] point of view in this connection in order to make the idea of truth perspicuous. The first-person point of view is the inquirer's point of view in which the beliefs which are doubt-free are taken as true, while from the third-person point of view, it can be doubted whether a belief is true or false. The latter gives rise to the demand for evidence or justification. Thus there is at least a point of view in which we demand no justification for beliefs. Both Rorty and Davidson do not accept the authority of the first-person point of view regarding truth and so rule out the authority of the inquirer about truth. Rorty's pragmatism is a third-person point of view, while Davidson makes truth a semantic notion from the third-person point of view. McDowell approaches truth from a first-person point of view so that truth is entrenched in one's logical thinking. We do not necessarily doubt our own beliefs unless otherwise prompted by our own intuitions. The so-called cautionary view of truth[57] mentioned by Rorty

55. Bilgrami, "Is Truth a Goal of Inquiry: Rorty and Davidson on Truth", in *Rorty and His Critics*, p. 256.

56. Ibid.

57. Rorty, "Universality and Truth", in *Rorty and His Critics*, pp. 4-5.

applies only to the beliefs of others because we are not sure which of the beliefs are true and which are false.

Realism, Anti-realism and Transcendental Idealism

The realism-anti-realism debate centres around the question whether truth can be viewed as correspondence or as some sort of warranted assertability. The classical realist position known also as metaphysical realism holds onto the idea that truth is something which establishes a relation between language and the world. A true sentence therefore is one which tracks the reality as it is. Such a notion is committed to the following:

1. Truth is independent of the cognition of the speaker or knower.
2. Truth is eternal in the sense that it is not subject to change in the mind of the knower.
3. Truth is absolute.

These commitments are manifested in the realist notion that language is a representation of reality and therefore all assertions in language are subject to the principle of bivalence, i.e. that they are either true or false.[58] The realist position in semantics has its metaphysical implication that the true assertions are the true representations of the world as it is in itself.

Like Dummett, Putnam is a critic of the realist position in semantics and metaphysics. Both argue that truth cannot be cognition-transcendent[59] and that it cannot be out of the bounds of the mind of the knower. Putnam especially has argued that if truth means that there is a complete description or representation of the world and that there is a readymade

58. Michael Dummett, "Truth", in *Philosophical Logic*, ed. P.F. Strawson, Oxford: Oxford university Press, 1967, pp. 49-68.

59. Ibid. See also Putnam, *Reason, Truth and History*, Chapter 3.

world to be represented, then such a theory of truth must be rejected, because there is nothing called the perfect representation of the world which exists independently of the human mind or his theoretical point of view.[60] Putnam puts forward the following anti-realist (or, internal realist) theses:

1. Truth is objective but is internal to the conceptual scheme of the speaker or knower.
2. Truth is not absolute in the classical sense, since it is relative to the conceptual scheme of the speaker.
3. Truth is different from any particular justification but it is not independent of all justifications.
4. Truth is internal to the cognition of the knower or the speaker.

Thus Putnam elaborates the framework of his internal realism which provides an alternative theory of truth.

Rorty agrees with Putnam's anti-realist stand that truth cannot be detached from the knowing mind and therefore there is no more to truth than can be provided by the knower in terms of justifications and evidences. He argues for a pragmatic notion of truth that broadly agrees with the anti-realist contention that there is nothing in truth that transcends justification. He is particularly critical of the representationalist notion of truth which tends to make truth inaccessible to the cognizing mind. For him, truth is pragmatically entrenched in the human practices and so internal to the social practices[61] of language and knowledge.

Much of what is claimed by the anti-realists and the pragmatists cannot be faulted, but what remains debatable is

60. Putnam, *Reason, Truth and History,* Chapter 3.

61. Rorty, "Representation, Social Practice and Truth", in *Objectivity, Relativism and Truth,* pp. 151-61.

whether truth can be jettisoned altogether as it has been argued by Rorty. Davidson argues against Rorty that truth can be rehabilitated without smuggling in the metaphysics and epistemology of the past, because truth is already there in the structure of our thinking and use of language.[62] Truth is a fundamental concept and hence it is indispensable in our language. Besides, the concept of truth also reminds of the fact that language is related to reality and that we have to depend upon the world for vouchsafing for the truth of our assertions. In that sense, we have to have truth in our logical vocabulary, whether or not we retain the idea of linguistic representations.

In this context, it is worthwhile to discuss the possibility of transcendental idealism[63] to which McDowell and Bilgrami make reference. McDowell broaches this idea in his defence of objectivity of truth, while Bilgrami brings it out in his theory of truth as the goal of inquiry. Both make the following claims:

1. Truth like justification is placed in the mind of the speaker or the knower because it cannot climb beyond the boundary of the mind. There is, in fact, nothing like climbing beyond the mind.
2. There is a definite world view which we inhabit and which is inescapable for all rational human beings.
3. All our beliefs constitute our world view and so they must be judged as either true or false.
4. Therefore, we have access to truth within our world view such that we have no occasion to doubt that most of our beliefs are true and that they are justified within our cognitive system.

---

62. Davidson, "Truth Rehabilitated", in *Rorty and His Critics*, pp. 65-74.

63. Bilgrami, "Is Truth a Goal of Inquiry?: Rorty and Davidson on Truth", in *Rorty and His Critics*, pp. 242-62.

5. So, it is not realism nor anti-realism which is true, but transcendental idealism.

In view of the above, transcendental idealism holds promise because it takes us right to the heart of truth and the world by denying that truth is beyond our grasp and that reality is beyond our cognitive categories. Like Kant, McDowell and Bilgrami argue that the idea of not having truth and thus not making any contact with reality in language does not hold good at all. Therefore the pragmatic notion of managing without truth and the world in the robust sense does not make any sense. We can recover truth and the world from the pragmatist's rejection of them. Bilgrami writes:

> This recovery may with some right be described as constituting a version of transcendental idealism. And it is a recovery of the world, which is compatible with Davidson's claim that we could never tell which of our beliefs is true. It is *only a global* recovery, and is, as it were, *an epistemologically blind* recovery, since no *particular* truth about the world is known to be a truth by inquirers. But recovery it is. Truth cannot any longer be described as being out of reach in the way a strict transcendental realism would have it.[64]

To put it succinctly, transcendental idealism of this sort is a ticket against scepticism on one hand and transcendental realism on the other. It brings us to the plain truth that truth matters and so does our representation of the world in language.

Why Representationalism is Still a Good Buy

Given the transcendental idealist framework, one can argue that we can retain representationalism without the

---

64. Bilgrami, "Is Truth a Goal of Inquiry?: Rorty and Davidson on Truth", in *Rorty and His Critics*, p. 247.

metaphysical baggage of realism and thus without the idea that truth and world are beyond our cognitive grasp. Rorty has argued against representationalism[65] in philosophy of language and truth for the reason that it brings in the concepts universally bracketed with metaphysical realism. He characterizes representationalism in the words of Brandom as that which "takes truth to be the basic concept in terms of which a theory of meaning, and hence a theory of language, is to be developed"[66] and also holds that "the essential feature of language is its capacity to represent the way things are".[67] Rorty radically changes the concept of language, following the later Wittgenstein, Heidegger and Dewey, into a form of life involving a set of social practices. From the latter point of view, language ceases to be a representation of reality and so the concept of truth loses its central place in philosophy of language.

The idea of language as a representation, however, does not disappear from philosophy because of the fact that there is no reason to believe that language ceases to be about reality and that truth loses its centrality in semantics and logic. Even Davidson who is willing to sacrifice the classical idea of truth as correspondence does not think that language has no relation with reality. He writes:

> The point is that I believe in the ordinary notion of truth: there really are people, mountains, camels and stars out there, just as we think there are, and those objects and events frequently have the characteristics we think we perceive them to have. Our concepts are ours, but that does not mean

---

65. Rorty, "Representation, Social Practise and Truth", in *Objectivity, Relativism and Truth*, pp. 151-61.
66. Ibid., p. 151. Quoted from Robert Brandom, "Truth and Assertibility", *Journal of Philosophy*, LXXIII (1976), p. 137.
67. Ibid.

> they don't truly, as well as usually, describe an objective reality.[68]

This shows that our concepts and our language are about the world, even if we do not say that they represent the world. Davidson, while rejecting the correspondence theory of truth concedes that "correspondence, while it is empty as definition, does capture the thought that truth depends on how the world is, and this should be enough to discredit most epistemic and pragmatic theories".[69] Thus the basic thesis of representationalism is preserved by Davidson in re-emphasizing that language is about the world which makes "truth the key to how mind apprehends the world".[70]

Now it is clear that representationalism is not the villain as it is made out to be by Rorty. Things have not gone wrong in semantics because of the idea that language is a representation of the world. In a sense it is a truism, so obvious that nobody should take note of it. But wrongly understood it can give rise to a realist metaphysics questioned by Putnam and others under the name of transcendental realism. But suppose we change the tone, as indicated by McDowell and Bilgrami, of the metaphysical language and introduce the concept of the world view (not the "conceptual scheme" in the pejorative sense) to which our concepts belong. These concepts are ours but they capture the way the world is without introducing an intermediary, thus ruling out the scheme-content distinction. Within such a world view, the world is very much our world in which we live and which is

68. Davidson, "Is Truth a Goal of Inquiry? Discussion with Rorty", in *Donald Davdson: Truth, Meaning and Knowledge,* ed. Uruzula M. Zeglen, London and New York: Routledge, 1999, pp. 17-19.
69. Davidson, "Truth Rehabilitated", in *Rorty and His Critics,* p. 73.
70. Ibid.

"ready-to-hand" and not "present-to-hand" in Heidegger's sense. The world is not epistemically separated from us as claimed by the realists, but which is constituted within our language and the social practices. Given this way of construing the world it is still represented in our language and made internal to our world view. McDowell puts it as follows:

> In this conception, being genuinely in touch with reality would in a radical way transcend whatever we can do within our practices of arriving at answers to our questions. Thus a familiar gulf seems to open between us and what we should like to be able to think of ourselves as able to get to know about.[71]

This shows how the linguistic practices alone cannot assure us of our relation with the world. We have other epistemic relations as well which can be guaranteed within our world view. If representationalism is associated with the epistemic relations alone then it is inadequate to make our world available to us, but it need not be so because what we represent we also constitute in terms of our interests as Heidegger, Dewey, Wittgenstein and Rorty argue. Representationalism is holistic in its texture by assimilating the epistemic, pragmatic and semantic components in our relation with the world.

Conclusion

The following theses may be noted for considering the availability of linguistic representations and truth in philosophy of language:

1. Language cannot cease to be representational if by it we mean that we cannot but see the world through language.
2. Linguistic representations are semantically and logically truth-centred.

---

71. McDowell, "Towards Rehabilitating Objectivity", in *Rorty and His Critics*, p. 115.

3. Truth takes us back to the world because that is how it is present in language.
4. The world discloses itself in language by virtue of the latter's creating the space of reasons for the world to be constituted.
5. Therefore, transcendental idealism is an ideal option to map the world onto our language, without pushing the world "outside our own minds".

In short, we can defend a version of representational view of language, truth and world without espousing Rorty's ethnocentric and pragmatic deconstruction of language and truth.

12

Epistemic Autonomy of Śabda-pramāṇa
Revisiting Classical Indian debates

K.S. Prasad

> We cannot suggest a novel theory which is highly original. Short-sighted as I am, I cannot discover even a blade of grass which my predecessors, logicians of keen insight, have failed to take notice of.[1]
>
> — Jayantabhaṭṭa, *Nyāya-Mañjarī*

FOLLOWING Jayantabhaṭṭa, I do not want to claim anything profound in what I am writing; rather I would like to reinterpret the age-old problem in such a way so as to make it more interesting in the contemporary context. Of course, my intention is not in anyway associated with the romance of reliving the past; rather, it is undertaken with the purpose of getting some insights from the past to understand the present better. As Bhartṛhari rightly suggests,

> The intellect acquires critical acumen by familiarity with different traditions. How much does one really understand by merely following one's own reasoning only? The learning of those who have not sat at the feet of the earlier

1. Jayantabhaṭṭa, *Nyāyamañjarī*, Āhnika I, tr. Janaki Vallabha Bhattacharyya, New Delhi: Motilal Banarsidass, 1978, p. 839.

> scholars but have flit from one idea to another do not attain complete definiteness.[2]

While many would agree that one of the most significant methods for transfer of knowledge is from testimony; however, arguments over its credibility do exist, with some scholars sceptical about its status as a legitimate source of knowledge. One of the problems concerning knowledge acquisition through testimony is that it does not seem to live up to the standards of knowledge. Even if it is acceptable as a legitimate source of knowledge there is a view that knowing from testimony is a form of complicated but disguised inference, on the basis of a repeated observation of connection between certain utterances and their associated meanings and the facts corresponding to them in the external world. Let me address this problem.

Mapping the Domain

Not many people know that in 1937, Gandhiji made a visit to Hyderabad and he did some sightseeing, paid a visit to Paradise Restaurant in Secunderabad, enjoyed the taste of chicken biriyani and learnt the technique of cooking chicken biriyani from the chief chef of the restaurant. There is sufficient reason why not many people know all this. The reason is that none of it is true. But the remarkable thing is that just as you read this sentence, let us say "*S*1", you understood it perfectly, whether or not you were ready to accept it and amazingly you did so with ease. But, the question is how you understood the sentence *S*1. Not by having seen or heard it before; I am sure that never in the history has anyone ever written or uttered that sentence until I did. Nor did you understand *S*1 by having seen a very similar sentence, since I doubt that anyone has ever written a sentence even remotely similar to

2. Bhartṛhari, *Vākyapadīya* II.484-485, tr. K.A. Subramania Iyer, New Delhi: Motilal Banarsidass, 1977, p. 205.

*S*1. Yet it is a fact that you understood the sentence S1 as natural as breathing or walking or eating. Now when I start reporting a news item from one of the credible leading national dailies such as "A car bomb blast in a busy shopping area in Peshawar in Pakistan claimed 90 lives", let us call this sentence "*S*2", you understood it perfectly and you are ready to accept it without any reservation. Both *S*1 and *S*2 generate cognitions, no doubt, but the cognition generated by *S*2 is considered as knowledge generated from testimony and is on par with knowledge generated by perception and inference while *S*1 is not. We need to draw a line between understanding the meaning of a sentence and knowledge acquired by it. True, understanding the meaning of a sentence is a necessary but not sufficient condition. Even if someone understands the content of the sentence *S*1, there is nothing incorrect about such simple understanding of what the sentence means. However such an understanding hardly amounts to knowledge as it is false. The crucial issue is how we are to differentiate a valid linguistic expression from an invalid one in the act of transmitting knowledge. However the role of testimony in acquiring and transmitting knowledge, according to C.A.J. Coady, has been a relatively neglected epistemological issue in the Western tradition.[3] It is generally believed that it is mainly due to the fact that traditional epistemologists in the West have had a marked individualistic approach in their excessive emphasis on the status of knowledge acquired from perception and inference. But in the classical Indian tradition it has been elaborately discussed for well over 2,500 years, that true utterances in a certain language can cause knowledge in the hearer who is trained in that language. By reading newspapers or books, listening to expert lectures, we come to know about such important pieces

3. C.A.J. Coady, *Testimony: A Philosophical Study*, Oxford: Clarendon Press, 1992, p. 6.

of knowledge like when Gandhi was assassinated or a particular star in the galaxy is the farthest of all, etc. Many of our beliefs that we hold have been gained through accepting testimony as a legitimate source of knowledge. In fact, with the increasing complexity in science and technology such as nano-science and the like, we have to depend more and more on testimony rather than trying to obtain directly either through perception or inference. By and large our justification in believing what people tell us comes from our experience of the constant and regular correspondence between the state of affairs linguistically expressed by people and the actual state of affairs.

In classical Indian philosophical tradition the role of testimony as a legitimate source of knowledge has been debated down the ages under the rubric of *śabda-pramāṇa*. The fundamental question involved in testimony is: Can we recognize testimony as an independent and irreducible source of *pramā* or valid cognition? This problem has attracted many scholars in modern times, to name a few, B.K. Matilal, J.N. Mohanty, Arindam Chakraborty, Purushottama Bilimoria and Mark Siderits. They have given a fair description of views and theories highlighting the different dimensions of testimony. The thrust of my paper is not to explain or elaborate the conditions of a valid linguistic expression or how the meaning of a linguistic expression is known; it is rather to establish the epistemic autonomy of *śabda-pramāṇa* in knowledge acquisition. In recent years J.N. Mohanty has presented a critique of the traditional view of *śabda* as a *pramāṇa*. He has raised doubts about whether language can deliver knowledge of actual state of affairs by itself.[4] Mohanty argues that when we obtain knowledge from a linguistic utterance either from

4. J.N. Mohanty, *Reason and Tradition in Indian Thought: An Essay on the Nature of Indian Philosophical Thinking*, Oxford: Clarendon Press, 1992, pp. 249-59.

radio or television or books or newspapers, such knowledge is not solely based on linguistic expressions but is always parasitic upon perception and inference. He writes:

> In all such cases we are said to know only inasmuch as the possibility of perceptual confirmation or inferential backing is taken for granted.[5]

Thus Indian philosophy is not able to provide any satisfactory account of how we can know something just from words.[6] Further, he suggests that in an age when faith in the infallibility of the scriptures is considerably weakened *śabda* is no longer useful as a *pramāṇa* in regard to physical or metaphysical reality, though it can be a valid means of communicating moral rules, which are conventional in nature.[7] In order to know what is factual, *pratyakṣa* and *anumāna* are all that we require. He suggests that *śabda* should not be held to be stronger than *pratyakṣa* and *anumāna*. In addressing these issues, I begin with a few standard definitions of testimony as recorded in Nyāya, Mīmāṁsā and Vedānta traditions to identify the domains of testimony. It is followed by an enquiry into the question: Can testimony be regarded as a means of acquiring valid knowledge? If it can, it will have to be regarded as a legitimate means of knowledge. Once we accept it as a legitimate source of knowledge then we are to address another serious question: Is the way the testimony gives knowledge different and distinct from what is known from perception and inference, no matter if the same object is known from perception or inference?

---

5. J.N. Mohanty, *Reason and Tradition in Indian Thought: An Essay on the Nature of Indian Philosophical Thinking*, Oxford: Clarendon Press, 1992, p. 252.
6. Ibid., pp. 251-52.
7. Ibid., p. 22 and p. 257.

What is Testimony?

Testimony is generally believed to be an activity wherein knowledge is passed on from one individual to the other. Under normal circumstances if someone knows something he can as well communicate what is known by him to the other through linguistic utterances intelligible to him. However, not all linguistic utterances generate knowledge. The speaker could be mistaken, might be lying or could be joking just as in the case of *S*1. Because of this, *Nyāya-Sūtra* defines verbal testimony as *āptopadeśaḥ śabdaḥ.*[8] This *sūtra* may be interpreted in two ways depending on whether one takes the compound *āptopadeśa* relational or qualificational. If it is taken in relational sense as *āptaḥ tasya upadeśaḥ*, it means the words of a "reliable person". On the other hand, if it is taken in a qualificational sense as *āptaścopadeśaḥ*, it means "reliable words". Mīmāṁsakas and Vedāntins support the qualificational interpretation and Naiyāyikas favour relational interpretation of the *sūtra*.

Vātsyāyana in his commentary on *Nyāya-Sūtra*s has explained the term *āpta* as follows:

> The person who has the direct knowledge of an object and intends to communicate correctly the result of his experience and is competent to express whatever he intends to communicate is known as *āpta*. The status of being an *āpta* is equally applicable to a sage, an Āryan or even a non-Āryan.[9]

8. *Nyāyasūtra* 1.1.7 tr. Ganganath Jha, *The Nyāya Sūtras of Gautama with Bhāṣya of Vātsyāyana and Vārttika of Uddyotakāra* vol. I, New Delhi: Motilal Banarsidass, 1984, p. 199.

9. *āptaḥ khalu sākṣātkṛtadharma yathādṛṣṭasyarthasyacikhya-payisiya prayukta upadeśa.* "That person is called *āpta* reliable, who possesses the direct and right knowledge of things, who is moved by desire to make known (to others) the thing as he knows it, and who is fully capable of speaking of it." *Ṛṣyaryamlechhanam samanam lakṣaṇam.*"This definition applies to sages as well as to Āryas and Mlecchas". — *Nyāya-bhāṣya* 1.1.7, tr. Ganganath Jha, pp. 199-200.

Thus the statement of a person prompted to speak from direct knowledge of something serves as a valid means of cognition to others. The elucidation in the *Bhāṣya* thus presumes three things:

1. The person transmitting knowledge linguistically must have first-hand knowledge of the things that he is speaking about.
2. He/she must have the desire to communicate this knowledge impartially to others without any distortion.
3. To be able to communicate whatever he/she intends to communicate.

As long as there is no reason to suspect the credibility of the speaker/writer, he/she can conventionally be taken not only to be one who expresses his/her knowledge of certain state of affairs but also to be one who communicates facts, giving us an opportunity to know such state of affairs as he/she has known it. This knowledge need not be sacred knowledge. In so far as the *sūtra* and its exposition in *Bhāṣya* are concerned, they exhibit no theological bias, though it does not summarily dismisses the possibility of such an interpretation. From this it follows that all linguistic expressions are not of the same value; only such linguistic expressions that emanate from a trustworthy source be recognized as a legitimate means of valid knowledge. The value of linguistic expressions in disseminating valuable experiences of the few among the masses in the form of information is sufficiently clear from the *sūtra* on *śabda-pramāṇa*. It is through language that the knowledge acquired by an expert in a particular field comes to be shared by others and becomes a public property. In fact, a vast mass of knowledge an individual acquires during one's own life is from information gathered from trustworthy linguistic expressions. Thus, we can comfortably place on record reports by reliable persons or media signified as one of the domains of the scope of verbal testimony.

Immediately after defining *śabda,* Gautama in his *Nyāya-Sūtras* 1.1.8 states, that (*śabda*) is of two kinds, according to its object being verifiable and non-verifiable by experience. While explaining the terms *dṛṣṭārtha* and *adṛṣṭārtha,* Vātsyāyana in his *Bhāṣya* states that of which the object is verifiable here is *dṛṣṭārtha* and that of which the object is verifiable hereafter, is *adṛṣṭārtha.*[10] According to this interpretation the distinction between *dṛṣṭārtha* and *adṛṣṭārtha* is to be considered as two varieties of *dṛṣṭa* — real and potential — which is very difficult to accept. If the expression *āptopadeśaḥ* is interpreted as suggested by Vātsyāyana, then there could be no verbal testimony in respect of imperceptible objects. In fact, the word *adṛṣṭārtha* in the *sūtra* signifies the absolute non-verifiable and not the possible verifiable as the *Bhāṣya* seems to suggest. If we take this as the true import of the expression *adṛṣṭārtha,* then all that fails to fall within the purview of *dṛṣṭārtha-śabda* will be considered as *adṛṣṭārtha-śabda* and in such a case testimony of transcendental objects forms the other domain of verbal testimony as these cannot be known by any other method other than verbal testimony. Uddyotakara in his *Vārttika* interprets it in a different way. For him the distinction between *dṛṣṭārtha-śabda* and *adṛṣṭārtha-śabda* should not be viewed in absolute sense. Indeed while heaven, hell, etc. are not perceptible to ordinary beings, they are very much objects of perception to seers or God. Ordinary individuals like us cannot be authoritative with regard to transcendental objects.[11]

10. *sa dvividho dṛṣṭādṛṣṭārthatvāt yasya dṛṣyaterthaḥ sa dṛṣṭārthaḥ yasyamutra pratīyate sodṛṣṭārthaḥ* — *Nyāya-Bhāṣya,* 1.1.8.

11. *yadi sākṣāṭkaraṇam arthasyaptiḥ svargapūrvadevatadin na kascit paśyatiti tatpratipādako vyavahāro na syāt tasmāt āptaścasavupadeśasca iti yuktam n āptasyopadeśa iti. naiśa dosaḥ, na brumosmadādinam pratyakṣa, svargadāya iti api tu yasya pratyakṣahtasyopadeśa iti.* — *Nyāya-Vārttika* 1.1.7.

Transcendental objects are known to ordinary individuals through scriptures which are by their very nature authoritative as they are from a trustworthy source, namely either seers or God. With regard to verifiability, our mundane objects of perception, etc. are verifiable here (*dr̥ṣṭārtha*), while transcendental objects such as rebirth, etc. are objects of inference.[12] Thus, the interpretation of the *Bhāṣya* and *Vārttika* brings in transcendental objects within the purview of verbal testimony and this forms the second domain of verbal testimony.

The Mīmāṁsakas lay immense emphasis on testimony because *dharma* which is their principal object of enquiry can be known only from scriptures. They define verbal testimony as the knowledge which flows from the comprehension of the meanings of the words, and is about an object which is not accessible to any other means of cognizing.[13] Significantly this definition dispenses with the reliable person as the validating source of verbal testimony and holds firmly that value judgements such as duty, etc. cannot be accessible through any method other than scriptural testimony.[14] This forms the third domain of testimony.

Thus the domains of verbal testimony may be identified as follows:

i. The knowledge of the objects of ordinary experience from the reports of reliable persons/source.

ii. The knowledge of transcendental objects from reliable persons/source.

---

12. *pratyakṣa upalabdhorthaḥ dr̥ṣṭārthaḥ, anumanata upalabdhorthaḥ adr̥ṣṭārthaḥ. Nyāya-Vārttika* 1.1.7.

13. *śāstram śabdavijñānadsannikr̥ṣṭe'rthe vijñānam. — Śābarabhāṣya on Mīmāṁsāsūtra* 1.1.5, p. 44

14. For Bhāṭṭa school of Pūrva-Mīmāṁsā apart from Vedic sentences, sentences uttered by truthful persons (*āpta*) can also be regarded as testimony. But Prābhākara school of Pūrva-Mīmāṁsā maintains that Vedic sentences alone can be treated as testimony.

iii. The knowledge of value judgements

What is important here is that a linguistic expression conveying some information must have an authentic source and as such free from defects.

Testimony and Knowledge Transmission

In any standard case of communicative use of language, knowledge transmission takes place. The following is the standard process outlined in Nyāya philosophy in knowledge transmission. A speaker primarily intends to communicate certain information which he himself had acquired through one of the legitimate methods of knowledge or issue certain instruction. This in turn makes him produce suitable utterance. The sentence he utters consists of a finite number of words properly ordered. If the words were different or differently ordered then it would be at best a different sentence, which would perhaps be unable to serve the intended purpose. On the other hand, if the words lacked the essential syntactic and semantic properties, then also they would have failed to serve the intended purpose for the simple reason that it cannot be regarded as a meaningful sentence. Thus whenever a competent speaker of a language uses language with some definite purpose or with the purpose of communicating a definite piece of information he/she utters appropriate words in an appropriate order and in unbroken or uninterrupted sequence. The causal efficacy of a particular intention is exhausted once a particular sentence appropriate for the occasion is produced. The Naiyāyikas hold that if the hearer knows the language the speaker is speaking, if he had earlier learnt the meanings of all the words occurring in the sentence such that from this word that would follow, then the process in question has three moments in it. In the first place, the hearer hears the words which the speaker utters. Thus the hearer has the auditory perception of the words of a sentence. In the second place, he recalls what he had already learnt in the past, the meanings of the words spoken by the speaker. Finally, the hearer has the knowledge of the expression uttered by the speaker. Thus through the words, the same piece of information as it were gets transmitted from the authentic knowledgeable speaker to the inquisitive hearer who has mastery over the language in question. We express our thoughts and share our feelings with others through language. The grasping of the content of a linguistic utterance on the part of the hearer who has the mastery over that language is instantaneous. In fact, it is the principal medium in knowledge acquisition. Since the scope of our personal experience is limited, it is the testimony that serves as a major source of knowledge.

Critique of Testimony

There is considerable difference of opinion among different schools of Indian philosophy with regard to the status of testimony as a source of valid knowledge. There are three major views:

i. Testimony can never be the legitimate source of knowledge.

ii. Knowledge from testimony can be reduced to either perception or inference.

iii. Testimony gives us valid knowledge and is an independent and irreducible source of knowledge.

There is a view in classical Indian tradition, particularly the view of the materialists that testimony can never be the legitimate source of valid knowledge because it often fails to give us a firm belief that this or that is the case. There is a strong belief that language can never give us the knowledge of the actual state of affairs. What it expresses and what exists, there is always a mismatch. Perception does not arise in the absence of the object it represents, while language can give us an idea of certain state of affairs that does not exist at all. For instance, the sentence, "The ox has delivered a calf" generates cognition in the listener by the meaning connected with it even though it is not connected with reality. It is true that perception at times fails to present the object as it is, but that is due to some defect or the other in the causal factors that give rise to it. On the other hand, when a false awareness arises from a sentence, the sentence which is the cause of the awareness is by and large without any defect. Even when one knows by the other methods of knowledge that what is expressed in sentence does not exist at all, still one can cognize it. Thus language always does not connect with the reality. However, one may wish to locate a defect in the speaker when it does not connect to the reality, i.e. the speaker is not competent or reliable, etc. But the speaker is merely the utterer of the words; it is still the words themselves that produce the cognition in question. In the light of this the critic may argue that language can never produce cognition with a firm belief in the existence of what it expresses, since there is always a doubt about its credibility. There is no justification for believing in anything and everything simply on the basis of linguistic expressions of a person. If it were so, we shall have to believe in many absurd and fictitious objects about which anyone may tell us.

This whole thesis of the critic rests on complete misunderstanding of the structure of testimony as a method of knowledge. What we need to understand is that we are to draw a distinction between knowledge of what is meant and knowledge by testimony. The sentence, "The ox has delivered a calf", fails to fulfil certain conditions of a meaningful expression[15] such as *yogyatā* in order to generate a valid verbal

15. *āsattiyogyatākāṅkṣātātparyajñāmisyate karaṇam*. "The knowledge of contiguity, consistency, expectancy and intention is the cause of (verbal comprehension)" — *Bhāṣāparicheda,* tr. Madhavananda, Calcutta: Advaita Ashrama, 1977. p. 166.

cognition even though we can very well understand the meaning of the sentence. True, understanding the meaning of a sentence is a necessary condition but not the sufficient condition to generate valid verbal cognition. What we are concerned here with is the firm belief in the existence of the state of affairs expressed by the sentence which alone can lead to valid verbal cognition. We are to draw a distinction between understanding a linguistic expression as something quite different from knowing that what it says is the case. On hearing the sentence, "The ox has delivered a calf", we do understand what it means but that does not translate into knowledge as the content of this expression does not correspond with the reality. However, a well-formed sentence that fulfils the formal conditions such as *ākāṅkṣā, yogyatā* and *āsatti* from a trustworthy source will definitely generate knowledge in the hearer who has the ability in understanding the *tātparya* or the intention of the expression.[16]

In fact, it is through linguistic expressions either in the form of news reports, books and journals or through conversation we constantly acquire new ideas and information. We cannot summarily dismiss testimony as a source of knowledge. Our perception has a limited scope. We have the ability to perceive the objects that are here and now, that is what is present to the senses. For the knowledge of what is beyond this limit we are to depend on, in principle either on inference from our past experience or on testimony. However the role of inference is also limited though it has much wider

16. An expression in order to be meaningful must fulfil the four formal conditions. The four conditions are: *ākāṅkṣā* or mutual expectancy that one word rouses for another; *yogyatā* or the semantic compatibility that the words of a sentence must be related meaningfully to yield a coherent sentence meaning; *āsatti* or the proximity that words of a sentence must be in juxtaposition and *tātparya* or awareness of the intention with which the sentence is uttered.

scope than perception. We can infer only what has been previously observed to be invariably connected to something that is being perceived. Since the domain of our personal experience is limited, it is the linguistic expressions of reliable source which serve as our main source of knowledge. Thus when I am told by someone at an unknown place that "this water is drinkable", it generates cognition in me that it can quench my thirst. This cognition is obviously not by perception or by inference or by any other method other than testimony. It is not a case of perceptual experience because even though the fact that this is water is perceptual, the fact that this water is drinkable is not a case of perception as I did not experience it. It cannot be a case of memory either, for there is no previous experience corresponding to my present experience of *this* water. I cannot now remember that this water is drinkable because I have not experienced this water to be such in the past. It is not a case of inference as the invariable relation which is crucial for inference is not possible here. What we are doing here is placing trust on the expert's or native user's explicit contextual linguistic expressions. Thus, when an astronomer tells me that "Neptune is eleven times larger than earth", I immediately come to know what it means. How is this possible? It is surely by testimony. We do not have to establish the separate trustworthiness of the source; it is sufficient if no evidence to the contrary is available. To put it in other words, we do not have to have reasons for believing it, only an absence of reasons for not to believe it. Sometimes cognition from testimony may lead to certain absurd consequences. That does not mean that we are to summarily dismiss testimony as a source of knowledge. If failure of our sensory inputs in generating perceptual cognition does not go against the validity of perception as a legitimate method of knowledge why should we refuse to assign the title "knowledge" to testimonial cognition on the ground that all understandable linguistic expressions could be generally false unless otherwise proved? Indeed it is the other way that all linguistic expressions, by and large, are correct unless otherwise proved and there is no reason to doubt the credibility of testimonial knowledge and we can place it on par with knowledge acquired through perception or inference. In fact the canvas of testimony is far larger than perception and inference. It is captivating to note that Gaṅgeśa in his *Tattvacintāmaṇi* questions the attitude of the Buddhists in denying testimony as a legitimate source of knowledge in an interesting way. He questions, if the Buddhists do not admit testimony as a source of knowledge, how do they derive the validity of their own expression, namely "linguistic expression is not a means of valid knowledge". Testimony being denied as a legitimate method of knowledge, their own linguistic expression cannot be proved as valid and hence they cannot use this linguistic expression as an argument against testimony. However, if their linguistic expression is admitted as valid, they will have to give up their contention that "linguistic expression is not a means of valid knowledge".[17] Thus it is simply unfair to doubt the credibility of testimonial knowledge. The question whether testimony is at all an admissible avenue of knowledge deserves an affirmative answer. However it remains to be seen whether knowledge from testimony is an independent and irreducible method of knowledge.

Irreducibility Thesis of Testimony as a Method of Knowledge

Gaṅgeśa in his work *Tattvacintāmaṇi* refers to the Buddhist view of reducing testimony to a kind of perception, namely mental perception.[18] However, it is not possible to have a direct

17. *Tattvacintāmaṇi* of Gaṅgeśopādhyāya quoted in S. Vidyabhusana, *History of Indian Logic,* New Delhi: Motilal Banarsidass, p. 445.

18. Ibid.

contact of the sense organ with its object from a linguistic expression. When a sentence such as "the cat is on the wall", is uttered, the listener would be able to get an immediate awareness of the fact of the existence of cat on the wall. This could be held because on hearing an expression there arises in the listener the knowledge of the recollection of the things signified by the expression which the listener must have actually perceived individually, the kind of objects talked about by the speaker on some previous occasion, and this recollection serves to establish a contact with the object and we actually perceive the thing through our mind. Thus the function of testimony being performed by mental perception there is no need to accept testimony as distinct method of knowing. Against this view Gaṅgeśa argues,

> Just as in the perception of a colour our eye is the means or instrument, its union with the colour is the intercourse, and the perceptual knowledge is the result, so in verbal testimony, speech is the means or instrument, the recollection of things signified by it is the intercourse and the verbal knowledge is the result. Speech therefore serves the same purpose in verbal testimony as the sense organs do in perception.[19]

Thus he argues that testimony cannot be reduced to perception. However, perception of a linguistic utterance is the starting point of a testimonial knowledge. But that does not lead to a situation of perceiving the objects about which information is orally transmitted. It is simple common sense that what we learn from a sentence is not immediately felt as something that we have seen but as something that we have heard and known. It is not something that is felt to be presentational or direct in nature which is an essential

19. *Tattvacintāmaṇi* of Gaṅgeśopādhyāya quoted in S. Vidyabhusana, *History of Indian Logic*, New Delhi: Motilal Banarsidass, p. 446.

prerequisite to consider it as perceptual. In fact, perceiving mere words can never give us perceptual knowledge of the reported fact. It is just a word-generated awareness of the meant relation between the word and its referent. In fact, perception may be defined as an immediate knowledge not brought out by any antecedent knowledge. On the other hand, testimony is the mediate knowledge which is brought out through the knowledge of the words. A person can understand the meaning of a sentence, "There is a bird's nest on the tree", without ever having seen a nest on a tree. As he hears or reads each word in the sentence he remembers its meaning which has already been known to him. This knowledge is gained for the first time through a linguistic utterance from a reliable source and not through perception. Testimony is not identical with auditory or visual perception though they play a significant role in the act of hearing or reading a sentence which facilitates in understanding the meaning expressed by it.

It has been held by a few thinkers in classical Indian tradition that knowledge from testimony is a form of inference. There are two main reasons to support this thesis:

i. The truth or falsity of a linguistic utterance is inferred from the character of the person who utters.

ii. The relation between a linguistic utterance and a certain state of affairs is similar to sign and signified as in the case of inference.

This whole exercise rests on complete misunderstanding of the essentials of the structure of inference and testimony. To determine whether testimony is an independent source of knowledge or not, we are only to see if it gives us a true knowledge of facts, and not how its truth is known or tested by us. The meaning of a linguistic utterance is grasped immediately on hearing the utterance for which no knowledge of its trustworthy character is necessary. In fact, we can very well know the meaning of a linguistic utterance even before we enquire into its source or even when the source of it is not known. It is only later on we take recourse to inference when the validity of the said linguistic utterance is doubted. Thus a distinction has to be made between apprehending the meaning of a linguistic utterance and apprehending its truth. If giving reasons for a belief count as an inference then we could even call perceptual knowledge as inferential. Naiyāyikas are very clear when they argue that validity of any cognition, be it perceptual or inferential or testimonial, rests both in respect of origin and ascertainment not by the same conditions that bring about that cognition but by some other conditions than those conditions that bring about that cognition. Thus they subscribe to the position of *parataḥprāmāṇyavāda*.[20]

Further the view that the relation between a linguistic utterance and a certain state of affairs associated with it, is similar to sign and signified as in the case of inference, does not hold water. In classical Indian tradition the Buddhists and the Vaiśeṣikas share a common platform in reducing knowledge from testimony to inference. At the surface level it seems as if there is no difference between the knowledge generated from inference and the knowledge generated from testimony. Both inferential knowledge and testimonial knowledge have no immediate object to reveal. Both depend on some relation to enlighten an object they indicate. Both of them indicate only general feature of an object. Further if the relation in question is not known, both fail to bring about their intended result. However on closer scrutiny we notice that there is an unmistakable difference between these two methods of knowledge.

20. *pramāṇatvam na svatogrāhyam, saṁsayanupapatiḥ*. 136. Viswanatha Nyāya-Pañcānana, *Bhāṣā-pariccheda with Siddānta-Mukātavalī*, tr. Swami Madhavananda, Calcutta: Advaita Ashrama, 1977, pp. 221-22.

Inference is a process wherein the perception of mark (*hetu*) in the subject (*pakṣa*) of inference leading to the cognition of the inferred (*sādhya*) in the subject (*pakṣa*) because of the invariable relation (*vyāpti*) that exists between the mark (*hetu*) and the marked (*sādhya*). In the classic example, the perception of smoke (*hetu*) on the hill (*pakṣa*) leads us to infer fire (*sādhya*) on the hill (*pakṣa*) because of the invariable relation between smoke (*hetu*) and fire (*sādhya*). This invariable relation is crucial for inferential knowledge. It is primarily this knowledge of invariable relation that is responsible for the cognition of the inferred through the perception of the mark. One who is not aware of this invariable relation, will fail to have the cognition of the inferred object though the mark is perceived. The supporters of reducibility thesis argue that knowledge from testimony is governed by the same fundamental law of reasoning. Let us recall a statement from *Padārthadharma-saṁgraḥ:*

> Verbal testimony is a form of inference in so far as it functions in the same way. In order to comprehend the meaning of a word one must recall a previously learned connection between word and meaning, just as one must remember the previously established connection between the mark and the marked in order to receive a cognition of the latter from the former.[21]

For instance the perception of a linguistic expression such as "there is a bird's nest on the tree" generates cognition in the hearer of the state of affairs connected with the utterance though these states of affairs are not perceived by the hearer. Thus to know these words is to know the objects denoted by

---

21. *śabdādinām api anumanentarabhāvaḥ samānvidhitvāt, yathā prasiddasamayasyāsaṅdighliṅgadarśanaprasiddhānusmaraṇābhayam atindriye'rthe bhavay anumānam evam śabdādbhyopiti. Praśastapādabhāṣya with the Nyāyakandalī*, ed. Durgadhara Jha, Varanasi: Sampurnanand Sanskrit Visvavidyalaya, 1977, p. 512.

them just as to know smoke is, for one who knows the universal relation between smoke and fire, to know the existence of fire in relation to it. Hence knowledge from testimony is not an independent source of knowledge. It can be reduced to inference. Śrīdhara echoes the same idea in his *Nyāyakandalī*. He remarks,

> Just as the inferential process functions through invariable concomitance, so do words also. . . . As a matter of fact, we know that a word never denotes anything until it is known for certain that it never fails in its concomitance with such denotation; and when it does denote an object after unfailing concomitance has been ascertained, it becomes an inferential sign pure and simple.[22]

This reducibility thesis suffers from serious objections. In fact, this whole exercise of reducing testimony to inferences turns and twists the very nature of testimony so as to make it conformable to the inferential process. In fact, inference depends on the knowledge of invariable concomitance (*vyāpti*) which is a natural relation of coexistence between two entities. We do not find such a natural relation between word and meaning. There is a natural relation between smoke and fire, so that the perception of smoke leads to the cognition of fire. But there is no such natural relation between the word "smoke" and the smoke itself. The relation between word and its meaning is conventional and it is quite different from that of the sign and the signified of an inference. Words mean certain objects, but do not coexist with them. A word may mean different things in different contexts. For instance, one may say, "I see no light" while listening to a sermon, or while entering a room at night. The same utterance has two different meanings on two different occasions. Similarly, the classic

22. *Praśastapādabhāṣya with the Nyāyakandalī*, ed. Durgadhara Jha, Varanasi: Sampurnanand Sanskrit Visvavidyalaya, 1977, p. 512.

example of the word *saindhava* which means both horse and salt is to be understood depending upon the context in which the word is used in a sentence. It may be argued that the knowledge of the meaning of a word may not be inferential but the knowledge of the meaning of a sentence is inferential. This view also does not hold water because when a novel sentence is uttered, which one may never have heard before, nor ever had an apprehension of the relation between the words in the sentence, there still is the possibility of apprehending the meaning of the sentence independent of inferential mechanism. However there has to be a recognition of the meanings associated with each word. But the interrelations between the words and their meanings are not of their having been invariably related in the particular sequence and the way they should be related in a particular sentence. Our experience suggests that those who are familiar with words and their meanings can easily make out the meaning of a sentence which they have never heard before, the moment they read or listen to it. But an inference necessarily presupposes the knowledge of the relation between the reason and the consequence which is not the case with testimony. Hence, we cannot reduce testimony to inference.

Gaṅgeśa's criticism on this reducibility thesis is quite interesting.[23] Suppose when some utters the sentence, "Mr. *X* has a mango garden", we can as well understand what it means as members of the same language community and for all practical purposes we believe that we know this fact through testimony. However the Vaiśeṣika tries to show that this is a case of inferential knowledge whose structure may be as follows:

---

23. *Tattvacintāmaṇi*, Book IV, *śabdaprāmāṇyavāda*. Quoted in Vidyabushana, *History of Indian Logic*, Delhi: Motilal Banarsidass, 1971, pp. 446-47.

Thesis (*pratijñā*)	: The sentence, "Mr. *X* has a mango garden" has meaning.
Reason (*hetu*)	: Because it possesses expectancy, competency, proximity and an intention.
Example (*dṛṣṭānta*)	: Any sentence that has expectancy, competency, proximity and intention has meaning, for example, "Bring the cow"
Application (*upānaya*)	: So this sentence is
Conclusion (*nigamana*)	: Therefore the sentence "Mr. *X* has a mango garden" has Meaning

Gaṅgeśa argues that the above inference does not involve the knowledge of actual things as in the case of testimony, but the knowledge of things recollected, i.e. the knowledge of knowledge of the things. Knowledge from testimony is not like in inferential knowledge, dependent on the knowledge of invariable concomitance between the words of speech and knowledge of the mutual connection of things signified by them, but results immediately from the words as soon as expectancy, competency, proximity and intention existing among them have been known. Further introspective evidence (*anuvyavasāya*) suggests that testimony is different from inference. When we know something from testimony, we say "I knew this from what he has said" and not "I inferred this from his utterance".

Further there is an unmistakable difference between inference and testimony. In inference we become aware that a certain locus, the subject of inference, so to say, *pakṣa* possesses certain property, namely the inferred object, so to say, *sādhya* on the basis of the perception of the mark, so to say, *hetu* in *pakṣa*. Let us recall the classic example of an inferential process where the perception of smoke (*hetu*) on hill (*pakṣa*) leading to the cognition of fire (*sādhya*) on the hill (*pakṣa*). If testimony is a kind of inference, then what would be the *pakṣa* or subject of this inference? Certainly the word is not the subject as it is the reason (*hetu*). Obviously the meaning is not *pakṣa*. Because in an inference the *pakṣa* is something that is already given wherein the *sādhya* is established through the presence of *hetu* in it. We seek to prove the hill we see is on fire because it is smoking. In this case the hill is the *pakṣa* which is already known to us along with smoke which is the *hetu*. The meaning of a word is what we become aware of through the word; it is not already given. So it cannot be the *pakṣa* or subject of inference. Can we say the speaker or the writer is the *pakṣa*. This is impossible because, the relation between sign (*hetu*) and signified (*sādhya*) of an inference is such that if the sign is present in a particular locus, the signified also must be present in it. That is where there is *hetu* there the *sādhya* exists. Assuming there is such a relation between words and objects denoted by them, we should expect to find the objects in the book in which the words occur or in the person who uttered those words, which is not the case. There is no such natural relation of coexistence between words and their meanings which would serve as the basis for inferential reasoning and hence testimony cannot be reduced to inference. The structure of an inference and testimony are different.

While defending the autonomy of testimony as an independent and irreducible source of knowledge, Nārāyaṇa in his work *Mānameyodaya* refers to the criticism of Prābhākaras on human testimony. Acçording to Prābhākaras scriptural sentences alone are valid. The utterances of human beings simply lead to the inference of the intention of the speaker and do not convey by themselves the meaning of a sentence. They argue

> The capacity for significance of words, although established at the time of learning, becomes blunt in the words of men

> with their profusion of inconstancies, of account doubt about those inconstancies. And there, so long as it is not inferred that the sentence has been stated by the speaker only after knowing such and such a meaning, doubt regarding its being otherwise does not vanish; and so, one ignores the sentence.... So without inferring the cognition in the speaker, there cannot be the determination of the purport and for this reason too, one ignores the sentence. Therefore the cognition in the speaker is first to be inferred. Then when one hears the sentence . . . one infers: "These words have been used only after cognizing the relation to these meanings, because they are words uttered by a reliable man, like the words, 'Bring the cow'".[24]

Thus an utterance serves as an inferential sign (*hetu*), of an intention (*vivakṣa*) of the speaker who utters it. From that intention of the speaker and from the fact that the speaker is trustworthy (*āpta*), one is able to infer in turn that the speaker possesses knowledge of the state of affairs of which he speaks. Finally, from this one is able to infer the existence of the state of affairs that speaker knows. Thus from an utterance one does not directly infer its meaning, rather being aware of the state of the mind of the speaker who employs it, and from that, given the speaker is reliable, infers its meaning. Buddhists by and large follow the same line of thinking. Followers of irreducibility thesis of testimony argue that when words are uttered, we become immediately aware of certain things are state of affairs without taking into consideration the state of mind, so to say, the intention of the speaker who utters them. Words convey their meanings prior to our apprehending the intention or knowledge of the one who speaks them, and in fact serve as the means by which we recognize what he or she has in mind. Indeed, only because the words a person speaks

24. *Mānameyodaya of Nārāyaṇa, pramāṇāni,* 13-15, tr. C. Kunhan Raja and S.S. Suryanarayana Sastri, Madras: The Adyar Library and Research Centre, 1975, pp. 105-08.

indicate a certain state of affairs, we are able to know that he is thinking of that state of affairs. Further if we can be aware of what a linguistic expression means without being aware of the intention of the source, then we can be aware of what it means without being aware of the credibility of the source. A sentence generates the same meaning when uttered by an untrustworthy person and also by a trustworthy person. In fact Naiyāyikas being committed to their theory of *parataḥprāmāṇyavāda* suggest that the truth of cognition, be it perceptual or inferential or testimonial, is to be known extrinsically, that is, after the cognition has arisen by means of confirmation by other cognition. Thus, the Naiyāyikas would appear to have the notion of an initial belief aroused by linguistic utterance itself that brings in certain state of affairs of the world, followed by a categorical awareness that one's belief is indeed true.

Epistemic Autonomy of Testimony

One of the explicitly used criteria in deciding the irreducible character of a particular method of knowledge (*pramāṇa*) in classical Indian traditon is "the uniqueness of the object (*prameya*) of a *pramāṇa*". We can say a *pramāṇa* is independent of and is irreducible to another *pramāṇa* if and only if there is at least one object that is known exclusively by that *pramāṇa* alone and not by any other *pramāṇa.* However this does not mean that the different *pramāṇa*s cannot be aimed at a common object. As a matter of fact many of objects are common to all *pramāṇa*s. But in the case of each *pramāṇa* there is at least one object which is the exclusive domain of that *pramāṇa* alone. Vātsyāyana in his *Nyāya-Bhāṣya* explicitly mentions this criteria:

> Have the *pramāṇa*s their objectives in common? Or is the scope of the *pramāṇa*s restricted within mutually exclusive limits?
>
> As a matter of fact, we find both ways of functioning among

> *pramāṇas*. For instance . . . in the case of fire, we find that — (a) when a trustworthy person says "there is fire at such and such a place", we have the cognition of fire by means of word; (b) drawing nearer to the place, if we happen to see smoke issuing, we infer from this the existence of fire; (c) actually getting at the place, we directly see the fire. On the other hand, in the case of certain things we find that one thing is amenable to only one particular *pramāṇa*; as for example, that "the Agnihotra should be performed by one desiring heaven", we can know only by the words of the Veda; the ordinary man of the world does not know of any indicative features of Heaven; nor is he able to perceive it directly; similarly when we hear the sound of thunder, from this, we infer the source of the sound; and in regard to this we have no perception, nor any verbal cognition; lastly of our own hand we have a direct perception and no inference or word is operative in this case.[25]

However there is a difference of opinion among different schools of Indian philosophy regarding whether a particular object is really a unique object corresponding to a given *pramāṇa.* At least in the case of testimony the criteria, "uniqueness of object" is explicitly applied to settle the question of its autonomy. The knowledge of scriptural statements and moral judgements are known exclusively through testimony. The authority of scriptural statements is not vitiated by its having been composed by a human being, who could not possibly have known the transcendental matters of which it speaks. It is valid because the initial sense of truth with which it is received is never contradicted. As long as it is not contradicted there is no harm in accepting it as valid. Further in so far as communicating moral rules there is no method other than testimony. Thus scriptural statements and moral rules are known to us exclusively through testimony.

There is a popular view that knowledge from testimony

---

25. *Nyāya-Bhāṣya* 1.1.3, tr. Ganganath Jha, pp. 101-02.

is considered to be less reliable than perception and inference. Because in the acquisition of verbal knowledge we have to depend primarily on the reliability of the speaker, his honesty and competence and these criteria to a large extent are uncertain. Contrary to our common belief, one should note that neither perception nor inference should be in any way better than verbal knowledge as far as reliability or certainty is concerned. For reliability of the sense organs, adequacy of the evidence of reason and trustworthiness of the speaker — all sail in the same boat. As far as Nyāya is concerned, none of them would be infallible. Each of them can, on occasion, mislead and generate error. But nevertheless, knowledge is generated from all these sources.

13

Minding Language and Languaging Reality

Manidipa Sanyal

idamandham tamaḥ kṛtsnam jāyeta bhubanatrayam |
yadi śabdāhvayam jyotirāsaṁsāram na dīpyate | |

— *Daṇḍī*

THE struggle for existence — the coping with and taming of the reality around us — has been the constant history of human life. In this process, the most lively phenomenon happens to be the relation between human beings — more specifically the human minds — and the outer world. History says that the debate between rationalism and empiricism as theories of the origin of knowledge ruled the world of philosophical thinking for two and a half century. It is in the early twentieth century that there occurred the "linguistic turn". This shift gave birth to many currents in "post-modern" thoughts. The relevance of language is better understood as playing the role of a mediator between human mind and reality. This relation may be strategically viewed in the following way. On the one hand, there is evidence in favour of linguistic representation mediating the duo. On the other hand, there is equally strong evidence for denying the role of a mediator. In this paper, the first section will focus upon the said denial of the role of linguistic representation. The second section deals with the necessity of language. The third section attempts to shed light on the mind – language – reality trio from the Western standpoint, while a survey of the same issue from Indian perspective will be the subject matter of the concluding section.

I

cakṣur-vijñānasamaṅgī nīlam vijānāti na tu nīlam iti
Diṅnāga, *Pramāṇasamuccaya*, ch 1,
Vṛtti under verse 4b

The chief argument in favour of redundancy of language in understanding the world around us is found in the philosophy of Buddhism. P.F. Strawson in his essay "Imagination and Perception"[1] has referred to the technical use of the word "imagination" by philosophers like Hume and Kant. In the context of philosophy of perception similar variation in meaning of the Sanskrit term *kalpanā* from common sense to technical one has been shown by B.K. Matilal.[2] The variation has been made with the help of the word *vikalpa* as is found in the distinction between *nirvikalpaka pratyakṣa* (perception without imagination) and *sa-vikalpaka pratyakṣa* (perception with imagination).[3]

The concept of *nirvikalpaka pratyakṣa* has been entertained by founders of many schools of Indian philosophy such as Nyāya, Bauddha, Mīmāṁsakas and Vedāntins. In all the interpretations, language plays a very important role. All of them agree that there is no need for the intervention of language at this stage of perception. There is a basic difference between the Naiyāyikas and the Buddhists about the nature of verbal reports. While the Naiyāyikas welcome the

1. P.F., Strawson, "Imagination and Perception", in *Freedom and Resentment and Other Essays*, London: Methuen, 1974, pp. 45-65.
2. B.K. Matilal, *Perception*, Oxford: Clarendon Press, 1986, pp. 312-13.
3. Matilal prefers literal translation as less misleading and the same may be referred to as "conception-free" and conception-loaded perception".

acceptability of verbal reports until found guilty, the Bauddhas mark them as always wrong. This has important impact on their theory of *nirvikalpaka* cognition. *Vikalpa* in its ordinary meaning stands for acceptable alternative constructs. Nyāya used *vikalpa* as thought-construct which may be a true construction that represents the structure of reality truly. But the Buddhists consider *vikalpa* as completely fictional as different from 'pure given' that provides the required foundation of knowledge.

For the Buddhists all cognitions are self-cognizable (*svasamvedya*). They are immediate, perceptual in nature.Their position with respect to perceptual cognition can be presented in the following way:

(a) Perceptual cognition is supposed to be produced by a sense organ and its appropriate object.

(b) Perceptual cognition can be only indeterminate or non-qualificative.

(c) Non-qualificative perception has qualityless, essenceless pure particulars (*svalakṣaṇa*) as its object.

They advance certain arguments against the possibility of qualificative perception:[4]

A. Neither the names are located in the objects nor they constitute the nature of the objects bearing the names. So perceptual cognition cannot reveal the object as associated with a name.

B. There may be a counter-argument of this form: a relation between words and objects can be established through some convention. Hence, a person, conversant

---

4. I am very much indebted to my teacher, Prof. Prabal Kumar Sen for using some of his unpublished writings on the Buddhists' arguments against perceptions associated with predicative construction.

with this relation, may recall the word by law of association. So sense organs, with the assistance of memory may produce another perceptual cognition where object perceived may feature as associated with the word that stands for it.

Admitting the possibility of such habitual association, the Buddhists will say that entities normally associated with words like "cow" are only common properties (*anugatadharma*) or universals (*sāmānya*). But such common properties are only imaginary constructions (*vikalpas*) which are devoid of causal efficacy. Besides, the proponents of the counter-arguments would agree that in such a cognition, awareness of words/names is due to memory, and not due to sense organs. So memory disrupts the functioning of sense organs and consequently the qualificative cognition resulting from memory cannot be perceptual, because it is not produced by the functioning of sense organs (as perception is).

C. In a qualificative cognition something features as qualificand, something as qualifier, and something as a relation which is to be grasped as a whole. All these, including linguistic convention, are not the works of sense organs. Hence it is not perception.

D. Many of the objects revealed in qualificative cognition are not ultimately real. Universals, supposed to be located in the individuals or substances, supposed to be the substrata of qualities, movements and universals are not real. Things which are not real lack causal efficacy and hence cannot be objects of perceptual consciousness. So qualificative cognitions are not perceptual in nature.

The main reason for discouraging language as imparting

any knowledge is, as B.K. Matilal observes,[5] a pantheistic theme that "language distorts reality by proliferating false concepts and images". The Buddhist model views language as a "colossal maze"[6] that conceals reality instead of expressing it. We have first of all concept-free awareness after which we conceptualize it through words and finally, in search of the meaning of words, we objectify concepts. According to them, this is wrong, because no such objectification is possible since it is a borrowed objectivity. There is no external object. Language therefore is used for convenience which spoils its own game. According to Nāgārjuna, concepts are relative, and hence, always dependent upon some other concepts (cause/effect, part/whole, left/right and such others). Dependence is indicative of essencelessness or unreality. Hence ultimate reality cannot be approached through concepts. Candrakīrti also means by *prapañca* only "speech" or language. The Buddhists actually approve only direct awareness or pure sense perception as probable means of having knowledge. We may have a parallel theory in Hume's conception of sensory experience, though unlike the Buddhists, Hume claims that there is an unbridgeable gap between the sensory evidence and the conclusion we reach in our ordinary perceptual judgement.

Buddhists like Diṅnāga and Dharmakīrti opine that no cases of "seeing as" should be properly called "seeing". The reason is, "seeing as" is a product of conceptual construction, but "seeing" truly should be free from any conceptual construction. There is no possibility of any verbal report of "seeing" truly.[7]

5. Matilal, op. cit., p. 309.
6. Matilal, op. cit., p. 310.
7. F.I. Dretske, in the conception of "non-epistemic seeing", speaks of a "pure" seeing free from all inferential, interactive discussion on associational elements. It finds an echo in Buddhism. F.I. Dretske, *Seeing and Knowing,* London: Kegan Paul, 1969.

Kumārila of the Mīmāṁsā school argues against the Buddhists to establish both immediate and mediate perception. According to him, each object has two aspects — a generality and a particularity. The immediate perception is that where we know the object as a whole by first sense-object contact, which includes both particular and general aspect. Mediate perception brings the object as qualified by a universal/attribute/action. Early Nyāya writers like Vācaspati Miśra accepted this view of Kumārila, but Navya-Nyāya school represented by Gaṅgeśa modified this version. Kumārila's idea of non-unitary pure sensation is not entertained by the Buddhists. There was a long controversy between the Naiyāyikas and the Buddhists, the strongest attack was made by Udayana against privatizing perception. He showed that the Buddhists' attempt to untie the lock between language and perception was in vain. B.K. Matilal has beautifully shown a strong defence of Udayana's position found in Kant's view that no object can be thought without understanding.[8]

The Buddhists claim that whenever conceptual awareness tries to transcend itself to reach the non-existent object, it commits a mistake. Udayana however agrees with the Buddhists to say that the truth of the conceptual awareness is in the revelation of object as it is, hence the truth of the awareness is identical with itself. But it remains a separate question whether that object really exists or not. Hence the conception-loaded awareness can be true and at the same time is a product of the working of senses and object just as conception-free awareness is.

The more elaborate and realistic conception of immediate

8. I. Kant, *The Critique of Pure Reason*, B75 A51, tr. Norman Kemp Smith, London: Macmillan, 1958, p. 93: "Without sensibility no object would be given to us, without understanding no object would be thought. Thoughts without content are empty, intuitions without concepts are blind.".

perception is found in the Nyāya school. According to the Naiyāyikas, perception, in the sense of perception of a concrete object, is not an abruptly happening event. The occurrence of the event of pure sense perception was readily accepted by the Naiyāyikas, but the question was raised regarding the actual awareness or awarenesshood of the pre-linguistic pre-conceptual, pre-construction perception. This doubt becomes strong because of Bhartṛhari's idea that each cognitive event is undeniably connected internally with concept or word.[9] It is the reason why perception without conception, i.e. mute perception is considered useless. The Buddhists are vocal in declaring the necessary self-awareness of this conception-free awareness. This is however questionable, because memory cannot be a proof for it. The reason is, memory of something cannot take place unless that thing is identified with a name. Nyāya, in its elaborate discussion of *savikalpaka* and *nirvikalpaka* perception, distinctly holds that there is no "knowledge" of such *nirvikalpaka* perception. They accept only word-impregnated nature of our awareness under the influence of powerful arguments given by Bhartṛhari. Unlike the older Naiyāyikas, the Navya-Naiyāyikas (Udayana, Gaṅgeśa and others) accept inference as a proof for such a pre-linguistic perception. The common justification of pre-linguistic perception found in the Naiyāyikas is that, in order to have an awareness of x as qualified by y, we need a prior conception of y.

This issue of conception-free perception in the background of Nyāya realism has not been overlooked by thinkers all around the world. Arindam Chakrabarti finds it important for Nyāya theory itself to do away with non-predicative

9. What Bhartṛhari called *Śabdabhāvanā*, *Vākyapadīya*, Bhartṛhari, ch. I, verses 123-24 and the *vṛtti* therein; quoted by B.K. Matilal, *Perception*, p. 342.

perception for seven reasons.[10] Chakrabarti's attack on what he calls "myth of the unqualified given"[11] is actually against the traditional Nyāya doctrine of indeterminate perception. As he claims, his objections are different from the objections against Gaṅgeśa's theory of pre-predicative perception made by the great Madhva logician Vyāsatīrtha in his book *Tarkatāṇḍava*. The main point of dissatisfaction with the pre-linguistic perception is this. Under normal circumstances people become aware of a mental state immediately after undergoing it. But pre-linguistic perception is nameless, featureless, qualityless and relationless. Hence, we can never be aware of them at all. Eventually he finds an endorsing note in J.N. Mohanty's view.[12] Mohanty discards any epistemic status to a pre-cognitive state which is pre-predicative (pre-prdicative awareness does not have basic epistemic feature of having an object-directedness or *viṣayitā*).

In answer to Chakrabarti's objections Stephen H. Phillips tried to defend Naiyāyika's position with reference to Gaṅgeśa's seminal work *Tattvacintāmaṇi* where one full chapter is devoted to the analysis of *nirvikalpaka pratyakṣa*.[13] Though there is no apperceptive evidence for such *pratyakṣa*, still it may be shown by an inference as the first step of a two-step argument. A perceptual cognition, viz. "a cat" is generated by a knowledge of the qualifier. The qualifier is to be available in

---

10. Arindam Chakrabarti, "Against Immaculate Perception: Seven Reasons for Eliminating Nirvikalpaka Perception from Nyaya", *Philosophy East and West,* v. 50, no. 1, January, 2000.
11. Chakrabarti, op. cit., p. 3.
12. J.N. Mohanty, *Reason and Tradition in Indian Thought : An Essay on the Nature of Indian Philosophical Thinking,* Oxford: Clarendon Press, 1972, p. 174.
13. Stephen H. Phillips, "There's Nothing Wrong with Raw Perception: A Response to Chakrabarti's Attack on Nyaya's 'Nirvikalpaka Pratyaksha'", *Philosophy East and West,* vol. 51, no. 1, January 2001, pp. 104-13.

its perception in the raw which is a causal factor of the later perception. It is just a "plain unadorned entity". Intricate arguments have been advanced for defending the case of indeterminate perception which is "transitional between inconscient workings of sensory instruments and conscious processes".[14]

Now, one thing is clear from the name that it is perception because it is a case of cognition, though it is at the same time indeterminate, i.e. different from other cognitions. Both reason and intuition provoke us to accept indeterminate perception as a valid one. One point to note here is this. B.K. Matilal observes that Gaṅgeśa's argument implies that there is no need to postulate a conception-free percepual awareness occurring indispensably at the beginning of a conception-loaded perception. But it should not be viewed as anti-Naiyāyika attitude. Matilal comments that Gaṅgeśa attempted to show that there is no logical necessity of having such a prior awareness, though in some cases, such an unstructured perception is "logically" and "causally" necessary to precede judgemental perception.[15]

It sounds rational to follow Matilal's line of argument here. We may term the pre-linguistic perception as "dim-awareness" or "subliminal awareness", but the possibility of an *unconceptualized* awareness-event points to the fact that it cannot be totally *unconceptualizable*, "since it is, though very modestly, conception-loaded".[16] What follows and what is relevant in the present discussion is that it is language which is somehow indispensable at least to talk about the possibility

14. Stephen H. Phillips, "There's Nothing Wrong with Raw Perception: A Response to Chakrabarti's Attack on Nyaya's 'Nirvikalpaka Pratyaksha'", *Philosophy East and West*, vol. 51, no. 1, January 2001, p. 112.
15. Matilal, *Perception*, p. 348.
16. Ibid., p. 354.

of indeterminate perception, because "conceptualizable" implies linguistically apprehensible. With this linguistic turn, it seems easier to switch over to the discussion of relevancy and indispensability of language mediating between mind and reality.

II

> If thought can corrupt language, then language can corrupt thought.
> — George Orwell

Can only a conversing creature contemplate? Is thinking essentially linked with expressing the thought through language? We can have an answer that reflects the common opinion found in the starting note of B. K. Matilal's book *The Word and the World*:

> It may be that we understand the world in terms of language, and this would imply that our thinking about the world necessarily involves the use of language.[17]

That our approach to the world is made in terms of language is evident from our ordinary experiences and behaviour.

It is also commonly held that human language is relevant because thinking is almost impossible without language. It is because communicability of thought is indispensable for human existence since nobody struggles at all about the issue of unexpressed thought. So, by analysing language we can analyse thought. The most interesting point is that language is the means which is used both to conceal and to express our thoughts. That there can be no separation between thought and language is a view which is shared by Wittgenstein and Quine. According to Wittgenstein, thinking is not a mental process , rather "the language is itself the vehicle of thought".[18]

17. Matilal, *The Word and the World*, Oxford: Oxford University Press, 1990, p. 3.
18. L. Wittgenstein, *Philosophical Investigations*, tr. G.E.M. Anscombe, London: Basil Blackwell, 1958, 329, p. 107.

It is a sharp comparison, as Dummett interprets, between the sense of a word and the power of a chess piece.[19] Sense "belongs" to word just as power "belongs" to a chess piece. To know a chess piece is to know its power, to know a word is to know its sense.

An anti-mentalist like Quine does not go to the extreme of saying that silent thinking is inaudible speaking (the muscular theory of meditation), but he emphasizes that when we speak of meanings meant or beliefs expressed, we are actually speaking of linguistic capacities and other behavioural patterns. Such a reductionist standpoint generalizes the view that thinking need not be some process distinct from the use of words. Such a nothing-buttery theory of thought and language is easily eclipsed by its opposite that language is the "contingent manifestation of thought".[20] It is to be noted that this view is not in that sharp opposition to Quine's theory as it is to the Nyāya theory of *nirvikalpaka jñāna*. The reason is, while the former at least admits the role of language as necessary, The Nyāya theory denies the role of language in the context of *nirvikalpaka*. We shall come to the Nyāya theory in the next section. Presently we concentrate upon the ontological priority of thought over language.

The popular view about the possibility of tongueless thoughts (mute meditations) says that the necessity of language lies in our wish to reach others in thought. This view gets support from the fact that thoughts may come in images, colours, daydreams as well as in words. Dummett expressed this view in the following way:

> We need language, on this view, only because we happen

19. M. Dummett, *Frege: Philosophy of Language*, London: Duckworth, 1973, p. 156.
20. Colin McGinn, *The Character of Mind*, Oxford: Oxford University Press, 1982, p. 59.

to lack the faculty of telepathy, that is, of the direct transmission of thoughts.[21]

Thus it is heuristically necessary to attend to language in investigating its content. This theory gets primary support from Socrates when he says that thinking is speaking to oneself. This theory, upholding private and independent status of thought, is termed as "inner saying" theory by Colin McGinn. According to him, to judge inwardly that snow is white is to be internally related to a sentence endowed with that meaning. In order to understand this theory it is better to draw an analogy between one language and another language or between a vernacular and a Morse-code on the one hand, and thought and language on the other.

According to this theory, thoughts are private entities, which are gradually translated into publicly audible language. When the hearer hears the sounds, she translates them back (or decodes them) into her own thoughts, and gets the message of the speaker. Hence, every language-user is an interpreter either of her own utterance or of the utterance of anyone else as expressions of thought. There are three presuppositions of this thesis:

(a) We can have thoughts independently of and prior to having or using language.

(b) Command over one's mother tongue is basically like one's command over a second language.

(c) Thoughts are private entities.

Against this thesis, Davidson points out a pertinent issue that inability for finding an appropriate word for a thought is no proof for the independent status of thought. On the contrary, such an inability indicates absence of clear idea of the content of thought. Frege vehemently opposes the third

21. M. Dummett, *Frege: Philosophy of Language*, p. 156.

presupposition by referring to the communicability of thought. The same thought is grasped by the speaker and the hearer of a particular sentence. Michael Dummett speaks of the vulnerability of both, the first and the second presupposition.

Against the first presupposition, it may be said that manifestability is the essential mark of grasping a thought. And it is better to mark this manifestation as linguistic manifestation so that the same behavioural mark could not have to represent different alternative concepts. Dummett gives an apt example of a dog's awareness of being chased by one dog and being chased by several dogs. It is hard to ascribe the awareness of "one" and "many" to the dog, though there is sharp distinction in its observed behaviour in these two cases, i.e. in the latter, tension is increased. A similar example is found in Wittgenstein. It is hard to believe that a dog expects his master to come home "next week" though its expectation of the master's "coming home" is comparatively easy to understand.

Dummett's attack on the second presupposition is much more important. Understanding a translational account of a second language involves two steps: (1) knowledge of the corresponding words in the new language is essential, (2) we must understand the basic language. This second step is important, because the ability to translate does not presuppose the ability to understand. If we know simply one-to-one correspondence between two sets of symbols, we can translate one by the other without knowing the meaning of either. In fact, this is the reason why a translational account is not a circular one, because in translating a second language from our mother tongue we have a prior knowledge of our mother tongue. Now such a translational account involving these two steps is hardly applicable in thought-language relation. The problem is, it is difficult to explain our command over the language of thought itself, without involving vicious regress. Hence, grasping a concept necessarily amounts to using linguistic capacity.

Failure of this theory enables us to consider the view that language is an essential vehicle of thought. The strong interconnection between language and thought may therefore be accepted, though we have to maintain a guard against the tendency to get rid of psychological terms altogether in any account of thinking.

III

> In sharing a language, in whatever sense this is required for communication, we share a picture of the world that must, in its large features, be true. — Donald Davidson

From what has been said so far, it may be granted that thought and language are essentially related to each other. There remains however, the obligation of relating language with reality. This relation is inevitably interwoven by the concept of meaning. Historical development shows that meaning has been identified with information or content in the modern terminology of natural science. In the initial stage of modern philosophy (classical empiricism and rationalism) the problem of the theory of meaning has been considered as an epistemological problem because of its connection with knowledge and justification, etc. With the development of modern logic (Frege, Russell, early Wittgenstein) the problem is viewed as more relating with ontology than to epistemology. (Frege's anti-psychologism and Wittgenstein's form of logical atomism.) There is another perspective where meaning is thought of as formal constructs. Here both epistemology and ontology become less important, while semantical interpretation gains prominence.

Coming to the present discussion, we may get a way out of the puzzle from language being either independent of thought or being essentially tied with the latter, as in Davidson's theory. It has the merit of connecting not only thought with language, but also language with reality, and thereby providing an easy way of relating mind with reality. Thoughts are not private entities, since otherwise a single thought cannot be accessible to all persons. A thought is considered to be the common meaning conveyed to every user of an expression. Hence the only capacity for grasping a thought is the capacity for learning to use and interpret the sentences used to express it. In the language of Davidson, "a creature cannot have thoughts unless it is an interpreter of the speech of another".[22] The argument behind this remark is this. The purposeful explanations behind observable human conducts depend essentially on the distinctions between thoughts of different articulate structures. These distinctions depend essentially on the expressive power of language. To cite Davidson's example, a dog which knows that its master is home, cannot know that Mr. Smith is home, though Mr. Smith is its master. Ability to use the words "Mr. Smith" is essential for having knowledge of Mr. Smith, and it is possible only for a member of speech community. This leads us ultimately to the revolutionary discovery by Davidson that thought is defined by a system of beliefs.

There is a vast controversy regarding non-verbal behaviour as evidence of thought or belief, but the issue there is focused on whether linguistic capacity is necessary for possessing thoughts or beliefs. As there is no question of immediately linking up reality with language and thereby with thought, the discussion of that point may be postponed in the present context.

Davidson's thesis reminds us of the Tarskian context of defining truth. According to Tarski, the necessary and sufficient cause of the truth of a sentence "*S* is *P*" is the real event of S being *P*. It reminds us that in general we attribute truth to a sentence, though there is no point in denying the

22. D. Davidson, "Thought and Talk", *Mind and Language*, p. 9.

fact that there is a distinction between mentioning a sentence and the sentence itself. And attribution of truth is relevant only in the context of the former. It has an exact echo in Davidson's argument against the code-theory of language. According to Davidson, through language, we reach not only our thought about reality, but also reality itself. The reason thereof is that in sharing a language, we share a picture of the world which is true. Hence metaphysics is better pursued through the study of the general structure of our language.[23]

This tie between thought and language on the one hand, and language and reality on the other, as conceived by the Western thinkers has been repeatedly and quite reasonably challenged by the problems of lapse of connection and miscommunication. It has, however, a good reason behind itself. Topics like mind, language and reality normally constitute subject matters of three different branches of study, viz. psychology, epistemology and metaphysics. These three subjects are too distinct from each other to be tied up by a single cord. At the same time, there is great truth in Davidson's thesis which provokes us to search for a genuine link between these three. And truly, yet surprisingly, such an attempt is found in the thought of a great Indian scholar Bhartṛhari.

IV

vāgrūpatā cedutkrāmedavabodhasya śāśvatī |
na prakāśaḥ prakāśeta sā hi pratyavamar śinī | |
— *Vākyapadīya*, 1.124

The notion of meaning — whether separate and distinct from

---

23. ". . . in making manifest the large features of our language, we must manifest the large features of reality. One way of pursuing metaphysics is therefore to study the general structure of our language." D. Davidson, "The Method of Truth in Metaphysics", *Inquiries into Truth and Interpretation*, Oxford: Clarendon Press, 1984.

that of language or not — appears to be the right approach to enter the philosophical thought of Bhartṛhari. Meaning is to be understood in the context of linguistic process. Being a grammarian of the Pāṇinian school he dared to discard the behaviouristic approach to the study of language. In his major work *Of Sentences and Words* consisting of three different volumes, he developed one unique theory of speech or language. For Bhartṛhari, as B.K. Matilal has discussed,[24] language is a type of activity in human beings. All thinking as well as all awareness are intertwined with "languaging". In order to understand this we have to be familiar with his *sphoṭa-nāda* conception in language. In a language, one has to distinguish between (1) utterance of a sentence and (2) the event of communication or conveying meaning to the hearer. As B.K. Matilal observes, "language, in this view, is a dispositional property of humans".[25] For Bhartṛhari, the "expressive word" is the sentence. This word is made explicit through a stretch of sounds uttered by the speaker. This stretch of sounds is received by the hearer who understands the sentence. *Nāda* is the stretch of sounds produced by the vocal organ. While hearing the stretch of sounds, the hearer also grasps the unity and the "sequenceless whole" (of sounds) which we call a sentence. In this way he has grasped the "linguistic unit" which is called *sphoṭa*. These two are distinguishable but not separable.

This theory is opposed to the theory of the Naiyāyikas who advocate distinction between language and what it signifies/conveys, i.e. its meaning. These meanings may either be external objects/facts, or thoughts. This duality of word and its meaning leads to the idea of pure meaning that remains

24. Matilal, *Mind, Language and Reality* (The Collected Essays of Bimal Krishna Matilal, ed. Jonardon Ganeri), Oxford: Oxford University Press, 2002, p. 334.

25. Ibid., p. 335.

constant. According to Bhartṛhari this duality may seem useful to explain mechanism of language, but "it is more a fiction than reality".[26] If we can dispense with the notion of pure or virgin thought, we can better explain the inseparableness of meaning or thought and language or its "verbal cloak". It is this inseparableness that prevents us to have exact translation of a language. And it is in this context that he differs from Quine, though both of them speak of untranslatability of language. While for Quine, it is a limitation of language, Bhartṛhari considers this untranslatability to be implied by essential properties of natural language. The essential property is that language is inseparable from what it conveys. It is the *sphoṭa* concept of Bhartṛhari where *sphoṭa* is explained, not as the meaning of a sentence, but the sentence itself at an implicit level of language. The transition from the implicit level to the explicit level may be explained in the following way.

According to Bhartṛhari, language initially resides in humans as speech potentials (*śabdabīja*). At that inarticulate stage *śabda* or "sound stretch" lies undifferentiated from *sphoṭa* or the "linguistic unit" (a sentence). This is called the pure non-verbal or unverbalized or *paśyantī* stage. After that there is the intermediate stage called *madhyamā*. It is like a stage of unexpressed verbal thought with the implication that if anyone conceives it, she would have a thought with exactly the same verbal content. In the imagery of Bhartṛhari, thought at this stage is what vibrates through language and language is what illuminates thought. This is the stage where thought and language are inseparable from each other, though they are distinguishable. The next is the stage of audible utterance that makes explicit the sentence and its meaning as distinct in the so-called sense. The last stage is *vaikharī*. This separation of

26. Matilal, *Mind, Language and Reality* (The Collected Essays of Bimal Krishna Matilal, ed. Jonardon Ganeri), Oxford: Oxford University Press, 2002, pp. 336-37.

śabda and *sphoṭa* is to be understood as temporary, though necessary for understanding the communicability of language. The hearer hears the sound stretch, i.e. *śabda* from which his own *sphoṭa* is aroused and he superimposes his *sphoṭa* upon (i.e. identifies it with) what he hears. It is this necessarily false identification which is instrumental to successful communication. According to Bhartṛhari, the duality of language and meaning is an illusion because people falsely identify *śabda* as language and require a separate meaning to be connected with it.

The ordinary relational view of meaning speaks of the conventional connection between linguistic expression and their so-called meanings. This connection depends highly on the customs of the speech community. The older grammarians and the Mīmāṁsakas consider the relation between the word and its meaning as eternally fixed or natural/uncreated. Bhartṛhari's *sphoṭa* theory views the relation between a sentence and its meaning as a causal relation. It is the transformation of a prior stage into a latter stage, and these stages, the prior appearing as the cause and the latter as the effect, are virtually not different from each other. Hence the sentence and its meaning are related by identity.

We have to remember that language is to be understood as essentially linked with the use of language. And from this perspective there has been a revolutionary change in the concept of meaning. In this context we get the concept of information exchange. This perspective of semantics as coming close to pragmatics has been prominently found in Stalnaker's works. It has a great influence on the theory of meaning, because the concepts of reference and truth, which are treated as essential concepts of ontology get different treatment here. There is the theory of direct reference, i.e. realistic notion of meaning. But this notion in possible-world-semantics is challenged by situation semantics where meaning is related with its naturalistic determinants. There has been found neuro-cognitive research which is an attempt to bridge the gap between the two. The result is, this rules out the possibility of a fixed concept of meaning.

While the Western philosophical thoughts are struggling much to bridge the gap in search of a better explanation, we may think of Bhartṛhari's attempt as a better solution even if pragmatics is brought into the picture.

14

Metaphoric Understanding and Mental Representations of Moral Concepts

Smita Sirker

Findings and theories in cognitive science have been increasingly important in many areas of philosophy, especially philosophy of mind, epistemology, and philosophy of language. The time is ripe to examine its potential applications to moral theory as well.

. . . the cognitive materials deployed by moral judges or evaluators in thinking about moral matters. The language of morals includes words like *good, right, fair, honest, just,* and so forth. What do users of these words mentally associate with them? How are the concepts of fairness and justice represented? Further, are such representations wholly determined by the cultural environment, or are there perhaps innate structures that dispose cognizers toward certain conceptions of fairness or just distribution, toward reactions of distaste or opprobrium *vis-à-vis* certain types of action, and so forth?

— Alvin I. Goldman, "Ethics and Cognitive Science" in *Readings in Philosophy and Cognitive Science*, p. 623

Something crucial is missing in this widely held conception of morality. What is missing is any recognition of the fundamental role of imagination in our moral reasoning. We human beings are imaginative creatures, from our most

> mundane, automatic acts of perception all the way up to our most abstract conceptualization and reasoning. Consequently, our moral understanding depends in large measure on various structures of imagination, such as images, image schemas, metaphors, narratives and so forth. Moral reasoning is thus basically an imaginative activity, because it uses imaginatively structured concepts and requires imagination to discern what is morally relevant in situations, to understand emphatically how others experience things, and to envision the full range of possibilities open to us in particular case.
>
> Moral principles without moral imagination become trivial, impossible to apply, and even a hindrance to morally constructive action."
>
> — Mark Johnson, in *Moral Imagination: Implications of Cognitive Science for Ethics,* Preface, pp. ix-x

PEOPLE lead lives in many different ways and participate in various different forms of life. There are no two individuals who lead their lives in exactly the same way. Furthermore, the beliefs that we have and share are not always similar. However, in many contexts, we do engage and participate in moral discourse where our goal is to share and exchange moral opinions, ideas and even moral judgements. We deliberate on moral issues and raise questions regarding morality of various actions, like whether adultery is morally bad, whether abortion is morally permissible, whether injustice is a moral violation, etc. Such engagements must at least presuppose that we share a common, minimum repertoire of moral concepts; moral values; moral beliefs; moral ideas; and in some sense a basic moral understanding. If one is not able to comprehend moral concepts, moral values, moral prescriptions, one cannot meaningfully participate in any moral discourse. There are many interesting dimensions of research on morality. There are many questions which are very important to address in order to understand how we actually participate in a moral life:

- How do we actually understand diverse moral issues and what kind of moral reasoning is reflected in our day-to-day moral decisions?
- What do we really understand of moral terms/concepts, like *good, bad, right, wrong, free will*, etc.?
- How are moral terms represented in human minds when we try to understand them?
- Are all moral representations of the same kind, i.e. are our understandings of the same moral issue alike?
- What does our ordinary moral discourse disclose about our moral understanding and moral reasoning?
- Why do different cultures have folklores and narratives as a medium to dissipate moral values amongst its members? Do these folklores reveal any similarity or dissimilarity amongst cultures in how they understand morality?

Our initiation to morality mostly begins with several moral prescriptions, which are of the form of "moral oughts". The question is how are the learnt moral prescriptions (especially "moral oughts"); moral concepts; moral values; moral evaluations applied in different life situations at different stages of life? How do children follow and understand "moral oughts"? An instance of a "moral ought" like, "You ought never to lie" ("You should not lie") is often justified by the following:

(i) lying is (universally) bad; and

(ii) lying often leads people into trouble (may be in terms of causing harm to oneself or others).

However, a child may "lie" just to avoid trouble (which defies the first justification, i.e. lying is not always bad) and "lying" seems the sensible way out (which defies the second justification, because lying is keeping the child out of trouble). We cannot presume that a child understands "moral oughts" like "lying as a universally bad action/lying as an immoral action" unless we are able to decipher how such universal moral norms (moral prohibitions/moral sanctions/moral prescriptions) are cognized by children. Even for adults, acceptance of "Lying as a morally bad act" is often hard to justify in all situations. Following Kant's theory, establishing the superiority of reason over emotion in every moral situation, advocating Supreme Principle of Morality and Duty, and rationalizing and translating subjective maxims into moral maxims by the function of Reason are difficult to validate in all moral contexts. I may extend my own moral reasoning to justify Kant's position but it is not without reflecting — why Kant's position seems counter-intuitive and difficult to defend at times. This is perhaps one of the primary reasons, why understanding the *nature of our moral understanding* is so intriguing. Any attempt to understand the nature of morality cannot be achieved without the understanding of the *nature of mental representation of moral terms and moral issues* (like, moral values, moral principles, moral decisions, etc). Over the past few decades, cognitive scientists have been involved in understanding the psychology of moral understanding and moral reasoning. They are engaged in unveiling the actual nature of both moral understanding and mental representation of moral concepts. Goldman's above quote highlights the contributions that cognitive science can make in the study of moral philosophy.

Inquiry into the nature of human cognition is one of the defining tasks of cognitive science. One of the fundamental assumptions of cognitive psychology and cognitive science is that any explanation of human behaviour makes reference not just to inputs and outputs but also to the information that is encoded in the brain. An attempt to give an information processing account of a particular cognitive act would require a description of how inputs, outputs and information are internally encoded. These encodings are often considered to depend on mental representation scheme or language. Fodor (1975)[1] calls this language as the *language of thought*, though different mental faculties may use different representational schemes. In study of ethics and moral reasoning, Goldman points out that there is an importance in addressing issues like "What do users of these words (as in language of morals) mentally associate with them?", "How are the concepts of fairness and justice represented?", and "Whether such representations are wholly determined by the cultural environment, or are there perhaps innate structures that dispose cognizers toward certain conceptions of fairness or just distribution, toward reactions of distaste or opprobrium *vis-à-vis* certain types of action, and so forth?" Thus, study of mental representations of moral terms and situations is important to understand the nature of cognition of morality and moral concepts.

The theory of moral imagination, proposed by Mark Johnson, dissects our ordinary moral discourse and brings out a crucial component of moral deliberations. Moral discourse is an important source of knowing how we understand moral terms and rationalize or justify our moral decisions and actions. Moral reasoning, like any other forms of reasoning, calls for an understanding of its pattern because it shows how moral terms are interpreted and applied by the reasoner in their moral argumentations and how moral contexts are interpreted and acted upon. Johnson (1993)[2] shows how analysis of moral language brings out the usage of metaphors. According to Johnson, our moral reasoning is an act of

1. Fodor A. Jerry, *The Language of Thought*, New York: Thomas Y Crowell, 1975.
2. M. Johnson, *Moral Imagination: Implications of Cognitive Science for Ethics*, Chicago: The University of Chicago Press, 1993.

constructive imagination that is primarily based on metaphoric concepts at two basic levels:[3]

(i) our most fundamental moral concepts (e.g. will, freedom, law, right, duty, well-being, action) are defined metaphorically, typically by multiple metaphoric mappings for a single concept;

(ii) the way we conceptualize a particular situation will depend on our use of systematic conceptual metaphors that make up the common understanding of members of our culture.

Thus, our moral reasoning about a particular situation is determined by the way we frame and categorize a given situation. How we frame a given situation will depend on what metaphorical concepts we are using.

In this paper, we will discuss only about how ordinary people think about moral attributes and moral issues. Johnson holds that moral psychology should broadly be understood as the *psychology of human moral understanding*, which includes empirical inquiry into the conceptual systems that underlie moral reasoning. He states:

> The psychology of moral understanding can give us profound insights into the origin, nature, and structure of our basic moral concepts and into the ways we reason with those concepts. There is no direct deductive link between such knowledge of our moral concepts and specific moral values (such as rules telling us why Nazism is immoral), and that is why moral psychology is not going to give us an exhaustive set of prescriptions for moral living. However, moral psychology will tell what is involved in making moral judgements.[4]

3. Johnson, 1993, p. 33.
4. M.L. Johnson, "How Moral Psychology Changes Moral Theory", in *Minds and Morals: Essays on Cognitive Science and* →

I

Metaphoric Understanding of Morality

According to Johnson, metaphors play a role in two particular contexts: (a) in our moral understanding; and (b) in our moral discourse which reflects the very nature of metaphorical understanding of moral terms. He argues that the use of metaphors and metaphoric understanding is pervasive in our moral deliberations and metaphoric application is involved in our moral reasoning. Metaphors are instrumental in imagining alternatives for resolving moral conflicts, to criticize our values and institutions.[5] He posits that metaphor is an integral part of our moral discourse and the nature of our moral understanding is also metaphoric. He examines a collection of fundamental moral concepts to show how these concepts are defined by metaphors. These concepts are considered to be systematically related to each other by metaphors and they form hierarchical levels of metaphoric systems. Johnson derives support for his theory from the linguistic evidence of how we ordinarily talk about morality, from the patterns of our moral discourse. He shows that our conventional language of ethical discourse is based on systems of metaphor that define our fundamental moral concepts. Further, he studies the patterns of inference in our moral reasoning that are based on metaphorical concepts.

Johnson holds that there are three primary clusters of metaphors that define our shared conception of morality. The first cluster of metaphors is concerned mainly with the action performed and that involves metaphorical structuring of our notions of action, purpose, law, duties, rights and so forth. The second cluster of metaphors includes those by which we

---

→ *Ethics*, ed. Larry May, Marilyn Freidman and Andy Clark, Cambridge, Massachusetts: MIT Press, 1998, p. 46.

5. Johnson, 1993, p. 33.

decide *what we owe others* and *what others owe us* as a result of our helping and harming each other. The third cluster contains metaphors by which we evaluate *moral character*. The categorization of these three clusters indicates the pervasiveness of metaphor usage in our thought and language. The presence of extended metaphoric systems is a striking feature of our language.

Use of metaphors and analogies in language are generally observed by most of us. When one says, *life is a journey*; it is an analogy drawn between two concepts, life and journey, that may be related in many different ways. The analogy "Mind is a computer" is widely used in philosophy of mind and cognitive science to bring out the analogical insight that the functioning of the mind can be understood in terms of computation. The computational theory of mind draws its theoretical insight from this analogy. In a typical use of analogy, an analogical mapping is drawn between a familiar situation (the *base* or *source*) and a less familiar situation (the *target*). Through the analogical mapping between the source and the target, the familiar situation suggests new inferences to be drawn about the less familiar situation. Analogical reasoning helps in drawing associations between two situations, cases, etc. and thereby deriving new information for the newer situation from the known one.

Metaphorical understanding would typically involve a kind of analogical reasoning. In order to understand what metaphorical understanding of moral terms is, we have to understand how metaphorical mappings are done. A conceptual metaphor is a mapping of conceptual structure from a source domain (which is typically some aspect of our concrete bodily experience) onto a more abstract or a less highly articulated target domain. The conceptual metaphors in our conceptual system have conceptual structures and these conceptual structures serve as the basis of our inference that we draw from the metaphor. This is similar to analogical reasoning, including how we draw upon relevant analogies and how we associate one analogue (the source or base) with another analogue (the target). The structure of the conceptual metaphor in the source domain determines our understanding of the target domain. The knowledge that we have in the source domain partly constructs our knowledge in the target domain. Let us consider the Moral Accounting Metaphor as explained by Johnson. The Moral Accounting Metaphor is primarily concerned with what we owe people to increase their well-being and what they, in turn, owe to us. According to Johnson, we understand our moral interactions metaphorically akin to a kind of transaction, more specifically, economic transaction. Conceptual mapping occurs between the source domain consisting of concepts of economic transaction and the target domain consisting notions of moral interaction. The conceptual structure of the concepts in the target domain is mapped onto the target domain. And how we understand moral interactions depend on the conceptual structure and our understanding of the concepts in the source domain. Let us follow the structure of the Moral Accounting Metaphor given by Johnson:

Source Domain **Commodity Transaction**		**Target Domain** **Moral Interaction**
Objects, commodities	⟶	Deeds (actions), states
Utility or value of objects	⟶	Moral worth of actions
Wealth	⟶	Well-being
Accumulation of goods	⟶	Increase in well-being
Causing increase in goods	⟶	Moral = causing increase in well-being
Causing decrease in goods	⟶	Immoral = causing increase in well-being

Giving/taking money	⟶	Performing moral/ immoral deeds
Account of transactions	⟶	Moral account
Balance of account	⟶	Moral balance of deeds
Debt	⟶	Moral debt = owing something good to another
Credit	⟶	Moral credit = others owe you something good
Fair exchange/payment	⟶	Justice

Johnson holds that this conceptual mapping between commodity transaction (the source) and moral interaction (the target) "provides us a conceptual basis for a large number of inferences that we draw in evaluating moral conduct".[6] Conceptions about certain features of a commodity transaction are drawn upon to understand certain aspects of moral interaction. In a particular context, we draw upon the basic knowledge of the source domain (economic transactions) to make moral inferences about the situation in the target domain of moral interactions. For example, justice can be understood as a "fair exchange in a transaction" which implies absence of cheating or exploitation between the parties involved. According to Johnson, our knowledge about *wealth* helps us to generate inferences about situations about *morality* via the Well-Being is Wealth Metaphor. For instance, "wealth" is understood as:

- something which can be earned by hardwork or can be acquired by inheritance
- an instrument that fulfils the needs and desires of someone and may contribute towards the enhancement of the quality of life

6. Johnson, 1993, p. 33.

- something when fairly distributed amongst people of the society/community/world gives fairness

Given the Moral Accounting Metaphor, we understand moral well-being as wealth, according to the following mapping:

Financial Domain		**Moral Domain**
Wealth	⟶	Well-being
Accumulation of goods	⟶	Increase in well-being
Profitable = causing increase in wealth	⟶	Moral = causing increase in well-being
Unprofitable = causing decrease in wealth	⟶	Immoral = causing decrease in well-being

Within the Moral Accounting Metaphor, the Well-Being is Wealth Metaphor gives rise to definite inferences about our moral obligations (i.e. we reason on the basis of the metaphor). Given the conceptual mapping from the source domain to the target domain and on the basis of our knowledge of the source domain, we subsequently develop a corresponding knowledge in the target domain and draw the appropriate inferences. Just as in the context of wealth, moral well-being can also be understood in different ways. As pointed by Johnson, one may consider moral well-being as something that can be earned by one's good actions. Some may consider moral well-being as something which can accumulate or even diminish. In the moral domain, moral actions would increase moral well-being whereas immoral actions would decrease moral well-being. Our ordinary moral exchange reflects some of the suggested metaphoric understanding, like, "She has had an undeservedly *rich* life"; "I have had a *wealth* of happiness in my life"; "She *profited* from her relationship with him. It made her become a better person".

Subsequently, the Moral Accounting Metaphor also gives

rise to a pattern of reasoning about our duties, rights and obligations. Based on this metaphor, we reason about what is fair, and our moral discourse reveals this underlying conceptual metaphor system. When one performs good acts then one accrues moral credit. However, when someone inflicts an injury upon me thereby diminishing my well-being, the person is expected to owe me a debt and return/pay back what the person has taken from me. Thus patterns of moral discourse are like "In *return* of your kindness, she gave us nothing but grief", "I *owe* you my life", "You must *pay* for your wrong deeds".

There are at least two levels of conceptual metaphor operative in our moral judgements.[7] The first (higher) level consists of metaphors for our moral interactions generally, such as the Moral Accounting Metaphor, which sets the parameters of our judgements about what is due to us and what we owe others. Metaphors at this level define our moral framework and fundamental moral concepts. However, in order to apply our moral framework to concrete situations, we need a second level of metaphor for conceptualizing the situations. Metaphors at this level help to apply our moral framework in a particular situation.

Johnson argues that our moral reasoning typically depends on the several possible metaphors we use at two basic levels. First, adopting a particular metaphorically defined framework to our interactions; and second, filling that framework with metaphors that connect it to the particular situation. These two levels must fit together to give concrete moral inferences. Johnson says,

> . . . conceptual metaphors are not merely optional ways of talking about morality. There is nothing optional about them at all, and they are not merely matters of words. They are the

7. Johnson, 1998, p. 55.

means by which we define our moral concepts. Although we may not be limited to just one unique metaphor system for a particular concept (for example, we have both WELL-BEING IS WEALTH and WELL-BEING IS HEALTH), neither can we use just any metaphor, especially since this is seldom a matter of conscious choice and the range of metaphors available is relatively small. Most important, the nature and structure of source domain constrains the inferences we make about the aspect of morality that is the target domain. The metaphor, in other words, sets limits on our reasoning about how we ought to behave and how we ought to regard others. If, for instance, we understand moral well-being as WEALTH, we will act and reason quite differently than if we understood it as HEALTH. The logic of the WEALTH metaphor contains notions of fair exchange, quantification, and balance, while the logic of moral HEALTH emphasizes avoidance of immoral people, staying pure, fighting moral disease, and maintaining moral disease.[8]

II

Mental Representation of Moral Concepts

Defining the fundamental moral notions such as justice, goodness, obligation, responsibility, equality, etc. has been a primary concern for many moral philosophers. Stich (1993)[9] points out that we find such exercise of defining moral concepts even in the Platonic dialogues. In the conversations of his dialogues, the speakers engage themselves in seeking proper definitions of moral concepts such as Justice, Good. Cephalus (in Plato's *Republic*) makes a continuing effort to give a proper definition of "what it is being 'just'" and each definition projects

8. Johnson, 1998, pp. 62-63.
9. Stich P. Stephen, "Moral Philosophy and Mental Representation", *The Origin of Values*, eds. M. Hechter, L. Nader & R. Michod, New York: Aldine de Gruyer, 1993, pp. 215-28.

a necessary condition for being "just". This is the typical classical theory of concepts approach, where correct definitions must provide necessary conditions that collectively would be the sufficient conditions for the proper understanding and application of (moral) concepts. Thus, for appropriate application of any moral concept, one must know all the conditions that define that concept and in order to judge whether an act is an act of justice or duty, then the act must satisfy the relevant set of conditions. The classical theory of concepts holds that most concepts have a definitional structure,[10] that is, most concepts encode necessary and sufficient conditions for their application. Consider the concept "bachelor". According to this theory, we can think of this concept as a complex mental representation that specifies necessary and sufficient conditions for something to be a "bachelor". So "bachelor" might be composed of a set of representations such as *is not married*, *is male*, and *is an adult*.

Each of these components specifies a condition that someone must meet in order to be a "bachelor", and anyone

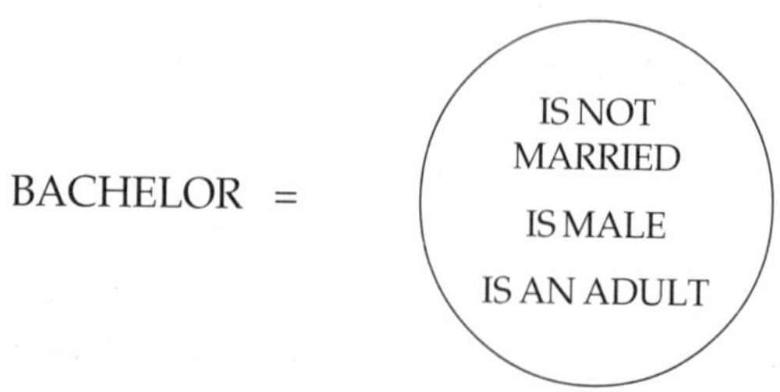

who satisfies all of them counts as a "bachelor". The classical

10. Eric Margolis and Stephen Laurence, "Concepts and Cognitive Science", in *Concepts: Core Readings*, eds. Eric Margolis and Stephen Laurence, Cambridge, Massachusetts: MIT Press, 1999, p. 9.

theory is usually associated with a specific theory of concept acquisition and of categorization.[11] Acquiring a concept would require the knowledge of the properties that are necessary and sufficient for belonging to this category. Categorization consists of checking whether the object (the target) to be categorized possesses the properties that are necessary and sufficient for belonging to this category. This theory posits that concepts or categories are defined by the list of features that an entity must possess in order to be a member of a particular category. For a category membership an entity is either *in* the category or *outside* it, depending on the condition satisfaction. However, one cannot rule out the possibility of borderline cases, and this is where the classical theory falls short. For this theory, since every member must possess all of the features on the list that defines the category, there is nothing in the structure of a category that could differentiate one member from another. They are all equal in the category.

In context of morality, such defining sets of properties would be akin to moral absolutism seeking absolute grounding and moral objectivity by giving a definitive set of moral rules equally binding on all rational beings, unchanging across cultures and throughout histories. If our fundamental moral laws and moral values are absolute then the concepts contained in these values and laws must be well-defined. The concepts must have a definite meaning, so that their application to concrete situations is simply a matter of determining whether the necessary and sufficient conditions defining the concept actually obtain in experience. However, actual moral contexts are not always without areas which are difficult to decide. There are many situations where the agent faces a dilemma — how to resolve and decide on a particular moral problem.

11. Edouard Machery, *Doing without Concepts*, Oxford: Oxford University Press, 2009, p. 78.

Cases of moral indecisions and moral dilemmas show that all moral contexts are not the typical ones, where one can without ambiguity locate the defining conditions and apply the appropriate moral laws. In *atypical* situations moral norms are not always directly applicable. There are many situations where we have to conceptualize the situation in a certain way. How we frame the situations and what perceptual lens we use make all the difference.

The classical theory of concepts is challenged by an alternate theory of concepts — *the prototype theory of concepts*. Eleanor Rosch and her colleagues discovered that there is typically a great deal of internal structure to a category. Not every member is equally central to our understanding of a given category.[12] For a particular category, for example, birds, some members (e.g. parrots, kingfishers) of this category turn out to be more central in our understanding of the category. These cognitive prototypes are important in defining our categories, but they do not exhaust the entire structure of the category, nor do they give us a list of necessary and sufficient conditions for category membership. In the bird category, other members will be less central or prototypical, such as chickens, emus, penguins, ostriches. In most cases there will not be a single defining set of features possessed by every member of the category. Different members can be related by what Wittgenstein calls family resemblance, rather than sharing a set of essential properties.

12. In one series of experiments it was shown that people can reliably order instances falling under a concept when asked how "typical" or "representative" the instances are. An apple will be rated as a more typical fruit than a lemon; a lemon will be rated as more typical than a coconut; and a coconut will be rated as more typical than an olive (Rosch, 1978).

    Eleanor Rosch, "Principles of Categorisation", in *Cognition and Categorisation*, eds. E. Rosch & B. Lloyd, Hillsdale, NJ: Lawrence Erlbaum, 1978, pp. 27-48.

The prototype theory considers concepts as prototypes.[13] A prototype of a class is a body of statistical knowledge about the properties possessed by the members of this class. While the classical theory assumes that when we categorize or when we reason, we have in mind some properties that we take to be individually necessary and jointly sufficient for belonging to the class at hand, the prototype paradigm of concepts assumes that we have in mind some properties that are characterized statistically — like, the properties that are believed to be typically possessed by the members of this class. For the prototype theory, concept application is a matter of satisfying a sufficient number of features where some may be weighted more significantly than others. For instance, if bird is composed of features such as flies, sings, nests in trees, lays eggs, and so on, then for the prototype theory, robins are in the extension of bird because they tend to have all the corresponding properties: robins fly, they lay eggs, etc. However, ostrich is also a bird because even though ostriches don't have all these properties, they have enough of them.[14]

We have seen that classical view of concepts poses restrictions which may prove problematic for defining moral

13. The term "prototype" is used to designate the most typical member of a category (e.g., Rosch and Mervis 1975) and the representation of a category (e.g., Hampton 1979).

14. For this theory, concept acquisition is more or less similar to that of classical theory. One acquires a concept by assembling its features. It is often assumed that the features correspond to sensory properties. The main difference is that on the prototype theory, the features of a concept express statistically prominent properties. So the mechanism of acquisition embodies a statistical procedure. It does not aim to monitor whether various properties always co-occur, but only whether they tend to. Prototype theorists model categorization as a similarity comparison process that involves operations on two representations — one for the target category and one for an instance. On these models, an instance is taken to be a member

→

concepts. It fails to accommodate *atypical* cases, cases where we are mostly faced with moral dilemmas and we need a way out of these difficult situations. Prototype theory of concepts suggests that our categorization includes not just typical but also atypical cases. Atypical cases call for non-normative solutions. Is moral imagination a way out for these cases, as it opens up the possibility of extending beyond the expected, prototypical cases? Johnson says,

> I view moral deliberation as expansive, imaginative inquiry into possibilities for enhancing the quality of our communally shared life. . . . I will urge that moral deliberation is better described as imaginative exploration and transformation of experience, instead of pigeonholing of cases under a set of fixed rules.[15]

Thus, if moral deliberation is an imaginative inquiry then restricting moral thinking with fixed norms along with predetermined sets of conditions may have to be questioned.

According to Johnson, prototypes can supply what we need to make intelligent moral decisions, especially in non-prototypical (atypical) cases. If we want to expand the moral laws to cover non-prototypical cases, we could not do it using rules alone because they have no internal resources for imaginative thinking (imagination). He lists some of the chief ways in which prototypes are important in our moral deliberations.[16] First, prototypes represent experientially basic types of situation. Given the kinds of bodies we have, the nature of our cognition, and the kinds of physical, interpersonal, and cultural interactions we engage in, certain

---

→ of a category just in case the representation of the instance and the representation of the category are judged to be sufficiently similar.

15. Johnson, 1993, p. 80.

16. Ibid., pp. 190-92.

types of situations will take on special importance for us in our attempt to function successfully in our physical and social environments. Second, prototypes are flexible in nature. A child's early experiences of fair and unfair distribution (say, of chocolates) give rise to a sense of justice. But such simple models of distribution alone will not suffice. Our moral deliberations about complex matters of justice will require grand extensions of our primitive models of fair distribution. Our prototype of the *bully, the good samaritan, fair distribution, breach of promise*, etc., must all undergo a series of imaginative extensions that change the meaning of those prototypes over time. Third, a central part of our moral development is the imaginative use of particular prototypes in constructing our lives. Each prototype has a definite structure, yet that structure must undergo gradual imaginative transformation as new situations arise. It thus has the dynamic character, which is what makes possible our moral development and growth.

Not much has yet been discussed about the nature of mental representation of moral concepts. We have so far focused on two theories of concepts which moral theorists presume in their moral theories. One kind of moral theory presupposes mental structures underlying moral judgements that are like definitions (necessary and sufficient conditions). Another kind of moral theory presupposes mental structures underlying moral judgements that are like prototypes. However, the nature of moral concepts does not tell the whole story about the kind of mental representations that we can have about these concepts. An account of mental representation of moral systems cannot be settled a priori. It is an empirical question. And probably venturing into this domain of mental representation of moral concepts and values would need an interdisciplinary approach from philosophers, linguists, anthropologists, etc.

III

A Triadic Representational System

The theory of moral imagination examines the pattern and nature of our moral discourse — which does say something about how we perceive different moral concepts such as an act of balance (fair distribution, justice, and injustice), act of revenge, moral well-being, etc. Johnson's theory provides an insight into how metaphors are useful in understanding and expressing moral concepts. The Moral Accounting Metaphor reflects a pattern of understanding which applies both in matters of economic exchange as well as moral exchange between agents. Analogical reasoning allows this kind of cross-domain conceptual transfer and inference drawing. Conceptual understanding in one domain can be shared in another domain if there is a structural or relational similarity between the two conceptual domains. Hence the mental mapping between the domains is possible, like in cases of economic transaction and moral transaction.

Each culture has its own metaphor database and hence a culture's/society's prevalent set of metaphors does contribute to its understanding of moral values, moral norms and moral contexts. This may be a possible explanation why there are differences regarding moral judgements across cultures. In matters of learning moral values, society and culture-specific metaphors help in disseminating moral education. Folklores of specific cultures play an important role in disseminating the moral values of that culture. Folklores are instrumental in imparting moral education to children. Thus, if one studies the prevalent myths and legends of different cultures one may locate the roots of the kinds of metaphorical usage.

Another area of research, apart from the role of metaphors, is regarding the nature of mental representation of the moral concepts. I think that studying the nature and mechanism of mental representation of moral concepts and values would require treatment from at least three levels:

i. *Internal System Level* — where there is the storage (in a metaphorical sense) of the representations/ understanding of moral concepts and moral values and from where retrieval is done in different situations.

   This is the most challenging level. Our learning of moral values and concepts begins from childhood. When children are first exposed to what I would like to call the "moral culture" of any society — the moral knowledge comes from more than one source. One source is fables, parables, mythological tales where moral knowledge is stored in the form of examples and stories. Another source is from one's own experience — like an unfair distribution of chocolates. The third source is, of course, the precepts that come from the elders of the society, which can be typically in the form of moral laws/moral rules.

   If we look at the first source, one learns in the form of examples and stories which can be stored in the form of exemplars. From the second source, which is one of direct experiences, one can either remember the incident itself if the event has greatly affected the child, or might extract the moral lesson from the experience. Here, the storage can be in the form of prototypes or can even be in the form of rule-extraction. The pattern of storage from the third source can be in the form of moral rules and moral values which can be stored in a rule pattern. The question is, how is knowledge from these different sources represented in the mind/brain; and is there a moral module in the brain which stores the different patterns of learning and which acts as a source of all our moral decisions?

ii. *The Network Level*: When one talks about moral judgements and tries to look into the kind of representation of moral concepts which led to the judgement — what is most important is how a moral situation is understood or interpreted by the individual. At the level of interpretation — it will not suffice to look only into the kinds of moral values that the person has, but a further inquiry is required to study the network of *association and dependence* between the moral knowledge-base and other non-moral beliefs. A belief set is a complex, intertwined hub of many different kinds of beliefs. And hence drawing upon any belief (at any particular context) may not be an outcome of a single selection. If one probes deep one may find links with some other beliefs which acted together in selecting that particular belief in that particular context.

    This kind of inquiry might be able to discover a pattern of dependence. Whether for every moral rule/lesson that is learnt one draws corroboration from his/her belief set? Or whether there is a core of moral beliefs/understandings which is directly applied? This is perhaps also an area which would be addressed when we deal with moral dilemmas. Is there a hierarchy of moral values starting with some core values?

iii. *Application Level*: The application level is concerned with the pattern of moral reasoning — how are moral values and moral principles applied in our moral reasoning? What kinds of justification do we seek — is it a justification from personal experience and personal beliefs or is it a justification from direct moral principles? A lot of current researches are being conducted on the psychology of moral reasoning. I think that these researches will contribute significantly

> in corroborating many of our moral theories. More detailed study of the structure of moral reasoning and moral justification will lend an understanding of the above two levels. Moral agreement is another interesting domain where we can look into how people from different cultures come to agree on a moral issue, burying cultural differences. Perhaps there is a minimal core of moral values which are shared universally. How does this minimal core of moral values get synchronized with specific, varied culture beliefs?

Debates and judgements about moral issues are an integral part of our day-to-day life as we go about making moral judgements and discussing moral issues without reflecting on deeper questions like "why" I made this moral judgement and "why" is there a difference in moral opinions. Is there something called "*the* morally right decision"? There are many questions which are to be simultaneously addressed if one wants to build a holistic theory of morality and moral understanding. Investigations into the nature of moral representation would give us insight into the underlying differences in our moral decisions. The theory of moral imagination gives us a novel perspective of how moral understanding takes place. The novelty lies in the inclusion of the "imaginative" faculty of cognitive agents. Moral decisions and moral understanding in the Kantian model have always been thought to be the function of reason. The possibility of imagination in matters of morality seemed to be too distant and feeble. However, it is interesting to note that Johnson has claimed that even understanding of Kant's five categorical imperatives is metaphorical. In the formulation of "Kingdom of Ends" imperative, one cannot but engage in a kind of metaphorical understanding. Otherwise, how does one understand the very concept "kingdom of ends" as there is corresponding reality to it? Our aim in this paper had been to discuss certain facets of research in morality which can together bring about a better and holistic picture of our moral understanding.

Acknowledgement

An earlier version of this paper was presented at the National Seminar on "Linguistic Representation: The Road Ahead". I am thankful to the members of the audience of the seminar for their insightful comments and queries. This has led me to revise this paper and work on the flaws of the initial draft.

15

The Mentalistic Turn in Analytical Philosophy

Madhucchanda Sen

MICHAEL Dummett says in his *Origins of Analytical Philosophy*,

> What distinguishes Analytical Philosophy, in its diverse manifestations from other schools is the belief, first, that a philosophical account of thought can be attained through a philosophical account of language, and, secondly, that a comprehensive account can only be so attained.

He then goes on to say,

> . . . Some recent work in the analytical tradition has reversed this priority, in the order of explanation, of language over thought, holding that language can be explained only in terms of antecedently given notions of different types of thought, considered independently of their linguistic expression. A good example of this new trend is Gareth Evan's posthumous book [*Varieties of Reference*]. . . . On my characterization, therefore, Evans was no longer an analytical philosopher. He was, indeed, squarely in the analytical tradition: the three pillars on which his book rests are Russell, Moore and Frege.[1]

I would like to contest Dummett's view on this mentalistic turn in analytical philosophy. Evans and others like him are

1. Michael Dummett, *Origins of Analytical Philosophy*, Cambridge, Mass: Harvard University Press, 1994, p. 4.

still analytical philosophers (not merely belonging to the analytical tradition). The question that is relevant here is not which has precedence over which: thought over language, or language over thought? We must realize that certain concerns that we have in Philosophy of Language converge with certain concerns that we have in Philosophy of Mind. Discussions in Philosophy of Language and Philosophy of Mind converge on particular issues. And this convergence can be understood *only* within Analytical Philosophy.

One of the key issues in Philosophy of Language is what would constitute the meaning of a sentence or the semantic content of an utterance. One of the key issues in Philosophy of Mind is what would constitute the content of an intentional mental state. It is in connection with the issue of the semantic content of an utterance and content of intentional mental states that discussions in Philosophy of Language and Philosophy of Mind converge. We now realize that there are issues that have to be discussed within the purview of Philosophy of Mind and Philosophy of Language *together*. This effort of doing Philosophy of Mind along with Philosophy of Language has often been seen as a Mentalistic Turn in Analytical Philosophy.

The mentalistic turn however is not that new a trend in philosophy. The trend was set by no less a person than Ludwig Wittgenstein in his *Philosophical Investigations*. When Wittgenstein offers his famous critique of Private Language, he is actually critiquing a particular view of the mind. He critiques a particular notion of subjectivity, which is actually Cartesian in its nature and origin.

This Cartesian view created a kind of orthodoxy which became an influential paradigm in the analytical tradition itself. This in turn gave birth to one of the most powerful isms in analytical philosophy: Descriptivism — a view which finds its best expression in the works of Frege and Russell. This is also a view that gave rise to another powerful ism: Representationalism.

The Cartesian view that I have in mind is the Self-Containedness Thesis. Descartes said that the mind is self-contained with respect to the world. This idea was reflected in Frege and Russell's treatment of empty terms and their belief that such terms have associated with them a description which is not satisfied by anything in the world. Hence, contents of thoughts whose expression make a use of such terms are to be seen in terms of narrow content (a content that can be specified without having to make any existential claims regarding the world and the objects in it). They also concluded that we may also see other terms in the same way. Hence, the Descriptivist Tradition in Philosophy of Language and Philosophy of Mind was born. All this gave birth to Frege's Theory of Sense and Russell's theory of Descriptions.

Descriptivism has been largely responsible for the birth of Representationalism in Philosophy of Mind and Language. We must remember that many philosophers within the analytic tradition, however, did not favour Representationalism. Donald Davidson says

> There is a picture of the mind which has become so ingrained in our philosophical tradition that it is almost impossible to escape its influence even when its faults are recognized and repudiated. In one crude, but familiar, version it goes like this: the mind is a theatre in which the conscious self watches a passing show (the shadows on the wall). The show consists of "appearances", sense data, qualia, what is "given" in experience. What appear on the stage are no ordinary objects that the outer eye registers and the heart loves, but their purported representatives. Whatever we can know about the outside depends on what we glean from the inner clues.[2]

This idea was reflected also in the works of Frege and Russell. Both Frege and Russell believed in the idea that "thought" (and

2. Donald Davidson "Knowing One's Own Mind", in *Subjective, Intersubjective, Objective"*, Oxford: Clarendon Press, 2001.

speech)

> relates to objects with an essential indirectness: by way of a blueprint or specification which, if formulated, would be expressed in purely general terms. Whether the object exists or not would then be incidental to the availability of thought. Underlying that idea is the following line of argument. When we mention an object in describing a thought we are giving only an extrinsic characterization of the thought (since the mention of the object takes us outside the subject's mind); but there must be an intrinsic characterization available (one which does not take us outside the subject's mind), and that characterization would have succeeded in specifying the essential core of thought even if extra-mental reality had not obliged by containing the object.[3]

Descriptivism, Representationalism and the idea of narrow content follow from Descartes' self-containedness thesis. Descartes claimed that the mind is "a substance whose whole essence is to think, and which does not depend on any place or material thing in order to exist".[4] Two things follow from this self-containedness thesis: (a) a person's mind is not only distinct from her body but is also distinct from all other bodies; and (b) "all mental characteristics are equally separable from, that is, could exist just as they are in the absence of, any body whatsoever".[5] What is important for us is that Descartes maintains that a person's mind is capable of having the mental characteristics, that it is independent of the existence of any other body whatsoever. This makes mind insulated from the

3. John McDowell, "The Sense and Reference of a Proper Name", in A.W. Moore (ed.), *Meaning and Reference*, Oxford: Oxford University Press, 1993.
4. *The Philosophical Writings of Descartes*, tr., J. Cottingham, R. Stoothoff, D. Murdoch, Cambridge: Cambridge University Press, 1984, vol. I, p. 127.
5. McDowell's "Singular Thought and the Extent of Inner Space" in Pettit and McDowell (eds.), *Subject, Thought and Context*, Oxford: Clarendon Press, 1986, pp. 146-58.

world as well as the other minds. This idea of a mind has been criticized by many especially Wittgenstein. He once said that under this characterization of the mind we would have to say that if God looked into our minds, he would not have been able to see there whom we are speaking of.

This idea however was not appealing to Wittgenstein and many others.

> Evidently that (mythical) repository is not the right place to look. God (or anyone) might see whom we have in mind . . . by . . . seeing whom we are looking at when we speak. The sort of thing — seeing relations between a person and bits of world, not prying into a hidden place whose content could be just as they are even if there were no world — is (in part) what seeing into a person's mind is.[6]

Hence some philosophers spoke of a different kind of content which can be understood only in terms of the relation that the subject bears with the world outside. This is called Broad Content. The two conflicting views that emerge here give rise to a debate regarding content. Actually, there are six famous puzzles regarding content which indicate that there may be more than one way in which content may be conceived.

David Chalmers in his paper "The Components of Content"[7] says that we can find at least six famous puzzles in philosophy which all indicate the necessity of admitting what might be called narrow content. They are:

(1) The first is the one that results from Putnam's Twin Earth Thought experiments. The question that Putnam answers is "Is content in the head?". And he answers this in the negative by showing that the twins across the worlds are

6. McDowell, "The Sense and Reference of Proper Names", in A.W. Moore (ed.), *Meaning and Reference,* Oxford: Oxford University Press, 1993.

7. In his *Philosophy of Mind: Classical and Contemporary Readings,* Oxford: Oxford University Press, 2002.

identical in the physical histories, but one's thought is about water or H_2O while the other's is about twin water or twater or XYZ. And hence the experiment demonstrates that the psychological histories do not supervene on the physical histories of the twins. This very example, however, has been used by internalists to vindicate their faith in narrow content as they say that the experiments also show that the cognitive similarities between the twins are striking. This might indicate that there is some wholly internal aspect of content that the twins share. And that might be what can be called the narrow content of their mental states.

(2) The second is Frege's puzzle, which speaks of the cognitive difference in our thought that Hesperus is Hesperus, and our thought that Hesperus is Phosphorus. These cognitive differences indicate conceptual differences, which might have serious bearing on the theory of content.

(3) The third is the puzzle about belief made famous by Kripke in his "A puzzle about belief". Frenchman Pierre is told in French that London is pretty, and he believes it. Later on he visits a city called London and he has no idea that the city he knew as Londres is the same as the one called London. Pierre however finds London ugly. We cannot take Pierre to be highly irrational and believing simultaneously that London is pretty and that London is not pretty.

(4) A similar kind of problem arises in propositional attitude ascribing contexts. Chalmers calls it "The mode-of-presentation problem". If Jimmy says, "Lois believes that Superman can fly", he speaks truly. If he says, "Lois believes that Clark Kent can fly", he speaks falsely, as Lois does not know that Clark Kent is Superman. But on many accounts, the proposition that Clark Kent can fly is the same as the proposition that Superman can fly. If so, it seems that to believe that Clark Kent can fly, it is not

enough to believe the corresponding proposition; one must believe it under an appropriate mode of presentation. Then the question is: What is a mode of presentation, and how can this be integrated into an account of belief ascription?

(5) The fifth puzzle is called by Chalmers "The problem of the essential indexical". Suppose I believe that I am in grave danger. If I believe this, I am most likely to take appropriate action. What is important is that this belief is essentially indexical in nature. I would not be driven to action, had I believed that *x* was in danger, even though (unknown to me) *x* was no one else but me. And so the question arises: "How can we square this indexical aspect with an account of the contents of thought?"

(6) The sixth puzzle is called by Chalmers the puzzle of the "contingent a priori". We have stipulated that one metre is the length of a stick kept somewhere in Paris. And so we can, in fact, know a priori that that particular stick is one metre long. But it is in fact a contingent fact that the stick is one metre, as the stick could well have been longer or shorter. And so we face yet another puzzle how "can one have a priori knowledge of a contingent truth?"

This led to the famous debate in Philosophy of Mind: Externalism and Internalism. Externalism and Internalism in the philosophy of mind are two conflicting theses about how intentional mental states are correctly individuated. Externalism about the mind is the thesis which says that there is a deep individuative relation between an individual's being in those states and the nature of her social and physical environment. The very existence of those states entails the existence and the nature of the objects towards which they are directed or entail that the physical or social environment of the subject is in a particular way. I am not taking any stand on the issue regarding whether all mental states are intentional or not. But I am going to discuss only the intentional mental states, as it is in the case of the intentional mental states that the externalist-internalist debate arises.

All this however presupposes that there is a great affinity between semantic content and mentalistic/intentional content.

Suppose: Galileo says "The earth is round".

The meaning of the utterance or the semantic content of the utterance is the proposition that *the earth is round*.

Suppose again: Galileo believes that the earth is round.

The intentional content/mentalistic content of Galileo's belief is the proposition that *the earth is round*. The meaning of Galileo's utterance is identified in terms of this proposition. The belief of Galileo is also identified in terms of this proposition. The key questions of meaning and identification of mental states converge when we search for a fuller understanding of this content (semantic and intentional). This convergence can only be seen within the Analytical tradition. Interestingly, we shall see that what view we have about content (semantic and intentional) will reflect our understanding of the relation between mind and the world.

It is clear why content is so important for theory of meaning. We shall now try to say why content is so important in understanding the mind and the mental. Here we are using content to make sense of one of the crucial mental phenomena: Intentionality. To understand this we shall refer to Fodor's *Psychosemantics: The Problem of Meaning in the Philosophy of Mind.* We find Fodor articulating the essence of propositional attitudes or intentional mental states in the first chapter of his book. He says that propositional attitudes or Intentional States are Semantically Evaluable.

> Beliefs are the kinds of things that are true or false; desires are the kind of things that get frustrated or fulfilled; hunches are the kind of things that turn out to be right or wrong; so it goes.

> I will assume that what makes a belief true (/false) is something about its relation to the non-psychological world. . . . Hence, to say of a belief that it is true (/false) is to evaluate that belief in terms of its relation to the world. I will call such evaluation "semantic". The idea of Semantic Evaluation and the idea of Content are intimately interconnected . . . Hamlet's belief that his uncle killed his father . . . has a certain semantic value; in particular, it's a *true* belief. Why true? Well, because it corresponds to a certain fact. Which fact? Well, the fact that Hamlet's uncle killed Hamlet's father. But why is it *that* fact that determines the semantic evaluation of Hamlet's belief? Why not the fact that two is a prime number. . . . Well, because the *content* of Hamlet's belief is *that* his uncle killed his father. . . . *If you know what the content of a belief is, then you know what it is about the world that determines the semantic evaluation of the belief*; that, at a minimum, is how the notions of content and semantic evaluation connect.[8]

Fodor also claims that propositional attitudes or intentional states have *causal powers*. In psychology, we want to explain and predict human behaviour and we do so by ascribing intentional states to subjects and claiming causal relations between such states and behaviour. Fodor claims that ascription of content and causal powers to intentional states go hand in hand. Fodor claims that we attribute "content and causal powers to the very same mental things" that we take to be

> semantically evaluable. It is Hamlet's belief that Claudius killed his father — the very same belief which is true or false in virtue of the facts about his father's death — that causes him to behave in such a beastly way to Gertrude. . . . In fact, there's a deeper point to make. It's not just that in psychology of propositional attitudes, content and causal powers are attributed to the same things. It's also that causal relations among propositional attitudes somehow typically contrive

8. Jerry Fodor, *Psychosemantics: The Problem of Meaning in the Philosophy of Mind*, Cambridge, Mass: Bradford Books, MIT Press, 1988, pp. 10-11.

to respect their relations of content and belief/desire explanations often turn on this.[9]

To take an example, Hamlet's belief that Claudius killed his father causes his belief that someone killed his father. If we ask ourselves why there is such a relation, the answer would be that "Claudius killed Hamlet's father" logically entails "Someone killed Hamlet's father". (Recall the simple rule of Existential Generalization). What is being said is that mental states have the causal powers they have in terms of having specific contents.

Now it is clear why contents are so important for both Philosophy of Language and Philosophy of Mind. The Six Puzzles about Content which we discussed also shows that this content may either be *broad* or *narrow*. The important question that we face now is whether we should opt for a narrow content theory or a broad content theory.

I would like to say that the mentalistic turn is not a break away from the analytical tradition. We realize that we are addressing the same problem in Semantics and Philosophy of Mind. It is the question regarding content which is at the same time semantic and mentalistic.

What we must realize is that we are here debating about one of the key questions in philosophy: What is the Mind-World relation like? We are here talking about the *Threefold Cord: World, Thought, and Language*. Descriptivism founded upon the Cartesian Thesis of Self-Containedness of Mind really makes the Mind-World Relation difficult to understand. It definitely makes the gap between the mind and the world insurmountable.

I would like to emphasize here that we can really trace a problem regarding meaning in the philosophy of mind. The kind of view regarding mentalistic content one will have depends upon her views in philosophy of language. I would

9. Jerry Fodor, *Psychosemantics: The Problem of Meaning in the Philosophy of Mind*, Cambridge, Mass: Bradford Books, MIT Press, 1988, p. 11.

like to take an example to demonstrate this claim. I take up the externalism-internalism debate. We shall see that the kind of externalist you will be depends upon which terms in language she takes to be genuine referring expressions.

Though in a very general way we can say that any externalist would believe that (some) of our mental states are constitutively or individuatively dependent on the external world, yet it would be wrong to think that externalism is just one uniform thesis. There are and can be several kinds of externalists and several kinds of internalists opposing their theses. The difference can be traced in various ways. In the literature we find very many different ways in which varieties of externalism have been conceived. Of all these, I find the most insightful the distinction that can be traced by looking into the answers that externalists give to three questions which are closely tied with the above-mentioned general description of their thesis. They are:

1. Which mental states, and more specifically which aspects of such mental states, are so constitutively and individuatively determined externally?
2. What do we mean by external? In other words, which are the external items that determine these mental states constitutively?
3. What kind of relation does one have to stand in with those external items in order to have such thoughts?

For our purpose, the first question is most significant. This is so because we shall see that some philosophers think that only singular thoughts have broad content. Some others think both singular and general thoughts have broad content. Let us see why they have such views. Philosophers who believe that singular thoughts have broad content believe that singular terms like proper names or definite descriptions or demonstratives alone are purely referring expressions. Those who think that general thoughts too might have broad content take general terms like "water", "tiger", "gold" to be referring expressions.

We will, for our own purpose, just discuss singular thoughts. I would like to discuss how an important insight that we find in Russell's theory of descriptions can help us in tackling the question, which kind of thought are we to be externalists about. The details of this particular kind of externalism will be discussed later, but here it would be worthwhile to make a note of the history behind this view. In doing so, I shall first discuss this insight of Russell's which will bring us to talk about his view about genuine proper names and genuine acts of referring. In this connection we shall discuss two important principles which have come to be known as Russell's Criterion and Russell's Principle. I shall then discuss how seriously this has been taken by philosophers like Gareth Evans and John McDowell and how this in turn has provided us a support for *a particular kind* of Content Externalism in Philosophy of Mind. This is why I want to call them Analytical Philosophers and this is why I differ from Dummett.

We shall start by articulating Russell's Principle and showing how this was extended, first by Evans, and then by McDowell in coming up with a particular brand of externalism about perceptual demonstrative thoughts.

We start off by discussing a point about Russell's idea of proposition. Russell did not take propositions as abstract meanings of sentence-types. Russell tied the notion of propositions with particular utterances of sentences. A proposition, under this view is, what is expressed by a particular utterance of a sentence. Stephen Neale in this connection wants to make an important distinction: the distinction between the linguistic meaning of an expression and the semantic value of an expression. He says that, on the one hand, we cannot speak of the value of an expression, rather we can speak of its meaning. On the other hand, we cannot speak of the meaning of an utterance, rather we can speak of the value of an utterance.

Neale takes Russell's view to be that the semantic value of the utterance of a sentence is a proposition. If this is the Russellian notion of the proposition, then we can ask how would Russell understand names, or demonstratives, or description, or any subsentential expression for that matter. Neale says that

> the semantic value of an utterance of a subsentential expression α is whatever the utterance of *a contributes to the identity* of the proposition expressed by the utterance of the sentence ∅ of which α is a constituent.[10]

If we accept this view, then we will have to say that the semantic value of an expression is just its *reference*.

What is peculiar to a demonstrative or an indexical expression is that there is a systematic dependence of its semantic value on the *context* of its utterance. In other words, the references of such expressions are systematically determined by the context of the utterance of the expression. Let us take the example of the utterance of the sentence "I have a cold". The semantic value of the expression "I" in the sentence and also the semantic value of the utterance of the sentence itself change from context to context. But note that the *linguistic meaning* of the expression and the sentence *do not* change from context to context. A person can very well know what the linguistic meaning of the word "I" is without knowing all the different semantic values that the expression can have in different contexts of its utterance. Neale says that,

> To know the linguistic meaning of the word "I" is to know something constant across utterances, roughly that the referent is the individual, using the word.[11]

This point was made (in somewhat different terms) by Russell in his *An Inquiry into Meaning and Truth*. He says that the

10. Stephen Neale, *Descriptions*, Cambridge, Mass: MIT Press, 1990, p. 66.
11. Stephen Neale, *Descriptions*, Cambridge, Mass: MIT Press, 1990, p. 8.

meanings of demonstrative and indexical expressions do not change with the context of their utterance but their *designations* do. We should remember that Russell might not have tied this distinction to another distinction, which is important here, viz. the distinction between expression types and particular token utterances of those expression types. Though the distinction is usually seen as one related to the distinction between expression types and utterances of those expressions.

Neale wants to say that the sentence of the form "that *f* is *g*" is very different semantically from the sentence "the *f* is *g*". He says that while the first expresses an "object dependent proposition", the second expresses an "object independent proposition".

For Russell, if we are to have singular propositions with genuinely referring expressions then they have to be, following Neale's terminology, object dependent propositions. It is here that we come to talk about Russell's Criterion, which tells us what can count as a genuinely referring expression (proper name).

In discussing Russell's Criterion we shall be drawing upon Gareth Evans' treatment of Russell's theory of singular term in his book *Varieties of Reference.* It is here that Evans introduces the discussion of what he calls Russell's Criterion which is actually a semantic criterion which helps us to distinguish two kinds of noun phrases. We ask a question in order to decide whether a noun phrase falls into one kind of noun phrase or it falls in another, viz.: If this noun phrase lacked reference, would that render atomic sentences in which it occurs meaningless as well? In case the answer is "No", i.e. in the case where the noun phrase's lack of reference does not render the sentences in which it occurs meaningless, the noun phrase will not count as a genuine *Russellian singular term.* Russell uses this criterion to distinguish definite descriptions from logically proper names. Definite descriptions, though look like singular terms, yet are not so because they were actually complex quantifiers (quantified expressions). Their lack of reference does not render the sentences in which they occur as meaningless and hence they are not genuine referring expressions for Russell.

The reason why Russell and, in fact, pre-1890 Frege believed is this that they took the main function of a genuine referring expression to be identifying an object — an object such that when it does not satisfy the predicate the sentence becomes false and when it does satisfy the predicate the sentence becomes true. In case there is no object identified by a (supposed) referring expression, then the sentence would become meaningless. So we may now state Russell's criterion:

> The grammatical subject of a proposition is a genuine proper name, i.e. a name directly representing some object, only if its failing to have a referent renders the proposition meaningless.

On this criterion we know how definite descriptions which were regarded as genuine referring expressions were found out not to be so. But what then is a genuine proper name? Russell was extremely strict in the application of this criterion and thought that even proper names like "Julius Caesar" or "Gottlob Frege" and even demonstratives were merely covert definite descriptions. What could be the reasons for which Russell took such a stringent view about what could count as a genuine proper name? It is here that we come to speak about what Gareth Evans calls Russell's Principle. Whereas Russell's Criterion is a semantic principle regarding what would count as a genuine proper name, Russell's Principle is an epistemic principle regarding what are the conditions that a subject needs to satisfy in order to entertain a thought about an object and be able to genuinely refer to it. Russell says that in order that a subject entertains a thought about an object the subject must know which object is in question.

Russell goes on further to say that this the subject can do in two ways. The subject could know the object as that which uniquely satisfies a particular description or the subject could actually be *acquainted* with the object. And it is only when a subject is *acquainted* with the object that one is said to have a genuinely singular thought and is able to make a genuinely singular reference. What is more, is that Russell goes on further to say that the only kind of objects with which the subject may be in a genuine acquaintance relation was private mental indexicals and demonstratives. This surely gives us an idea about what Russell took to be genuine or "logically proper" names. Russell felt that ordinary proper names and even indexicals failed to be in this sense logically proper names as there would be a violation of Russell's Principle in their cases. We shall now go into a discussion of this pricinple and, in fact, disagree with Russell and go beyond his view to say that there can be genuine singular demonstrative thoughts in which the subject is in an acquaintance relation with an object which is not just a private mental indexical. After discussing this we shall see how this new and more relaxed interpretation of Russell's Principle will go hand in hand with a particular brand of content externalism and will provide a solution to one of the questions that the externalism-internalism debate concerns itself with.

In discussing Russell's Principle we shall be discussing how Gareth Evans speaks of this principle in the second chapter of his *Varieties of Reference.*[12] Russell's Principle, as it is called by Evans, is a principle regarding the conditions that a person has to satisfy in order that he makes a judgement about something. It is said that in order to make a judgement about an object, the object should somehow be the one that the person in question has in mind, in the sense that the person has to know who or what or which the object is. But it is perhaps too much to ask of a person. The knowledge required should not be characterized as "knows which". One may quite well be able to make a judgement about an object which she knows in acquaintance without having the faintest idea about which the object is. (Evans

12. Gareth Evans, *Varieties of Reference*, Oxford: Oxford University Press, 1982.

says that one may have the same kind of knowledge about oneself without having any clue to who one really is!) But none the less, there must be some kind of restriction that the principle imposes upon the subject in order that the subject can legitimately claim that she knows the object (in whatever sense of the word). Otherwise, the principle would be too "trivial", as "anyone who is prepared to ascribe to a subject the thought that *a* is *F* in the first place will also be prepared to ascribe to him the thought, and presumably the knowledge, that it is *a* that he is thinking about". In other words, the subject should be capable of telling us which object he has in mind.

Now what would make the principle non-trivial? The requirement might be that in order to make a judgement about an object one has to have a discriminating knowledge about the object, i.e. the subject has to be able to distinguish the object from all the other objects in the world. But is that enough? What may be regarded as the sufficient condition for having discriminating knowledge? There may be at least three such sufficient conditions: (1) if one can perceive it at the present time; (2) if one can recognize it once it is presented to the person; (3) if one knows certain distinguishing facts about the object.

But there seems to be a problem in conceiving each of these as sufficient conditions. Evans offers us an example where one has satisfied conditions (1) and (2) and yet we cannot say that one has discriminating knowledge. Evans speaks of such a counter-example of Russell's Principle in *Varieties of Reference*. We shall, however, for the purpose of the paper, not go into this. But if we look back into Russell's own construal of the principle, then we will be faced with the question once again as to what kind of object can be the object of such a discriminating knowledge. And as we have already said, Russell would restrict the range of such objects to such mental entities to which we can make a demonstrative reference and entertain a demonstrative thought.

We shall have to first understand why Russell was so stringent in construing this principle, i.e. why did he think that we could genuinely refer only to private mental indexicals. In understanding this we shall at once enter the terrain of the Externalism-Internalism debate. Gareth Evans says that the most important reason for which Russell wants to restrict the genuine cases of referring to private mental demonstratives is that Russell is loyal to a Cartesian idea, viz. that we can never be mistaken about whether we are having a thought.

However, this is where the externalists like Evans will come in and say that it is quite possible to be mistaken about whether I, as a subject, have indeed succeeded, in a particular case, in having a genuine thought.

We find in *Varieties of Reference* an argument in support of the coherence of the idea that we might be mistaken about whether we indeed have a thought. We shall first try to understand the argument that Evans gives and then we shall see what consequences we can derive in philosophy of mind from this.

Let us first point out that if we take Russell's Principle stringently and believe that we can only make genuine reference to our private indexical mental states, then we would have to say something rather bizarre, i.e. we would have to say one can succeed in making a genuine reference only in a private language. Keeping in tune with Wittgensteinian reservations about the plausibility of the notion of a private language, Evans is critical of this over-stringent conception of genuine reference that Russell is speaking about. Of course, at this point one could ask the question:

> Which is a more absurd idea, the idea of a private language or the idea that we may be mistaken about whether we are having a thought?

We must understand that if we give up this stringent

interpretation of Russell's Principle, we are forced to believe that we might be so mistaken about whether we are having a thought, and this is something that must have disturbed Russell a great deal. This is why we find Russell limiting the scope of a genuinely referring expression to those demonstrative thoughts whose objects were private mental items, as it seemed quite absurd to Russell that one could be wrong about whether one was really entertaining such a thought.

Evans is with Russell also in believing that there is a special kind of thought that is involved in the case of demonstrative expression, a thought which may be rightfully called a demonstrative thought. But in extending this Principle, Evans claims that we can definitely say that we can demonstratively identify not only mental entities but also physical objects. And in case one makes a demonstrative reference to an object which in fact does not exist but the subject takes it to exist, then we shall have to say that the subject is actually mistaken in thinking that she has a demonstrative thought. And it is here that the stringency of the Russell's Principle is given up. We have to keep in mind that Evans is not saying that in such situations the subject's mind is totally empty — what he says is that whatever state the person is in will not qualify as a genuine thought at all. So, what Evans is saying is that if a subject truly has a demonstrative thought, then that entails that the object of her thought actually exists. And also that there is a constitutive relation between the object and such a thought as there would be no thought in the absence of such an object. This brings us right into the discussion of externalism about demonstrative thoughts.

So we have now seen how our understanding of what would count as genuine referring expressions in our language will dictate what sort of externalist I will be. This is just one instance of the Problem of Meaning in Mind. This particular Mentalistic Turn is truly a philosophical stance taken by philosophers within Analytical Philosophy.

16

Limits of Linguistic Representations

Wittgenstein and the Unrepresentable that Shows Forth

Muhammad Maroof Shah

> Wittgenstein's philosophical reflections are in large part, however indirectly, readings between the lines of the story of the soul in the Western metaphysical tradition.
>
> — Fergusson Kerr in *Theology after Wittgenstein*, p. 166

> I am not a religious man but I cannot help seeing every problem from a religious point of view.
>
> — Wittgenstein

> My thoughts are 100 per cent Hebraic.
>
> — Wittgenstein

Linguistic Representations and Dialogue with the Mystical

WHAT do linguistic representations aim at? Mirroring reality? Or they constitute an autonomous play that gives us no insights into the most important foundation for culture? The dream or motivation has often been access to reality, however imperfect that may be. Strangely, there now seems to be an increasing consensus over the thesis that language and reality are two different things and the latter is either opaque for the former or far too rich a thing to be captured in the net of the former. From Nāgārjuna to Wittgenstein and Derrida, many thinkers have denied language and thought access to reality. The question is what do mystics say about this problem? Could the path ahead for philosophers dealing with linguistic representations be opening for a cross-disciplinary study with mystical philosophers or philosophers of mysticism? My contention in this paper is that it should be so. Particularly focusing on Wittgenstein, it is argued that the royal road to reality is not through language and thought but modes of perception that bypass them. The most important point is that what matters at the end of the day is ethics and answer to the fundamental existential questions, the problems that *Culture and Value* embodies and for these questions we need to explore other languages than the one ordinarily known. This language is the language of the Self. Wittgenstein fundamentally preoccupied himself with this problem though this concern has been largely sidelined by Wittgenstein scholars and those working on philosophy of language. The present paper pleads for a dialogue with this ignored Wittgenstein to contemplate the possibility for breaking fresh ground in tackling the nagging problems in the debate on language and reality.

There is hardly any difference in early and late Wittgensteins on the question of the mystical and the ethical. He remained Tractarian till the end in his mystical viewpoint. He did abandon parts of the *Tractatus* later but there was no evolution — and in fact could not by the very logic of mystical experience that converts its subjects for good. The mystics solve — for themselves at least — all important intellectual and existential problems. In fact, experiencing God dissolves all problems. For logical positivists what mattered most was what is in *Tractatus* but for Wittgenstein himself what mattered the most was what was not in there, the unsaid part. That was not in the *Tractatus* because language could not handle that. That something is neither linguistic nor representable in any other way. However, that shows itself and thus need not be spoken of or represented. Wittgenstein's most decisive move was thus away from linguistic representations and the most important job for the philosopher was to delimit what can be represented and thus related to what only shows itself. Ethics and aesthetics and the mystical, all belong to this second category. Man does not live by bread of facts (science, instrumental rationality) alone but needs supernatural manna embodied in ethical/aesthetical/mystical. It is ironic that what mattered most to him has not been given due attention by his successors. All his endeavour was to save the intelligence from the bewitchment of language. He was all for transcendence so that man becomes himself and lives truly, joyfully. In his search for happy life, life lived *sub specie aeternitatis*, he paid great attention to working of language, how language fails to represent reality and leads us astray by creating problems that are not there. It is how men lived that interested him rather than their speculative exercises. This alone solves the riddles of life. Language has no answers and answers can only be found when we step outside language.

As Wittgenstein was more interested in what *cannot* be linguistically represented his conclusions are radical. The most important things cannot be talked about. Ethics, religion and aesthetics are transcendental. The very fact that things exist, is mystical or linguistically and conceptually unrepresentable. We can only gaze at it and get lost in wonder. We can dissolve into this primordial mystery, love and celebrate it. Wittgenstein lived almost like a saint. He is the most mystical of the greatest philosophers of the modern Western history. He tried to show exit to philosophy. He found no problems once we let intelligence operate naturally and it shatters linguistic cobwebs. He fought against pervasive bewitchment of intelligence by language.

However he also realized all-pervasiveness of language and how it constructs the world for us. It hardly needs to be argued that we have nothing but linguistic representations even when we seek to talk about transcendence. Man, as has been observed in the classical ages, is a speaking animal. Language is the house of Being. In language the divine and the human meet. Prophets and saints too have spoken. Even the Buddha, the Prophet of silence, spoke even if it is about the impossibility of speech in matters transcendental. Man is condemned to speak and even speak to God and receive the speech of God in turn, as scriptures narrate. Scriptures are all filled with linguistic representations of that which though ideally resists getting represented nevertheless is largely accessible though not quite adequately through language. Masses do not know silence and even saints can't afford it for too long. Man lives in dialogue, I and Thou dialogue. The absolute stillness is superhuman and for most humans synonymous with death. It is not given for man to conceptually know Truth or represent the divine. But nevertheless, he has no other window to higher worlds. Language though imperfect is normally indispensable for humans. Later Wittgenstein is all about appreciating how divine suffuses and expresses in religious language, how ordinary use of language is steeped in the transcendental world.

We must not confuse two senses of the term transcendental in Wittgenstein. Logic too is transcendental and we can only show rather than speak about/represent the correspondence between two pictures. To say the correspondence between language and reality would require an intermediate language which in turn will require the same, but then that language would also require the same, *ad infinitum*. This kind of transcendence has logical or intellectual function only and did interest Wittgenstein but what mattered for him both personally and as a philosopher is transcendence in ethical/

aesthetic/mystical experiences, in the primordial encounter with the world and finding that things exist. The present paper is about this transcendence. As there can be no propositions about what is not in the world or, is transcendental, we shall have to focus more on life and experiences of the transcendent than on analysis of some theses regarding language or language games to make our point.

Wittgenstein's Mysticism

Wittgenstein's protests against being misunderstood notwithstanding, a great industry propounding a version of him he would strongly resent, has been flourishing. What he considered more important has been relegated to the background. There is great agreement between scholars on almost everything except that what mattered most to him. His motive for doing philosophy and living philosophy have been absent amongst his admirers, not to speak of detractors. His life has not been taken seriously as an aid in clarifying his basic theses and commitments. He has been read as philosopher of language though for him transcendence is more central for culture and value realization. The mystical in Wittgenstein has not been duly noticed and if noticed not quite well understood. His religious thought has been misunderstood and not read in continuation with his fundamentally mystical outlook. All kinds of theories have been put forward for accounting for his scattered mystical statements and observations on religion. The mystical is central for Wittgenstein and his philosophy and he has stated it in his *Tractatus, Notebooks,* "Lecture on Ethics" and in fact most of his writings develop this theme in many novel ways, in so subtle a manner that few can notice. His attitude towards religion, often understood in connection with the thesis of language game, is to be put in proper context by foregrounding the empirical mystical foundation that he gives to religion. Wittgenstein scholars have not generally succeeded in integrating his mysticism with his view of religion, culture and aesthetics. Mysticism is in the background of many a theses of later Wittgenstein as well and not just the *Tractatus*. Even in *Philosophical Investigations* Wittgenstein's central arguments that foreground illusoriness of the self, critique mentalistic picture of the soul, dissolve subject-object duality and plunge headlong into the world which is all there to alert us of dangers in asserting or making propositions on anything that transcends language.

Wittgenstein deserves a comparison with great mystical thinkers. If we understand that God is what is and is missed when we attempt to think or imagine or make images of Him or attempt to comprehend the Mystery, we can understand Wittgenstein. According to mysticism God is the case. The only thing is we don't see. We verbalize and babble and create theologies and metaphysics. Wittgenstein is a metaphysician in the same way Buddha is or Krishnamurti is. God is above speech. "The Absolute has never been defiled by speech." But by metaphysics is here meant living or breathing the noumenal world, dissolving into it and not speculating about it with conceptual schemes. Metaphysics as the knowledge of the supraphenomenal reality is the soul of all traditional cultures or "epistemologies". Man is made for the Absolute, to die in It and thus to eternally live. Certainty is the requirement of intelligence and man is not absurdity. If man fails to access the most certain, the indubitable, the absolutely safe in Wittgenstein's terms, he has failed as a man. God is the greatest certainty — the greatest and most palpable of the present facts in Whitehead's words — and a philosophy or epistemology that doesn't account for this does not deserve to be called a philosophy. It is failure and betrayal of philosophy and of man and his intelligence if the real is not knowable though of course not conceptually knowable. Modern philosophy, that is largely ignorant of God, can't qualify as a genuine philosophy, as Indians or great traditional philosophers from other traditions understand philosophy as *darśana*, as seeing or vision.

Wittgenstein had mystic experiences of both the ecstatic and nature-mystical kind. Seeing creation as wondrous is what Einstein correctly defined as religious or mystical attitude. God is attention without distraction as Simone Weil would say. He is the Mystery at the heart of everything. For Wittgenstein God is approached in all these ways and doubting our experience of wonder, of mystery, of eternity, of the ethical or unconditional goodness or his urge for it is absurd. Indeed God is the case and only the fools say in their hearts there is no God. Nasr has remarked that if it were possible to teach (traditional) metaphysics to everyone there would be no atheists around. Modern man has failed to understand what traditions meant by God. God is Reality for traditions and it is absurd to ask is there a reality. Only mystics can, however, say this so genuinely and Wittgenstein is a mystic. As ethics or aesthetics is transcendental and yet quite human and real, concerns that constitute the grounds of all that we value most, so is religion understood as living/talking God (to be distinguished from talking about God or mere propositional belief statement) so characteristic of human endowment that it is absurd to question it. In fact, as the Quran says, no question or doubt can be entertained regarding God. God is love, superabundant joy, beauty that kills, sweetness of every sweet thing, green in the leaves and red in the golden rays and mystery that surrounds us. This is not pantheism which is a heresy for traditions but our experience of God out of the world, so to speak — and of course we also need to note that *saṁsāra* is *nirvāṇa* and this very garden is the Garden of Eden for the seeing or who know. Debating about God is height of folly like debating about pleasures of love by eunuchs. Against this folly Wittgenstein asserted what normal men have always taken to be the case that God is reality or Reality and only saints truly live life. Wittgenstein was a saint though not of the order of great Western saints like Eckhart. Saints don't talk about God but talk God, live God, breathe God and share the great joy that God is with lesser mortals. The real question for traditional philosophies is how we become Godlike (*theosis*) or prepare for death in life (which is the same thing or means for it) or live and move and have our being in God. All else is vanity. Wittgenstein stood for this primordial heritage of man and that is why was misunderstood by most of his friends and foes alike. Needless to remark that he didn't consider the Western civilization that refused to fully countenance the reality of the sacred as something of a monstrosity and like Gandhi a laughable "interesting" idea. He complained of Russell, the paragon of modern rationality or philosophy — to have fatally misunderstood him. In fact, what he considered most important has been dismissed by many a modern thinker as folly. God (understood mystically or more precisely metaphysically) is the meaning of life for all religions including transtheistic one as for Wittgenstein. I wish to argue the point that Wittgenstein is to be read alongside great traditional philosophers that saw God above everything, had little use for fashionable pursuits of today, considered ethics as first philosophy and metaphysical discoveries as fruits or realizations of real ethical life, were centred on God rather than man and saw quintessentially human in living up to the divine image in him, in transcending himself. There is nothing new or original in Wittgenstein's mysticism as, in fact, there can't be anything new in matters transcendental. One can refer to many mystics while explicating central statements of his. So far we have read — with few exceptions — Wittgenstein as a philosopher or failed to appreciate how mysticism informs/grounds his philosophy.

Wittgenstein is not only a philosopher of mysticism but a

mystic, a practical mystic of great standing. All his work was dedicated to the "glory of God" as he once said to his friend Dury (Rhees 1984: 168) — an expression quite unexpected from modern profane philosophers. He didn't like philosophizing as a speculative/analytical exercise, as an academic pursuit as is the case now in modern academies or universities, but something that Plato would appreciate or other ancient traditional philosophers would prescribe as a way of life and nothing short of preparation of death. That he wanted his legacy to be of changed attitude towards ethics is hardly surprising.

> I am by no means sure that I should prefer a continuation of my work by others to a change in the way people live which would make all those questions superfluous.
>
> — Wittgenstein, CV: 61

Philosophy, as pursued by his contemporaries or even today, is a disease of modern form of life that needs cure. And that cure is ultimately provided by seeing the futility of the game called philosophy. For ancients it was ethics and a vision and had little to do with language or concepts. It was, most probably, his deep conviction borne from experience regarding sacrality of the world and thus the truth of the supernatural/eternal that made him loathe modern civilization that had banished the sacred. It is in light of mysticism that we can understand his unconventional attitude towards secular careers or vocations, his renunciation of his property, his austerity in life and manners, his casual attitude towards dress, his independence in thought and action, his nostalgia for peasant life in Russia, his alienation from his times that he characterized as dark ages and many puzzles in his biography. His view of philosophy's aim, his attempt at transcending it for getting the vision of the things as they really are, his rejection of the claims of conceptual analysis or linguistic analysis as explaining reality, his rejection of classical dualisms that have bedevilled Cartesian and post-Cartesian thought, his plea for convergence of the ethical and the aesthetic, his view that ethics is transcendental, his rejection of doing science and mathematics as the ideals of philosophizing, his critique of psychologism and rationalistic attempts at building a metaphysics and our addiction to use metaphysical notions in ordinary discourse at rational plane are all threads in the fabric of mystical tapestry that he has so subtly woven. He rejected theological representations, as many others before have done, but he never rejected the symbolizandum. He said there is no theoretical content in religious doctrines. This is, in a way, easily understandable. God is not a thing, an entity, a being among other beings or existence. "God is not" as Eckhart would put it. God is Nothing as Buddhism would put it. God is all that there is as Sūfīsm and Taoist mysticism see it. *Saṁsāra* and *nirvāṇa* are really one.

There can be no doubt about the mystical in Wittgenstein. Amongst the most loved books of him are included William James's *Varieties of Religious Experience* and Tolstoy's *The Gospel in Brief*, Augustine's *Confessions*, Dostoevsky's *Brothers Karamazov* in which Father Zossima figures, and writings of George Fox and Plato. He claimed that Vienna circle people didn't understand *Tractatus* and that few will understand it and in fact his learned commentators still mostly miss its kernel, its last pages and especially the closing proposition. His only public lecture is through and through a mystical piece. His only published book during his lifetime is an attempt to delineate the sacred realm and prevent its debasement by speculative metaphysics and exoteric theology. His notebooks are marked by the mystical passion. His *Culture and Value* criticizes modern Western civilization on precisely religious-mystical grounds. His *Philosophical Grammar, Blue Book and Philosophical Investigations* have mysticism in the background and, in fact, pave way for it. The most important questions of life that science or logical positivism or any reductionist philosophy miss need, according to him, to be treated mystically. His respect for religion as a form of life — though this belongs to the exoteric part of his work — and his refusal to take cudgels on behalf of theologians are explainable through the thesis of the mystical that he values above everything. If we don't comprehend such typical mystical statements as "*saṁsāra* and *nirvāṇa* are one", "God is what is", "I see nothing but God everywhere", "God is the Hidden and the Manifest", "God is our ultimate concern", "Eternity is the present moment", "Don't prat about God; God is not", "God is neither good nor true", "God is the sweetness of all sweet things", "God is Beauty and Truth", "God is the real Doer", "It is God that sees and listens rather than we", "God is the knownest of the Known", "No doubt can be entertained regarding God", "God is the Light of the World", "God is the Totality, the Whole", "God is the most immediate of the present facts and unattainable quest" we can't comprehend mysticism of Wittgenstein. He saw everything from the mystical (what he wrongly called religious) point of view. His metaphysics of experience is built on the foundations provided by mystical attitude towards life and the world. The central doctrines and conceptions of religion or theology are understood in the light of mystical interpretation that informs Wittgenstein.

Review of Works on the Mystical in Wittgenstein

The problem with most of the works done on this theme is that they have not been done by the students of mysticism but of philosophy and that too a very hostile antimetaphysical antimystical philosophy. How deeply ironic it is that Wittgenstein would be understood as supporter of the manifesto of logical positivism that banished as nonsense everything which concerned Wittgenstein the most. Science for Wittgenstein has not and could not even touch the problem of life, the problem of meaning, the problem of transcendence.

His critique of psychologism meant saying goodbye to one of the most fashionable reductionist approaches to spiritual reality. His denial of self was negation of everything for which secular humanism and modern individualism stand. His characterization of scientific-technological civilization as dark ages places him squarely with other great religious critics of Enlightenment thought. For him modern positivist civilization lacked culture and therefore was cursed. He lamented that Russell, Carnap and many others who were so close to him didn't really understand him and those who claimed to be his followers didn't make the spiritual endeavour share the spiritual vocation that moved him. He was every inch a mystic and no doubt should be entertained regarding this. Both Russell and Carnap accused him of mysticism and, in fact, none of the Wittgenstein scholars or biographers has denied the element of mystical in him, but none has been able to see how mysticism is the key to his whole thought; not excluding the latter Wittgenstein. Logic is a tool for paving the way to the supralogical or transcendental. In fact, mystical is the case for him and needs no arguments. The unrepresentable shows forth. It is there to be contemplated, breathed and enjoyed. God is everywhere and nowhere. Man is not. He lives and moves and has his being in God. My purpose here is to make some general remarks on the centrality of the mystical in Wittgenstein and thus help to put in perspective the critical writings on his religion besides clarifying why it should matter in any discussion of him. I shall particularly focus on his *Notebooks* (1914-16) to argue my case, though I shall not ignore the *Tractatus* which has been much, though still inadequately and often not quite rightly, commented upon from this perspective.

Amongst those who have sympathetically written on his mysticism Russell Nieli should be counted as the most important and balanced author. Atkinson reads him as a pantheist as if Wittgenstein had not placed transcendence outside the world in so clear terms. Malcolm and some other critics who have written on his view of religion as a language game have missed the mystical core of his religiosity — his metaphysics of transcendence — to recall Pradhan's title of his very useful book — I believe it is Indians who can better comment on Wittgenstein because the metaphysics that he affirms — metaphysics as suprarational intuitive or intellectual instead of speculative rational affair — belongs to India especially. (Indians have no difficulty in understanding Buddha as a mystic and Buddhism as a great metaphysics, even if Buddha refused to answer the metaphysical questions.) Brian McGuinness has made a useful small study and there are valuable insights in Kerr's *Theology after Wittgenstein.* Mark Lazenby in *The Early Wittgenstein on Religion* pays attention to the mystical in him and rightly points out that McGuinness's view that Wittgenstein is a nature mystic in the *Tractatus* is not correct and instead argues that he is actually a theistic mystic. He notes that there are two worlds in *Tractatus,* namely the factual and the spiritual and points out that realizing this is in order to understand how there can be value inside the world. Lazenby develops this position by arguing that the factual world is the everyday one which logic characterizes and that value lies outside this world. The mystic looks back upon this world after transcending it and once it has been transcended there is nothing to say and hence silence ensues. Engleman, Dury and other acquaintances of Wittgenstein have also pointed out the profundity of his mystical outlook. In fact, logical positivist camp soon discovered that he is not amongst them. Wittgenstein's differences with Russell and positivist friends are largely attributable to his mystical-ethical convictions. Many papers have been written to argue the point that Wittgenstein had mystical convictions but very few studies have been able to convincingly link his life and work and interpret him consistently on mystical lines. He has been approached more from theological/religious than from mystic-metaphysical viewpoint. The present paper seeks to fill the gap.

K.C. Pandey's edited collection *Perspectives on the Unsayable* shows a glimpse of confusion on Wittgenstein's fundamental contributions to the debate on religion or transcendence. There are disagreements over the nature of his religiosity, cognitive status of religious claims, central metaphysical notions, such as the self in relation to God, the meaning of the unsayable, etc. Wittgenstein has been approached as a philosopher and not as a mystic and this contributes to confusions. So far few scholars specializing in mysticism have written on Wittgenstein and this has complicated problems. Wittgenstein is a mystic and a metaphysician of a different order — he does metaphysics as many traditional philosopher-sages have been doing it. It is a non-rational route for doing metaphysics that he takes. I think the best guide to understanding traditional non-rational metaphysics is the trinity of perennialist metaphysicians Rene Guenon, Ananda Coomaraswamy and Frithjof Schuon. For Wittgenstein — to refute his postmodernist appropriations that argue he is a prisoner of language and textuality — what can't be said is the case. The world is not explained by science or philosophy or anything that employs language.

In a remarkable book *Wittgenstein and the Mystical: Philosophy as an Ascetic Practice* Fredrick Sontag sets ten themes that run throughout Wittgenstein's work. The "themes" dominated Wittgenstein's life and, Sontag argues, provide a way to understand Wittgenstein's work. The themes are, as his reviewer puts it: (1) Philosophy as an ascetic practice; (2) The philosopher as existentialist/pragmatist; (3) The monk's isolated search for forgiveness; (4) The penitent's search for forgiveness; (5) The struggle with God as an unknown object; (6) Philosophy as a "religious" way of life; (7) Philosophy as a life of courage; (8) Serious philosophical pursuit has an affinity to mysticism; (9) Language has a mystical quality; (10) Insight can be imparted only to one who is serious and dedicated.

The Mystical in Wittgenstein's Texts

I focus here particularly though not exclusively on *Notebooks* (1914-16) and then subsume those observations and comment on them from mystical viewpoint. Some statements from *Tractatus* are too well known and well commented upon to need quoting here. Almost all the statements on religion, ethics and aesthetics in the *Notebooks* need to be kept in focus for appreciating our reading. Here only a few statements can be quoted or alluded to while commentary proceeds. These statements are scattered throughout his early work:

> Ethics is transcendental.
>
> The work of art is the object seen *sub-species aeternitatis* and the good life is the world *seen sub-species aeternitatis.* This is the connection between art and ethics.
>
> The urge towards mystical comes after non-realization of our wishes by science. We feel that even with all possible scientific questions answered our problem is still not touched at all.
>
> It is true: Man is the microcosmos.
>
> There is no such thing as the act of the will. Will is the attitude of the subject to the world.
>
> World in itself is neither good nor evil.
>
> Everything is perfect.
>
> Objects I can only name.
>
> Where in the world is the metaphysical subject to be found?
>
> There is no riddle.
>
> How things stand is God.
>
> . . . my will is world will.
>
> There can and must be mentioned of I in a non-psychological

> sense in philosophy.
>
> Scepticism is *not* irrefutable, but *obvious nonsense* if it tries to doubt where no question can be asked.
>
> For doubts can only exist where a question exists; a question can only exist where an answer exists, and this can only exist where something can be said.

The fact that Wittgenstein had personal mystical experience is well attested. His description of being absolutely safe and seeing creation as a miracle are so compelling that we hardly need to entertain any second opinion about the mystical in him or his encounter with the mystical. The cognizance of the fact that there is a world is enough to make one dance with ecstasy and wonder. Wonder is the beginning and the end of human wisdom.

According to him philosophy is not one of the natural sciences. He made the aim of philosophy more a vision than anything else (Pradhan 1981: 237). His aim was to get

> vision of things as they are and therefore he aimed transcending philosophy itself. Philosophy could be transcended only after it has given us the correct vision of the world. As we have said earlier, this vision consists in man's knowledge of the world, or in other words, in the metaphysics.

Although metaphysical interpretation of Wittgenstein's thought has been disputed we can still say that he does argue for a new way of looking at the world which involves a kind of transcendence quite similar to the one advocated by mystics. After enlightenment the world continues to be the same but we have one foot above the ground as famous Zen anecdote recounts. This is the whole burden of a remarkable work titled *Wittgenstein: A Way of Seeing*. To quote only one statement from *Philosophical Investigations*

> What you have discovered is a new way of looking at things.

> As if you had invented a new way of painting; or again a new metre or a new kind of song. —401

Wittgenstein is a metaphysician in a special sense. He is a philosopher of transcendence. This point may need a clarification.

Metaphysics as conceived by its greatest masters across traditions from Nāgārjuna to Śaṅkara to Lao Tzu to Eckhart and Ibn Arabi consists in a vision that transforms our ordinary perception or attitude regarding the world. It is not necessarily a vision of beyond in the sense that involves moving out of oneself and talking of an abstraction or higher world ontologically distinguishable from the world we all know. It always presupposes *saṁsāra-nirvāṇa* or world-heaven equivalence. The immediate is the ultimate and path is the goal as Zen tradition would put it. God is the green in the trees and the red in the sunrays. Transcendence could well be construed as true being of beings as Heidegger would tell us or mystery of things or depth dimension of things. Everything is within according to all traditions. There is no other in the absolute sense. All are one. Ibn Arabi's words "you are everything, in everything, and from everything" express the vision of all great mystical thinkers. Thus all the higher worlds are part of the Self or consciousness. Ken Wilber has been emphasizing this point especially in almost all his writings. To be open to revelations of transcendence is simply to keep the sense of wonder alive. Philosophy begins in wonder and mysticism makes this wonder a permanent state. The highest stage in the path is the stage of wonder or getting lost as Ibn Arabi says. Nietzsche was right to emphasize loyalty to this earth. In fact, father Zosima in Dostoevsky's mystical work *The Brothers Karamazov* sees every garden as the Garden of Eden. He says:

> We don't understand that life is a paradise [at present], for

> we have only to wish to understand this and it will immediately appear before us in all its beauty.

Rabbi Herschel has made the same point in different terms "Just to be is a blessing, just to live is holy."

The quarrel between transcendentalists and anti-transcendentalists of almost all hues is largely a verbal quibble. Platonic ideal world is not a separate world, an abstraction. But the world ordinarily thought to be world is also not the whole world but just a mental construction. Blake sees eternity in an hour or infinity in a grain of sand. In fact, for the mystics everything is, as it is infinite. Eternity is not an abstraction or some new realm as opposed to time but the present moment. To live in eternity is to live in the present, to live moment by moment. What characterizes a philosopher of transcendence is he continues to find a depth in the world, something that excites wonder, something that invites our response and even love. Wittgenstein lucidly made this point in these words:

> Some philosophers (or whatever you like to call them) suffer from what may be called "loss of problems". Then everything seems quite simple to them, no deep problems seem to exist any more, the world becomes broad and flat and loses all depth, and what they write becomes immeasurably shallow and trivial. Russell and H.G. Wells suffer from this. — Zettel, 456

His remark about Ayer after listening to his debate with Father Copleston that "he has a point but he is shallow" underscores the same sensibility. His remark that "The I, the I is what is deeply mysterious" (*Notebooks*, p. 80) is in line with this viewpoint. Though he granted that only strictly scientific statements are meaningful, he cautioned against positivists that natural science could never touch what was really important in human life, the mystical.

That would have to be contemplated in silence. For

"whereof one cannot speak, thereof one must besilent/" as the last proposition of the *Tractatus* declared. We can understand his famous statement "I am not a religious man but I cannot help seeing every problem from a religious point of view" in this light. In fact, religions don't aim at even vision but advocate a discipline that makes us open or vulnerable to reality, to richness of being, to thingliness of things as Heidegger would have it, to essences of things that get expressed through things when looked at rather than thought. Wittgenstein would recommend looking instead of thinking. Transcendence of thinking is what contemplation/meditation is all about. It appears to me that Wittgenstein says nothing because nothing needs to be said. He advocates no position or privilges no point of view because this can't be done. All his endeavour, like the mystics and prophets, is to emphasize that we need to see with open eyes, unburdened by memories or anxieties of thought. We need to see through God's eyes. And that consists in non-egoistic vision and this makes it possible to assert that "How things stand is God".

Wittgenstein gave great attention to language in order to show that what constitutes us and what we value most is delimited from what could be expressed in language, from profane textual domain. The *Tractatus*'s design was expressly determined by this consideration. For him the metaphysical self that constitutes us transcends the world, the urges that move us point beyond the world, experiences that we cherish most are of the world beyond the ordinarily familiar world, our ethical and aesthetic dimensions are anchored outside the world. For him both the willing subjects and the knowing subjects are one and both are outside of the world, and are the source of our language and world-cognition. However, as in mystical traditions, transcendence is not consummated; it remains an unfulfilled quest. It is movement, perpetual movement and not reaching anywhere. It is the limit that can never be reached. Absolute is inexhaustibly rich. Man must perpetually travel. Experiences are open-ended and self is perpetually creative. Our search for transcendence, like our need to engage with philosophy is, as Pradhan has noted,

> merely an ideal never to be fulfilled, because the metaphysics of experience as unfolded through our subjectivity has to be constantly guarded against unclarity and confusion through language itself. Therefore, philosophy can never ultimately be transcended, since transcendence of language itself is a continuing activity which is performed by philosophy.
>
> — Pradhan: 230

It means one can never stop worshipping or glorifying God and travel on the plane of servitude or perfect his surrender or state of innocence or vulnerability to reality. Mystics, as true philosophers (as traditionally understood activity), are always striving to remove the veils of language and thought in order to reach the still centre of existence that transcends language and thought. Wittgenstein is quite clear on the point that conceptual analysis can teach nothing about reality. Nor resolve the puzzle of how we should understand the world and how we should live. He leaves all questions open and thus paves way for alternative approaches that bypass conceptual analysis and science for understanding or living the great mystery of life. As Paul Johnson notes:

> The conclusion of a Wittegenstein investigation still has all great questions open. As far as the Inner is concerned, in one sense it will always remain as mysterious as life itself.
>
> —Johnson: 239

This is precisely mystical attitude towards mystery of life. No question is answered. Only our plane of seeing life shifts and dissolves the ordinary sense of questions. We consent to unlearn. The learned ignorance.

The mystic is an extraordinarily ordinary person. He is a

> non-knower, non-caner. The human need for account for the world and our place in it will not disappear, because traditional metaphysics has been shown to be flawed . . . accepting these points doesn't involve embracing relativism and is close to a moral argument. — Pradhan, 239

It means the mystic, the artist, the poet, the scientist, shall ever be busy and man needs to be humble. Let Reality speak to him. Let him learn to be receptive. Imposing conceptual structures is violence. We need to learn to be still so that God speaks to us in silence. This opening up, surrender of self, emptying out and polishing our receptivity is what is the crux of Vedānta as Som Raj Gupta has argued in his largely ignored but superb work *Word Speaks to the Faustian Man* (1991). In fact, all religious and mystical traditions are agreed on this point.

Wittgenstein's statement that "God is the meaning of life" is quintessentially mystical and best understood in light of mystical writings. Underhill's explication of the meaning of life in mysticism is best commentary on this statement. One can't be more God-intoxicated to equate the most significant thing in life with God. Wittgenstein's statement that man is a microcosmos is comprehensible only in mystical world view. He also observed that "As a thing among things each thing is equally insignificant. As a world each one equally significant" (NB: 83) which reminds of Blake's seeing the heaven in a grain of sand. Mystics have never doubted the significance of the meanest flower or blade of grass seeing everything as the face of the Absolute, as participating in everything.

Wittgenstein famously remarked that the riddle doesn't exist and the solution of the problem of life is seen in the disappearance of the problem of life. For mystics God is the Light of the world. The question is how to live and that dissolves the problem or riddle. Life is not a riddle to be solved but a mystery to be lived, dissolved in. Riddle exists for those who want to conceptually approach life that resists all logic. The problem of meaning of life is the problem of how to live, how to live so that life stops being problematic. For him good life is world seen in a certain way rather than in a way of behaving. For him there is no value in the world (*TLP* 6.41). It is impossible to be there for proposition of ethics (*TLP* 6.42). The problem of how to live becomes for him not some epistemological inquiry into the problem of how to look at that world, the problem of how to find the right spirit in it.

Wittgenstein assigns key importance to art, on the ground that art alone can express the meaning of life. Only the artist can teach the things that matter most in life. For him art is the solution. Compare this with Coomaraswamy or Schuon on art and aesthetics and we get the full import of the statement.

Wittgenstein has categorically stated the error of moderns for believing that laws of science explain nature. The world is suffused in mystery that is divine. The very fact that there is a world is incomprehensible and metaphysical. God has been conceived as mystery, as given, as something that is — "what is" in Augustine's and Krishnamurti's phrase. Who can afford to deny the "gratuitous" universe? Philosophy begins and ends in wonder explaining nothing and demanding our opening up towards the transcendent miracle of existence. Modern man's key problem in engaging positively or creatively with religion/mysticism arises from felt absence/hiddenness of God in contemporary experience. But taken as synonymous with Reality the complaint seems to lose all warrant. God is the only Experiencer, Knower and Actor. For Ibn Arabi, the great sūfī metaphysician, we don't see but God sees and we don't hear but God listens. God is immanent in every experience. As he says:

> If we gaze, it is upon Him; if we use our intelligence, it is towards Him; if we reflect, it is upon Him; if we know it is Him. For it is He who is revealed in every face, sought in

> every sign, worshipped in every object of worship, and pursued in the invisible and the visible. The whole world prays to Him, prostrates itself before Him and glorifies His praise; tongues speak of Him, hearts are enraptured by love for Him, minds are bewildered in Him. —*Futūhāt*, III: 449-50

For Wittgenstein these lines of Ibn Arabi would be perfectly comprehensible given his notion of metaphysical subject and its role in constituting experience, his view of the world as my world. Here I propose to compare Wittgenstein and Ibn Arabi by keeping Ibn Arabi's explication in the background while applying the same for understanding Wittgenstein. Agnosticism and scepticisms of various orientations in the contemporary world have a point if understood as the declaration of impossibility of conceptually knowing the Reality, Transcendent Principle, the Ground of existence, the whole Truth, the Mystery. However these are often presented in cruder versions that deny men any knowledge of the supraphenomenal or the very existence of the sacred for which Wittgenstein and Ibn Arabi will have zero tolerance. The Pure Absolute or Essence (*Dhat*) in its fundamental aspect — and thus Meaning/Truth/Presence/Identity/Reality *per se* — is beyond the human quest and all attempts to reach It, track it, pinpoint It, catch It in the net of language or realm of the finite or time, to conceptualize It, to imagine It, to speak about It, to affirm anything of It are doomed. Before the Ipseity or *Dhat* one can only be bewildered according to Ibn Arabi and Wittgenstein. The world is ultimately a Mystery, a Mystery of Mysteries and no rational or scientific approach could finally and completely demystify it. The world being ultimately a mystery that resists being demystified by means of conceptual intellect is what transcendence implies as Stace has explained in his *Time and Eternity* (1952). There is no humanely discoverable ultimate truth. All representations of the Real are provisional. Godhead/Absolute/*Zat-uz-Zat* is opaque, deep, deep darkness, impenetrable, the absolutely inscrutable, unknowable Other. Gnosis consists in knowing that God can't be known as Abu Bakr is quoted time and again by Ibn Arabi. As the world is not-He and man ever a worshipper of *his* Lord or conditioned by his belief — a notion subsumable under the concept of form of life in Wittgenstein — and nothing is ever repeated as God's theophanies change ceaselessly, imply that the world will never cease to be an object of wonder and fascination and Beauty never cease to be worshipped and act as an efficient net through which God catches most of his servants as Plato also noted.

Rationalization, familiarization, demystification and descaralization of the world that ultimately make it inhuman, alienating and absurd and disrespectful towards the Big Other can't happen in the Akbarian/Wittgensteinian perspective that sees the mysterious, sacred divine face in everything. The Western philosophy, as Heidegger pointed out, is oblivious to the ground of Being. It is not open to the sacred mystery of Being. It is not the philosopher but the poet who can show the track of the holy, to the sacred mystery of Being. Nothing in the world of known can express the Divine Darkness. All quests end in wonder. In the last analysis man knows nothing to its depth by means of senses, language and reason. Other modes of knowledge such as intellectual intuition give us another kind of knowledge, that instead of making things comprehensible dissolves the knowing subject in the object, preserving the ultimate mystery of things in the process. If to comprehend means to have discursive conceptual knowledge we comprehend nothing ultimately. All our explanations, analyses stop at a certain point. Things are as they are. There is something instead of nothing. Being or *wajūd* is in the last analysis a miracle or a scandal to reason. Why should there be a knowing subject and why should our universe be comprehensible are perhaps unanswerable. Man knows but little and this applies to everything from God to quarks. God is incomparable, transcendent. Symbols are all we know. We can only name things and that is all but things escape us as Wittgenstein would say. God alone knows or is Knowledge. The knowledge of reality given to mystics and prophets is of a different order. God remains inscrutable and the sacred inapproachable. Man's prerogative is to contemplate and dissolve in the mystery of Being. Though Being is aware of itself this awareness has no analysable or knowable structure.

We are here and there is no cure for it. But, more precisely, we are not. Only God is. Only the play of divine names is and man happens to be a locus of their action rather than some independent subject or agency. The cloak of mystery can't be removed from the universe. All human knowledge is progressive unveiling of the ultimate impenetrability of the veil that disguises Reality. Essences are not discursively known. Existence is a mystery and its grandeur and sublimity defy our reason and its categories. Rereading of Kantian sublime by such writers as Derrida or Lyotard is based on increasingly felt inability of reason to contain the brutal power of imagination. We can't conceptualize or represent in language the infinity which human beings do encounter. The highest station is that of bewilderment according to Ibn Arabi and Wittgenstein. All this implies that dogmatisms are unwarranted. Exoteric theologies need to be on guard and take Wittgenstein seriously as Kerr has also argued in *Theology after Wittgenstein.*

It is God and not the name of God that religions seek. Exoteric theologies may not distinguish between the Truth and the descriptions or representations of Truth. Nothing can capture the Reality in rational propositional framework. Even ethical propositions are not possible for Wittgenstein. This means we can only know our inability to know God and will do good on our own, and this means humility in the face of the Great Mystery that God is. This vetoes all self-righteous fundamentalist ideologies. Jaina doctrine of Syādvāda is a corollary of the fundamental mystery and transcendence of the First Principle, the Absolute. This rules out all totalistic or totalitarian claims. Ideological conflicts are based on one's exclusive claim to have access to truth and denying one's fallibility. Religions by relegating truth to transcendent realm and its access to transcendent intellect (which is in us but is not ours) veto all quarrels about accessibility to it of any worldly ideology and self-centric person. Secular philosophies that require no moral purification on the part of the philosopher are barred from entering the doors of the great King or Truth.

The essential ethics of Wittgenstein like that of Ibn Arabi is constituted by such virtues as disinterest, self-denial, charity and love which form the ethical core of all religious/mystical traditions. God is experienced by everyone who sincerely cultivates these virtues. (Post)Modernity has essentially no argument against these values and indeed affirms them. Ibn Arabi has nothing to argue for and against — he only invites us to experience things afresh, to be open to the Real which alone is really experienced in every experience. Wittgenstein's endeavour is similar in his invitation to transcend language and thought in order to see what is, to see things *sub specie aeternitatis*, to see solution in aesthetics, to live rather than think the mystery that life is. God is not a hypothesis that one needs to prove or could question — He is the ground of every perception, every imagination, every conception or thought, every experience. As Wittgenstein puts it, there is no answer as there is no question where nothing can be said.

Wittgenstein is not himself a philosopher in the modern sense of the term which sees reason as the chief if not the only tool for understanding or approaching reality. His view of modern philosophers could not but be largely negative. For projecting Ibn Arabi or Wittgenstein as a philosopher we need to refer to perennialist conception of philosopher and philosophy. His denunciation of rationalism and much of what today passes for intellectuality aligns him to perennialist critics of modern thought. It is not a prerogative of *ratio* or mental faculty of reason but of *nous*, the supraindividual universal faculty of intellect. For Wittgenstein knowing and willing subjects are one and man is knowledge, so to speak. Instead of conceptualizing we can see and in order to pave way for that direct seeing he removes the traps and cobwebs that language builds. Philosophy should not be a mere theoretical rational inquiry, a conceptual analysis or analysis of language as an end in itself but a realization, intellection or noetic vision that transcends subject-object duality and demands something like ethical discipline that Plato argued for. Philosophy as an abstract philosophical discourse based on rationalistic scientific method and its methodically obtained "truths" is what Ibn Arabi and Wittgenstein often critique. Philosophy for Wittgenstein is not a method to discover truth but a sort of shock therapy to prepare us for receiving truth, to make us innocent or children again. It is a sort of death to the linguistically/conceptually constructed self. Philosophy implies for all of the ancients a moral conformity to wisdom: only he is wise, *sophos*, who lives wisely as Schuon notes (8: 136). Living happily is living wisely. Living in such a way that problem disappears and there is no more sorrow and one partakes of eternity by living in the present is what Wittgenstein is all about. Philosophy in the traditional Orphic-Pythagorean sense is wisdom and love combined in a moral and intellectual purification in order to reach the "likeness to god". (Uzdavinys 2005). It is contemplation of Beauty and Good. This is attainable by gnosis. By philosophizing ancients meant "both noetic activity and spiritual practice". Wittgensteinian conception is remarkably similar.

In Ibn Arabi's understanding the Real alone is and there

is no distance between us and It. We are already there in the lap of God — we have never been really away and cannot be away from It. God has never been missed. We have forgotten or fallen asleep but this doesn't alter the fact that God is our very being, our inmost reality. Man is inwardly God and outwardly a creature according to Ibn Arabi. The world is God's visible face. The real, the obvious, that which is always with us, has been always with us, will always be with us, is God. God is the world. God is how things are as Wittgenstein would put it. But this doesn't make him a pantheist as he has categorically stated also that God is outside the world, the world constructed by language, by a self that sees it as the other. God is the Isness of things. He is the Meaning of everything as Wittgenstein said. God constitutes all-pervasive Environment (*al-Muhit* in the Quranic parlance) in which normal man lives, moves and has his being.

Realizing that everything is perfect this very moment or, in Buddhist (Nāgārjunian) terminology, that *saṁsāra* is *nirvāṇa* is realizing God. Wittgenstein's transcendence of good/evil binary and pleading for a vision of perfect harmony between the self and the "alien will" called God and seeing everything as unalterably perfect makes the same point. Such notions as "Ground of being", "depth of life", "mystery of things or existence" which many moderns have advocated as substitute metaphors for what used to be conventionally called God and most often pictured with a human face by anthropomorphic idolatrous imagination seem to be given some representation in this fundamentally Unitarian view of God as Totality, as Reality.

God is not an epistemological problem at all that our mind/ reason can investigate. He is a percept rather than a concept for Ibn Arabi and Wittgenstein. In more poetic terms, He is a song to be sung rather than an abstract Being, a Being among other beings but a Being of beings. God is "the knownest of the known" and so close that we only need to open our eyes, to cleanse the doors of perception to see how. Belief in God is not a proposition for Ibn Arabi and Wittgenstein but a matter of tasting, experiencing the divine (or the revelations of sheer Being), which, to them, presents itself in all experiences every moment and for everyone — in fact God is the Hearing and the Seeing as is often reiterated in the Quranic verse — and not just to a select few in the so-called religious experience which is a Jamesian construct uncritically accepted by many modern philosophers of religion. All the roads lead to His abode as they proceed from it. God is the name of "that which is". He is not something within isness, he himself is that which is.

Knowing oneself after denying the illusory desiring ego one comes to subsist in God. All beliefs and disbeliefs are in the realm of duality and need to be transcended. Ibn Arabi's and Wittgenstein's Unitarian Metaphysics is transtheistic and transcends both theism and atheism. This Unitarianism leads to the realization that the world is ultimately none other than the Absolute and thus finding everything perfect this very moment or seeing eternity here and now.

Modern man's problems are primarily with a constricted dualistic theological view of God and static absolutes of idealistic philosophies. Ibn Arabi's and Wittgenstein's conception of divinity is not vulnerable to these standard critiques of theistic and idealistic philosophical pictures. Most empiricist-positivist-postmodernist critiques look beside the point and are based on faulty construction of religious experience. Modern philosophy of religion seems to have gloriously misunderstood the central experience of religion if Akbarian exposition is accepted. It is not a subject that sees something which constitutes the essence of religious experience or mystical vision for Wittgenstein or Ibn Arabi. It is more a discovery or insight into things as they are, an attitude, a way of seeing the world rather than a particular or extraordinary experience.

Wittgenstein, like traditional philosopher-sages, is more concerned about certainties "seen" or "lived" by the immanent Intellect, as did the best of Greeks than about building rational speculative metaphysics. Cracks, crises and emasculations of the discipline of philosophy in the modern West could have been avoided if the West had not opted for Latin Averrorism and Cartesian rationalism and consequent dualisms and irresolvable problems that still haunt its epistemology and other areas like ontology.

Wittgenstein, like Ibn Arabi, provides a possible exit point from the choking morass of sceptical thought currents which otherwise doom us to abysmal ignorance regarding our most important questions in life including possibility of certain knowledge and knowledge of good life or good action.

"The final end and ultimate return of the gnostics . . . is that the Real is identical with them, while they don't exist", said Ibn Arabi. Wittgenstein arrives at similar conclusions through a different route. It is through the metaphysical realization that one realizes that the Self withdraws from the "servant-Lord" polarity and resides in its own transpersonal being. The subject-object dichotomy is transcended by virtue of pure intellect or Spirit, which is identical with the divine Essence" (Qaisar 2002: 133). Once the soul or *nafs* has withered away in the experience of *fana*, the self-identity of mystic realization is transformed into the Self-identity of metaphysical realization. In the metaphysical perspective the reality of the "I" doesn't belong to man or *nafs* but to the Spirit which is the divine spark at the centre of man's being identical with the unmanifest consciousness or Divine Essence. The crucial distinction between soul and Spirit is necessary to understand the Akbarian-Wittgensteinian metaphysical conception of religious experience. This distinction is largely forgotten by most philosophical critics of religious experience. Numerous misunderstandings and debates of theological *vs.* mystical debate in religions and meaning of such notions as soul/spirit, God/man, could be resolved if we keep these key points in mind. A fruitful dialogue with critics of religion and mysticism and in fact with secular thought in general is possible if we keep in mind ingenious interpretations put forward of many exponents of non-dualism in the contemporary world.

Love of the World and Discovering God as Unutterable Joy

For Wittgenstein happy life is life divine and the great moral prerogative. It comes by loving the world, by *amor fati*. It comes from transcending the principle of ego which judges from self-centric perspective. Jesus said "judge not". For Wittgenstein joy accompanies this surrender of vanity of the self in the All-Embracing Divine Environment or "alien" Cosmic Will. He defined God as the Other, the Great Other that dictates terms, that constrains one, that embodies principle of Necessity.

One is reminded of many writings and especially the following from Augustine's commentary on Psalm 32 in one of his sermons.

> As the harvest, in the vineyard, wherever men must labour hard, they begin with songs whose words express their joy. But when their joy brims over and words are not enough, they abandon even this coherence and give themselves up to the sheer sound of singing. What is this jubilation, this exultant song; It is the melody that means our hearts are bursting with feelings, words cannot express. And to whom does this jubliation most belong? Surely to God, who is unutterable. And does not unutterable mean what cannot be uttered? If words will not come and you may not remain silent, what else can you do but let the melody soar?
>
> — Qtd. in Kerr 1986: 167

In mystical perspective God is joy and awareness of God is joy and thus awareness of reality in which all association with the self is put aside. If it is possible to access Reality or God nihilism is overcome. Weil has an ingenious argument to show that awareness of reality is joy and despair or sadness is a loss of contact with reality. This is her expression of old mystical/metaphysical viewpoint which identifies God as *ānanda* (bliss). Simone Weil expresses the identity of joy with the awareness of reality. Since beauty is manifest appearance, the striking sign of reality, joy can only be a feeling, an awareness of reality. Weil describes sadness as a loss of contact with reality. Through sadness we cannot fulfil our vacation — to understate misery of our condition and to accept our reduction to what we truly are: nothing. The memory of the revelation of reality through joy keeps us from plunging into despair, and the joy felt in our nothingness can be inscribed in our sensibility only by suffering. "Joy and pain are equally precious gifts both of which must be savoured fully, and each in its purity. . . ." (Weil 1951: 132).

Simone Weil best captures the essence of many ideas that Wittgenstein only briefly touches. I think her observations allow us to make sense of Wittgenstein's many observations from a mystical perspective. I reproduce some of her observations to put Wittgenstein in perspective and make him comprehensible.

Wittgenstein maintained that God is the Meaning of life and one must love the world unconditionally to appropriate this meaning. Weil is at her best in showing how one creates the meaning in life by renouncing all personal meanings, by complete acceptance of submission to the order of the world. One loves the order of the world by renouncing all personal interests. This is, in practice, close to Spinoza's view of love of God by renouncing every vestige of personal interest. Freedom lies in recognizing our utter dependence on Totality, on God and in fact giving up sense of illusory autonomy or freedom that we associate with a separate individuality. We are not asked to do something against which our heart or head rebels but just shifting the perception in accordance with the nature of things. One is just asked to accept or recognize the obvious fact that there is the order called necessity, which exists prior to us and which is there for reasons not necessarily understandable in human terms. Reality is there that transcends all our estimates, evaluations, desires and constitutes the given and man has no choice but to accept it by renouncing that which would have led him to rebellion — the sense of individuality and freedom outside God. "Where there is complete, authentic, and unconditioned consent to necessity, there is the fullness of love of God" (Weil 1956: 267). Other texts identify the supernatural faculty in us as consent. For Weil that consent is always consent to the good, and, as such, it is the good itself. Faith is itself this faculty of submission or consent according to her. Absurdism rejects this notion of consent as a species of bad faith. Affirming the principle of autonomy and freedom in man independent of God it can't but reject consent and consequently suffer alienation, *angst* and all those things with which absurdist literature is suffused.

All traditions emphasize remembrance of God. Modern mystics such as Krishnamurti translate it as attention or choiceless awareness. Weil has a similar understanding.

> Attention bridges division of subject and object, knower and known. Attention consists in suspending thought, in making it available, enmity, penetrable by the object. . . . Thought must be empty, waiting, not searching for anything, but ready to receive in its naked truth the object which will penetrate there. — Weil 1951: 92-3

For her God is attention without distraction. It is living as a witness, a detached subject or awareness that watches every moment, that lives in the present by transcending thinking which distracts one from the given, the present. Living beyond the mind, in what has been called as the space of no-mind where time doesn't enter and thus is neither fear nor hope nor any need of consolation. God is what is in Krishnamurti's phrase and to live in God is to be aware of what is without judgement, without condemnation, disinterestedly. Wittgenstein pleaded for seeing without the conceptual glasses, seeing things as they are after transcending philosophy. He meant something similar. Contemplation is a means of transcending confusions created by use or misuse of language.

Giving up the centre of one's own value system is harder, but when we succeed, the very sensibility changes and we become capable of a new way of seeing. We are able to "empty ourselves of little false divinity, deny oneself, to renounce being at the centre of the world, to discern all the points of the world as being centres in the same title and the veritable centre as being outside the world". Wittgenstein was all for this ascesis, this transformation in attitude and not correcting one's views by updating our knowledge of history or science. By saying that God is outside the world or aesthetics is transcendental, he meant adopting the divine perspective of seeing things from outside the world. This necessitates transcendence of individuality and human way of seeing and judging. When we are no longer centres we can't condemn anything and can justify the world

Weil argues that one shouldn't desire particular things or pray for particular things because that is slavery. Her argument practically converges with the formula of *amor fati* and loving everything as if there is eternal recurrence. This alone ensures unconditional love. Total renunciation is demanded for loving the order of the world or affirming everything unconditionally. To quote her:

> Nothing can be produced unless the conditions for its production are brought together.

> Such and such a thing calls for such and such a condition. But if one thinks: everything can be produced, given the conditions, and everything is equivalent. . . .
>
> If one desires a particular thing one becomes enslaved to the series of conditions. But if one desires the series itself, the satisfaction of this desire is unconditioned.
>
> That is why the one and only liberation is love of the order of the world.
>
> Christ on the cross, the greatest harm inflicted on the greatest good [can anything be more absurd and more revolting]: if one loves that, one loves the order of the world.
>
> — Weil 1970: 143-44

Nietzsche suggests a similar way of overcoming nihilism. Affirming the order of the world, praying for nothing, or letting one consent to the order of the world, freedom from the self that seeks consolation and this or that thing — these are the strategies common to Weil and Wittgenstein and in fact is the mystical position. Eckhart teaches the same thing.

Man has only two choices — to affirm his will, his autonomy or to affirm divine or cosmic will and his creatureliness, his nothingness. The first choice pits him against God and against cosmos and leads him to wail and despair for that which is thwarted, which is not honoured in the scheme of things. When one renounces free will and thus choice between good and evil one no longer wishes good against evil to be done to him. Everything is justified because both good and evil are really one. (This relative understanding of good and evil is to be distinguished from that supreme value which Plato calls Good which stands above all relative distinctions.) Camus finds Christianity based on great injustice as an innocent lamb was sacrificed. Weil leaves no scope for any such reading. We too are asked to consent to die, to be crucified, to love God in utter desolation of the Spirit when He seems absent as He was when the Christ cried.

Wittgenstein wanted us to see things from God's perspective or *sub specie aeternitatis*. Weil asks for adapting the perspective of God or the non-perspective of supraindividual faculty of intellect (*nous* as distinct from *ratio* or discursive reason). For attaining this perspective one has to die first. One starts from the Absolute and from the perspective of the Absolute man, his free will, his dreams, his autonomy is an anomaly, a state of disequilibrium. If individual is engulfed in the Absolute as critics of perennialists point out or as existentialists argue against monists, it is something for which nothing can be done. If we are concerned with truth and not sentimentalism there is no escape from the tragic fact that individual or ego doesn't count in the face of the Absolute. Are we after truth as such or truth as it appears to our subjective predispositions, to our heart? God is Truth and man may be in need of consolation though truth need not be necessarily consoling. From perennialist/Weil's perspective the need for consolation is a weakness and a species of bad faith. This also explains Wittgenstein's critique of conventional prayer as petition. We need to be iron-willed, capable of facing utter solitude or Void (*Neant*). It is only the strong man, the superman, who can unconditionally affirm and love fate — a fatalist in this higher sense is a man of strong character — or consent to eternal recurrence. Weil thus advocates the perspective of God in contrast to man-centric perspectives that individualist subjectivist thought currents advocate. This appropriates Keatsian negative capability, Nietzsche's perspectivism and Jainism's Syādvāda as all these imply openness to infinitely nuanced and multidimensional character of reality or truth.

Meaning of Providence

Wittgenstein observed in *Tractatus:* "How things in the world are a matter of complete indifference to what is higher. God does not reveal himself in the world." He rejected conception of prayer as petition. He, however, attempted to make sense of religious person's trust in God and religious language that expresses care of God. Weil explains this difficult problem in her own characteristic way. We need to note that nothing is gratuitous and nothing is meaningless and nothing is out of God's control, care and mercy in God-centric view though nothing is respectful of human egoism which wants things according to the self's desire. Not a sparrow falls except by the writ of providence. There is no role for chance. God is equally present everywhere, in all circumstances. Even raindrops fall in a measured quantity and angels accompany every drop. This is the conviction of all religions, even those who have no personal God to look into the affairs of the world. However, these statements are best understood by those who are familiar with the strange language of God. One can approach such statements not as cognitive verifiable statements that positivist or empiricist could handle but only by being within a "form of life" and mastering the rules and conventions of the particular game. Despite the fact that God is "absent" for Weil there is providence, the mystery of which is not decipherable to the uninitiated, to those profane inquirers who refuse to be annihilated in God and insist on seeing things outside God. The following account is irrefutable on its own terms by outsiders.

> All the events of life, whatever they may be, without exception, are by conventions or signs of God. God establishes a conventional language with his friends. Every event in life is a word of this language. These words are all synonymous but, as happens in beautiful languages, each of them has its completely specific nuance, each of them is untranslatable. The meaning common to all these words is: I love you.
>
> A man drinks a glass of water. The water is God's "I love you". He is two days in the desert without finding anything

> to drink. The dryness in his throat is God's "I love you".... Those who are beginning to learn this language think that only some of its words mean "I love you". Those who know the language know that it has only one meaning
>
> — Weil 1970: 128-29

There is no providence that pertains to our created nature which itself is a result of injustice because by definition it tends to be autonomous and in opposition to the whole, the totality that the term God designates. What transcends the world is indeed indifferent towards the concerns of the world as Wittgenstein would say. To be born is indeed a sin according to both Christian and Eastern traditions, because it involves separation from the ground and thus a kind of fall. (Redemption consists in, according to Weil, consenting to return to God what is His, i.e. our very being or existence. Metaphysically our being is a non-being and God alone is truly real and the illusory dream of separate existence must be given up and this constitutes salvation.) Providence has, as in Beckett, only a negative meaning, of ensuring decreation so that the dust returns to dust and the uncreated Spirit comes to its own glory. Because creation is abandonment it necessarily implies subjection to necessity and thus, in a sense, absence of providence in the usually accepted sense of the term.

> God abandons our whole entire being — flesh, blood, sensibility, intelligence, love — to the pitiless necessity of matter and the cruelty of the devil, except for the eternal and supernatural part of the soul.
>
> The Creation is abandonment. In creating what is other than Himself, God necessarily abandoned it. He only keeps under His care the part of Creation which is Himself — the uncreated part of every creature. That is the Life, the Light, the Word
>
> — Weil 1970: 103

God himself can't prevent what has happened from having

happened. What better proof that the creation is an abdication? What greater abdication of God than is represented by time?

We are abandoned in time. God is not in time.

God emptied himself of his divinity and filled us with a false divinity. Let us empty ourselves of it. This act is the purpose of the act by which we were created.

At this very moment God, by his creative will, is maintaining me in existence, in order that I may renounce it (Weil 1970: 140).

One doesn't ask of providence to take care of this and that because if one loves the order of the world one transcends it with all its misery. Love is transcendence. It is we who are asked to redeem or justify ourselves in relation to the Totality. Love of the world takes all its pain. Love, in the final analysis, is the one thing needful that solves all problems. Here Rumi comes to mind who says love cures all ills. As Weil says: "It is sufficient if we consent to this order of things." Faith is precisely this demand for loving the world which God has made and found good. Faith is trust in the order of things. It is gratitude towards Existence. It is self effacement before the whole, the Totality, the Tao. It is renunciation of all claims to a separate selfhood over and against the Whole.

Meaning of Time and Eternity

Weil has a time-tested mystical mechanism of ending of time called decreation. Decreation, according to Weil, means the "end of time". There is an eternal and hidden part of soul which has the reservoir of energy "beyond time". Through it one lives beyond time. Nihilism is overcome by those prepared to live it to the hilt by annihilating themselves, by eliminating the seeking self which lives in time and rising above the mind which lives in past and future and never beyond time, in the moment. Cultivating the faculty of undistracted attention and intelligence one breaks through the prison of time. Weil is convinced as is Beckett that there is a timeless dimension which is our home.

The entire life of the self is directed towards the future because its substratum is supplementary energy, "produced" only by motives whose ends are in the future (or in the past) (Weil 1956: 184). One should live in the present breaking the ties with the future and the past. Here Heidegger comes to mind who sees life as project into future. Being reduced to the present moment also implies a sinless state, since sin is essentially a claim to mastery over the future, the refusal of future love or suffering, or the refusal to repent of an evil act committed in the past:

> If we contemplate ourselves at a specific moment — the present moment, cut off from past and future — we are innocent. . . . Isolating a moment in this way implies forgiveness. But this isolation is detachment.
>
> — Weil 1956: 216

Remarks on His Ethics and Suffering

In 1939 Wittgenstein said,

> The fact that life is problematic shows the shape of your life does not fit into life's mould. So you must change the way you live and, once your life does fit into the mould, what is problematic will disappear. Or shouldn't I say rather: a man who lives rightly won't experience the problem as sorrow, so for him it will not be a problem but a joy rather; in other words for him it will be a bright halo around his life, not a dubious background.
>
> — CV: 27

This is the crux of mystical theodicy. This is what Buddha said in a different way. Eliminate desire and you will be in peace. Wittgenstein said this quite clearly and wondered what for are amenities. He was the monk in the true sense.

"Ethics", Wittgenstein says, "has nothing to do with

punishment and reward in the ordinary sense" (*Tractatus*, 6.422) and he adds that

> the ethical consequences must lie in the action itself. If we assume that it is a person's actions and the way those actions are performed that create a life, then the ethical desert of those actions is simply that life itself, and since life and the world are said to be one, the ethical reward is nothing else but the fact with which the world looks back at you. To complete the account let us remember that the face that looks back at our is your own: it is tempting to speculate that your ethical reward is no more nor no less than the discovery of your own character.

From Lao Tzu to Ibn Arabi and Eckhart mystical ethics and its eschatological significance have been almost similarly understood. For mystics like Ibn Arabi people choose their stations in the other world. God only unveils their reality. People judge themselves in the light of the Absolute. Choosing to live inside the cocoon of limiting self amounts to obstructing Divine Mercy or choosing separation from the Real. Prayer establishes the dialogue between the self and transcendence. Refusing to pray — which is, for Ibn Arabi, simply gratitude to Existence for the gift of life — amounts to condemning oneself to self-referring and self-enclosed windowless subjective space. Hell is self-love and nothing burns there but self will as one Christian mystic has said.

Modern world is largely convinced that ethics is relative and everything is permissible. There is no ontological foundation for ethics. There are some isolated thinkers who challenge dominant model but in almost all spheres of secular life there are no imperatives like those bequeathed by religions. In contrast Wittgenstein's ethics, like mystical ethics, is grounded in ontology. Noble character traits are not merely extraneous qualities that have no bearing upon our mode of existence. They define our mode of existence and the extent to which we participate in the fullness of the Light of Being. He accepted and further developed by including aesthetics also in it Moore's definition of ethics as a discovery of the Good or Divinity. Ethics, he said, is transcendental. The moral law within is not a biological or cultural product. It is the voice of God. Values are from the transcendental world. His disagreements with Plato come to end here. Ethical commandments have to be observed if man desires felicity. Modern wishy-washy do goodism or absolutization of ethical relativism or ethics complicit with Capitalism and other power-centric ideologies are not compatible with Wittgensteinian theomorphic ethics. Capitalism and State Capitalism disguised as Marxism have little room for attributes of beauty. There is no warrant for ignoring the Scale of the Law interiorized in conscience which provides the norm. Antinomianism which has been popularized by certain libertine *gurus*, has no place here. Men with all their limitations and imperfections can't claim to be infinitely beyond this world and thus beyond good and evil which we encounter at every stage of existence. Man must always separate divine viewpoint which is corollary of his incomparability from his own human, all-too-human viewpoint which is a corollary of divine similarity as Ibn Arabi would insist. However, all this should not be construed to imply that he countenances moralism which is typical modern heresy. The deadly criticism of Nietzsche on morality doesn't apply to his view of ethics. Wittgenstein read *Gospels in Brief* by Tolstoy and then read *Anti-Christ* of Nietzsche and could not be moved an inch from his commitment to Tolstoy's Christian ethical universe. Postmodern problematization of ethics and modern scientific discoveries implicating relativism of morals can't problematize Akbarian-Wittgensteinian position as they too, like Nietzsche's *Zarathustra*, speak from the high mountains of the Spirit which transcends all actions, good or evil. Wittgenstein emphasizes that man is not an agent of action. He can't will to do good. This is explainable by reference to God as the Only Doer or what Taoism calls *wu wei wei*, actionless action. Evil action in ordinary parlance is possible only when man is under the dominion of ego or lower self and Wittgenstein's demand for possibility of ethics is transcendence of this principle of egoism.

It is religion taken as a metanarrative, a system, an ideology explaining things, as privileging of the other world or eternity at the cost of this world and time here now and privileging of soul over body, elaborate creedal formulae coached in terms of propositions privileging the religious as distinct from or opposite to the secular, as unqualified belief in the representation of Reality and their absolutist exclusivism that Ibn Arabi and Wittgenstein plead for transcending by virtue of their Unitarianism that puts the Real at the centre while questioning absolutization of all conceptions and theorizations of It. The world is one. And It must be affirmed *in toto*. Language and thought divide the One of experience and integrity of unitary subject and the world. The Real is the essence of everything and no dualistic apprehension or categorical framework can capture it. It is the totality of all existents, a metaphysical whole that can't be reduced to an object of knowledge by a subject that is thought to be separate from the object. All this implies that meaning closure, epistemic chauvinism, totalistic thought and consequent war on the basis of a particular conception or delimitation of the Reality/Truth are unwarranted. Truth rather than discourse *about* Truth which is the prerogative of exoteric theology and rational philosophy is what the gnostic comes to realize and as it is the One and All it necessarily follows that the knower transcends all particular beliefs and views. Living Truth, dissolving in Truth, rather than talking about it and fighting for it is the way to end all conflicts that arise from dualistic theological and rationalistic philosophical approaches.

For Wittgenstein religion gives one new eyes so that everything looks different and redeemed by and suffused with love. God is wherever love is, beauty is, blessedness is and grace is. In fact, God is these things and not an abstraction or object. This solves the important problems of theology as well without making it pantheism either. Seen with the eyes of love, trust and faith everything appears God. God is not the name of a person or entity but the very thingness of a thing, the beauty of beauty, the goodness in the good. As Weil puts it:

> God not as I love, but as emerald is green. He is "I love". And I too, if I were in the state of perfection, would love as emerald is green. I would be an impersonal person (like God).
>
> — Weil 1970: 129

God speaks these words through all of us who love and more effectively through those who love so intensely and selflessly as to become love. What differentiates a *bhakti* mystic or *sūfī* from ordinary mortals or non-mystics is their capacity to love and it is this love which redeems them. All positive experiences — aesthetic, moral, cognitive — are bridges to God-realization.

Representation or Practice of the Self?

Wittgenstein is concerned, above all, with the happy life and that he links with transcendence of desiring or willing self. His problem is ethical and existential and his proposed solution too is on these planes that have little to do with language or representation business. His solution involves contemplating, looking, wondering, loving rather than thinking or questioning. He is struggling with/against language rather than doing business with it. His object (ethical/aesthetical/religious or mystical) is not in the world, is untouched by scientific discoveries or any speculative exercise. His concern is metaphysical and metaphysical is what he calls mysterious, mystical, outside the world, supernatural. He was interested in speaking without words — "conveying thoughts by themselves without words" (*CV*: 15). He thought, with Goethe, that we need to learn from contemplation of untrammelled nature rather than laboratory experiement and hypothesis that distort the truth (*CV*: 11). Like Heidegger he found the richness of being to which poets rather than philosophers point out the key to salvation.

Wittgenstein was supremely religious man and it is because he is religious in every important sense of term (rather than only in a trivial sense as G.H. von Wright claims) that he said he is not a religious man. Humility is the supreme virtue of a religious man. He had not only respect for religion (including even its rituals) but moulded his life by its dictates. One of the things Christianity says, Wittgenstein thinks, is that all sound doctrines are of no avail. One must change one's life (or the *direction* of one's life). According to him Christianity didn't talk about what has happened or will happen to man but what happens daily to him, every moment (*CV*: 28). Existentialist theology and demythologization movement have been emphasizing this point as have been mystics in all climes. For all religions the greatest obstacle in one's journey to God or beatitude is pride/ego and Wittgenstein was supremely concerned about this thing all his life and many of his biographical details can be understood in this light only.

His remarks about symbolic significance of rituals and how they embody our search for the sacred in *Culture and Value* and elsewhere show how profound his religious sensibility is. His dismissal of Frazer and defence of "primitives" at many points against moderns show what kind of a man he was. His critique of modernity and European civilization is fundamentally on religious grounds. He found in it loss of respect for mystery, the idea of progress, lack of culture and direction or purpose, and the cult of the ugly in its art, objectionable. All his beloved writers and philosophers have been religious/mystical. God was his ultimate concern as shown by exemplary moral life he lived and his wish to have been able to dedicate all his work to the glory of God. His biographer, Brian McGuinness, reports that before doing any action, he prayed like this: "God be with me!", "The spirit be with me". Sin and thus hell were terribly real for him. He thought about sin as seriously if not more as about logic as his reply to Russell to the question regarding what he was thinking about when he came to meet him during night. Explanations, reasons, justifications *come to an end* in religious thinking for Wittgenstein. Wittgenstein, like the mystics before and after him, did not favour a cosmological conception of a Deity. For mystics theology is in fact autology. He was, like Spinoza, God-intoxicated and standard reading of him as fideist or non-cognitivist is far off the mark. His considering himself wretched and in need of infinite help and never ceasing to scrutinize the desires, vanity and all that religion cautions against shows how seriously he took religion and what grounds it.

Wittgenstein's stand on different aspects of ethics is the following. Ethics deals with absolute value; value judgements that we often use can be reduced to facts. We can re-formulate them as hypothetical judgements of if . . . then form and make them to be statements of facts. Paradoxically, Wittgenstein states that we can experience value. An experience is an event, and hence ought to be factual. It seems strange that Wittgenstein maintains that values are absolute and transcendental and yet we can experience them. Ethical values cannot be spoken or discussed about since they are transcendental. There are explicit statements of Wittgenstein that militate against any kind of fideist interpretation, extreme or moderate versions of it. For him God is the case. How things are is the mystical. These imply Wittgenstein can't be framed in either ethical or conventional religious frameworks.

He is fundamentally a mystic who has made metaphysical claims in the sense metaphysics is understood by perennialists. He has made cognitive claims of mysticism though not of religion. What better argument for cognitivity or knowledge claim and against fidiest interpretations than his assertion that the mystical shows forth?

Wittgenstein scholars have not paid due attention to the distinction between the religious/theological and the mystical and confounded the two in approaching him resulting in quite divergent interpretations. I have foregrounded the mystical in him which grounds his religiosity and this gives us a heremeneutical tool to make sense of his different observations on religion. I argue that he is an absolutist and we should not approach him from the lens of *Philosophical Investigations* and then attempt to show that religion is a language game, a foundationless discourse making no cognitive or knowledge claims and a matter of faith. If Śaṅkara or Eckhart or Augustine are absolutists, Wittgenstein too is an absolutist for whom God/eternity is absolute certainty, the first principle and is experienced rather than merely believed.

The Unrepresentable Shows Forth

In a letter from the Russian front dated 9 April 1917, to his friend Paul Engelmann, who had sent him a poem by the early nineteenth-century poet Johann Ludwig Uhlan, Wittgenstein wrote:

> The Poem by Uhlan is really magnificent. And this is how it is: if only you do not try to utter what is unutterable then nothing gets lost. But the unutterable will be — unutterably — contained in what has been uttered!
>
> — Qtd. in Kerr 1986: 166

Though one can't clearly state what he means similar things in the writings of mystics that emphasize how God speaks when we become silent and how everything is lighted up by

God and God is meaning of everything, how transcendence and immanence or *nirvāṇa* and *saṁsāra* are ultimately linked and even one. The unrepresentable shows forth and the gnostic sees nothing but That which is also the Light of the world, the light that is neither of the sea nor of the land but light that lights everything.

Though we should guard against the identification of the inexpressible and the mystical, it is nevertheless clear that the really mystical, for Wittgenstein, transcends the world but can be accessed in ethical life rooted in transcendence and mystical and aesthetic experiences and concretely lived in religious forms and rituals. If the Unrepresentable were not accessible there would be no meaning for Wittgenstein's taking cudgels on its behalf and judging modern intellectual thought currents from religio-mystical viewpoint. Wittgenstein rejects all the important modernist myths such as that of progress and criticizes reductionism in anthropology and psychologism to pave the way for faith. He judges modernity in the light of faith. It means how cognitive an affair religion is for him. He takes Frazer and his likes to task for rationalistic interpretation of traditional ritual. He pointed out that many religious practices are not generated by any views that one could censure or verify. He saw university educated intelligentsia of the West carriers of moral and spiritual corruption that had thrusted human civilization into a new dark age.

For Wittgenstein

> Symbolism of Catholicism is wonderful beyond words. But any attempt to make it into a philosophical system is offensive. All religions are wonderful, even those of the most primitive tribes.
> — Qtd. in Kerr 1986

Nothing of this sort could come out from an agnostic. Like mystics he rejects literalism and believes in symbolism. He seems to appreciate the transcendental unity of religions by emphasizing mystical core at the heart of them. Religion for him is deed and not theory. This was so for Buddha also and, in fact, mystics have seen religion as transformative therapeutic towards a good life. Like mystics, he underscored non-anthropomorphic character of belief. God for him is not a thing, a being, a superbeing, an existence.

Conclusion

No doubt can be entertained regarding Wittgenstein's commitment to religion even if he didn't deem himself pure enough to be called a religious man. He looked at every problem from religious point of view. He liked to call himself as "a truth seeker", and he had found it, though one can't claim that he had reached the peaks that advanced mystics have access to.

> It strikes me that religious belief could only be something like a passionate commitment to a system of reference, hence though it is belief and assessing life. It is passionately seizing hold of this interpretation.

If religion is a method of assessing life, it is in a way cognitive. If one takes it seriously, it means one takes it to be truth of a certain kind. For Wittgenstein religion was a matter of life and death. He was not a phenomenologist observing it with a detachment of a scientist. He plunged passionately into God and found the treasure. He meant business when he talked about religion or philosophy. He had faith and learnt wisdom in the end, the wisdom of an Oriental sage who cultivates detachment. For him it is wisdom that he finds nowhere in his contemporary professors of philosophy doing sort of a work as it appears in *Mind* that really counts. To conclude there is a path that bypasses language and thought for accessing that which really matters, for realization of what has been eternal quest for values. Wittgenstein has outlined this path that needs to be kept in mind while we ponder on the limits and approaches to linguistic representations. No confusion needs to be entertained in understanding Wittgenstein, essentially his religious/mystical outlook. He was not a great mystic but, no doubt, a great mystical philosopher. He had very few intense mystical experiences. He often behaved in a way that is not expected of a mystic. Contemplating committing suicide, extreme agitated mind at times, sense of gloom that obsessed him are not the attributes of a great mystic. He didn't take himself to be a saint but had the saintly ideal of moral purity to which he tried to conform. However, if religion or mysticism are centred on deeds or practices we can't but see him as a great soul who renounced wealth, fame, amenities and other guises that self-love takes. He did find for himself the truth he sought and for him indeed philosophy has been love of wisdom. He has more wisdom than faith which is passionless and that is a sign of maturity of religion. His fundamental stance can be expressed in few sentences that express a world view that is 100 per cent Hebraic and 100 per cent mystical. I conclude by quoting and commenting on these few sentences.

The problem of life is "seen in the disappearance of the problem". This means that the answer is not known, but seen and need not be known, as the problem doesn't demand an answer as it disappears. In fact, the question can't be asked. Vanishing of the problem is only found through a way of knowing other than language. "To believe in God means to understand the question about the meaning of life" (*NB*: 74). To believe in God means to understand that there is more than facts (*NB*: 74). For him to pray is to think about the meaning of life. Further, explaining the meaning of mystical prayer he says that "I can't bend the happenings of the world to my will; I am completely powerless. I can only make myself independent of the world." It is impossible to know God through what can be said. What one knows about God is that this world exists. To be outside the world means to be outside what can be put into words. "I am my world" (*Tractatus* 5.63). Atkinson beautifully explains it:

> The separation between the thinker and the thought, or the eye and the object of sight, occurs in language, not in the event itself. Thus the idea of the personal self or subject in terms of a thinker of the thought among others. The subject is not a thing in the world and the thought one has of it does not correspond to a fact. — Atkinson 2009: 133

The difference between seeing the object together with and in space and time is a matter of seeing the world from either the outside or the inside. From the outside it is to see the world like one's eye in its visual field (*NB*: 73). To see the object *sub specie aeternitatis* from the outside is to see it from outside the world and language. Being outside language there is nothing that can be said about an object. Wittgenstein states that there are things that can't be put into words. These things show themselves. They are the mystical (*Tractatus* 6.522). These things "don't point to another world outside the world, but show themselves as the mystical". The metaphysical interpretation of the *Tractatus* has been forcefully criticized by a host of scholars including Atkinson. The mystical is what one finds immediately in reality. What "can't be put into words shows itself as the world that is and what shows itself must be coordinated with the solipsistic self in the moment of experience. This moment, I have argued, is to feel the world as a limited whole" (Atkinson 2009: 69).

We need not advocate metaphysical interpretation and can remain contended with the fact that there is something that science can't handle, there is a joy of the spirit available to a happy man who has consented to be nothing, the world is full of beauty, there are no problems and man's hunger for higher things can be quenched. It hardly matters where we precisely locate transcendence that gives meaning to life and grounds ethics and aesthetics — beyond the world or immanently within its depths. Interpretations, theological and metaphysical, ultimately can differ but what matters is what Wittgenstein achieves. He achieves the similar end that religions and mysticisms across traditions have sought. He gets the riddle dissolved and puts thoughts or philosophy to peace and that is the end of philosophical/mystical quest.

Abbreviations

NB : *Notebooks*, 1914-16
TLP : *Tractatus Logio-Philosophicus*
CV : *Culture and Value*

References

Atkinson, James R., *The Mystical in Wittgenstein's Early Writings*, London: Routledge, 2009.

Johnson, Paul, *Rethinking the Inner*, London: Routledge, 1993.

Ibn Arabi, 1972–91, *al-Futûhât al-makkiyya*, 14 vols., ed. O. Yahia, Cairo: al-Hay'at al-Misriyyat al-ūmma li'l-Kitāb, (Quotes and translations are mostly from Chittick and Chodkiewicz.)

Lazenby, Mark, *The Early Wittgenstein on Religion*, Continuum, 2006.

Kerr, Fergus, *Theology after Wittgenstein*, Oxford: Blackwell, 1989.

McGuinness, Brian, "Mysticism of the *Tractatus*", *Philosophical Review*, 75, 1966.

Nieli, Russel, *From Mysticism to Ordinary Language Philosophy: A Study of Viennese Positivism and the Thought of Ludwig Wittgenstein*, New York: SUNY, 1987.

Pradhan, R.C., *Language and Experience: An Interpretation of the Later Philosophy of Wittgenstein*, Meerut: Anu Prakasan, 1981.

Qaisar, Shahzad, *Iqbal and Khawja Ghulam Farid on Experiencing God*, Lahore: Iqbal Academy, 2002.

Schuon, F., *Understanding Islam*, tr. D.M. Mattuson, London: George Allen & Unwin.

Sontag, Fredrick, *Wittgenstein and the Mystical: Philosophy as an Ascetic Practice*, Oxford University Press, 2000.

Stace, W.T., *Time and Eternity: An Essay concerning Philosophy of Religion*, 1952.

Weil, Simone, 1970, *First and Last Notebooks*, tr. Richard Reese, New York: Oxford University Press (Here in the text referred to as *F.*)

———, *Waiting on God*, 1951, tr. Emma Caruford, New York: Putnam, 1951 (referred as *WG*).

———, *The Notebooks of Simone Weil*, 1956, tr. Arthur F. Mills, 2 vols., Putnam (referred as *N*).

Wittgenstein, Ludwig, *Notebooks, 1914-16*, 2nd edn., ed. Wright and Ascombe, Oxford: Blackwell, 1961.

———, *Culture and Value*, ed. G.H. von Wright, tr. P. Winch, Oxford: Basil Blackwell, 1980.

———, *Tractatus Logico-Philosophicus*, tr. D.F. Pears and B.F. McGuinness, London: Routeledge and Kegan Paul, 1961.

17

Hermeneutics and Language Analysis*

Gadamer and Wittgenstein on the Nature of Language

Sreekumar Nellickappilly

Introduction

FOR both Wittgenstein and Gadamer, arguably the most prominent proponents of two different philosophical positions that considered language as perennially significant, the question of understanding meaning occupies a central place. For finding an obvious common denominator, it is easier to approach the problem negatively; what happens when we lack a proper understanding?

When we fail to understand something, we find ourselves in a foreign territory, or a thick forest where there are no signboards to give us directions. We begin navigating through the tides with great difficulties, often losing ourselves and ending up in whirlpools. But no terrain is absolutely unfamiliar. We gradually start negotiating and at some point will start becoming comfortable with the initially unfamiliar territories. We then become a native! We realize that we are back home, or we make a new home in what was initially a foreign land. In any case, understanding meaning amounts to be an

* An earlier version of this paper was published in the *Indian Philosophical Quarterly*, vol. 34 nos. 2-4, April-December 2007, pp. 83-103.

experience of returning home. Since we encounter meanings infinitely, we keep on adding to our existing structure, only to realize that we do not actually "add", but only "discover" hitherto unknown facets of our own most intimate possession, i.e. language. In every new discovery the otherness of language becomes a familiar terrain for us. Yet it keeps on enticing us by unravelling new dimensions.

Gadamer and Wittgenstein treated language as our "natural" home in similar ways (though not in the same way). By affirming the essential linguisticality of man and by making language part of man's natural history, both Gadamer and Wittgenstein adopt for some forms of phenomenological paths that examine human nature and link it with the nature of language in fundamental ways. For Gadamer, this process primarily requires certain context of preunderstood meanings or "prejudices" with which we encounter the unfamiliar and for Wittgenstein, our "natural" ability to participate in a diversity of language-games. Gadamer expects hermeneutics to take us back into language and Wittgenstein envisages language analysis to take us back to the domain of natural use of linguistic expressions. As Christopher Smith says,

> the concerns of hermeneutical enquiry and of language analysis are the same; getting clear about what we say, about meanings in language as it is spoken, about the meanings of ordinary language. Smith concludes that a good part of what Gadamer is doing is translatable in terms of ordinary language philosophy.[1]

But, while for Gadamer this "driving home" essentially involves interpretation, Wittgenstein sees only a minimal role to the latter. This has led many to think that Wittgenstein, in

1. P. Christopher Smith, 1991, *Hermeneutics and Human Finitude: Toward a Theory of Ethical Understanding,* New York: Fordham University Press, p 106.

spite of his recognition of the rootedness of language use in the multitude of life contexts that resist any essential predetermined structure, was nevertheless affirmed following certain intersubjectively determined rules as an essential feature of all language-games. Patrick Rogers Horn observes that, even while resisting essentialism, Wittgenstein was never able to free himself of the notion that language is a sort of calculus, although he did abandon the notion of language as one great calculus and embraced the idea that language is a collection of different calculi.[2]

Gadamer, on the other hand, derives the inevitability of interpretation from the essential historicality of all linguistic expressions; the essential enrootedness of language uses in specific historical contexts. For both Gadamer and Wittgenstein, meaning, understanding and truth are not connected with a subjective mind and are to be essentially discovered in the contexts of actual praxis. But, while Wittgenstein seeks to identify certain rules that everyone who participates in a particular form of conversation needs to honour and follow in order to foster understanding, Gadamer links the questions of meaning, understanding and truth to the whole history and prospects of linguistic traditions that participate in the process of understanding. According to him, the truth of a proposition, ultimately

> . . . depends upon the genuineness of its enrootedness and bond with the person of the speaker in whom it wins its truth potential, for the meaning of the statement is not exhausted in what is stated. It can be disclosed only if one traces its history of motivation and looks ahead of its implications.[3]

---

2. Patrick Rogers Horn, *Gadamer and Wittgenstein on the Unity of Language,* Hampshire: Ashgate, 2005, p. 112.
3. Hans-Georg Gadamer, *Reason in the Age of Science,* tr. Frederick G. Lawrence, Cambridge: The MIT Press, 1981, 9.44.

WITTGENSTEIN AND THE HERMENEUTIC PROBLEM

Wittgenstein's later thought was often conceived by many as adopting a position very close to the thinkers of the hermeneutic tradition. For both the early Wittgenstein and the later, the problems of meaning and its understanding occupy a space of cardinal importance. Wittgenstein, during the earlier phase of his thought, was concerned solely with the so-called logical structure of language, which is essentially ahistorical. Hermeneutics, on the other hand, always conceptualized the issues that gained relevance when we encountered textual meaning in a historical context. But Wittgenstein's later thought brought the semantic content of language into the diverse life situations where the later is being employed. The contextuality of language use and discourse units abolished the sharp boundaries between concepts.[4] This paradigm shift had raised certain conceptual issues which were much similar to those which the hermeneutic thinkers encountered when they addressed the problem of historicity.

This paper examines the views of the hermeneutic philosophers, particularly Hans Georg Gadamer and later Wittgenstein with an objective to understand the nature of language in their philosophies. It briefly examines the positions of the Romanticists like Frederick Schleiermacher and Wilhelm Dilthey and the philosophical hermeneutics of Gadamer, in order to evaluate the hermeneutic problem. The similarities in their approaches towards the question of alien meanings and towards the notion of "alienness" itself will be focused. Wittgenstein approaches these problems with a concept of "rule following", which would not only account for the diversity of human life activities, but also would tackle the problem of "alienness" and therefore bypass the

4. Cf. L: Wittgenstein, 2001, *Philosophical Investigations* (hereafter *PI*), tr. G.E.M. Anscombe, Malden: Blackwell Publishing, # 68 and 76.

hermeneutic problem by making "interpretation" practically less relevant. He affirms that, ". . . there is a way of grasping a rule which is *not* an *interpretation*, but which is exhibited in what we call 'obeying the rule' and 'going against it' in actual cases".[5] For him, understanding meaning becomes a participatory effort. We participate in the playing of a game, where the movements are monitored by means of intersubjective rules.

The views of Schleiermacher and Dilthey are different from this, though they too bypass the hermeneutic problem with an idea of "reproduction" of the original meaning with the assistance of a methodological procedure. But while they seek to locate meaning in a subjective environment — in the psychic life of the author — Wittgenstein categorically opposes any form of mentalism that links meaning and truth with the subjective mind. Instead, he proposes to look into the socially constituted forms of life. By rejecting the idea of "private language" Wittgenstein affirms the essential "public" nature of rules that participants in a game need to follow. This view comes incredibly close to Gadamer's conception of language that makes the latter a domain of public participation.

With Gadamer, hermeneutics goes beyond the limits set by the concept of method. It envisages understanding traditions and with this, not only are texts understood, but insights are gained and truths are acknowledged.[6] Gadamer attempts to expose the ultimate futility of the idea of "objective comprehension" by showing how all our encounters with textual meanings are historically situated. It redefines the concept of meaning and shows that it is not a phenomenon that evolves from individual intentional acts, nor is it

5. L: Wittgenstein, 2001, *Philosophical Investigations*. # 201.
6. Cf. Hans Georg Gadamer, 1975, *Truth and Method* (hereafter *TM*), New York, The Seabury Press, p. xi.

understood with the learning of certain fixed rules, but is essentially something that is discovered in a common language of conversation. Gadamer places meaning in an ever-dynamic process of language-use and in order to explain the process of understanding meaning, emphasizes the dialogic process between the text and its interpreter. He argues that, in conversations between different people, meaning is located in a common language. Comprehension of meaning is facilitated through such an interaction where one not only participates in the "playing of a game", but also works for the creation of a common language between the participants.

The Hermeneutic Problem

The central characteristic feature of the hermeneutic approach is the recognition of historicity, which Gadamer reinforced by means of the notion of linguisticality. It recognizes man's life as bounded by specific historical and cultural life situations. Though this feature has wider implications, for our analysis we confine this analysis to the issues associated with conceiving the nature of language in certain peculiar ways and the consequent problems related to the understanding of meaning.

For the early hermeneutic philosophers Schleiermacher and Dilthey, the hermeneutic problem attracts attention owing to the text's and the interpreter's different situatedness in history.[7] Dilthey particularly conceived it as a methodological problem when he raised the issue of "objective comprehension" of meaning in the context of the human sciences and the historical phenomenon. Intentional and imaginative categories are actively at work for the constitution of the historical phenomenon, and for Dilthey, historical reality was

7. F.D.E.: Schleiermacher, "The Aphorisms on Hermeneutics From 1805 and 1809/10", in *The Hermeneutics Tradition, From Ast to Ricoeur* (hereafter *HT*), Albany: State University of New York Press, p. 62.

constituted of these intentional human acts. Since the being of man is organically related to it the historical phenomena cannot be approached in a detached manner. All these imply a different kind of experience and knowledge for the historical phenomenon, which radically differs, from that which relies on the subject-object relational pattern.[8] Man's being and his situations are intimately interconnected.[9] This shows that meaning and understanding are intimately associated with the dialectical relationship between the human self-making process and the historical situation. Subsequently, the notion of understanding the text in the sense of objectively comprehending its meaning appears problematic as meaning of the text in this context, depends on the nature of the dialectical relationship which will be different in different historical situations.

As a solution to this issue, Schleiermacher and Dilthey conceived meanings as determinate and unchanging by locating them in an ahistorical horizon outside the syntactical arrangement and the conventional usage pattern of the linguistic signs. In short, meanings have to be placed well outside the linguistic system, which is necessarily a historical product. As E.D. Hirsch puts it:

> If a meaning can change its identity and in fact does, then

---

8. Dilthey here refers to Husserl's distinction between two forms of experience, *erlebnis* and *erfahrung* where the former refers to the lived experiences, which are characterized by the "subjective" response to the world and are given immediately to the consciousness as things themselves in their subjective modes of givenness, See Georgia Warnke, 1987, *Gadamer: Hermeneutics, Tradition and Reason*, Stanford: Stanford University Press, pp. 26-28.
9. See my article "Language and the Evolution of the Self", in *Indian Philosophical Quarterly*, vol., XXIX, no. 2&3, April-July 2002, pp. 319-33.

> we have no norm for judging whether we are encountering the real meaning in a changed form or some spurious meaning that is pretending to be the one we seek. . . . To the interpreter this lack of a stable normative principle is equivalent to the indeterminacy of meaning.[10]

Schleiermacher placed meaning in the total intentional life of the author and Dilthey identifies the human subjectivity as its location. Hirsch reasserts these insights and proclaims that meaning is an affair of consciousness and not of words.[11] Meaning, according to him, is whatever someone has willed to convey by means of language.[12] This process of locating meaning in the author's intentional life is, in effect, a process of taking meaning outside the language of the text and therefore, outside the historical and self-making process. Meaning is thus made ahistorical.

Schleiermacher further asserted that meaning is not an exclusive product of the author's subjective will and highlighted the intimate relationship between the subjective and objective meaning (individuality and totality), both in the linguistic and in the psychological realms. Schleiermacher affirms that everyone shares certain universal traits and every person has a susceptibility to intuiting others, in addition to his sharing many human characteristics.[13]

Meaning is not found in an isolated and single unit of language but has to be located in the totality of the text and even further in the context of a literary tradition of the time of the text, where the work is essentially related with other

---

10. E.D. Hirsch, 1967, *Validity of Interpretation*, New Haven: Yale University Press. p. 46.
11. Cf. Ibid., p. 4.
12. Cf. Ibid., p. 31.
13. F.D.E. Schleiermacher, 1990, "The Hermeneutics: Outline of the 1819 Lectures", in *HT*, p. 98.

works with which it shares certain common features in terms of historical contexts and situations.[14] Again, meaning is not exhausted with the linguistic signs employed to convey them but depend on the author in vital ways.[15] These signs require primarily a unifying subject to give them life by performing the necessary "act of intending" which in turn will make the unity of the text possible. This reference to individuality is the mark of an artistic thought.

Thus the individual author is the ultimate locus of meaning. But all individuality is a manifestation of universal life and hence everyone carries a tiny bit of everyone else within himself.[16] Understanding consists of an objective reconstruction of meaning, which demands a comprehensive knowledge of the language as the author, and his original audience used it and a subjective reconstruction, which involves a divinatory method where the interpreter imaginatively transforms himself to the author's inner life.[17] With these methods, Schleiermacher asserts, the interpreter can understand the discourse, just as well and even better than its creator.[18] Therefore, the problem for Schleiermacher is, as

14. F.D.E. Schleiermacher, 1990, "The Hermeneutics: Outline of the 1819 Lectures", in *HT*,, p. 94.
15. Cf. F.D.E. Schleiermacher, 1990, "The Hermeneutics: Outline of the 1819 Lectures", pp. 93-94. Also see H.G. Gadamer, *TM*, p. 164. Gadamer argues that, though Schleiermacher views both grammatical and psychological interpretation as important, the latter's particular contribution is psychological interpretations. This stresses the importance Schleiermacher ascribes to the individual act.
16. Cf. Ibid., p. 166.
17. Cf. Ibid., p. 93.
18. Cf. Ibid.; Dilthey, while discussing the hermeneutics of Schleiermacher brings out this aspect more clearly and argues that this idea is the necessary consequence of the doctrine of unconscious creation. Cf. Wilhelm Dilthey, 1990, "The Rise of Hermeneutics", in *HT*, p. 113. Also see Gadamer, *TM*. p. 169.

Gadamer observes, not that of historical obscurity, but the obscurity of the "Thou".[19]

Like Schleiermacher, Dilthey too locates meaning in the author's individual creative act, which is subsequently related to his historical situation and for him understanding meaning calls for a process of reliving the author's intentional life. It is a reproduction of the author's meaning by imaginatively transforming to his historical situation.[20] For Dilthey particularly, understanding presupposes the ability to reflect on the voice that reaches from the past by successfully locating it in its original context and reproduce the original import of the text as it is intended by the author.[21] In other words, interpretation aims at comprehending every historical moment in itself, and not by simply submitting it to the measure of the historical situation that conditions the interpreter. The interpreter, therefore, has to disengage himself from his own situation in history. As Gadamer observes, for Dilthey, the real task of historical consciousness is a victory gained over its own relativity; thus justifying objective knowledge in this domain.[22] This victory is achievable because historical consciousness is critically self-reflective. Both Schleiermacher and Dilthey envisage the possibility of making a direct access to the horizon of the text, by placing the interpreter in the former. This involves a participation in the horizon of the text by overcoming the conceptual grip of the interpreter's horizon so that the meaning of the text will be understood without tampering it.

19. Cf. Gadamer, *TM*. p. 168.
20. Cf. Dilthey, *IHS*. pp. 438-39.
21. Cf. Gadamer, 1979, "The Problem of Historical Consciousness" (hereafter PHC), in Paul Rabinov and William Sullivan (eds.): *Interpretative Social Science: A Reader*, Berkeley: University of California Press, pp. 121.
22. Ibid.

Language plays a minimal role in the frameworks of these early hermeneutic thinkers. For them, the parameters of enlightenment philosophy remained sacrosanct and they craved for the latter's proclaimed objectives of objectivity and universality. Nevertheless, language was assigned a very important place and the difference between various horizons of language was recognized to be creating serious problems in communication. Dilthey particularly was attempting to resolve these problems by a rational method that postulates "historical reason" and "historical consciousness" as instrumental in attaining objective comprehension of alien texts by interpreters and communication between different people.

It was in Heidegger and Gadamer we find a greater role assigned to language and they radically reformulated the hermeneutic problem by providing it an ontological dimension. Language in their philosophies, not only determines our situatedness, but also gives us a world and reality with meaning, significance and aspirations.

Gadamer's Reformulation of the Hermeneutic Problem

With Gadamer's reformulation of the problem of historicity in terms of linguisticality, this image of reliving and the idea of reproduction looked problematic. On the one hand, with the greater role assigned to language, the focus on subjectivity — author's intentional life — appears as a defective and distorting image. Gadamer shows how linguistic horizons evolve as the product of traditions that are linguistic in nature and hence are necessarily intersubjective and are a common property of the community of language users.

Again, according to him, the reproduction of meaning by a process of reliving, which involves an overcoming of the gulf between the horizons appears to be an impossible task. The recognition of historicity leads to the experience of facticity as a characteristic feature of hermeneutic experience. The horizon of the text distances itself from the horizon of the interpreter in fundamental ways. Here historicity is explicated in terms of linguisticality and even man's being is explained in terms of this principle. Language, Gadamer says, is the element in which we live and which we can never objectify to the extent that it ceases to surround us.[23] Language is,

> . . . nothing like an enclosure from which we could ever strive to escape. The element of language is not a mere empty medium in which one thing or another may be encountered. It is the quintessence of everything that can encounter us at all.[24]

Hence language is ontologically significant and it functions as the essential hermeneutic medium, which we cannot disperse with at all. Every experience happens in language or more precisely, in a historically situated linguistic horizon and hence is never pure and objective. Therefore, our access to the world and reality presupposes language. Gadamer introduces the notion of prejudices to unravel the nature of human experience and the nature of linguistic constitution of man's being as well as the world. Referring to Heidegger's idea of fore-structures or fore-meanings, Gadamer shows how all our understanding of a text necessarily relies on a "projection" of meanings. The hermeneutic process that enables understanding is essentially a process of "working out the fore-projection, which involves projection of meanings and a revision of these fore-projections after encountering the text's otherness. Gadamer maintains that this is a constant process, as every movement of understanding and interpretation involves such subsequent projection of new meanings.[25]

---

23. Cf. Gadamer, 1981, *Reason in the Age of Science* (hereafter *RAS*), Cambridge: The MIT Press, p. 50.
24. Ibid., p. 50.
25. Gadamer, *TM*, p. 267.

This position, therefore, amounts to the categorical rejection of the traditional idea of "pure perceptions" and subsequently proclaims that perception necessarily includes meaning. Every encounter with meanings and their understanding therefore, does not only involve the intervention of language, but also happens in it. According to Gadamer:

> The phenomenon of understanding, then, shows the universality of human linguisticality as a limitless medium that carries *everything* within it — not only the "culture" that has been handed down to us through language, but absolutely everything — because everything (in the world and out of it) is included in the realm of "understandings" and understandability in which we move.[26]

To make prominent the historical and social dimensions of man's ontological status in the light of the essential linguisticality of understanding and existence, Gadamer explains how in the linguistic character of our access to the world we are implanted in a tradition.[27] He thus connects the realm of pre-understood meanings and the various modes of world-disclosures to a historically constituted linguistic tradition and to the very being of man who encounters the textual meanings in the constantly moving and evolving hermeneutic process. Understanding is the interplay of the movement of tradition and the movement of the interpreter, says Gadamer. The foresights or anticipation of meanings that govern our understanding proceed from the communality that binds us to the tradition. He writes:

> Tradition is not simply a precondition into which we come,

---

26. Gadamer, 1975, *Philosophical Hermeneutics* (hereafter *PH*), tr. David E. Linge, Berkeley: University of California Press, p. 25.
27. Cf. Gadamer, *RAS*. p. 50.

> but we produce it ourselves, inasmuch as we understand, participate in the evolution of tradition and hence further determine it ourselves.[28]

This reveals some other very important dimensions of language; dimensions that disclose the sense in which Gadamer affirms the ontological significance of language. Heidegger's idea of fore-structures constitute one important insight in developing the ontological structure. But perhaps a more important inspiration comes from Hegel, who has emphasized the dialectical element in human experience and has proclaimed that only the whole is true. Gadamer refuses to adopt Hegel's idealism and absolutism but derives from the latter the idea that no single perspective gives us a complete picture of reality.

The incompleteness of our knowledge urges us to look further and not settle with a finality that would fix the meaning of the text to some ahistorical location like the author's intentional life. He thus places it in language, which is understood as a constantly evolving conversation among participants. Our search for common grounds with Gadamer and Wittgenstein takes us to a domain of common language employed by participants who are engaged in an eternally unwinding string of praxis. But while Gadamer allows this common language to evolve in a fashion that entails no finality to it and thereby allowing participants to move legitimately in different directions on different occasions (to understand is to understand differently), Wittgenstein insists upon certain rules that freeze the participants to certain intersubjective moments of understanding.

Wittgenstein and the Hermeneutic Problem

Wittgenstein encounters the problem of alien meanings and proposes his theory of language — that gives an account of the nature of language and also describes the way we are

28. Gadamer, *TM*, p. 261.

related to the latter — in order to resolve it. With an emphasis on the link between meaning and the various contexts where language finds its use, Wittgenstein envisages a coming together of the world, language, and the being of man, as man's engagement in the various language games determine not only how the world is constituted, but also how we constitute ourselves through such language games. The dualistic notion of language as a medium as different from the world comes under suspicion and consequently the idea of a subject who objectively apprehends the world also becomes contestable. Language, in a unique way, brings together the self and the world, and this coming together, nevertheless, is also revealed in language. It is evaluated as a normative field that shapes not only the reality around us but also our very being. In this sense, it is not just a medium, which has a fixed task to perform, but is our quintessential ontological horizon.

The concepts of "language-game" and "form of life" are introduced in order to bring this coming together of a larger context that binds people together by means of verbal and non-verbal actions, intentions, objectives, and accomplishments. It brings a dynamic life context into action.

The idea of language-game also suggests how the various forms of life determine our knowledge about reality and subsequently frame our very selfhood. Each language-game we play reveals a unique individual dimension of reality, by bringing into life a possible intersubjective context, or in other words, by enliving a form of life. The plurality of language-games suggests that reality is essentially multidimensional. Wittgenstein places meaning in the dynamics of these multitude of language-games and understand them essentially by participating in them. A move in the language-game cannot be understood without familiarizing with the rules of that game and also by participating in it. As Wittgenstein puts it, "the term '*language-game*' is meant to bring into prominence the fact that the speaking of language is part of an activity or of a form of life".[29]

For the hermeneutic philosophers, the recognition and examination of historicity ultimately reveals the nature of human knowledge and understanding its essential finitude and facticity. Very similar to this, we will find in Wittgenstein the recognition of the intimate link between human existence and language that is intersubjectively constitutive. He attacks the notion of "private language", as any legitimate language requires others. He asserts that sounds made in a regular fashion would not qualify to be called language, unless they were shown to have consequences or they were used as signals to others in the community. He opposes the view which claims that languages are learned by means of personal sensations and various mental states through a process of introspection. Wittgenstein categorically asserts that, learning to name an inner experience is essentially connected with public behaviour and necessarily presupposes a background in society. This is because, naming demands that a word should be consistently used on the basis of certain agreements among people, i.e. it is used according to rules.[30] And the use of a word necessarily presupposes the context of a language-game, which has its own peculiar inner dynamics. The rules reflect this dynamics and subsequently provide a criterion for correct use. Words acquire sense and meaning only when we use them in our conversations and to use in this way, a definite amount of socialization, knowledge about conventions and practices which make up the functioning of the society, are essential. Any concept to be displayed requires the existence of the other.

The problem for Wittgenstein — corresponding to the

29. Gadamer, *TM*, p. 25.

30. Cf. Wittgenstein, *PI*, p. 199.

hermeneutic problem — is, how to understand the meaning of expressions, as they appear in the context of different language-games where they are used differently. Wittgenstein here proposes a way by which these differences are grasped, so that the meanings are properly understood. To understand the meaning of an expression, we have to understand its use in the particular language game, or the rule that governs its use. In other words, Wittgenstein bypasses the problem of understanding meaning by a concept of "rule-following".

With the examination of the hermeneutic problem in the previous section and the Wittgensteinian notion of understanding meaning in terms of rule following, the relevance of the participatory effort in the process for all these thinkers become evident. Schleiermacher and Dilthey, propose to overcome the hermeneutic problem by participating in the historical life of the author by "reliving it", in order to have a direct access to the latter's intentional life. Thus the reproduction of the textual meaning is materialized. What makes this participating role important is the fundamental historicity of our language and existence. This solution not only does bridge the historical gap between the author and the interpreter but also ensures the objective comprehension of meaning. Underlying this view is a concept of meaning where it is taken as fixed — in the intentional life of the author for Schleiermacher and Dilthey, and in the form of life determined by intersubjective rules for Wittgenstein — and hence is available for objective comprehension.

Gadamer and Wittgenstein

But unlike for Schleiermacher and Dilthey, Wittgenstein highlights linguisticality as an ontological category and assigns a greater role and significance to language. Though he never completely gave up the idea of fixed meanings, he nevertheless opposed associating it with the subjective intentional life of an individual and placed it in the intersubjective domain of a multitude of language-games. Gadamer, as we have seen, too has insisted on the depsychologizing of meaning and asserted that it is located in the public domain of language. But, though Wittgenstein makes linguisticality primary to human existence, the ontological significance of language has never come to full realization in the framework of his language-game theory. For him the whole process of understanding meaning can be explained in terms of the concept of rule-following. Learning rules amounts to participation in language-games.

Again, though both Wittgenstein and Gadamer do away with the image of the intentional life of a subjective mind with their emphasis on linguisticality, Wittgenstein fails to see the strong hermeneutic element that determines our understanding of the rules of the language games we encounter. Chris Lawn points some difficulties in Wittgenstein's conception of rule-following, particularly when Wittgenstein insists on the relatively insignificance of interpretation while one follows a rule. Rules, according to him, are formed on the basis of agreements. But for Wittgenstein, the agreements have no rational or empirical justification and they are simply part of the fabric of our inherited past.[31] Lawn points out that, there is an element of arbitrariness about the agreements we arrive at, which suggests the scope of interpretation. Again Wittgenstein conceives rule-following as a matter of custom.[32] Citing this, Lawn observes that, since customs emerge from the structures of social life they have a historical dimension linking the user to a collective past and Wittgenstein neglects these temporal and historical dimensions to the notion of the customary.[33]

---

31. Chris Lawn, *Wittgenstein and Gadamer: Towards a Post-Analytic Philosophy of Language* (hereafter *W&G*), London and New York: Continuum, 2004, p. 73.

32. *PI*: #199.

33. *W&G*, p. 74.

Wittgenstein's concept of rule-following with its stress on intersubjectivity fails to notice the significant ontological differences between the horizons that actually need to participate while a language-game is played. These horizons, since being rooted in different traditions, will necessarily project their own ontological schemata and attribute their own meanings to whatever they come to encounter. The problem in this context is triggered by historicity and not by mere differences in rules as even these rules themselves are interwoven with historically situated horizons.

Gadamer's dialogic model envisages bridging the gulf between the different linguistic horizons, not by merging one with the other, but by bringing them together and facilitating a mutual exploration of truth and meaning. The dialogic mode of conversation enables the interpreter to go beyond the boundaries of its subjective life. Like Wittgenstein who refutes the idea of private language, Gadamer stresses on the essential I-lessness that every language fosters.The I-lessness is an essential feature of the being of languages. He continues,

> . . . speaking does not belong in the sphere of the "I" but in the sphere of the "we" . . . the spiritual reality of language is that of the *pneuma*, the spirit, which unifies I and Thou . . . the actuality of speaking consists in the dialogue. But in every dialogue a spirit rules, a bad one or a good one, a spirit of obdurateness and hesitancy or a spirit of communication and of easy exchange between I and Thou.[34]

The entry to this sphere of the "we", the common language, is materialized only when participation is facilitated through interpretation; by making oneself open to the claim to truth of the otherness encountered in the text and attempting to bridge the gulf with the creation of a common language of conversation. This language of conversation is where Gadamer

34. Gadamer, *PH*, pp. 65-66.

situates his understanding. Since conversation is a continuous process, understanding too is a continuous process which renews itself endlessly. Gadamer observes:

> Every conversation presupposes a common language, or, it creates a common language. Something is placed in the centre, as the Greeks said, which the partners to the dialogue both share, and concerning which they can exchange ideas with one another. Hence agreement concerning the object, which it is the purpose of the conversation to bring about, necessarily means that a common language must first be worked out in the conversation.[35]

The horizon that evolves from this new communion will definitely be a more comprehensive one, as it will contain the perspectives of both the text and the interpreter in a unique way. Gadamer thus conceives understanding meaning as an essential mode of the being of man.

Ultimately Gadamer's philosophical hermeneutics contends that understanding consists in application. This is also the culmination point of the interpreter's participatory role. Here understanding meaning reveals one more dimension of the interpreter's possibilities and hence it essentially is a form of self-understanding. This self-understanding as well as the conception of understanding as application jointly owe to the openness of the interpreter to the horizon of the text and its truth claim and to his acceptance of ignorance. All these are derivations from the recognition of the ontological significance of language, which both Schleiermacher and Dilthey had failed to realize.

Wittgenstein recognized this, but failed to realize its full import. As Karl Otto Apel points out, Wittgenstein's language game theory revitalizes possible meaning to possible

---

35. Gadamer, *PH*, p. 341.

functioning language games but the dualistic scheme of the transcendental difference between the logical form and the possible content of the world, which dominates the *Tractatus*, is not really overcome in it, but is only differentiated.[36] Apel adds that for this reason, Wittgenstein ". . . cannot actually apprehend what is *historical* in understanding, the mediation between the disintegrating and the emerging language-games (the normal phenomenon of the mediation of tradition) and, on the other hand, mediation over the ages, the revitalization of the past and its assimilation into the present life-form."[37]

Nature of Language

> Language is the house of being. In its home human beings dwell. Those who think and those who create with words are the guardians of this home. Their guardianship accomplishes the manifestation of being in so far as they bring this manifestation to language and preserve it in language through their saving.[38]

Gadamer's conception of language is very close to this. The implication of this ontological significance of language reflects in the view of truth Heidegger advocates; truth as *alethia* or "unconcealedness". Heidegger shows how truth is uncovered to the ontological condition of man's being and his standpoint redefines man's relationship with the rest of the world. According to him, this relationship is characterized by what he calls "care" or "concern", as everything reveals to the being

36. Karl-Otto Apel, 1980, *Towards a Transformation of Philosophy*, tr. Glyn Adey and David Frisby, London: Routledge & Kegan Paul, p. 37.
37. Karl-Otto Apel, 1980, *Towards a Transformation of Philosophy*, tr. Glyn Adey and David Frisby, London: Routledge & Kegan Paul, p. 37.
38. Martin Heidegger, *Letter on Humanism*, available at http://www.archive.org/stream/Heidegger LetterOnHumanism 1949/Heidegger-LetterOnHumanism1949-djvu.txt

of man who approaches them from the context of certain projects and forestructures. In Gadamer's framework these forestructures are articulated as prejudices, which shares some similarities with Wittgenstein's rules.

The most important difference between Wittgenstein's and Gadamer's concept of language lies in the way they conceive its nature. Wittgenstein conceives language as the "part of man's natural history".[39] He emphasizes on a diversity of forms of life and to accommodate the legitimacy of language use in different contexts, introduces the notion of "rule-following". An individual participates in different language-games by employing different sets of rules, which s/he has mastered as a result of socialization. S/he may be able to play different games in a succession or even simultaneously, as social life demands that. Here he sees the role of philosophy — to show the fly its way out of the bottle — as "language analysis" may help one to resolve the possible confusions. To master a language, for Wittgenstein, is to master a technique.

But for Gadamer, language is the ultimate ontological horizon, to which we belong and hence in a sense is our dwelling place. Understanding is a process where the world is continuously uncovered to us. It is continuous because, on the one hand, no understanding can claim completion owing to human finitude, and on the other hand, every new context of encountering the text potentially offers a new uncovering. This is because, language, which is our dwelling place constitutes all perspectives. In a sense language "limits" us by defining our facticity and historicity. But this facticity is our very existential situation and the very condition for all transcendence. It places us in a space where we encounter infinity, as the real limit of human conversation is infinity. It enables us to transcend our facticity as language is not just

39. Wittgenstein, *PI*, # 25.

one perspective, but all perspectives. Because of its universality, and because of its essential conversational nature, language brings to the subject and makes available to it all the perspectives and horizons. It is in this sense Gadamer says that the spiritual reality of language unifies I and Thou.[40]

Perhaps the essential difference between them lies in the way the historicity of linguistic traditions is understood by both of them. Wittgenstein recognizes that language-games and rules are not rigidly fixed and are based on agreements between people. For him there is a plurality of rules and why it is so is not a genuine problem to be addressed. They are simply so. Gadamer's ontological exploration of language and its being, identifies in language what constitutes the most conditioning as well as enabling aspects of our being. Language for him is not just an bility or a technique, but constitutes a tradition which constantly fuses a collective past with a dynamic present and an unknown but anticipated and aspired future.

Language for Gadamer is an endlessly fascinating terrain and tradition, as it is the house of being and the being we understand and live with. It appropriates all alienness from its unique perspective, which redefines its horizonal norms with every assimilation and appropriation. In this sense, there are no rules that are merely followed. Every event of understanding is a discovery of new facets of meaning and new possible interpretations.

---

40. Hans-Georg Gadamer, *Philosophical Hermeneutics,* tr. David E. Linge, Berkeley: University of California Press, pp. 65-66.

18

The Nature of Linguistic Representations

C. A. Tomy

LINGUISTIC representations play a significant role in our socio-cultural and intellectual life, and it is no exaggeration to say that linguistic representations constitute a complete representational system in the sense that whatever can be represented in any other representational medium can be represented in language too. Perhaps, this is why a number of philosophers consider it the most basic of all our representational systems. With respect to the question which representational system is the most basic, the only contender to the claim made earlier is the system of mental representations. However, it may be argued that linguistic representations are more basic because anything that can be thought of or mentally represented can be represented in language as well. But, this argument by itself does not help us decide issue in favour of the primacy of linguistic representations, for one may argue that the representational power attributed to language is derived from the representational power of the mind and, therefore, that the latter is the complete and the most basic of all representational systems.

Those who are committed to the primacy of mental representations argue that there is a fundamental difference between the ways we approach linguistic and mental representations. Linguistic representations are publicly available. However, mental representations are not available the way linguistic representations are; one may even wonder whether they are available to us even privately at all. The function of mental representations, it is argued, is to explain human behaviour in general and the syntactic and semantic features of linguistic behaviour in particular. According to this explanatory perspective adopted with regard to the question of primacy, the status of linguistic representation and that of mental representations are different. The linguistic phenomenon is a part of the *explanandum*, the phenomenon to be explained, whereas the mental representations form a part of the *explanans*, the facts and principles invoked to explain a given phenomenon. The position that mental representations are primary because they are invoked to explain linguistic behaviour, among other things, is often countered by pointing out that when mental representations are postulated to account for the syntactic and semantic aspects of language, mental representations are structured like linguistic representations and that they possess the semantic or the representational features the way language possesses them.[1] In short, the argument is that since mental representations are conceived after linguistic representations of which we have a better grasp and hold, they cannot be considered primary.

Given that there are equally strong arguments in support of both the claims of primacy, it seems difficult to settle the dispute on the basis of these arguments alone. So in this discussion about linguistic representations, I do not take sides with issue of primacy. Rather I concentrate on the nature of linguistic representations *per se*, especially the conditions of their possibility. My emphasis is on the following questions:

1 A classic example is Fodor's language of thought hypothesis. See Jerry Fodor, *Language of Thought* (Cambridge, Mass.: Harvard University Press, 1975).

(1) What is it for a representation to be called a linguistic representation? (2) What are the necessary and sufficient conditions a linguistic representation must satisfy in order to represent what it is purported to represent? To answer these questions I propose, programmatically, a general argument to the effect that it is impossible to conceive of linguistic representations without granting ontological status to linguistic universals and that the notion of meaning often invoked to explain the representational power of language must be understood in terms of the notion of universals instantiated by the objects or state of affairs that these linguistic expressions pick out or identify. Thus, in the final analysis, what makes linguistic representation possible is our appeal to the notion of universals — at the level of linguistic expressions themselves as well as at the level of what they stand for. Linguistic representations form a sub-class of representations in general. So we stand to gain from an understanding of the general notion of representation. With this view in mind, before we go ahead with our discussion of linguistic representation, I shall briefly explicate the general notion of representation.

Representation

In philosophical literature, a representation is defined as something that represents something. It does not require much effort to note that this definition is circular: it uses the verb "represents" to define what representations are. Hence, this definition does not tell us what it is to represent. Despite being circular, the definition succeeds in identifying three important components involved in an instance of representation. They are: (a) something that represents; (b) something that is represented; and (c) a relation of representation held between what represents and what is represented. Let us call these components *medium*, *object* and *relation* of representation. To understand the nature of representation, then, it is important to understand the nature of these constitutive elements of representation.

Initially, it appears that the media of representation could be of diverse nature: cultural or national symbols, linguistic expressions of diverse kinds and forms such as words, phrases and sentences, either written or spoken, pictures, images, gestures, etc. are used for the purpose of representation. Similarly, it would be easily conceded that anything that is conceivable could be objects of representations: they could be physical objects, properties they possess, state of affairs or situations, abstract objects like numbers, immaterial substances like souls or spirits. They could even be non-existent things like Santa Claus and unicorns. It seems, then, that there are no limits to the kinds of things that could be objects of representations.

In the context of a discussion on representation, some questions that strike us as relevant are the following: how do various media of representation manage to represent their objects that are of diverse nature? Is there anything that is common to various media by virtue of which they become representational media? Or, is it the case that what makes something representational varies in accordance with the variations in the media and their objects of representation? Since the media and their objects are of diverse nature, it is unlikely that we will succeed in answering these questions through a scrutiny of the media or the objects. So, our only hope when it comes to understanding the nature as well as possibility of representing lies in a precise characterization of the relation of representation.

What, then, is the nature of the relation of representation? The relation of representation, which is supposed to unravel the nature and possibility of representation, must hold between diverse media, on the one hand, and diverse kinds of objects, on the other hand. So, it is natural to ask whether it is one and the same kind of relation that does this trick for us in every kind of representation or if the kind of relation varies depending on the media of representations and/or the objects of representations.

The diversity of media as well as their objects seems to suggest that the relation of representation is not a single unitary relation, but a plurality of relations, and that the nature of the relation that we invoke depends on the nature of the media and the objects. It may be thought, for example, that when the medium of representation involved is an image or a picture, the relation of representation may be considered as a relation of resemblance. The resemblance relation demands that what represents must be a replica of what is represented. In the case of analogue representations such as these, it seems that there is a tacit assumption, namely that what represents and what is represented must be alike. Though the relation of resemblance seems like a natural choice in accounting for how a picture or an image represents, it is well known that resemblance relation is neither necessary nor sufficient for pictorial representations.[2] Even if we grant that the relation of resemblance succeeds in explaining how pictures and images represent, it is obvious that, in the case of a non-analogue medium of representation like language, the relation of resemblance would be of no use in accounting for its representational power. So the nature of the relation of representation invoked in the case of linguistic representations must be different from the one that is appealed to in the case of pictures or images. Even if one were to argue that the relations of representations at work in both kinds of media are not radically different, it would at least be conceded that

2 For a lucid argument to this effect, see Tim Crane, *The Mechanical Mind: A Philosophical Introduction to Minds, Machines and Mental Representation* (Routledge, London, 2003): pp. 13-20.

the story that would satisfactorily explain the representational capacity of linguistic expressions would be much more sophisticated than the one we have for the representational power of pictures or images. In this paper, I shall focus on the representational power of the language and try to explore how language succeeds in representing.

Linguistic Representations

Language, we know, is nothing but a physical symbol system, that is to say, linguistic expressions considered in themselves are nothing but some kinds of physical patterns: they are either acoustic vibrations or marks on some writing material. There is nothing in the symbols themselves which would reveal what they represent or how they represent. The representational power of a physical symbol system, therefore, is not its intrinsic property.[3] Hence, there must be something other than the physical patterns that make them bearers of meaning.

To understand how a medium represents, we need to examine how the medium and its objects are related to each other and also specify the features of this relation. Since medium under consideration is language, we must look at linguistic expressions and how they are related to their objects of representation. Statements form a class of linguistic expressions about whose representational power we have simple but powerful and fairly articulate philosophical theories. A statement, we know, represents a situation or a state of

3 This is true not just of linguistic representations but of representations in general. That is, given any representational medium, there is nothing intrinsic to the representational medium as such which would tell us what it represents. This has been noted by philosophers like Berkeley who says that the picture of Julius Caesar taken in itself consists only of certain colours, lines and shapes. So there must be something over and above these lines and shapes which suggests that the picture represents Julius Caesar.

affairs. If Wittgenstein's story about how a statement represents a state of affairs is correct, what accounts for the success of the representation is the formal structure that a statement shares with the state of affairs it represents: a statement represents because of the relation of structural isomorphism that holds between the statement and the state of affairs it represents.[4] With sufficient ingenuity, an account of representation in terms of structural isomorphism can be extended to cover various kinds of linguistic expressions. It could even be argued that it has the advantage that it is general and comprehensive enough to explain the representational power not only of language, but also of other representational systems such as pictorial, imagistic and diagrammatic. That is, whenever a medium represents, we can identify a certain sort of structural isomorphism holding between medium and its objects. Within this framework, the structural form shared between the media and their objects is responsible for the representational features. The relation of isomorphism holds because the structural form, which is abstract in nature, is being instantiated by both media and the objects represented.

Though the attempt to explain the representational power of media in terms of the structural forms they share with their objects is appealing at first sight, a reconsideration of the same shows that this approach lands us in serious difficulties. A major problem associated with this account of the representational power of linguistic representations is that the relation of representation construed in terms of structural

4 See Wittgenstein's remarks: "There must be something identical in a picture and what it depicts, to enable the one to be a picture of the other at all" (2.16) and "What a picture must have in common with reality, in order to be able to depict it — correctly or incorrectly — in the way it does, is its pictorial form" (2.17) in Ludwig Wittgenstein, *Tractatus Logico-Philosophicus*, trs. D.F. Pears and B.F. McGuinness (New York and London: Routledge, 2002): pp. 10-11.

isomorphism does not help us distinguish between the media and objects of representation. Since the structural form is instantiated by both medium and its object, we find it impossible to say what represents what.[5] Moreover, there could be a number of state of affairs that instantiate the same structural form, and, hence, any of those state of affairs could be considered as either medium or the object of representation. Representing, we know, is an asymmetric relation: *X* may represent *Y*, but it is not necessary that *Y* represents *X*, whereas, structural isomorphism is necessarily a symmetric relation. This means that, though, in the case of complex linguistic representations like statements, structural isomorphism resulting from instantiation of structural form is necessary, it is not sufficient. The talk of representation makes sense only from a particular point of view, from the point of view of an epistemic subject for whom the media — whatever they are — are presented as representations, as things standing for something. Representations are those things from which an epistemic subject is able to move to or access the objects of representation. That is, by accessing the representations, a subject must be able to access the objects of representations and what makes such a move possible, at least partly, is the structural isomorphism between the complex linguistic representations and their objects, namely state of affairs. However, this is not the whole story.

If structural isomorphism by itself cannot help in demarcating between representation and its objects, what can? What other factors can determine this move from one system of objects to another, which is structurally isomorphic, making the former a representational system and the latter, objects of representation? To understand this, we must unravel the

5 Wittgenstein's remark in *Tractatus Logico-Philosophicus*, "A picture is a fact" (2.141) is worth remembering in this context.

meaning of the expression "structurally isomorphic". A system is structurally isomorphic to another if and only if both of them have the same structural form. A structure is a set of objects ordered by a certain set of relations and what determines the structural form are the ordering relations and the number of elements involved. A representational system instantiates a structural form and, therefore, it is a structure. If the structure as a whole should represent a state of affairs, then the elements of the representational structure must be able to represent the elements or the constituents of the state of affairs. The question is: can we succeed in moving from one element in a structure to a corresponding element in another structure, so that the former can be considered as the representation and the latter may be taken as its object? If a complex linguistic representation, like a statement, were to represent, its constituent elements must pick out their objects correctly.[6] Though constituent elements of a simple statement fall into various grammatical categories, the elements of a statement have only one function from a logical point of view, namely to refer to or to pick out their objects falling into various categories such as individuals, properties and relations and, for this reason, they could all be considered as names. Thus the question of linguistic representation comes down to the question of how names pick out their objects.

Naming as Representing

How does a name pick out its object(s)? It is generally believed

---

6 Wittgenstein is aware that if structural isomorphism were to explain the representational power of complex representational entities like an atomic statement, then the constituent elements of such statement themeselves must be representational. He says: "In a picture the elements of the picture are the representatives of the objects." (*Tractatus Logico-Philosophicus* : 2.131). He, however, does not give an account as to how they turn out to be representational.

that a name picks up its object(s) because of an explicit decision by a few members of a community of speakers to use the name to denote an object, and the acceptance of this decision by other members of the concerned linguistic community, which, in turn, results in establishing a convention such that subsequent uses of the name help the members refer to its object. One advantage of viewing names as conventionally adopted mechanisms to refer to objects is that it can account for how names that are radically different in nature from their objects succeed in referring. For example, the word "chair" and the chairs beside me do not resemble in any relevant respects for me to say that it refers to chairs on account of the resemblance between them. Nor does the word "chair" represent the chairs because the set of letters that make up the word is structurally isomorphic to chairs. There is nothing common between the word "chair" and chairs. Yet the term "chair" represents chairs as a result of a decision to adopt a particular order of phonemes or English letters as standing for chairs. Linguistic conventions express socially constructed norms or regularities to be followed by members of the linguistic community. Our success in referring to the objects named, by the use of the names, is explained by appealing to such conventions. But do appeals to convention really succeed in accounting for our use of names to pick out their objects? Alternatively we may ask: How are linguistic conventions that establish a link between names and the objects possible? In what follows, I shall argue that, for establishing linguistic norms and conventions, we must grant existence to universals, linguistic or otherwise. That is, to explain the possibility of linguistic representation, it is necessary to invoke universals. An ontology that grants only particulars cannot explain how we succeed in naming objects.

The philosophical position that there are only particulars and we can do well in theorizing about the world without swelling our ontological baggage with universals is indeed a respectable one, with a long history of its own. Within the framework adopted by this line of thinking, all that exists are particulars. If there are only particulars, names and objects also must be particulars, that is, each term that one utters and each object that an utterance refers to must also be particulars. How, then, shall we make sense of our talk about general terms, terms that are applicable to a *class* of objects? Those philosophers who are committed only to the ontology of particulars argue that even the so-called general term is a particular and that a particular term is considered to be a general term when it is made to stand for a number of particulars. Thus, for example, the term "chair" is a particular and it is considered an abstract general term when it is made to stand for a number of chairs. In my opinion, these philosophers fail to note that we cannot use a name as standing for a large number of particular objects unless the notion of universal is somehow smuggled in. I shall attempt to show why this is so by examining the steps involved in the process of naming.

We know that word "chair" represents or stands for a number of chairs because of two reasons: (1) the initial baptismal ceremony when a convention of using the word "chair" to stand for chairs was adopted; (2) the decision of the other members of the community to follow this convention. In order to proceed with our analysis, let us consider a hypothetical case where chairs are being named. Let us assume that the task of naming has been assigned to a committee whose members grant existence only to particulars and that they name objects presented to them in a baptistery in front of them. The speech act they perform in the naming ceremony of chairs may run as follows: "We hereby name the objects before us with this particular collection of phonemes occurring in this particular order as 'Chair'." That is, in the course of the naming ceremony, a particular collection of phonemes occurring in a certain order is made to stand for the set of objects that was presented before the committee. The question is, whether the naming committee succeeded in naming them as chairs? In my opinion, the answer is a clear *no*. The reason is as follows: the naming committee used a particular ordered set of phonemes as standing for a particular set of objects presented to it. However, can we say that the phonemes, the committee uttered, really stand for chairs? Being spatio-temporal particulars, with a short lifespan, the phonemes disappear soon after they were uttered. Hence those phonemes cannot any longer stand for the objects named. Even if the members of the committee make an effort to repeat the name they gave earlier, say, for the sake of those who were not present at the ceremony, it would be of no use because they would be uttering a numerically different collection of phonemes. The members of the naming committee, let us assume, soon realize this. They decide to have something abiding in the place of ephemeral phonemic events so that they can repeatedly use the same set of particular physical objects as standing for the objects presented in the baptistery. So they come up with letters of the alphabet and decide upon the order in which the letters occur for the representation of particular objects. They decide that the set of letters {A, I, C, H, R} would be used in this particular naming and they also decide on the order in which the members of this set have to occur in order to name the objects before them. They decide that this "C" must be followed by this "H" and so on. Since they do not want this name to disappear, as in the earlier case of phonemeal naming, they also decide to write down the particular ordered set of letters (C, H, A, I, R) on a register. Now, they can point out to those who were not present at the baptismal ceremony the particular ordered set of letters, direct their attention to the objects in the baptistery, and explain to them that the particular ordered set of letters they see before them stand for the objects they see in the baptistery. The question that arises here is whether the committee has succeeded in naming chairs through this manoeuvre.

It does not require much effort to see that the ordered set of letters written down on the register is a particular collection of token letters. What the naming committee decided is that this particular ordered tokens of letters stand for the particular objects present before them. If we go by the procedure of naming, as understood here, a numerically different token of the ordered letters (C, H, A, I, R) cannot be used as the name of the objects before them. Suppose, for example, people in the neighbourhood come to learn from the committee the name for the objects. The members of the committee point to the written letters in the register and tell them that these letters stand for the objects before them. The literates among the visitors decide to copy down the name so that they do not forget it. Moreover, they do not want to come back to have a relook at the register whenever they want to refer to those objects. But, unfortunately, the ordered sets of letters they copy from the register form different sets of tokens, and, as a result, they cannot stand for objects the committee named. If the tokens of the ordered set of letters (C, H, A, I, R) copied from its original in the register were to refer to the objects on the baptistery, it is not sufficient that the committee accepts the causal-historical account of reference.[7] In addition, the naming committee should decide that this letter order (C, H, A, I, R) and the letter orders of this *kind*, namely the other instances of the word type (**C H A I R**) shall refer to the objects on the baptistery.

The foregoing discussion suggests that it is not possible

---

7 See Saul Kripke, *Naming and Necessity* (Cambridge, Mass.: Harvard University Press, 1980).

to use a name to refer to its objects without conceiving a given name as some sort of linguistic universal. However, the notion of linguistic universals and the allied notion of linguistic particulars are not sufficient for us to be successful in naming objects. This is because the purpose of giving the general names like "chair" is not to just refer to objects to which the name was initially given, but also to other similar objects that are not presented to the naming committee. If the name is to be applicable to other objects, they must be similar in relevant respects to those objects to which the name was initially given. A set of objects can be similar to one another only if all of them share among themselves at least some common properties. From a realist's perspective, a class of objects shares properties if and only if they instantiate the same set of universals. It is indeed the properties that a class of objects possesses that make them worthy of the name. Using an alternative vocabulary, we may say that a general name hit a particular class of objects as its referent because all the members of the class instantiate a particular set of universals that make them the *kind* of objects that they are. Thus, in adopting general terms to be applied to classes of objects, the naming committee should also stipulate that the objects presented are merely a representative sample and, therefore, the initial letter order they have devised for naming the objects presented to them and their copies refer not only to the objects presented to them but also to the objects of the same kind. That is to say, in order for "general-naming" to succeed, the naming committee has to conceive names as types and also consider the objects they name as types or kinds. This is what they do when they stipulate that the initial token of the letter order they devised and their copies thereafter would refer to objects of the *kind* or type presented before them. What makes a certain object the kind of object that it is, is the specific collection of universals instantiated by the object. The universals such as these may be characterized as the meaning or sense of the names that help us in determining their references. Without positing such meanings or senses our attempt to fix the reference for names by adoption of a convention would not be successful at all.[8]

In short, if each token of a given general name succeeds in referring to objects that are presented and also to objects of the same kind, it is because these name instances are tokens of a given type-name. This would mean that names are formal in the sense that in each name-type, i.e. phonemes of a certain kind or letters of a given type in a particular language occur in a certain order or structure. Thus, an important aspect that makes it possible for us to repeatedly refer to the same object or objects of the same kind with our names is their formal character with possibility of repeated instantiation. However, this is only one part of the story, the part of the story concerned with the medium of representation. The other side of the story is about the objects that are referents of the names. In order that we may adopt a convention that would establish a link between names and their objects, the objects that we encounter must be considered as tokens belonging to certain type or kind. They can be considered as belonging to a type or a kind only if these instantiate a set of universals. The specific set of universals or properties that a name signifies would be considered as the meaning or the sense of the name, which must be satisfied by any objects in order that the name

---

8 This goes counter to Quine's claim that we can understand the notion of linguistic representation without appealing to the notion of meaning: "Actually we can acknowledge a world full of objects, and let our singular and general terms to refer to those objects in several ways to our heart's content, without ever taking up the topic of meaning." W.V. Quine "The Problem of Meaning in Linguistics" in Jerrold J. Katz, ed., *The Philosophy of Linguistics* (New York: Oxford University Press, 1985), p. 48.

may be applicable to them. Thus if our names were to succeed in naming, which is an act of establishing a convention, it is necessary to conceive names as well as their objects as types having many instances or tokens. That is, for a name to refer successfully both universals and particulars equally must be invoked; a particular or a universal by itself cannot refer or represent.

Proper Names

It might be objected that the above account about how names represent their objects is applicable only to general terms but not to proper names. However, I am sure, it would be conceded that each occurrence of a proper name is an instance of a type, and, hence, any proper name must be considered as a linguistic universal capable of being instantiated several times. Consider the name "Aristotle"; it can be repeated any number of times and each occurrence is a token of the word-type *Aristotle*. In order to use the word "Aristotle" to name something or someone, it is necessary to conceive each occurrence of the word an instantiation of a linguistic universal. Without such presupposition it is not even possible for us to say that at each occasion one utters the word "Aristotle" one is using the same word. More generally, it may be said that in order to consider two utterances as utterances of the same name, it is necessary to grant that names — general as well as proper — are linguistic universals capable of repeated instantiations. For successful use of names, it is necessary to invoke this assumption.

Naming is essentially a socio-linguistic act of establishing reference. As an act, it could be either successful or unsuccessful. An act of naming is successful when the name used has a referent corresponding to it, and unsuccessful if the object named is absent or non-existent. However, the presence or existence of the object or the individual named alone would not determine the success of an act of naming.

There are other factors that contribute to this success. What are these other factors? Our answer to this question depends upon what we mean by naming. It is possible to distinguish between a narrow and a broad sense of "naming". Taken in a narrow sense, the act of naming merely amounts to labelling. If a name (i.e. an ordered set of phonemes or letters) and an object are arbitrarily brought together on an occasion, the act of labelling the object may be said to have taken place successfully. I might name, for example, the sensation of sound that I experience at this very moment "0072", and, in so far as I have succeeded in arbitrarily relating "0072" to the sensation I am experiencing now, I have succeeded in naming it in the narrow sense of naming. In addition to the presence of the object named, the success of naming in the narrow sense depends on the availability of a linguistic expression to be used as a name and the establishment of a relation between linguistic expression and the thing named. In its narrow sense, naming appears to be a private, individual, and momentary act. One might even wonder whether it is naming in the proper sense of the term. In its broad sense, however, the success of an act of naming consists not only in bringing together a name and an object, but also the subsequent use of the name, in a communicative context, to refer to the object thus named. That is, in the broad sense, an act of labelling does not succeed in naming an object if the name cannot be used on a later occasion to refer to the object in an interpersonal communication. For example, by the use of the word "0072", I do not succeed in naming the sensation I had at a particular moment because this sensation being momentary and private cannot be re-identified. Taken in the broad sense, naming is essentially an act of establishing a social convention. In a social context, referring would be successful only if the members of the community use the name to identify or to refer to an object. The members of the community are able to do this on account of a shared criterion for the use of the name. Whatever those shared criteria may be, in principle, they must be available to all members of the community of speakers. In addition to the presence of the object named and the availability of a linguistic expression, what establishes the relation of reference between a name and its object is the accessibility of a shared criterion that enables the community of speakers for the repeated use of a name.

In the case of general names, the shared criterion for the use of name for the identification and re-identification of a class of objects is a certain set of properties that the objects possess. An important question that may arise here is whether the same account is applicable in the case of proper names as well. More specifically, we may ask: does a proper name refer to an object uniquely on account of a unique set of properties that it possesses, or is it the case that a proper name refers to its object without invoking any of the properties that it possesses? Depending on the way we answer this question, we have two alternative theories about naming, particularly about the nature of relation between name and the thing named. The first theory says that there is a natural relation between the name and what is named, and this natural relation is established on the basis of certain properties that the object possesses. The second theory, on the other hand, says that the relation between a name and what is named is an arbitrarily constructed relation. That is, for the choice of a name, there are no absolute criteria in the object itself. These two theories about the relation between a name and its object have different conceptions about what a name is. The first one would conceive a name as an abridged description of the properties that its object possesses, whereas, the second one implies that name does not signify any properties in the object but are merely "rigid designators" available on account of the decision of the linguistic community to use the name as referring to a unique object or a kind of object.

In my opinion, each of these two theories provides only partial accounts. As far as the relation of reference established between a name and its object is concerned, both natural and arbitrarily constructed aspects can be clearly deciphered. I shall explain it with the example of the natural kind term "cow". The relation between the general name "cow" and the natural kind, *cow*, is arbitrary and contingent in the sense that another name, say "tiger", could have been used to name it. Once the name "cow" is given to a class of animals, the subsequent use of the name "cow" to refer to cows is determined by certain natural properties that cows possess. That is to say, it is the identification of natural properties that a class of animals possesses that enables us to subsequently apply the name "cow" to cows. Once a naming relation is established between a word and its object, the name can be applied only to things that are worthy of the name, and what is worthy of the name is determined on the basis of what is there in the object. This means, in addition to the arbitrarily relation between name and its object established at the time of the initial baptism of the object, there is also a natural relation between name and the object because of which we are able to repeatedly use the name to refer correctly to its objects.

That the relation between a name and its object is a combination of natural and arbitrarily constructed relation is true not only of natural kind terms but also of property names. Let us consider the naming of a class of objects that are white. The class could have been christened "yellow" instead of "white". So the relation between the name and the class of objects is an arbitrary one created merely by the will of the name-givers. Once the reference is established, the relation between them is no more arbitrary because, in the subsequent use of the name "white" in labelling an object, one is informing us what is already there in the object. This is possible only if there is a natural relation between the name "white" and the class of objects named white.

Let us now proceed to examine the nature of the relation between proper names and their objects. Some philosophers subscribe to one of the two different theories about the nature of relationship between names — general as well as proper — and their objects. Others adopt one for proper names and the other for general names. Saul Kripke, for example, thinks that the theory that is applicable in the case of natural kind terms would be of no avail in the case of proper names. Hence, he adopts two different sets of criteria for the application of natural kind terms and proper names. Criteria for the use of natural kind terms are certain essential properties that the natural kind in question possesses. Consider the natural kind name "cow". We need a reliable criterion for the correct use of the word "cow" so that it is applied to cows and nothing else. This criterion specifies a set of properties without the possession of which nothing qualifies to be considered cows. This set of properties that enables us to use the same natural kind term "cow" on different occasions may be called cow-*ness* or the essence of the natural kind, *cow*. But proper names are neither adopted nor used on the basis of a similar criterion. A proper name names a unique particular and, in so far as it is a particular object, it does not have any essential properties whatsoever. The initial naming of the object is entirely arbitrary. There is nothing in the object that suggests the name it should be given. Whatever name that is given to it, is given on the basis of the decision of the name-givers, and the subsequent use the name to refer to the object is not based on any essential properties of the unique particular. That is to say, we do not use of the proper name, for example, "Aristotle" on the basis of the property of "Aristotleness". For its use, there is no such basis other than Aristotle himself. This means that Kripke advocates a thoroughgoing nominalism as far as the meaning of proper names is concerned, whereas he is a committed realist when it comes to natural kind terms.

It is, however, unlikely that the act of bestowing a proper name would be successful by arbitrarily bringing together a proper name and a unique singular object with the additional stipulation that proper names are rigid designators. If we are to use or apply the name, say, "Aristotle" in a communicative context to refer to the person so named, there must be certain criteria though it may not be an invariant essential property belonging to Aristotle. This can be clarified as follows: Suppose, I use the name "Aristotle" in the presence of an audience that has never heard the name. In such a situation, do I succeed in naming Aristotle by uttering the name? Not at all, for the members of the audience might ask me: "Who is Aristotle?" In answer to their query, I normally give a description like "the great Greek philosopher who is a disciple of Plato and a teacher of Alexander the Great". By providing descriptions of this sort, I invite my audience to a certain epistemic situation; the description epistemically empowers them so that they can identify the person when they encounter him. The ability to identify the object named is a necessary condition for the success of naming or referring. This ability can be exercised only if there are certain shared criteria for the success of naming, criteria for the identification and re-identification of the objects named.

General terms, I have been arguing in this paper, succeed in picking a class of objects of a certain kind through the mediation of meaning. Meaning of a general term is understood as a particular set of universals it signifies. The extension of a general term or the class of objects to which a general term is applicable is determined by identifying the objects that instantiate the set of universals signified by the general term. Can a similar strategy work in the case of proper names? One may object by saying that a similar strategy would not work in the case of proper names because they stand for unique particulars. But if Frege's and Russell's approach to proper names are correct, the way a general name determines its extension and the way a proper name refers to its unique object are not radically different. They argue that proper names too have senses or that they signify definite descriptions which convey their meanings and that these proper names refer through the mediation of their senses or meanings. The meaning of a proper name could be understood as a theory or a story that is true only of the unique object or person named and of nothing else. A story about an individual can be conceived as a description that signifies a unique set of properties. Thus, a proper name could be considered as signifying a unique set of universals. But if a proper name were to succeed in referring, its sense or the unique set of universals it signifies must be instantiated by one and only one individual. There is nothing in the set of universals *per se* that would dictate that only one individual can instantiate these universals. What really determines that the set of properties belongs only to one individual is the universe of discourse adopted by a community of speakers in a given context. Consider, for example, the proper name "Moses" and this name-type signifies a set of properties that *Moses* alone possesses in a given situation. We refer to Moses using token of the proper-name-type "Moses" because in the given context only Moses possesses the set of properties. We can clarify it as follows: Suppose one of contemporaries of Moses sees Moses approaching him and he utters: "Here comes Moses". The next day he sees Moses passing by and utters: "Moses passes by". On both the occasions, our speaker is supposed to have used the name "Moses" to refer to same parson. The first time, he uses the name to refer to the person only because he must have already been familiar with the person and his name. On the second occasion, he uses the name because he sees a person who, from his poiunt of view, is indistinguishable from the person whom he saw the previous day. He considers the person to be indistinguishable because the person is similar in the relevant respects to the person he saw the previous day. We may say that the speaker uses a token of the same name to refer to a person on that day, because he finds that the person possesses the same set of relevant properties as the individual he saw the previous day possessed. Thus even proper names refer and represent only because universals are granted. In saying that universals are appealed to in fixing the reference of even proper names, I do not intend to propose that there is a grand story associated with each proper name, something like a complete individual notion that Leibniz was speaking of. Rather, the story in question can still be incomplete and two speakers who use the same name may not share exactly the same story. However, there are some common elements in their stories that it is possible that would help the speakers uniquely identify the referent of the proper name given its context of use.

I have been arguing that the representational power of language cannot be accounted for without positing universals and that naming (both general and proper) is not possible if our ontology consists only of particulars. However, linguistic universals by themselves are not representational. To be successful in naming, we must grant universal and particulars at both the ends of the representational relation, namely the medium of representation, i.e. language, and the objects of representation. It is a particular that instantiates a universal which represents, and what is represented, namely the object of representation, too, is a particular instantiating universals. However, the set of universals instantiated by particulars at the two ends of the relation of representation is not necessarily the same. In the case of linguistic representations, the particulars that act as the media invariably instantiate some linguistic universals. When a statement represents a state of affairs, it is necessary both the medium and its object share the same structural form. This sharing of the structural form is possible because the components of a statement, i.e. names, represent their objects. So in the context of linguistic representation, the fundamental question is how names represent or are directed towards their objects. The naming relation has two features. The first is that the relation between the name and its object is an arbitrarily constructed relation in which a linguistic particular is associated with another particular. The second is that once established, this relation is a stable one, making the object worthy of the name. My concern, in this paper, has been how this stability becomes possible in a naming relation so that a name may stand for its object. What makes the naming relation stable, I have been arguing, is the sets of universals the media as well as their objects partake in. This stability factor is responsible for our success in repeatedly using the same names to refer again and again to the same (kind of) objects. The story developed above about how names represent their objects can be told not only of general terms but of proper names as well.

Contributors

P.R. Bhatt teaches philosophy at the Department of Humanities and Social Sciences, IIT, Bombay.

Bijoy H. Boruah teaches philosophy at the Department of Humanities and Social Sciences, IIT, Delhi.

Sadhan Chakraborti teaches philosophy at the Department of Jadavpur University, Kolkata.

Nirmalya Narayan Chakraborty is Member-Secretary at Indian Council of Philosophical Research, New Delhi.

Amitabha Dasgupta teaches philosophy at University of Hyderabad.

Lakshminarayan Lenka teaches philosophy at the North-Eastern Hill University, Shillong.

Ram C. Majhi teaches philosophy at Ravenshaw University, Cuttack.

Muhammedaly P.P. is a freelance writer in philosophy in Hyderabad.

Sreekala M. Nair teaches philosophy at Sree Sankaracharya University of Sanskrit, Kalady.

Ranjan K. Panda teaches philosophy at the Department of Humanities and Social Sciences, IIT, Bombay.

R.C. Pradhan teaches philosophy at University of Hyderabad.

K.S. Prasad teaches philosophy at University of Hyderabad.

Manidipa Sanyal teaches philosophy at Calcutta University.

Madhucchanda Sen teaches philosophy at Jadavpur University, Kolkata.

Muhammad Maroof Shah is a freelance writer in philosophy in Jammu and Kashmir.

Smita Sirker teaches philosophy at Jadavpur University, Kolkata.

Sreekumar Nellickappilly teaches philosophy at the Department of Humanities and Social Sciences, IIT, Madras.

C.A. Tomy teaches philosophy at the Department of Humanities and Social Sciences, IIT, Delhi.

Index

Absolute autonomy, 21
abstract thinking,
    complexity of, 165
act of,
    addressing, 204
    communication, 204
    linguistic representation, 205
    naming, 429
    telling, 204
    transmitting knowledge, 250
ādheyata, 78
*adhikaraṇa*s, 80
adṛṣṭārtha, 255
adṛṣṭārtha-śabda, 255
advanced mystics, 386
āharaṇa, 86
ākāṅkṣā, 77-79, 81, 260
    jñāna, 79
    relation, 79
alaukika, 80, 84
Alaukika perception, 80, 84
alaukika pratyakṣa, 80
alaukika sannikarṣa, 80
Alexander the Great, 434
alien meanings, problem of, 404
alienness, notion of, 394
alternative vocabulary, 427
An Inquiry into Meaning and Truth (Russell), 331
analysis of,
    language, 364
    linguistic understanding, 87
    meaning, 207
    nirvikalpaka pratyakṣa, 282
    reflective knowledge, 82
analytic statements, 23
analytic tradition, 321
Analytical Philosophers, 330
Analytical Philosophy, 319, 337
Analytical tradition, 326
ānanda (bliss), 369
anayānaṁ, 79
ancient traditional philosophers, 346
animal languages,
    syntax of, 26
another thing (*anvaya*), 77
Anscombe, 68
antecedent knowledge, 264
anthropomorphic character of belief, 386
Anti-Christ of Nietzsche, 379
anti-reductionist Nyāya, 86
anumāna, 252
anumititva, 83
anvaya, 86
    knowledge of, 79
anvaya (*sadbhāva*), 81-82

anvaya relation, 77
anvaya-vyatireka, 82
anvayabodha, 77, 79-82, 84
appearance of, 83
cause of, 79-80
form of, 79
objects of, 85
theorists, 83
Apel, Karl Otto, 410
appearance of,
anvayabodha, 83
reality, 112
application of,
(moral) concepts, 308
laws, 26
āpta, 253
āptaścopadeśaḥ, 253
āptopadeśaḥ, 255
śabdaḥ, 253
Arabi, Ibn('s), 354, 359-61, 363-67, 378, 380
conception of divinity, 366
Aristotle, 95, 429, 433-34
Aristotleness,
property of, 433
arrangement of simple objects, 169
Artificial Intelligence, 20
āsannā, 77
āsatti, 77-78
ascription of,
content, 327
mental attributes, 64
āśraya,
knowledge of, 80
Atkinson, 349, 388
attributes of beauty, 379
auditory sensation, 21
Augustine, 368, 384
Austin, 197, 199
autonomy,
principle of, 370
availability of,
linguistic expression, 430-31
linguistic representations, 246
awareness of self-identity, 72
background condition of language, 214
bādhajñāna, 79
bādhita, 79
bahnikaraṇakatva, 79
basic fact, 210
basic notion of human ability, 26
basis of communication, 43
Bauddha, 276
bearers of meaning, 419
beauty,
attributes of, 379
Beckett, 375
Bhāṣya, 254-55
interpretation of, 256
bhakti mystic, 381
Bhartṛhari, 248, 281, 290, 292, 294
philosophical thought of, 291
sphoṭa concept of, 292
sphoṭa theory of, 293
Bilgrami, 236, 238-39, 242-43
birth of Representationalism, 321
Blake, 355, 358
boundary of communicative intentionality, 212
Brandom, 93, 244
Brentano, 95-96
Brian McGuinness, 350, 383

brute fact(s), 210
  statement of, 197
Buddha, 343, 350, 377, 386
Buddhism,
  philosophy of, 276
Buddhist (Nāgārjunian) terminology, 365
Buddhists, 265, 271, 276-80
building-blocks of human languages, 106
Camus, 373
Candrakīrti, 279
capacity of linguistic expressions, 419
Carnap, 105, 349
Carnapian phenomenalism, 107
Cartesian dualism, 220
Cartesian idea, 336
Cartesian rationalism, 367
Cartesian scepticism, 220
Cartesian Thesis of Self-Containedness of Mind, 328
Cartesian thought, 347
causal perception, 28
causal power of utterance, 212
causal powers, 327
causal relations, 327
cause of,
  anvayabodha, 79-80
  laukika perception, 84
causation,
  intentionalization of, 212
cautionary view of truth, 239
Chalmers, David, 323, 325
characteristic feature of hermeneutic experience, 401
characteristics of human cognition- productivity, 156
Chomsky, 188
Christ, 373
Christian traditions, 375
Christian mystic, 378
Christianity, 373, 382
Churchill, Winston, 123-24
Claim of knowledge, 89
classical conditioning,
  theory of, 27
classical dualisms, 346
classical Greek philosophy, 95
classical idea of truth, 244
classical Indian philosophical tradition, 75, 251
classical Indian tradition, 258
classical realism, 110
classical theory of concepts, 308, 310
classification,
  principle of, 31
closure of intentionality, 212
cluster of metaphors, 301
code-theory of language, 290
cogency of argument,
  idea of, 92
cognition,
  explanation of, 153
  indication of, 153
cognition of morality,
  nature of, 299
cognitive activities, 165
cognitive phenomena of object recognition, 165
Cognitive processes, 160
cognitive psychology, 183, 195, 298
cognitive theory, 95
collection of phonemes, 425

collective intentionality, 212
commentary on *Nyāya-Sūtras*, 253
common language,
  creation of, 396
common language of conversation, 409
communicability of thought, 284
communicate values, 214
communication,
  basis of, 43
  intentional attitude of, 201
  logical structure of, 198
  means of, 182
  notion of, 210
  preliminary condition of, 206
  realm of, 214
communication identity of being, 213
communication intention, 201
  property of, 207
communication of self-consciousness, 70
communicative act,
  nature of, 204
communicative intention, 200-01
communicative intentionality, 197, 201, 207, 214
  boundary of, 212
  notion of, 197
communicative intentionality of language, 213
communicative use of language, 257
communicative utterance, 203
  nature of, 203
community of language users, 401
community of speakers, 431
complex linguistic representation(s), 421-22
complexity of abstract thinking, 165
components of,
  statement, 437
  representa-tionality, 97
compositionality,
  principle of, 157
compositionality of,
  human cognition, 157
  mental representation, 158
  sentences, 158
Comprehension of meaning, 396
comprehensive knowledge of language, 399
computational theory of mind (CTM), 154, 165
concept(s) of,
  discrete representation, 155
  economic transaction, 303
  form of life, 405
  God, 178
  information exchange, 293
  language, 244
  language-game, 405
  mediated under-standing, 88
  reference, 94
  rule following, 394, 407
  truth, 242
concept-learning, 187
conception of knowledge, 87
concepts,
  classical theory of, 308, 310
conceptual analysis, 346
conceptual mapping, 304
conceptual metaphor(s), 302

structure of, 303
conceptual statements, 23, 25
conceptual structures, 302
conceptual system, 302
conceptualization,
level of, 155
concession to scepticism, 89
concomitance (*vyāpti*), 267
condition of,
language, 179
solicitation, 207
Confessions (Augustine's), 347
configuration of simple objects, 169
connectionism,
developmental stage of, 165
connectivity,
patterns of, 160
consciousness,
intrinsic feature of, 200
subject of, 68, 74
consciousness of object, 70
constant exposures to language, 210
constative expressions, 199
constituents of speech act semantics, 200
constitutive rule of language, 211
constitutive rules,
Searlean notion of, 212
content,
ascription of, 328
content of thought, 286
content theory, 328
contextuality of language, 394
Contiguity (*āsatti*), 79
contingent statements, 32
conventional linguistic meaning, 131
conventional perception, 28
conventions of language, 18
convergence of information, 100
conversation,
common language of, 409
linguistic field of, 201
conviction of all religions, 374
Coomaraswamy, Ananda, 351, 359
corpus of observational utterances, 188
counterfactual statement, 20
cow (*go*), 83
creation of common language, 396
criticism of Prābhākaras, 270
critics of,
religion, 368
mysticism, 368
critique of modernity, 382
culture-specific metaphors, 314
darśana, 344
Daśaratha, 40
Davidson, Donald('s), 108-09, 217-21, 227-28, 230, 236-39, 242, 244-45, 286, 289-90, 321
distal theory of meaning, 108
distal theory of reference, 108-09
theory, 288
Davidsonian distal theory of linguistic representation, 109
decision-making,
function of, 21
declarative sentence,
meaning of, 23

definite description, 34
delimitation of,
  Reality, 380
  Truth, 380
demonstrative thought(s), 337
denial of realism, 118
Dennett, 125
deontic power of language, 214
Derrida, 54, 168, 176-82, 339, 362
Descartes, 321-22
  self-containedness thesis of, 322
Descriptivist Tradition, 321
Destruction of object, 169
determinate reference,
  notion of, 118-19
development of language, 207
Developmental psychology, 165
developmental stage of connectionism, 165
Devitt's semantics, 94
Dewey, 244, 246
dharma, 256
Dharmakīrti, 279
different linguistic horizons, 409
different linguistic instruments, 60
Dilthey, Wilhelm, 394-98, 400-01, 407, 410
dimensions of reality, 21
Diṅnāga, 279
direction of fit,
  Searlean notion of, 208
disclosure of meaning, 213
discrete representation, 163-64
  concept of, 155
  necessity of, 155
  notion of, 164
  scheme(s) of, 163-64
discreteness of mental representation, 159
discussion of,
  externalism, 337
  linguistic representation, 20
distributed representation, 164
  notion of, 160
diversity of,
  language-games, 392
  media, 418
Divine Darkness, 361
Divine Essence, 367
divinity,
  Wittgenstein's conception of, 366
doctrine of unhappiness, 199
domains of verbal testimony, 256
dṛṣṭa,
  varieties of, 255
dṛṣṭārtha, 255-56
dṛṣṭārtha-śabda, 255
dualistic notion of language, 405
Dummett, Michael, 240, 285, 287, 319, 330
Eastern traditions, 375
Eckhart, 354, 373, 378, 384
economic transaction,
  concepts of, 303
egoism,
  principle of, 380
emphasis on linguisticality, 408
empirical propositions,
  meaning of, 18
empirical psychology, 184
empirical statement(s), 18-19, 23
  truth-values of, 32

Engelmann, Paul, 384
enlightenment philosophy parameters of, 401
epistemic autonomy of *śabda-pramāṇa*, 251
epistemology of retained knowledge, 90
essence of religious experience, 366
essential nature of reality, 112
establishing reference,
    socio-linguistic act of, 429
Etchemendy's representational semantics, 94
ethics,
    possibility of, 380
European civilization, 382
Evans, Gareth, 330, 332-36
examination of hermeneutic problem, 407
existence (*astitva*), 83
existence of external reality, 104
Existentialist theology, 382
expectancy (*ākāṅkṣā*), 76
experience of *fana*, 367
explanation of,
    cognition, 153
    human cognition, 155-56
    meaning, 208
    understanding, 208
explicit assertion, 149
explicit statements, 383
exponents of non-dualism, 368
expression,
    linguistic meaning of, 331
    meaning of, 43, 407
    semantic value of, 331
expressions of language, 165
external reality,
    existence of, 104
    inferential knowledge of, 103
externalism,
    discussion of, 338
Externalism-Internalism debate, 329, 334, 336
extra-linguistic factors, 25
facets of meaning, 413
Failures of perception, 101
fana,
    experience of, 367
feature-based semantics, 162
fiction,
    language of, 19
first-personal pronominal constructions, 65
first-personal pronoun, 66, 69-71, 73
first-personal self-reference, 62, 66-67, 70
First-personal self-referential statements, 74
fixed concept of meaning, 294
fixed meanings,
    idea of, 407
Fixing of reference, 123
Fodor('s), 156, 158, 184-86, 191-93, 195-96, 327
    language of thought hypothesis, 154
    notion of semantics, 94
form(s) of,
    anvayabodha, 79
    grammar, 45
    linguistic intentionality, 197, 211
    phenomenalism, 104
    representationalism, 98, 102

scepticism, 121
self-understanding, 410
form of life,
concepts of, 405
formal semantics, 20
forms of statements, 23
formulation of realism, 128
formulation of law, 25
Fox, George, 347
fragrancehood (*saurabhatva*), 81
fragrant sandalwood (*surabhi candanam*), 80
Frazer, 382, 385
Frege('s), 286, 288, 320-21
approach to proper names, 434
puzzle, 324
Theory of Sense, 321
function(s) of,
decision-making, 21
mental representations, 415
language, 23, 25, 30, 212
referring, 21
representational system, 160
functioning of,
language, 30, 223
logic, 223
fundamental concept of being, 54
Gadamer, Hans Georg('s), 391-94, 395-96, 400-04, 408, 410, 412-13
concept of language, 412
conception of language, 395, 411
dialogic model, 409
ontological exploration of language, 413
philosophical hermeneutics, 410
Galileo, 326
Gandhi, Ramchandra, 197-98, 203-06, 208, 210-12
Gandhian perspective of linguistic representation, 209
Gandhiji('s), 249, 251
notion of communication, 212
gaṅgā, 78
gaṅgāyāṁ ghoṣaḥ, 78
Gaṅgeśa('s), 263, 268-69, 280-81, 283
theory of pre-predicative perception, 282
Garden of Eden, 344, 354
Gautama, 255
Gelder, 154, 160, 162-63
general notion of representation, 416
General statements, 23-25
general term,
Meaning of, 434
ghaṭa, 79-80, 86
ghaṭatva, 80
residence of, 80
goal of intellect, 227
God,
concept of, 178
knowledge of, 178
notion of, 178
perspective of, 373
Unitarian view of, 365
God-realization, 381
Goldman, 298
grammar,
form of, 45
knowledge of, 76
grammar of language, 225
grammatical rules, 18

gravitation,
    law of, 26
Grice, 129, 133-34, 136-40, 142-47, 151
Gricean analysis, 142, 145
Gricean condition(s), 133-35, 139, 145, 147, 150-51
Grice's account of meaning, 129
Guenon, Rene, 351
Harré, 159
Hegel('s), 404
    absolutism, 404
    idealism, 404
Heidegger('s), 244, 246, 354, 377, 382, 401, 411
    idea of fore-structures, 402, 404
Heraclitean flux, 177
hermeneutic experience, characteristic feature of, 401
hermeneutic problem, examination of, 407
hermeneutic thinkers, 394
hermeneutic tradition, 394
hierarchy of moral values, 316
higher cognitive processes, theory of, 185
Hirsch, E.D. 397-98
historical consciousness, 401
historical reason, 401
holistic theory of morality, 317
Horn, Patrick Rogers, 393
human ability,
    basic notion of, 26
human civilization, 385
human cognition, 159, 165
    compositionality of, 157
    explanation of, 155-56
    nature of, 298
    productivity of, 156
human cognition-productivity, characteristics of, 156
human communication, 204, 207, 212
human communicative attitude, 206
human conversation,
    limit of, 412
human egoism, 374
Human intentionality, 211
    linguistic elements of, 214
human language(s),
    building-blocks of, 106
    nature of, 52
human thought, 186
human wisdom, 353
Hume('s), 94
    conception of sensory experience, 279
hypothesis formation,
    process of, 196
I-statements, 63
idea of,
    cogency of argument, 92
    community, 234
    fixed meanings, 407
    language, 244
    linguistic representation(s), 218, 228, 242
    objective comprehension, 395
    private language, 409
    reference, 126
    reproduction, 395
    truth, 239
idealistic philosophies, 366
identification of,
    object, 434

natural properties, 432
Identity (*abheda*), 77
identity of joy, 369
Ideological conflicts, 363
illocutionary force, 202
illusory perception, 102
immediate cause of linguistic understanding, 78
immediate presence of objects, 79
implicit assertions, 149
impossibility of private language, 107
impression (*saṁskāra*), 83
incarnation,
metaphor of, 71
inception of language, 106-07
indeterminacy,
Quine's idea of, 126
indeterminate perception,
Nyāya doctrine of, 282
Indian philosophical tradition, classical, 75, 251
Indian philosophy,
schools of, 258, 273
indication of cognition, 153
individual objects (*viṣakalika*), 83
inevitability of interpretation, 393
inferential knowledge, 103, 268
inferential knowledge of external reality, 103
information exchange,
concept of, 293
influential assumption of metaphysical realism, 122
infrahuman organisms, 187
initial stages of object recognition, 165
inner language, 183
inner representations, 103
knowledge of, 103
relationship of, 104
input language, 192
institutional facts, 203
statement of, 197
integral part of speech act theory, 199
intellect,
goal of, 227
intended meaning, 202
Intention (*tātparya*), 79
intention (*vivakṣa*), 271
intentional attitude of communication, 201
intentional content of linguistic representation, 209
intentional form of language, 207
intentional representation of language, 207
intentional structure of linguistic field, 201
intentionality,
closure of, 212
intentionality of,
language, 214
linguistic field, 201
intentionalization of causation, 212
internal representation, 102, 186
internal structure of representation, 162
interpretation,
inevitability of, 393
level of, 316

interpretation of Russell's Principle, 337
interpretation of,
  Bhāṣya, 256
  sūtra, 253
intersubjective moments of understanding, 404
intersubjective rules, 395
intrinsic feature of consciousness, 200
introspection,
  process of, 406
introspective self-acquaintance, 73-74
introspective self-intimation, 73
invariable relation (*vyāpti*), 266
invocation (*maṅgala*), 76
issue of linguistic representation, 22, 25, 107
issue of reference, 50
Jagadīśa, 75-77, 81-83
Jaina doctrine of Syādvāda, 363, 374
jala, 86
Jayantabhaṭṭa, 248
jñāna lakṣaṇa, 80, 84-85
  pratyāsatti, 80
Johnson, Mark, 299, 300-01, 303-06, 312, 314
Johnson, Paul, 357
judgement of self-recognition, 72
justification of linguistic representations, 220
Kant, 26, 98, 103-04, 230, 243, 298, 317
Kantian thing-in-itself, 227
kāraṇa, 78
karaṇatva, 86
karmatva, 79, 86
knowledge,
  method(s) of, 259, 262, 265
knowledge of,
  anvaya, 79
  āśraya, 80
  block (*bāddha niścaya*), 86
  God, 178
  Grammar, 76
  inner representations, 103
  meaning (*vākyārthabodha*), 76
  metameta language, 191
  mutual fitness (*yogyatā jñāna*), 79
  Nyāya, 76
  reality, 233
  saṁsarga, 79
  scriptural statements, 273
  supraphenomenal reality, 343
  vahnikaraṇakatva, 79
  word(s) (*padajñāna*), 76, 78, 82, 84, 86-87
Kripke, Saul, 32-34, 49, 433
kṛtiḥ, 79, 86
Kumārila, 280
lakṣaṇa (metaphorical meaning), 76, 78
lakṣyārtha, 78
language(s),
  analysis of, 224, 364
  background condition of, 214
  code-theory of, 290
  communicative intentionality of, 213
  communicative use of, 257
  comprehensive knowledge of, 399
  concept of, 244
  condition of, 179

constant exposures to, 210
constitutive rule of, 211
contextuality of, 394
conventions of, 18
deontic power of, 214
development of, 207
dualistic notion of, 405
expressions of, 165
function(s) of, 23, 25, 30, 212
functioning of, 30, 223
grammar of, 225
Human, 20, 26, 45, 50, 186
idea of, 244
inception of, 106-07
inner, 183
input, 192
intermediate, 341
internal, 186, 190
intentional form of, 207
intentional representation of, 207
intentionality of, 214
Learning of, 106
legitimate, 406
limits of, 182, 223
logical structure of, 394
means of, 398
misuse of, 371
nature of, 53, 173, 396, 404
necessity of, 275
normative framework of, 197
normativity of, 197
ontological significance of, 408
Philosophy of, 87, 93-94, 209, 244, 246, 320-21, 328, 339
possibility of, 176
power of, 94, 219, 222
pragmatic deconstruction of, 247
predicates of, 190
realm of, 214
references of, 170
relevance of, 275
religious, 341
representational power of, 416, 436
representative, 187
rootedness of, 393
rules of, 18, 168, 170
semantic content of, 394
semantic power of, 214
single unit of, 398
speaker of, 31, 257
speaking of, 406
spiritual reality of, 413
syntax of, 18, 157
systematicity of, 157
theory of, 404
untranslatability of, 292
use of, 111, 124, 153, 171, 242, 341
user of, 19
veils of, 357
Western philosophy of, 109
Wittgenstein's notion of, 179
Wittgenstein's view on, 176
language comprehension, 157
language entry rule(s), 21, 29-30, 39, 57-58
nature of, 30
language exit rule(s), 21, 29-30, 57-58
language of,
fiction, 19
Self, 339
text, 398
Language of Thought (LOT), 154, 156, 160, 165, 187, 191, 193,

195-96, 299
notion of, 187
ontological status of, 195
language-game(s) theory, 408
concepts of, 405
diversity of, 392
multitude of, 405, 408
plurality of, 405
thesis of, 342
language-learning, 192
language-reality relationship, 110-11
nature of, 128
language use,
normative case of, 202
process of, 396
language users,
community of, 401
language universals,
system of, 188
laukika, 80, 84
perception, 84
sannikarṣa, 80
laukika perception,
cause of, 84
law(s) of,
gravitation, 26
logic, 29
nature, 20, 25-26, 29, 50, 53
Lawn, Chris, 408
learning,
patterns of, 315
Learning of language, 106
legitimate language, 406
legitimate means of knowledge, 252
legitimate source of knowledge, 249, 251
level of,
conceptualization, 155
interpretation, 316
Light of Being, 379
limit(s) of,
human conversation, 412
language, 182, 223
logic, 223
linguistic analysis, 346
linguistic behaviour,
semantic features of, 415
linguistic communication, 146, 151-52, 198, 201
primary form of, 200
linguistic community, 423
linguistic convention(s), 28, 278, 423
linguistic elements of human intentionality, 214
linguistic expression(s), 201, 252, 254, 257, 260-61, 272, 392
availability of, 430-31
capacity of, 419
linguistic field, 213
intentional structure of, 201
intentionality of, 201
notion of, 213
linguistic field of conversation, 201
linguistic forms of life, 207
linguistic freedom, 19
linguistic interpretation, 76
linguistic intentionality,
form of, 197, 211
linguistic licence, 19
linguistic meaning of expression, 330
linguistic perception, 282

linguistic policies, 194
linguistic practices, 232
linguistic relation, 131
linguistic representation(s), 18, 21-22, 26, 56-58, 98, 168, 200, 204-05, 208-09, 216-17, 219-20, 246, 275, 338-39, 387, 414-16, 418, 436
    act of, 205
    availability of, 246
    discussion of, 20
    idea of, 218, 228, 242
    intentional content of, 209
    issue of, 22, 25, 107
    justification of, 220
    meaning of, 207
    model for, 20
    nature of, 415
    necessity of, 216
    philosophical theories of, 98
    problem of, 216
    puzzle of, 108
    question of, 422
    representational power of, 420
    role of, 275
    Searlean perspective of, 209
    types of, 200
    various forms of, 197
linguistic rule(s), 168, 178
linguistic rule of representation, 172
linguistic signs, 399
Linguistic understanding (*śābdabodha*), 77, 79, 84
    Analysis of, 87
    immediate cause of, 78
    non-inclusion of, 81
    objects of, 85
linguistic universal(s), 427, 436
linguistic utterance, 131, 251, 264-65
    meaning of, 264-65
    perception of, 263
linguistic vocabulary, 19
linguisticality,
    notion of, 396
literal meaning, 202
logic,
    functioning of, 223
    laws of, 29
    limits of, 223
logical form,
    Wittgenstein's ontology of, 222
    Wittgenstein's theory of, 223
logical positivism,
    manifesto of, 348
logical semantic properties, 209
logical space of reasons, 229
logical statements, 23-25
logical structure of communication, 198
logical structure of language, 394
logical system of symbols, 232
love of God,
    Spinoza's view of, 369
Lyotard, 362
machine language, 192
madhyamā, 292
magical theory of reference, 123
Malcolm, 350
Mānameyodaya (Nārāyaṇa), 270
manifestation of universal life, 399
manifesto of logical positivism, 348

mark (*hetu*), 266
maturity of religion, 387
McDowell, John, 228-30, 233, 238, 242-43, 245-46, 330-31
McGinn, Colin, 286
meaning,
  analysis of, 207
  bearers of, 419
  Comprehension of, 396
  explanation of, 208
  facets of, 413
  fixed concept of, 294
  Quine's proximal theory of, 108
Meaning in Mind,
  Problem of, 338
meaning(s) of,
  declarative sentence, 23
  empirical propositions, 18
  expression, 43, 407
  general term, 434
  linguistic utterance, 264-65
  linguistic representation, 207
  sentence, 260, 268
  symbols, 154
  word(s), 30, 54, 70, 268
meaningful sentences, 19
means of,
  communication, 182
  language, 398
  representation, 171
media,
  diversity of, 418
media of representation(s), 417-18
mediated understanding, concept of, 88
medium of,
  representation, 186, 428, 436
  thought, 187
memory (*smṛti*), 83
mental attributes,
  ascription of, 64
mental language, 165, 187
Mental representation(s), 98, 208
  compositionality of, 158
  discreteness of, 159
  function of, 415
  nature of, 313
  philosophical theories of, 98
  primacy of, 414
  semantic structures of, 157
  study of, 98
mental representation of moral concepts, 313
mental states, 329
mentalistic content, 328
Mentalistic Turn, 337
metameta language,
  knowledge of, 191
metaphor(s),
  cluster of, 301
  culture-specific, 314
metaphor of incarnation, 71
metaphor usage,
  pervasiveness of, 302
metaphoric concepts, 300
metaphorical mappings, 302
metaphorical usage, 314
metaphysical interpretation of Wittgenstein, 353
metaphysical notions, 351
metaphysical realism, 111-12, 115, 117-18, 120-22, 126, 128, 244
  influential assumption of, 122
  untenability of, 119

versions of, 116
metaphysical realization, 367
method(s) of knowledge, 259, 262, 265
methodological procedure, 395
Microfeatures-based schemes, 162
Mill, 125
Mīmāṁsā, 252
Mīmāṁsakas, 253, 256, 276
Mind and World (McDowell), 228
Mind-World Relation, 328
Miśra, Vācaspati, 280
misuse of language, 371
modalities of perception, 99
mode of self-acquaintance, 66
model for linguistic representation, 20
modern civilization, 346
modern individualism, 349
Modern philosophy of religion, 366
modernity,
critique of, 382
monolithic picture of reality, 127
moral absolutism, 309
Moral Accounting Metaphor, 303, 305-06, 314
Moral agreement, 317
moral argumentations, 299
moral beliefs, 296
moral character, 302
moral concepts, 296, 301, 313, 315
mental representation of, 313
representation of, 316
moral corruption, 385
moral credit, 306
moral decisions, 312, 315, 317
moral dilemmas, 316
moral ideas, 296
moral imagination, theory of, 314
moral indecisions, 310
moral inferences, 306
moral issue(s), 297, 317
moral judgements, 306, 313
moral life, 297, 383
moral notions, 307
moral opinions, 317
moral oughts, 297
moral philosophers, 307
moral philosophy,
study of, 298
moral problem, 309
moral reasoning, 297
pattern of, 316
moral rules, 309
moral terms, 297
moral thinking, 312
moral understanding, 318
moral values, 296-97, 315, 317
hierarchy of, 316
morality,
holistic theory of, 317
Supreme Principle of, 298
multitude of language-games, 405, 408
mystery of Being, 361
mystic experiences, 344
mystical convictions, 350
mysticism,
critics of, 368
philosopher of, 345
Myth of Given, 228
Nāda, 291

nafs, 367
Nāgārjuna, 279, 339, 354
Naiyāyika(s), 77, 253, 257, 265, 272, 276, 280-82
natural language(s), 45, 158, 160, 186-87, 192-93
natural law, 24
natural meaning, 129-30
natural properties,
  identification of, 432
nature,
  laws of, 20, 25-26, 29, 50, 53
nature of,
  cognition of morality, 299
  communicative act, 204
  communicative utterance, 203
  human cognition, 298
  human language, 52
  knowledge, 233
  language, 53, 173, 396, 404
  language entry rules, 30
  language–reality relationship, 128
  linguistic representations, 415
  mental representation, 313
  objects, 96
  truth, 216
Navya-Naiyāyikas, 281
Navya-Nyāya school, 280
Neale, Stephen, 330
necessary statements, 24
necessity of,
  discrete representation, 155
  language, 275
  linguistic representations, 216
negative meaning, 375
negative theology, 178
neurophysical account of perception, 102
neurophysical theory of perception, 103
new meanings,
  projection of, 402
Nieli, Russell, 94, 288, 320, 322, 332, 334-38, 345, 349-50, 383
Nietzsche('s), 372
  Anti-Christ of, 379
  perspectivism, 374
nirvāṇa, 344, 347-48, 365, 385
nirvikalpaka, 285
  perception, 281
nirvikalpaka cognition,
  theory of, 277
nirvikalpaka jñāna,
  Nyāya theory of, 285
nirvikalpaka pratyakṣa (perception without imaginatoin), 276
  analysis of, 282
niścaya jñāna, 79
non-dualism,
  exponents of, 368
non-epistemic notion of truth, 118
non-inclusion of linguistic understanding, 81
non-linguistic assertions, 205
non-moral beliefs, 316
non-natural meaning, 129-30, 150
non-phonetic script, 178
non-verbal organisms, 187
Norman, 164
normative case of *language use*, 202

normative framework of language, 197
normativity of language, 197
Notebooks (Wittgenstein), 342, 349, 352, 355
nothing-buttery theory of thought, 285
notion of,
  ability, 210
  addressing, 204-05
  alienness, 394
  communication, 210
  communicative intentionality, 197
  determinate reference, 118-19
  discrete representation, 164
  distributed representation, 160
  God, 178
  language of thought, 187
  linguistic field, 213
  linguisticality, 396
  object, 68
  performance, 198
  performative expression, 197
  private language, 406
  propositions, 330
  representation, 153-54
  rule-following, 412
  superposed representation, 164
  telling, 205
  testimonial knowledge, 75
  universals, 416
Nyāya,
  knowledge of, 76
Nyāya-Bhāṣya (Vātsyāyana), 272
Nyāya doctrine of indeterminate perception, 282
Nyāya philosophy, 80, 252, 257, 274, 276, 281
Nyāya school, 281
Nyāya theory, 285
Nyāya theory of *nirvikalpaka jñāna*, 285
Nyāya writers, 280
*Nyāya-Sūtra*s (Gautama), 253, 255
  commentary on, 253
Nyāyakandalī (Śrīdhara's), 267
Naiyāyikas, theory of, 291
object (*padārtha*), 78
object (*viṣaya*), 77
object-consciousness, 7
object dependent proposition, 332
object independent proposition, 332
object language predicates, 191
object recognition,
  cognitive phenomena of, 165
  initial stages of, 1650
object-use, 66
objective comprehension,
  idea of, 395
objectivity of,
  rules, 170
  truth, 117, 233
objects (*artha*), 80
objects of,
  anvayabodha, 85
  linguistic understanding, 85
  representation(s), 417-18, 421, 436
observable statements, 23
observational utterances,
  corpus of, 188
occasion meaning, 146

ordinary language,
semantics of, 19
On Certainty (Wittgenstein), 168
ontological significance of language, 408
ontological status of Language of Thought (LOT), 195
ontology of representation, 209
operational definitions, 21
Origins of Analytical Philosophy (Michael Dummett), 319
output language, 192
Padārthadharma-saṁgraḥ, 266
pakṣa, 269-70
Pāṇinian school, 291
paradigm of concepts, 311
parameters of enlightenment philosophy, 401
parataḥprāmāṇyavāda, 265
theory of, 272
particular set of universals, 434
pattern(s) of,
connectivity, 160
learning, 315
moral reasoning, 316
proximal stimulation, 108
paśyantī, 292
Pavlov, 27
perception,
Failures of, 101
modalities of, 99
neurophysical account of, 102
neurophysical theory of, 103
perception(s) of,
linguistic utterance, 263
words, 257
reality, 22
perceptual demonstrative thoughts, 330
perceptual knowledge, 264
perceptual similarity, 105
private standards of, 106
standard of, 105
Performative expressions, 198-99, 201
notion of, 197
theorization of, 199
performative utterances,
Searle's theorization of, 198
perspective of God, 373
pervasiveness of metaphor usage, 302
phenomenalism,
form of, 104
phenomenological paths, 392
philosopher of,
mysticism, 345
transcendence, 354-55
philosophical hermeneutics, 394
Philosophical Investigations (Wittgenstein), 168, 169-70, 178, 224, 320, 343
philosophical issues, 50
philosophical literature, 56, 416
philosophical theories, 419
philosophical theories of mental representation, 98
philosophical theories of linguistic representation, 98
philosophical thought of Bhartṛhari, 291
philosophical/mystical quest, 389
philosophy,
role of, 412

philosophy of,
  Buddhism, 276
  Language, 87, 93-94, 209, 244, 246, 320-21, 328, 339
  Mind, 228, 302, 320-21, 325, 328
Phlogiston theory, 38
phonemes,
  collection of, 425
phonetic script, 178
picture theory of meaning, 113
Pierre, 324
Plato, 346-47, 361, 373, 434
Platonic dialogues, 307
Platonic ideal, 355
Platonic variety,
  pure objects of, 115
plurality of language-games, 405
possibility of,
  ethics, 380
  language, 176
possible-world-semantics, 293
post-Cartesian thought, 347
power of language, 94, 219, 222
Prābhākaras, 270
  criticism of, 270
pragmatic deconstruction of language, 247
pragmatic notion of,
  objectivity, 234
  truth, 241
prakāraka, 79-80
pramā, source of, 251
pramāṇa, 251-52, 272
prapañca, 279
pratiyogitva, 78
pratyakṣa, 252, 282
pratyāsatti, 80-81
pre-linguistic perception, 281
predicate (*prakāra*), 83
predicate (*viśeṣaṇa*), 78
predicate-expression, 63
predicates of language, 190
predicative knowledge (*viśiṣṭa buddhi*), 83
preliminary condition of communication, 206
presence of objects (*padārthopasthiti*), 80
pre-understood meanings,
  realm of, 403
preverbal organisms, 187
primacy of mental representations, 414
primary form of linguistic communication, 200
principle of,
  autonomy, 370
  classification, 31
  compositionality, 157
  egoism, 380
private representations, 195
Private Language, 193, 320
  idea of, 409
  impossibility of, 107
  notion of, 406
private standards of perceptual similarity, 106
problem(s) of,
  alien meanings, 404
  historicity, 394, 401
  life, 358
  linguistic representations, 216
  meaning, 348
  Meaning in Mind, 337
  transcendence, 348

theology, 381
process of,
hypothesis formation, 196
introspection, 406
language-use, 396
understanding meaning, 396
product of traditions, 401
productivity of human cognition, 156
programming language, 192
projection of new meanings, 402
property of,
Aristotleness, 433
communication intention, 207
propositional meanings, 186
propositions,
notion of, 331
proximal stimulation,
patterns of, 108
psychological predicates, 65
psychological processes, 160
psychological theories, 185
Psychosemantics: The Problem of Meaning in the Philosophy of Mind (Fodor's), 326
public language(s), 194
use of, 194
public representations, 195
pure objects of Platonic variety, 115
pure perceptions,
traditional idea of, 403
Putnam, Hilary('s), 44, 46, 111, 117-28, 232-33, 240-41, 245
theory of reference, 115
Twin Earth Thought experiments, 323
puzzle of linguistic representation, 108
Pylyshyn, 156
qualificative cognition, 278
question of,
linguistic representation, 422
reference, 45
Quine('s), 105-08, 126-27, 284-85, 292
Davidson conflict, 109
idea of indeterminacy, 126
naturalism, 107
proximal theory of meaning, 108
proximal theory of reference, 108
Quran, 344
rajas, 54
Rāma, 40
realism,
denial of, 118
formulation of, 128
unreal nature of, 119
realistic notion of meaning, 293
reality (*tattva*), 76
appearance of, 112
delimitation of, 380
dimensions of, 21
essential nature of, 112
knowledge of, 233
monolithic picture of, 127
perceptions of, 22
realm of,
communication, 214
language, 214
pre-understood meanings, 403
reasons,
logical space of, 229
recognition-condition, 148, 151

recognition of,
  historicity, 396
  meanings, 268
reference,
  concept of, 94
  Fixing of, 123
  idea of, 126
  issue of, 50
  magical theory of, 123
  question of, 45
  relation of, 432
  theory of, 111
  Varieties of, 335-37
reference in language, 120
reference(s) of,
  language, 170
  term, 127
referring,
  function of, 21
reflective knowledge (*anuvyavasāya*), 82, 85
  analysis of, 82
reflective testimonial knowledge (*śabdānuvyavasāya*), 85-86
regulative rules,
  Searlean notion of, 212
re-identification of object, 434
relation of reference, 432
relationship of inner representations, 104
relevance of language, 275
religion,
  critics of, 368
  maturity of, 387
  Modern philosophy of, 366
religious language, 341
religious experience,
  essence of, 366
reorganization condition, 148
representable language, 158
representable statements, 20
representation(s),
  general notion of, 416
  internal structure of, 162
  linguistic rule of, 172
  means of, 171
  media of, 417-18
  medium of, 186, 428, 436
  notion of, 153-54
  objects of, 417-18, 421, 436
  ontology of, 209
  semantic property of, 209
representation intention, 200-01
representation of,
  meaning, 176
  moral concepts, 316
  object, 176
representational power of,
  language, 416, 419, 436
  linguistic representation, 420
Representational realists, 185
representational system,
  functions of, 160
representational theory of mind (RTM), 94, 154
Representationalism,
  birth of, 321
  form(s) of, 98, 102
representationality,
  components of, 97
representative language, 187
reproduction,
  idea of, 395
reproduction of textual meaning, 407
Republic (Plato's), 307

requirement of intelligence, 343
residence of *ghaṭatva*, 80
response-soliciting, 210
retained knowledge,
  epistemology of, 90
role(s) of,
  convention, 27
  language, 18, 168, 170
  linguistic representation, 275
  philosophy, 412
  statement making, 209
role-playing games, 27
rootedness of language, 393
Rorty('s), 226-28, 230-31, 233-39, 241-42, 244-47
  idea of no-truth, 235
Rosch, Eleanor, 310
rule following,
  concept of, 394, 407
  notion of, 412
  Wittgenstein's concept of, 409
  Wittgenstein's conception of, 408
rule-governed behaviours, 183
Rumelhart, 154, 164
Rumi, 376
Russell('s), 320-21, 332-36
  approach to proper names, 434
  Criterion, 332
  idea of proposition, 330
  Principle, 330, 333-35, 337
  theory of Descriptions, 321, 330
Russell's Principle,
  interpretation of, 337
Russellian notion of proposition, 331
Russellian singular term, 332
Ryle, 95
śabda, 252, 255, 292-93
  traditional view of, 251
śabda-pramāṇa, 251, 254
  epistemic autonomy of, 251
Śābdabodha, 77-78
śābdabodha in Nyāya, 77
śabdaśakti, 76
Śabdaśaktiprakāśikā, 75-76
śabdatva jāti, 83
sa-vikalpaka pratyakṣa (perception with imagination), 276
saindhava, 79, 268
sākāṅkṣa, 81
śakti, 78
śakyārtha of *Gaṅgā*, 78
sāmānya lakṣaṇa, 80, 84
  perception, 84
sāmarthya, 76
Sāṁkhya, 54
saṁsāra, 344, 347-48, 365, 385
saṁsāra-nirvāṇa, 354
saṁsarga,
  Knowledge of, 79
saṁśaya, 79
Śaṅkara, 354, 384
saṅketa, 78
sannidhi, 77, 81
sannikarṣa(s), 80, 84
Santa Claus, 417
Sarasvatī, Goddess, 76-77
Sartre, 95
sattva, 54
savikalpaka perception, 281
Scale of Law, 379
scepticism,
  form of, 121
scheme(s) of discrete representations, 163-64

Schiffer, 147, 152
Schleiermacher, Frederick, 394-95, 397-400, 407, 410
Schlick, 95
schools of Indian philosophy, 258, 273
Schuon, Frithjof, 351, 359, 364
scientific fiction(s), 22, 39, 41, 44, 46
scientific law, 24
scientific statements, 355
scientific-technological civilization, 349
scriptural statements,
  knowledge of, 273
Searle, John('s), 138, 146, 197, 199, 202, 208-14
  above hypothesis of speech act theory, 203
  biological naturalism, 209
  theorization, 207
  theorization of performative utterances, 198
  theorization of speech act, 197, 200, 202
  theory of communication, 197
Searlean notion of,
  constitutive rules, 212
  direction of fit, 208
  regulative rules, 212
Searlean perspective of linguistic representation, 209
Second World War, 138
secular humanism, 349
Self,
  language of, 339
self-acquaintance,
  mode of, 66
self-ascription, 65
self-ascriptive judgements, 64
self-awareness, 67, 72, 74
  subject of, 70
self-consciousness, 70-72
  communication of, 70
Self-Containedness of Mind, Cartesian Thesis of, 329
Self-Containedness Thesis, 321
self-contradictory statement, 26
self-identity,
  awareness of, 72
self-love, 378
self-recognition,
  judgement of, 72
Self-reference, 67
self-referential statement, 44, 72
self-understanding,
  form of, 410
Sellars, 228-30
semantic content of,
  language, 394
  statement, 201
semantic features of linguistic behaviour, 415
semantic power of language, 214
semantic property of representation, 209
semantic structures of mental representations, 157
semantic(s) value of,
  communication, 206
  expression, 330-31
  ordinary language, 19
  utterance, 331
semantic values, 331
sense of naming, 430

sensory receptors, 99
sensual things (*atīndriya*), 80
sentence(s),
  compositionality of, 158
  meaning of, 260, 268
set of universals, 435-36
Shoemaker, Sydney, 64-65, 74
simple objects,
  arrangement of, 169
  configuration of, 169
simulation psychology, 183
sincerity condition, 149
single unit of language, 398
situation semantics, 293
Smith, Christopher, 392
Smolensky, 154, 161
smṛtitva, 83
socio-linguistic act of establishing reference, 429
Socrates, 286
solicitation,
  condition of, 207
source(s) of,
  knowledge, 82-83, 92, 258, 260-61
  pramā, 251
space of,
  reasons, 90-91
  representations, 163
speaker of language, 31, 257
speaking of language, 406
specific collection of universals, 427
specific set of universals, 428
spectrum of representations, 216
Speculative psychology, 184
speech act(s),
  Searle's theorization of, 197, 200, 202
  theoretical framework of, 203
speech acts semantics, 202
  constituents of, 200
speech act theory,
  integral part of, 199
  Searle's above hypothesis of, 203
sphoṭa, 291-93
sphoṭa concept of Bhartṛhari, 292
sphoṭa-nāda, 291
Spinoza's view of love of God, 369
spiritual corruption, 385
spiritual reality of language, 413
Stalnaker, 293
Stampe, 134-35
standard of perceptual similarity, 105
statement making,
  rules of, 209
statement of,
  brute facts, 197
  institutional facts, 197
statements,
  forms of, 23
statistical knowledge, 311
status of testimonial knowledge, 75
Stich, 307
stipulative definitions, 21
Strawson, P.F., 135, 147, 152, 276
structure(s) of,
  conceptual metaphor, 303
  sentences, 157
  testimony, 259

study of,
 mental representation, 98
 moral philosophy, 298
subject (*pakṣa*), 266
subject (*viśeṣya*), 83
subject of,
 consciousness, 68, 74
 self-awareness, 70
subject-object dichotomy, 367
subject-predicate (*viśeṣya-viśeṣaṇa*), 81
subject-use, 66
success of,
 naming, 430, 434
 referring, 430, 434
sūfī, 381
supraphenomenal reality, knowledge of, 343
superposed representation, 163
 notion of, 164
Supreme Being, 178
Supreme Principle of Duty, 298
Supreme Principle of Morality, 298
sūtra, 253-54
 interpretation of, 253
Syādvāda, Jaina doctrine of, 363, 374
symbol system of CTM, 164
symbols,
 logical system of, 232
 meanings of, 154
syntactic rules, 20
syntax of,
 language, 18, 157
 animal languages, 26
system of language universals, 188
systematicity of language, 157
tamas, 54
Tao, 376
Tarski, 289
tātparya, 260
Tattvacintāmaṇi (Gaṅgeśa's), 262, 282
terms of truth-condition, 23
testimonial knowledge, 91-92
 notion of, 75
 status of, 75
testimony to inference, 268
text,
 language of, 398
textual meaning,
 reproduction of, 407
The Brothers Karamazov (Dostoevsky's), 347, 354
The Divine Interpretation (*devī pakṣa*), 76
The Early Wittgenstein on Religion (Mark Lazenby), 350
The Gospel in Brief (Tolstoy's), 347, 379
theology,
 problems of, 381
Theology after Wittgenstein (Kerr's), 350, 362
theoretical framework of speech acts, 203
theorization of performative expressions, 199
theory of,
 classical conditioning, 27
 higher cognitive processes, 185
 language, 404
 meaning, 293
 moral imagination, 314

Naiyāyikas, 291
nirvikalpaka cognition, 277
parataḥprāmāṇyavāda, 272
reality, 116
reference, 111
truth, 235, 241
thesis of language game, 342
third dogma of empiricism, 227
third-person fact, 63
third-personal self-reference, 67
thought-language relation, 287
Time and Eternity (Stace), 360
timeless meaning, 146
totality of text, 398
Tractatus (Wittgenstein's), 94, 112, 342-43
traditional idea of pure perceptions, 403
traditional philosophers, 344
traditional view of *śabda*, 251
traditional vocabulary, 115
transcendence,
philosopher of, 354-55
problem of, 348
transcendental idealism, 243
transcendental notion of meaning, 180
transfer of knowledge, 249
translation procedure, 192
transmitting knowledge,
act of, 250
true or false statements, 218
truth theory, 232
truth-condition(s), 23-24, 117
terms of, 23
truth-values of empirical statements, 32
types of linguistic representation, 200
Tzu, Lao, 354
Udayana, 280-81
Uhlan, Johann Ludwig, 384
ultimate locus of meaning, 399
understanding of meaning, 396
process of, 396
unique (*vilakṣaṇa*), 82
Unitarian view of God, 365
universal life,
manifestation of, 399
universal statements, 23-25
unreal nature of realism, 119
untenability of metaphysical realism, 119
untranslatability of language, 292
upamititva, 83
Urmson, 133
use of,
language, 111, 124, 153, 171, 242, 341
public language, 194
use-theory of meaning, 170
user of language, 19
utterance,
causal power of, 212
semantic value of, 332
utterance(s) of sentence(s), 184, 331
vahnikaraṇakatva, knowledge of, 79
Vaiśeṣika(s), 265, 268
vaikharī, 292
vākyārthabodha, 77
Varieties of Religious Experience (William James's), 347

variety(ies) of,
    dṛṣṭa, 255
    Reference, 334-36
    disciplines, 183
various forms of linguistic representation, 197
various modes of world-disclosures, 403
Vārttika, 256
Vātsyāyana, 253, 255
Vedānta, 252, 358
Vedāntins, 253, 276
vehicle of communication, 187
veils of language, 357
verbal cognition, 260
verbal testimony,
    domains of, 256
veridical perception, 102
versions of metaphysical realism, 116
viśeṣaṇa, 80
viśeṣya, 79-80
vikalpa, 277
Visual information, 99-100
visual perception, 28, 100-01
visual sensation, 21
vṛtti, 78-79
vyabhicāra, 85-86
Vyāsatīrtha, a Madhva logician, 282
vyatireka (*asadbhāva*), 82, 86
    relation, 86
wajūd, 361
Weil, 369-70, 373, 376, 381
Western civilization, 345, 347
Western philosophy of language, 109
Western thinkers, 290
Western tradition, 250
Wilber, Ken, 354
Wilson, 143-45
Wittgenstein('s), 24, 29, 44, 59-60, 63-64, 74, 94-95, 113-15, 168-76, 178, 180, 182, 189, 193-94, 221-26, 244, 246, 284, 287-88, 310, 323, 339-45, 347-52, 356, 360-67, 369, 371, 373-75, 377, 379-86, 388-89, 391-95, 404-13, 420
    concept of rule-following, 409
    conception of divinity, 366
    conception of rule-following, 408
    ethics, 378
    language game theory, 410
    metaphysical interpretation of, 353
    mysticism, 345
    notion of language, 179
    ontology of logical form, 222
    terminology, 43
    theory of logical form, 223
    Unitarian Metaphysics, 366
    view on language, 176
Wittgenstein and Mystical: Philosophy as an Ascetic Practice (Fredrick Sontag), 351
Wittgenstein scholars, 342
Wittgensteinian, 107
Wittgensteinian notion of abnormality, 177
word(s),
    meaning(s) of, 30, 54, 70, 268
    perception of, 257
wordness (*śabdatva*), 85

world-disclosures,
  various modes of, 403
yogaja, 80, 84
  perception, 84
yogīs, 81
yogya, 77, 79
yogyatā, 77, 78, 81, 259-60
  jñāna, 79
Zahavi, Dan, 67
Zarathustra (Nietzsche's), 379
Zen tradition, 354
Zossima (Father), 347